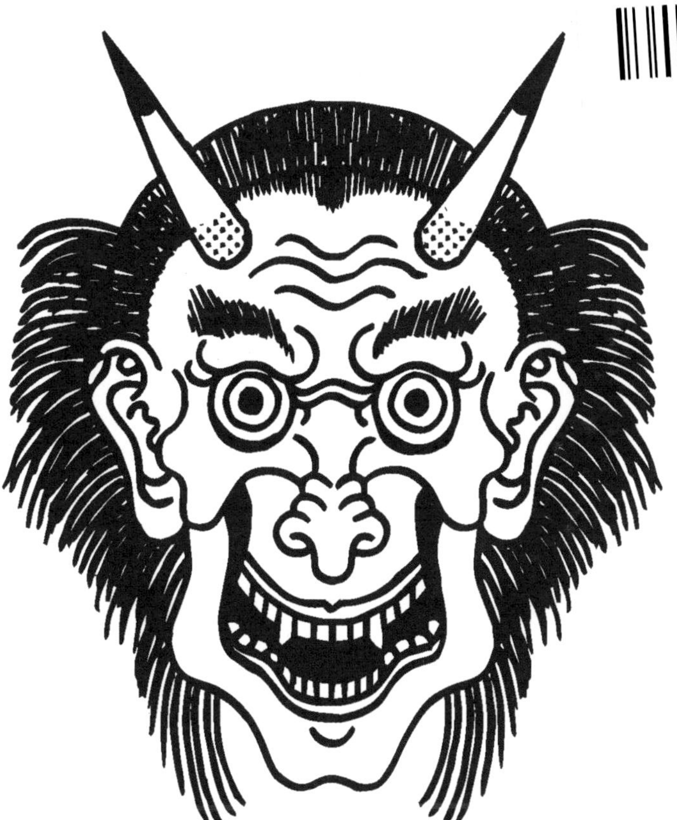

ALEXANDER HEIR

SACRED BONES BOOKS

WARRR2k∞/Work 2015-2017

Copyright © 2018 Alexander Heir

All rights reserved. No part of this publication may be reproduced,
stored in a retrieval system, or transmitted in any form or by any means,
electronic, mechanical, photocopying, recording, or otherwise,
without written permission of the publisher.

ISBN: 978-0-9996099-2-7

Published by Sacred Bones Books

First Edition

1 2 3 4 5 6 7 8 9 10

All requests and correspondence can be addressed to

Sacred Bones Books
144 N. 7th Street #413
Brooklyn, NY 11249

Printed in Canada

When I was a kid, I worshipped firecracker packaging. Later, that same fascination moved on to outsider art, the alchemical and religious drawings of Jakob Böhme, the stamps found on drug packaging, and other fringe art styles. I think something is successful if it looks like the symbol a drug lord will stamp on blocks of exported opium.

I've seen the theory that Lenin invented branding. All that great red propaganda art took graphics into a new frontier of modernism. The brand was Soviet communism and they really had an awesome logo that totally helped their marketing. During the Second World War, the Germans picked up the Russians' ideas and ran with them — and later, so did the Chinese. But credit where due: The Soviets were killing it with the state-controlled pop culture graphics from day one. The U.S. never really "got it," always drawing on Norman Rockwell-type baroque images. That stuff for me never had the streamlined approach. Also, I would imagine there was an attempt by American propagandists to stay away from Soviet-style elements.

In the '50s and '60s, various resistance movements created emerging graphic styles that led directly and indirectly into street art and graffiti. Protest moved from group to individual expression and lots of people were out tagging. I'll always remember watching a New York City tourist commercial that had shots on the stairs in the Statue of Liberty, and there in the background was Taki 183 painted on the wall.

The punk music scene produced very developed and specific style elements. Gig flyers for bands and related street art was quickly co-opted and embraced by the mainstream. So of course I'm attracted to Alex's stuff, its occult significance, and the outlines it creates around our culture of gentrification. It's still subversive and dangerous, which is a difficult standard to maintain in a period where everything is consumed, made safe, and spit back out at the speed of light. Alex made a piece with a skeleton and an executioner sharing a space in a tarot card-like relationship. I have a big poster of it framed in my house that I see daily, and it always makes me happy.

-Chris Stein (Blondie,) 2018

SECTION A:
COMISSSIONS

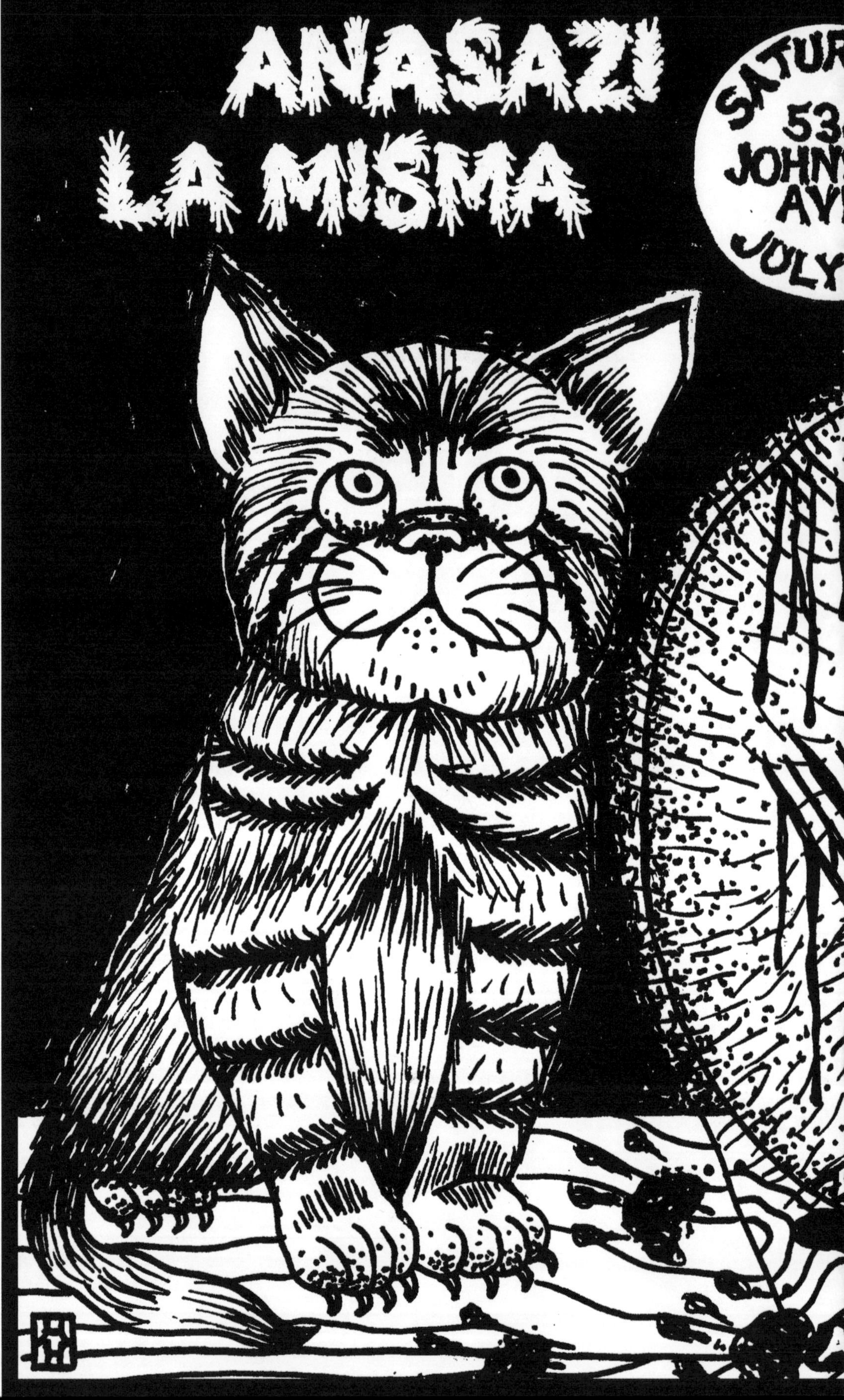

ANASAZI
LA MISMA
SATUR
53
JOHN
AV
JULY

GOOSEBUMPS
NOMAD G.M.K.
NEFIT FOR EMPTY CAGES COLLECTIVE

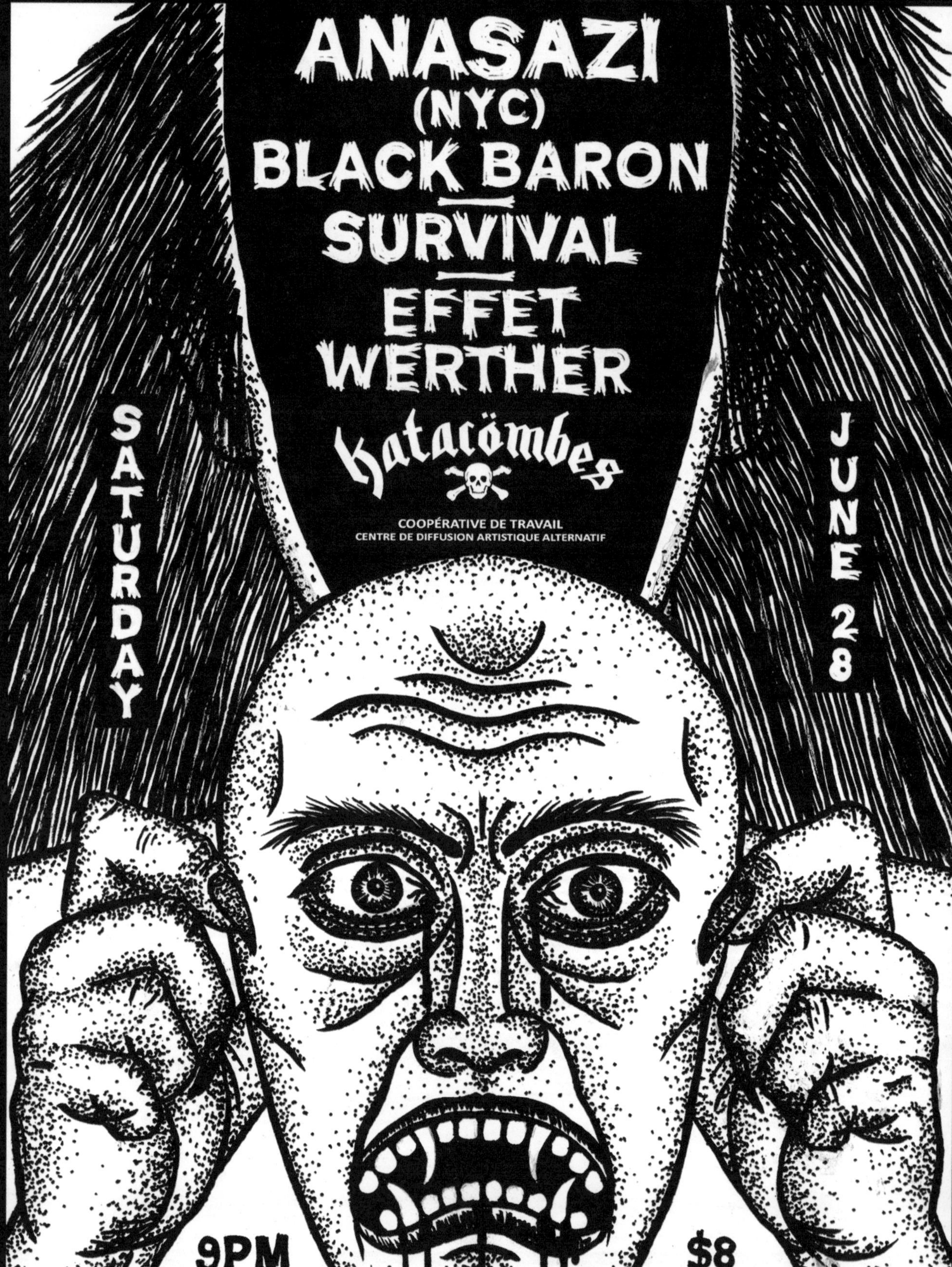
ANASAZI
(NYC)
BLACK BARON
—
SURVIVAL
—
EFFET
WERTHER
Katacömbes
COOPÉRATIVE DE TRAVAIL
CENTRE DE DIFFUSION ARTISTIQUE ALTERNATIF
SATURDAY
JUNE 28
9PM
$8

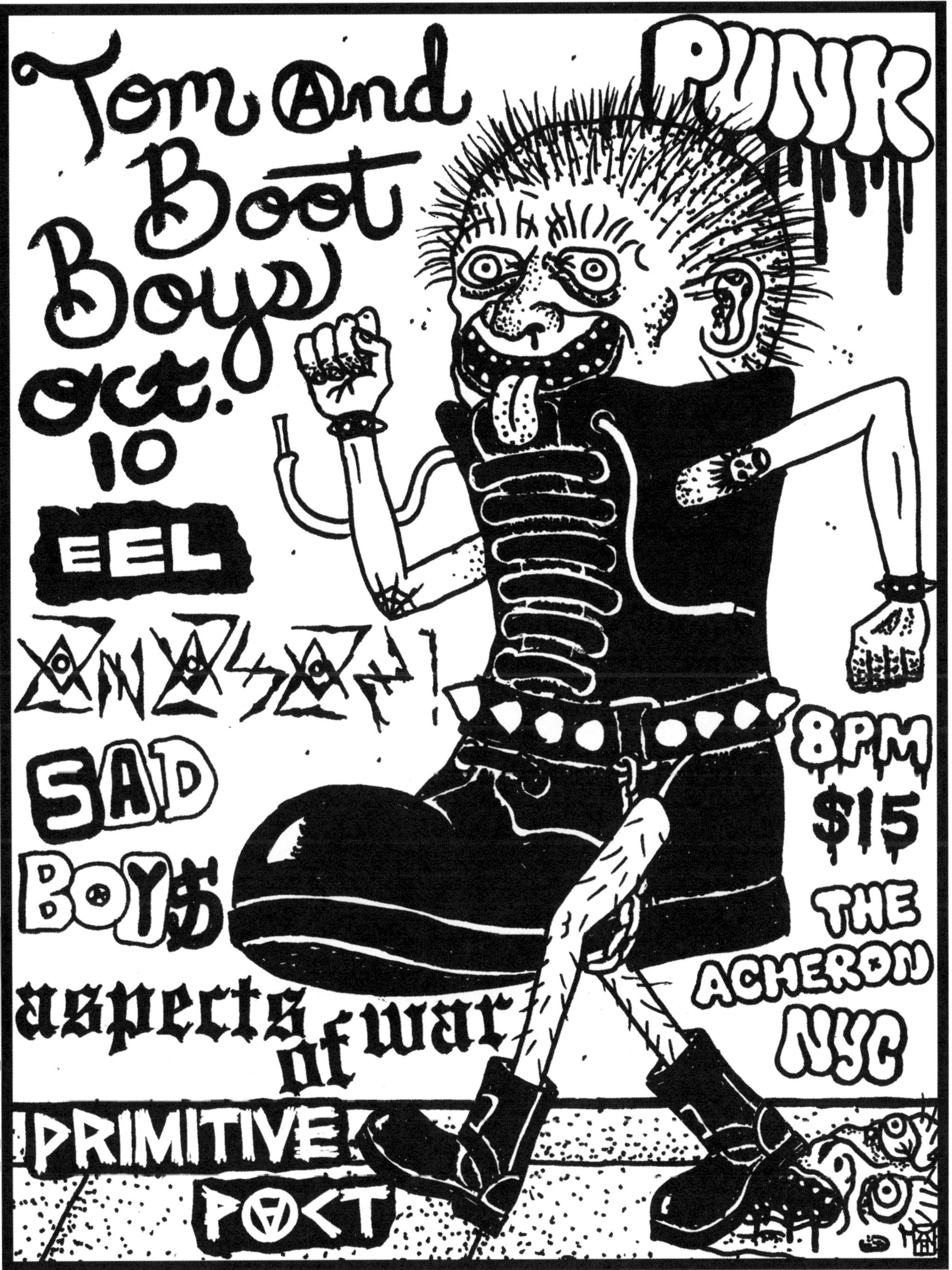

Tom And Boot Boys
Oct. 10
EEL
SAD BOYS
aspects of war
PRIMITIVE POCT
PUNK
8PM
$15
THE ACHERON
NYC

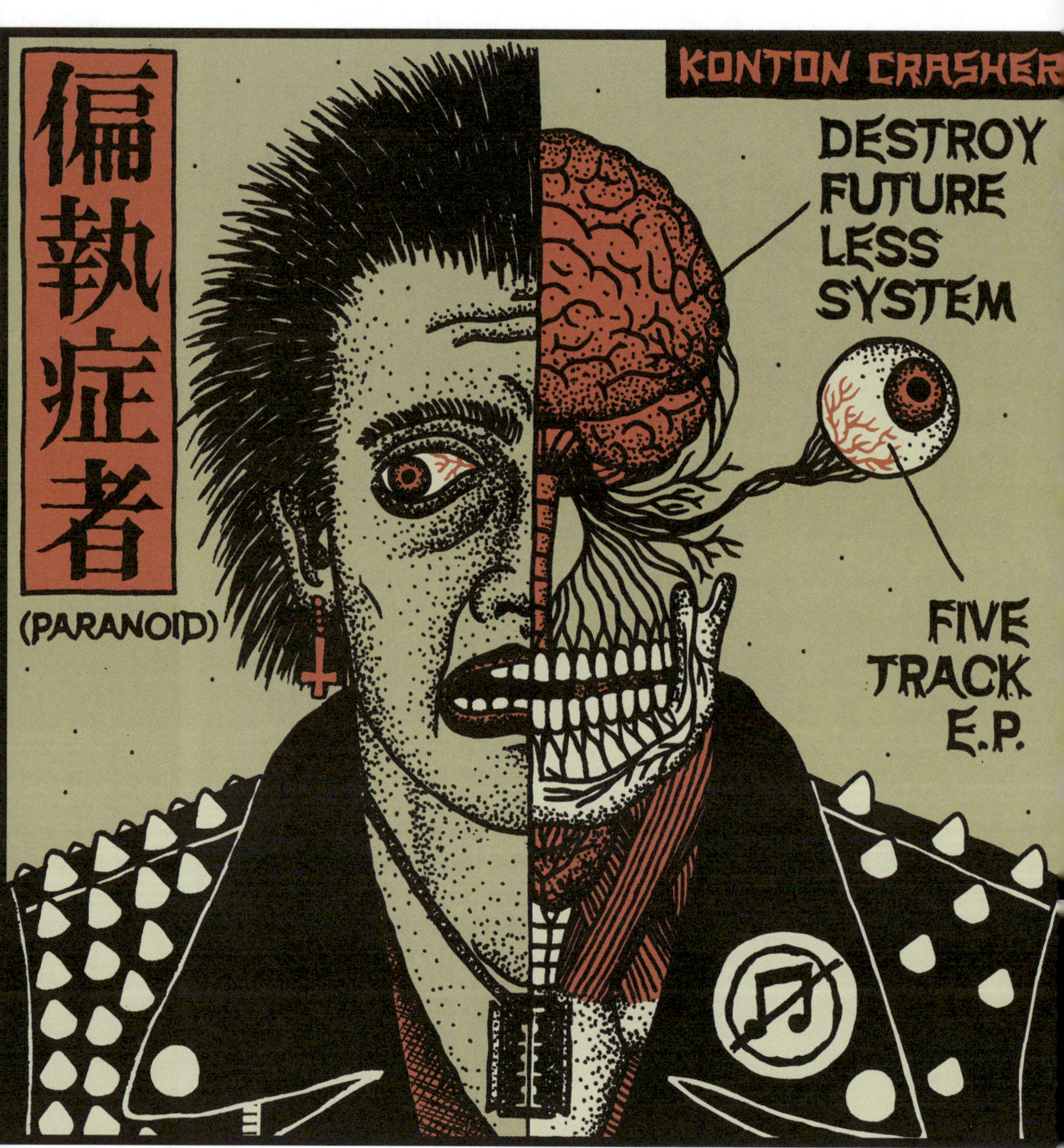
偏執症者
(PARANOID)
KONTON CRASHER
DESTROY FUTURE LESS SYSTEM
FIVE TRACK E.P.

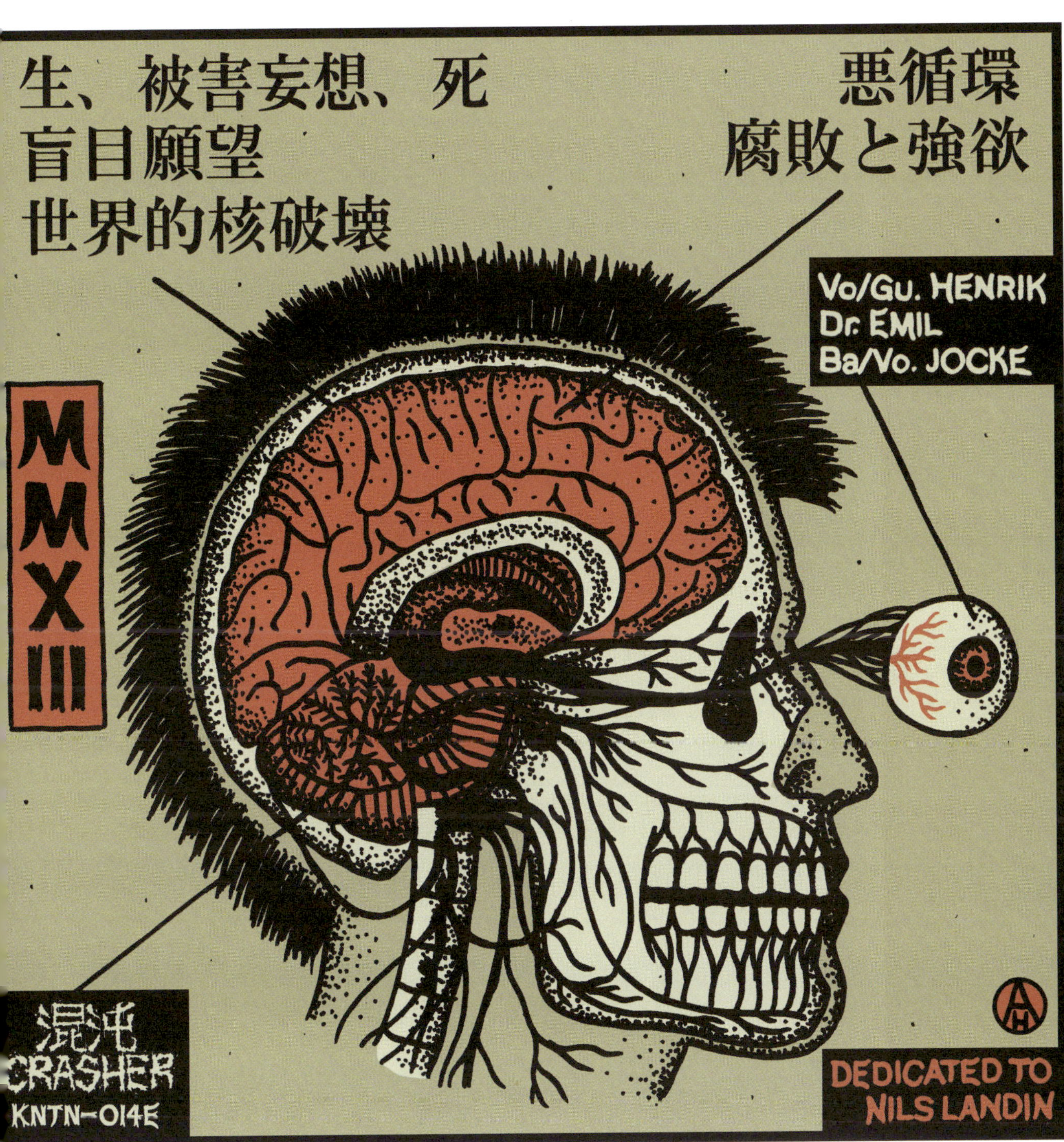
生、被害妄想、死
盲目願望
世界的核破壊
悪循環
腐敗と強欲
Vo/Gu. HENRIK
Dr. EMIL
Ba/Vo. JOCKE
MMXIII
混沌
CRASHER
KNTN-OI4E
DEDICATED TO
NILS LANDIN

偏執症者
(PARANOID)

NORTHERN WINDS OF BRUTAL HELL MANGEL

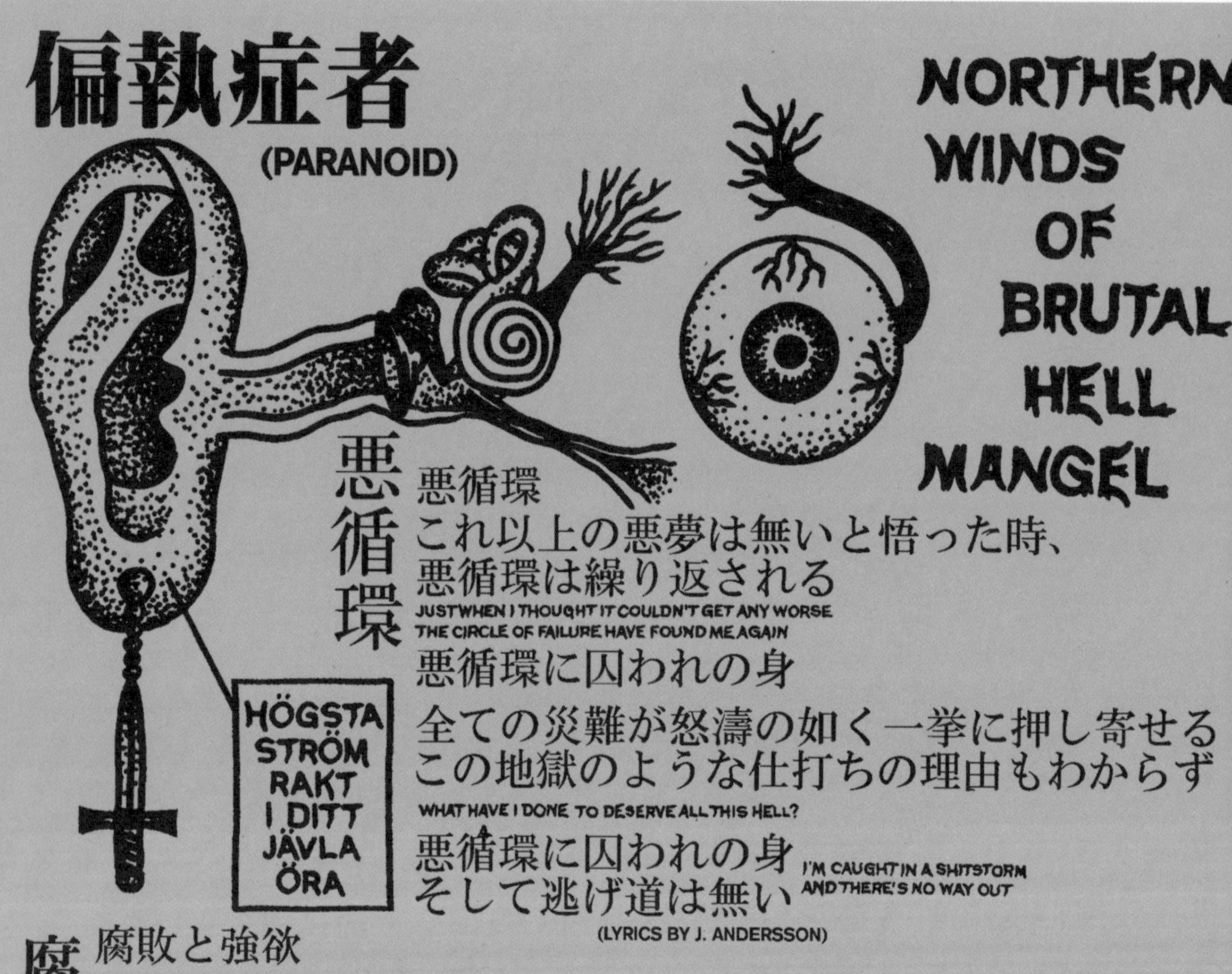

悪循環

悪循環
これ以上の悪夢は無いと悟った時、
悪循環は繰り返される
JUST WHEN I THOUGHT IT COULDN'T GET ANY WORSE
THE CIRCLE OF FAILURE HAVE FOUND ME AGAIN

悪循環に囚われの身

全ての災難が怒濤の如く一挙に押し寄せる
この地獄のような仕打ちの理由もわからず
WHAT HAVE I DONE TO DESERVE ALL THIS HELL?

悪循環に囚われの身
そして逃げ道は無い
I'M CAUGHT IN A SHITSTORM
AND THERE'S NO WAY OUT

(LYRICS BY J. ANDERSSON)

HÖGSTA STRÖM RAKT I DITT JÄVLA ÖRA

腐敗と強欲

腐敗と強欲
皆がなぜ目覚めないのか尋ねることに気づいているか？
もういい加減、たくさんだ

腐敗と強欲
CORRUPTION AND GREED
度の過ぎた反抗にやつらは身を滅ぼす
利益の渇望は消え去る事無く、
苦悩の叫びは沈黙の価値
YOUR THIRST FOR PROFIT CAN NEVER BE QUENCHED
SCREAMS OF THE TORTURED IS THE PRICE OF YOUR SILENCE

2014

KONTON CRASHER
PO BOX 393
LAKEWOOD, OH
44107
USA

KNTN-014E

生、被害妄想、死

生、被害妄想、死

生と被害妄想と　　生と被害妄想と
生と被害妄想と　　生と被害妄想と、
そして死
永遠の破滅へ
試験管で生まれ、
籃で育った現代の庶出の子
BORN IN A TEST TUBE RAISED IN A CAGE

精神障害　　精神障害
精神障害　　精神障害、そして死
終わる事の無い生き地獄
LIFE IS A NEVER ENDING HELL

盲目願望

盲目願望

自らの決断に溺れ、時は流れ
標無き道を辿る
盲目願望！
LET ME BE BLIND!

過ちの絶望における障碍者
目に映るは公認された未来
見渡す限り、指針に満ちる
WHEREVER I LOOK, I SEE A WAY OF LIFE

漂い、
どこかへたどり着くことを願う
I WANT TO DRIFT AND LAND ANYWHERE

(LYRICS BY N. LANDIN)

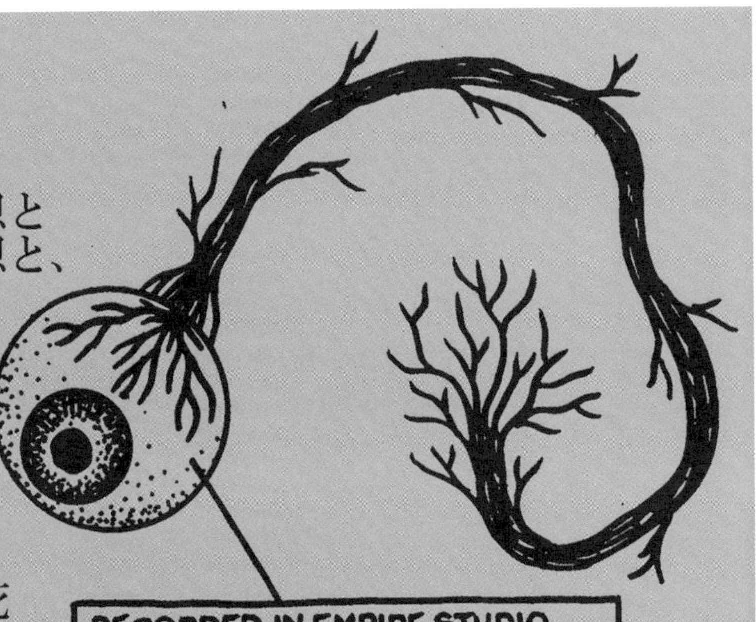

RECORDED IN EMPIRE STUDIO,
FRÖSÖN, SWEDEN, JANUARY 2014
ENGINEERED & PRODUCED BY
JOCKE D-TAKT
MIXED AND MASTERED BY KENKO
AT COMMUNICHAOS MEDIA
ART BY ALEXANDER HEIR

世界的核破壊

世界的核破壊
世界的核破壊
人類(ヒューマンレース)
人類消滅(ヒューマンイレース)
HUMAN ERASED
太陽を凌駕する大爆発
EXPLOSIONS TEN TIMES HOTTER THAN THE SUN
人類(ヒューマンレース)
人類消滅(ヒューマンイレース)
生命が残存は不可能
核による大虐殺へ
TO NUCLEAR HOLOCAUST WE'RE CAST

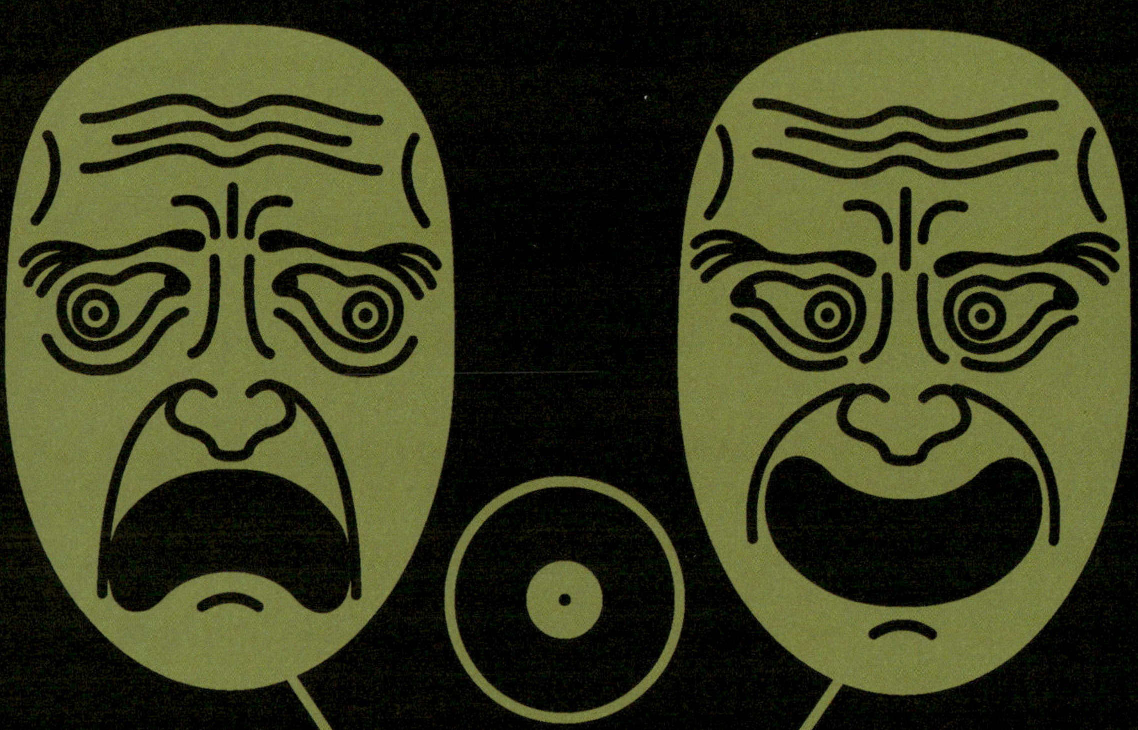
ARCADE
ACADEMY
RECORDS

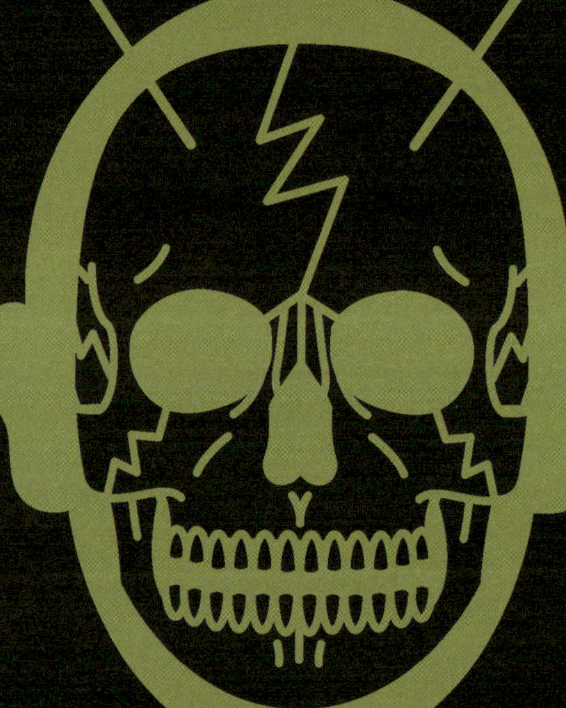
ARCADE
ACADEMY
RECORDS
NYC

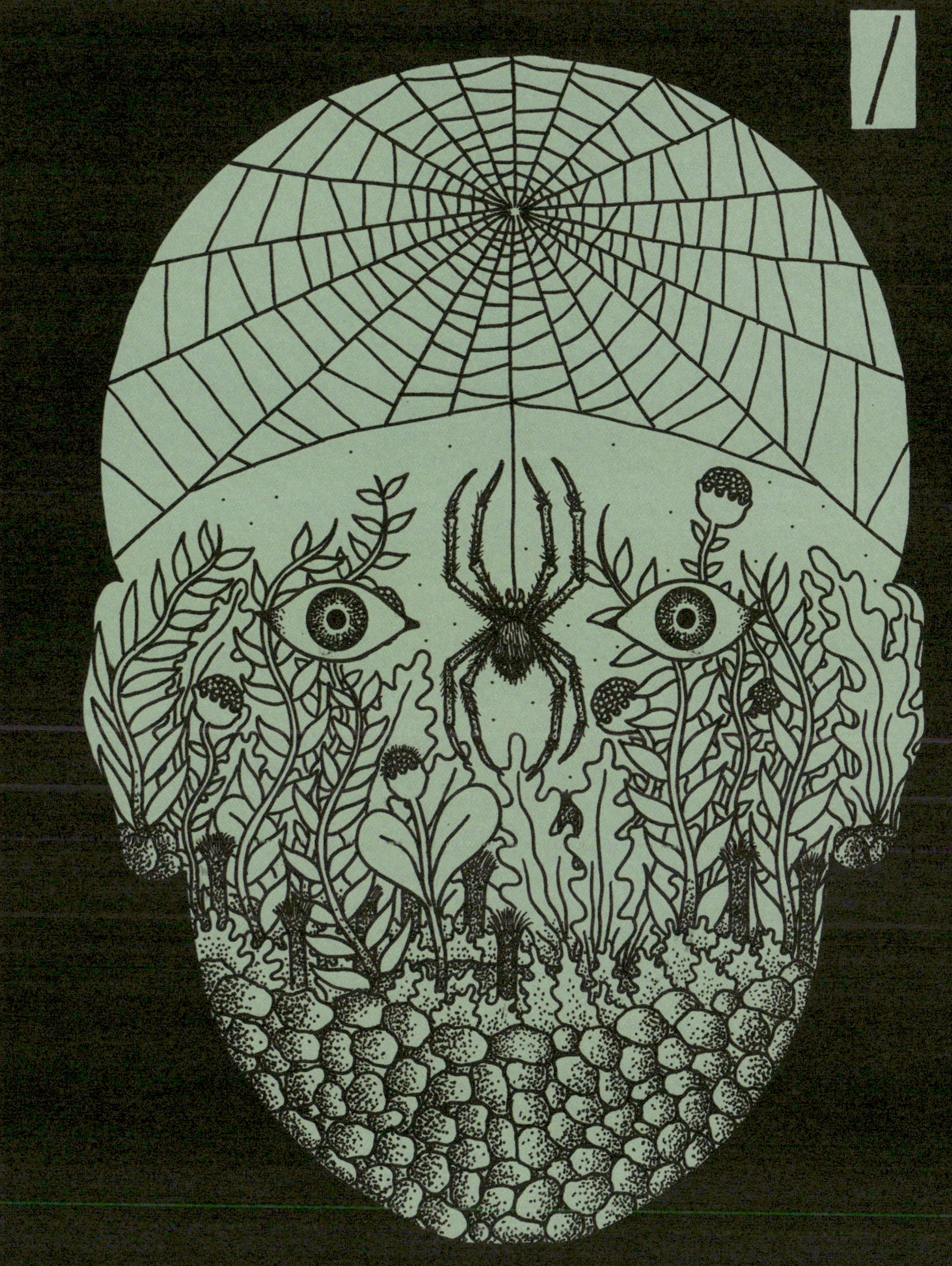
1
CAPTURED TRACKS

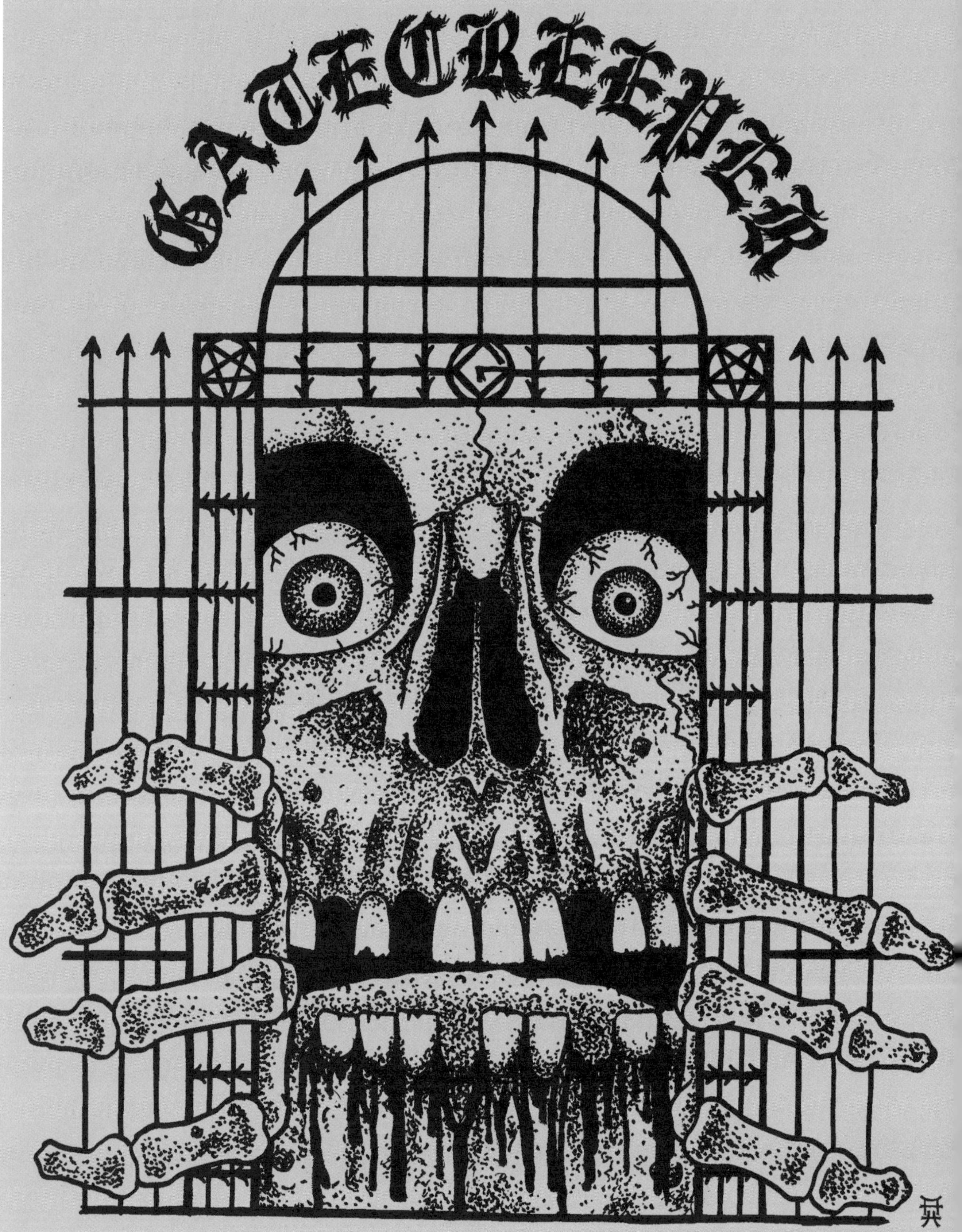

GATECREEPER

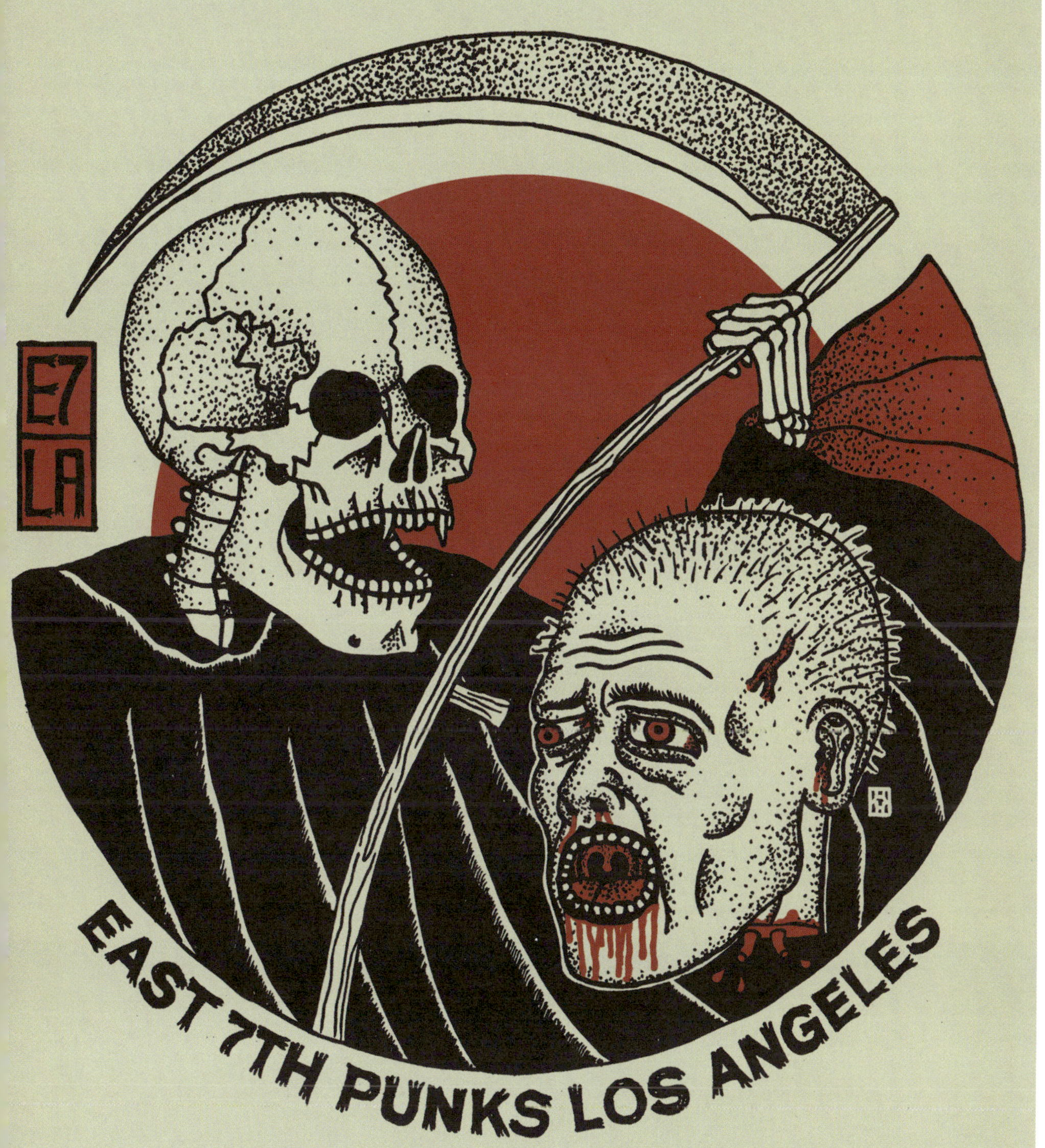
E7
LA
EAST 7TH PUNKS LOS ANGELES

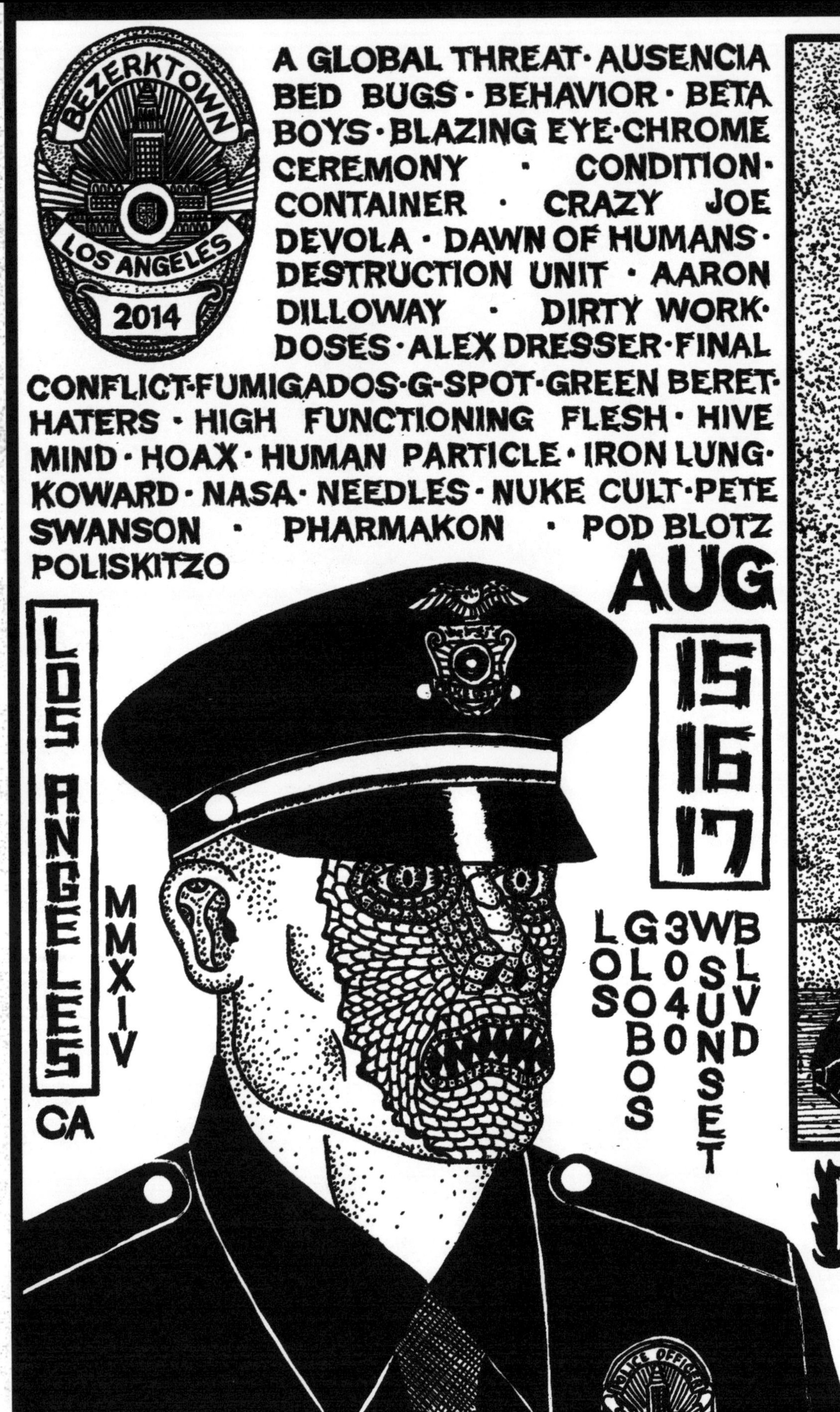

BEZERKTOWN
LOS ANGELES
2014
A GLOBAL THREAT · AUSENCIA
BED BUGS · BEHAVIOR · BETA
BOYS · BLAZING EYE · CHROME
CEREMONY · CONDITION ·
CONTAINER · CRAZY JOE
DEVOLA · DAWN OF HUMANS ·
DESTRUCTION UNIT · AARON
DILLOWAY · DIRTY WORK ·
DOSES · ALEX DRESSER · FINAL
CONFLICT · FUMIGADOS · G-SPOT · GREEN BERET ·
HATERS · HIGH FUNCTIONING FLESH · HIVE
MIND · HOAX · HUMAN PARTICLE · IRON LUNG ·
KOWARD · NASA · NEEDLES · NUKE CULT · PETE
SWANSON · PHARMAKON · POD BLOTZ
POLISKITZO
AUG
15
16
17
LOS ANGELES
MMXIV
CA
LGOLOSOBOS
3WBO040
SLUNSET
BLVD

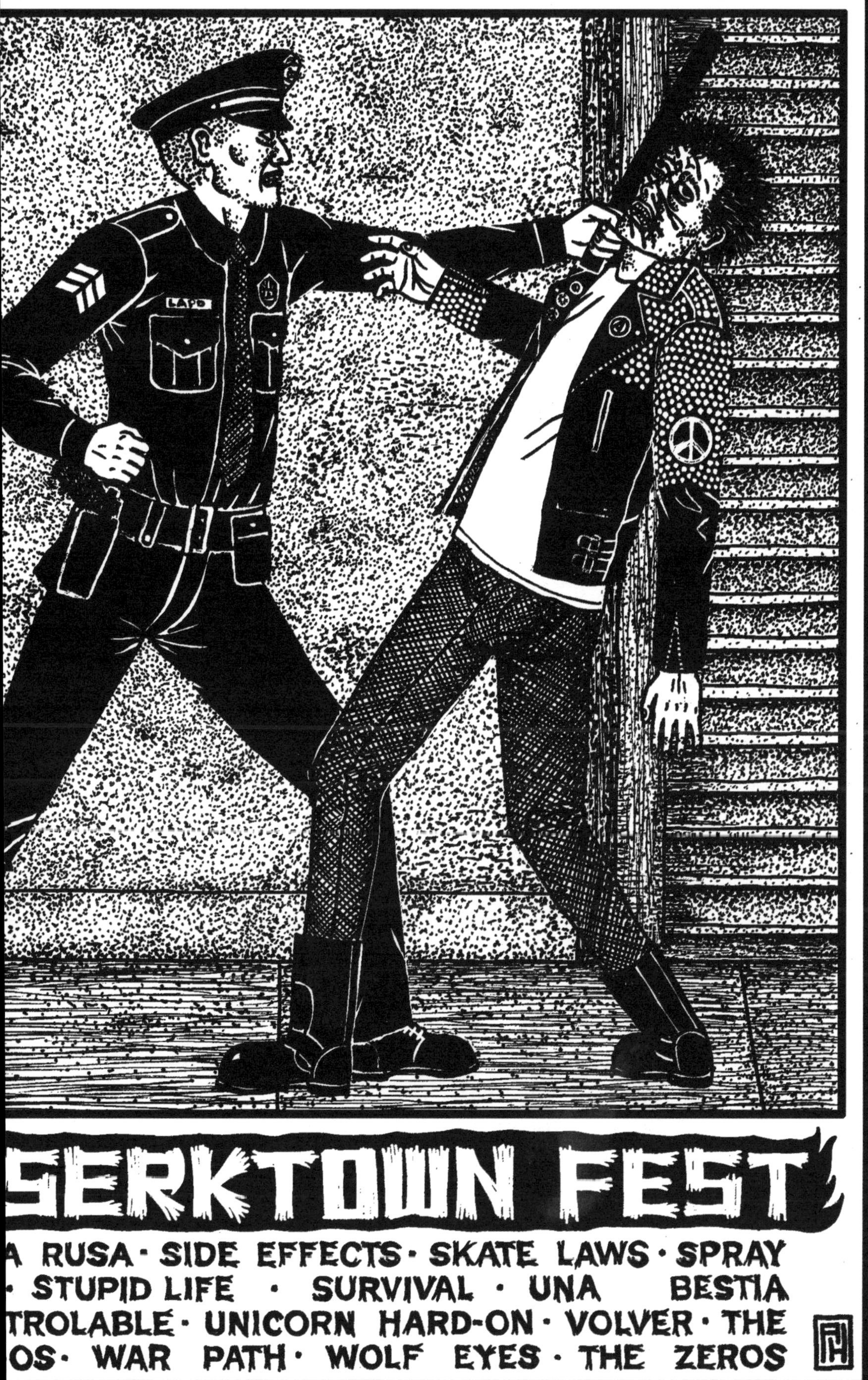

SERKTOWN FEST
A RUSA · SIDE EFFECTS · SKATE LAWS · SPRAY
· STUPID LIFE · SURVIVAL · UNA BESTIA
TROLABLE · UNICORN HARD-ON · VOLVER · THE
OS · WAR PATH · WOLF EYES · THE ZEROS

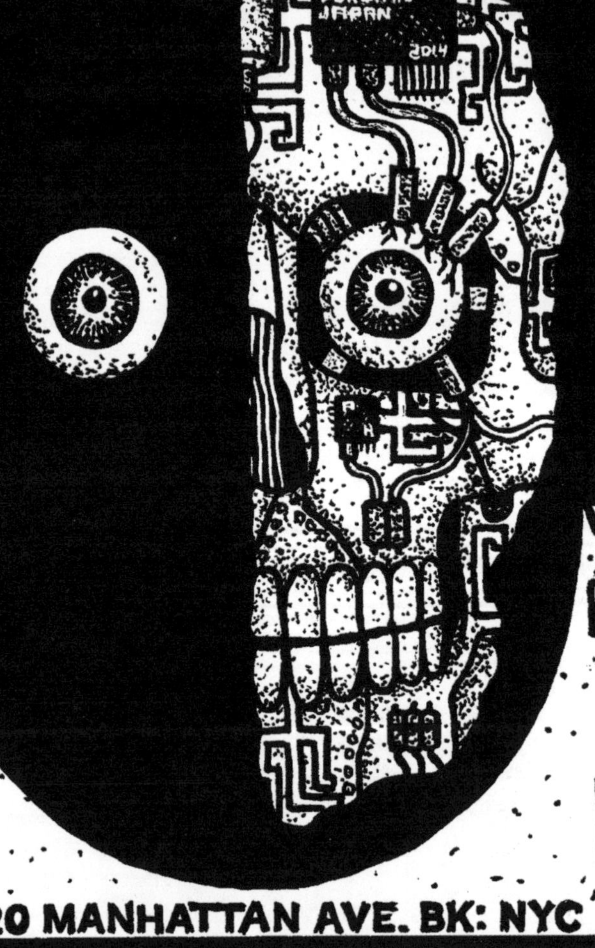

FORWARD
HARDCORE GIG
JAPAN
VOL 226
MONDAY
NOV.17
GREEN BERET
2014
SAINTS VITUS
NIGHT BIRDS
1120 MANHATTAN AVE. BK: NYC
LONG KNIFE
8PM
$10
21+

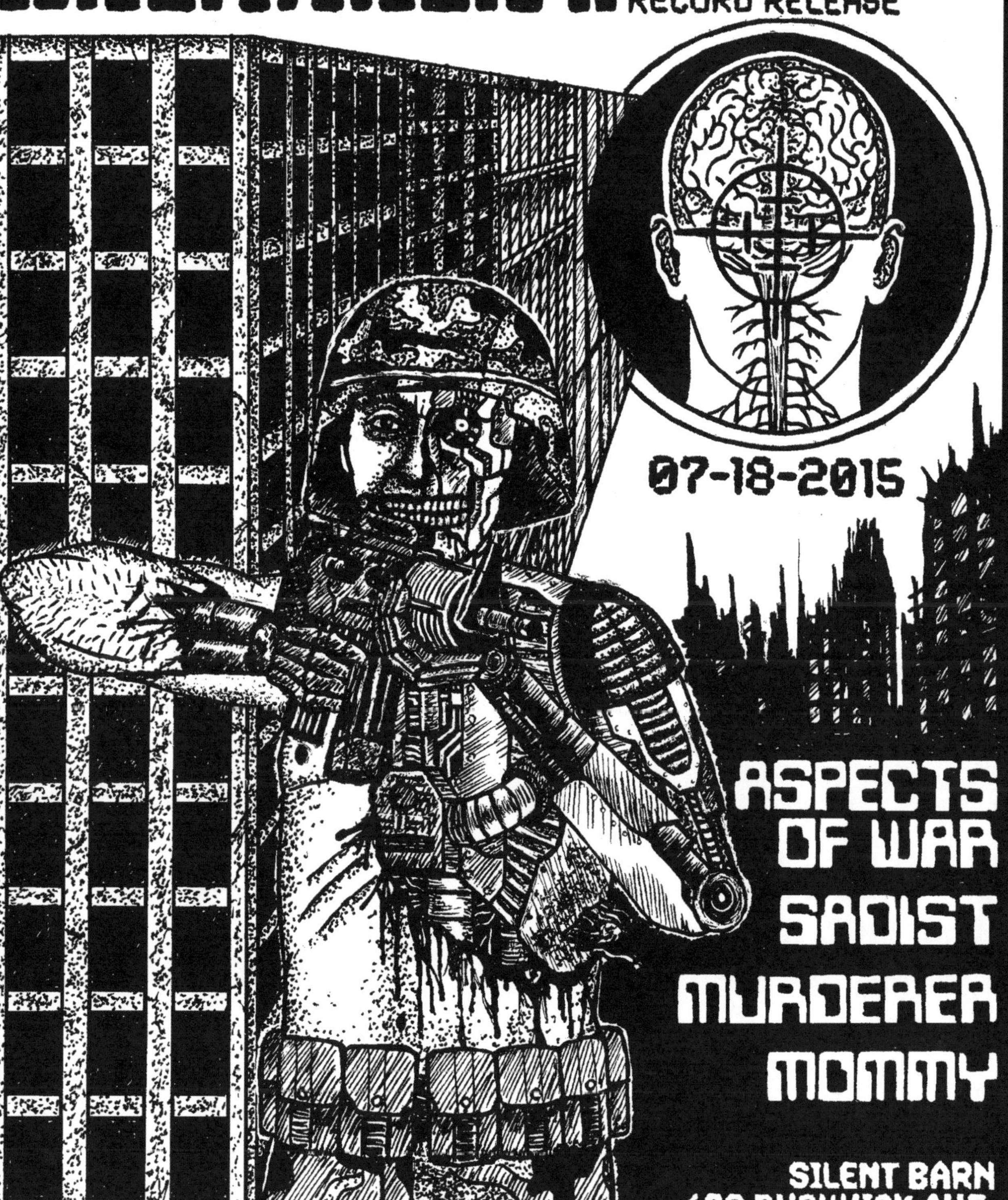
L.O.T.I.O.N.
DIGITAL CONTROL AND
MAN'S OBSOLESCENCE
RECORD RELEASE
07-18-2015
ASPECTS
OF WAR
SADIST
MURDERER
MOMMY
SILENT BARN
603 BUSHWICK AVE.

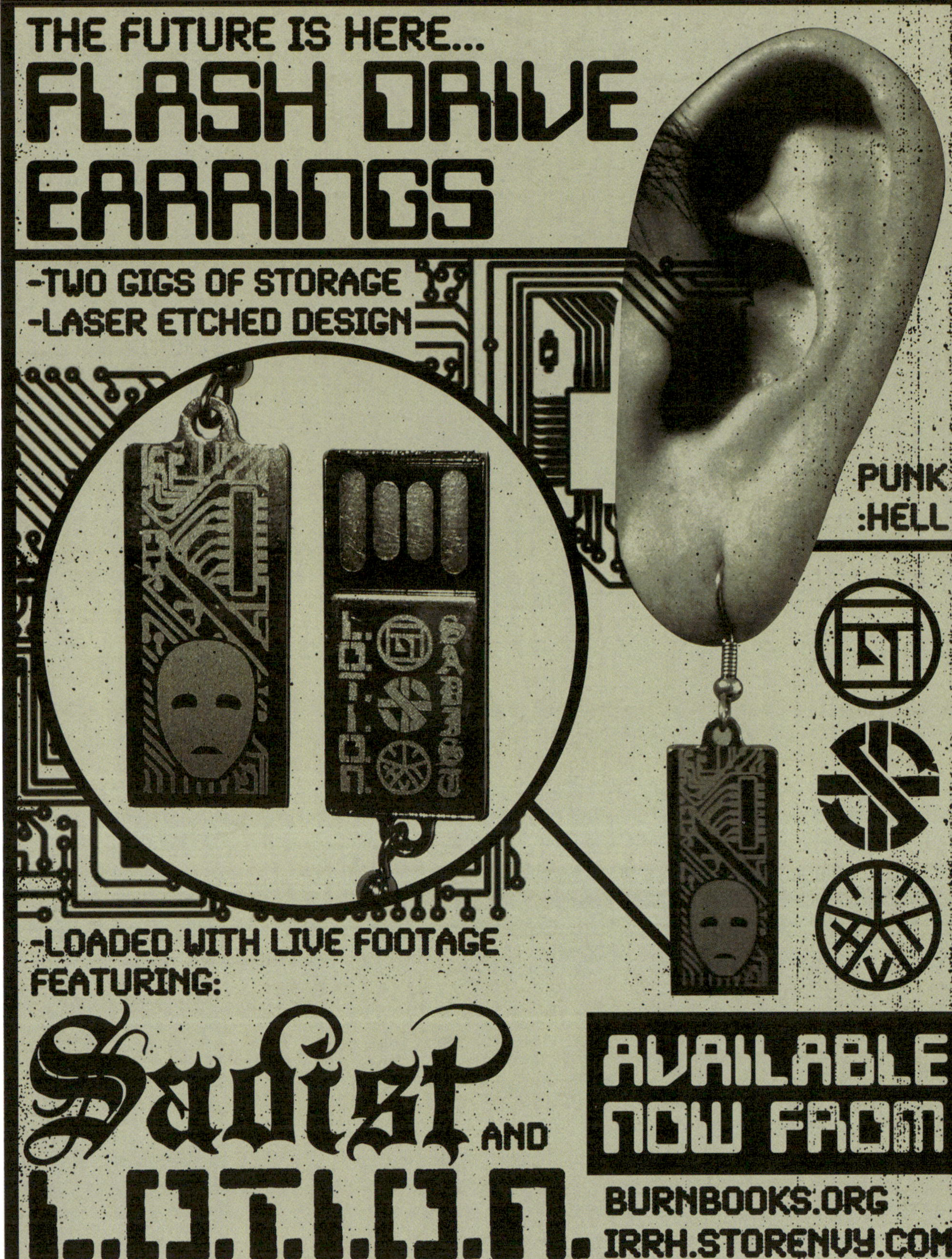

THE FUTURE IS HERE...
FLASH DRIVE
EARRINGS

-TWO GIGS OF STORAGE
-LASER ETCHED DESIGN

PUNK
:HELL

-LOADED WITH LIVE FOOTAGE
FEATURING:

Sadist AND
L.O.T.I.O.N.

AVAILABLE
NOW FROM

BURNBOOKS.ORG
IRRH.STORENVY.COM

L.O.T.I.O.N. 2015

PROJECTED DATES FOR INTERNATIONAL EXPANSION

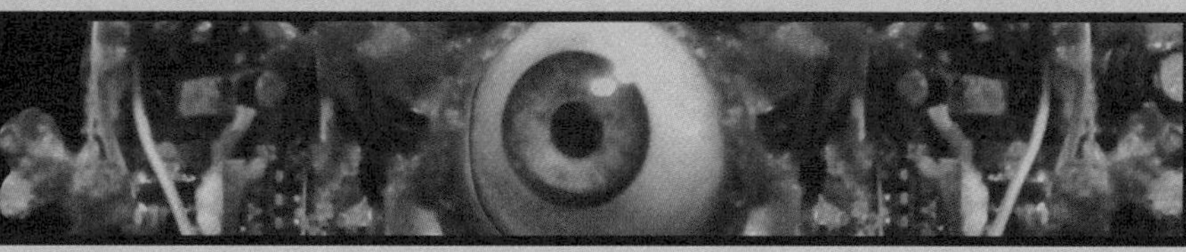

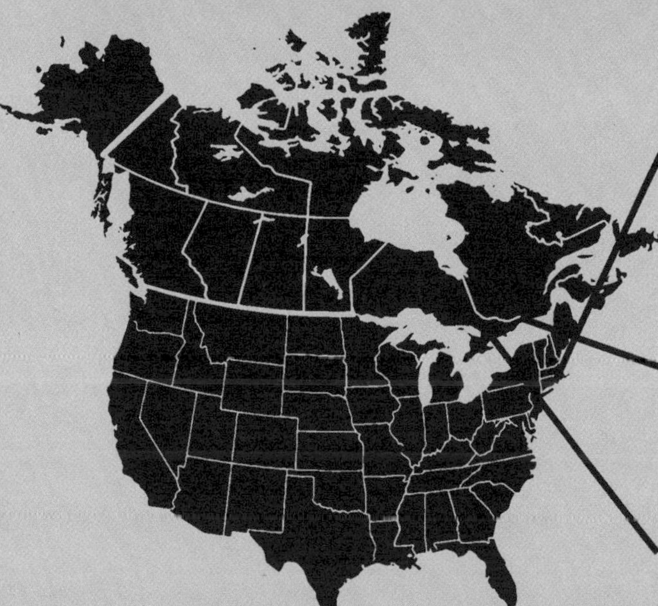

12.11:
PROVIDENCE, RI
MACHINES WITH MAGNETS

12.12:
MONTREAL, QC
CASA DEL POPOLO

12.13:
TORONTO, ON
SMILING BUDDHA

WITH
LIGATURE
V SINCLAIR
SAVAGE BLIND GOD

WITH
LIGATURE
TRIAGE
DEATH KNEEL

WITH
LIGATURE
UN REGARD FROID
CROCHE
ANUSOL

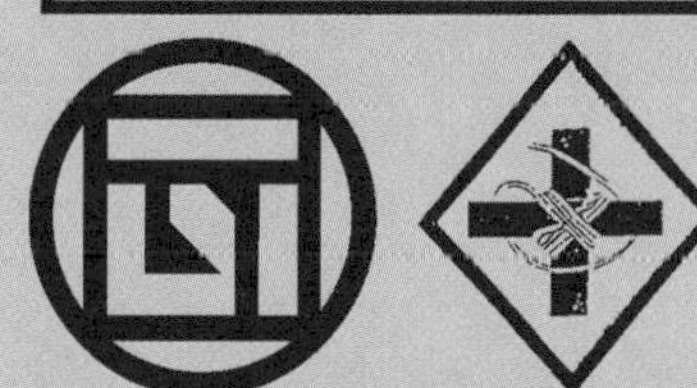

IN CONGLOMERATION WITH LIGATURE LTD.

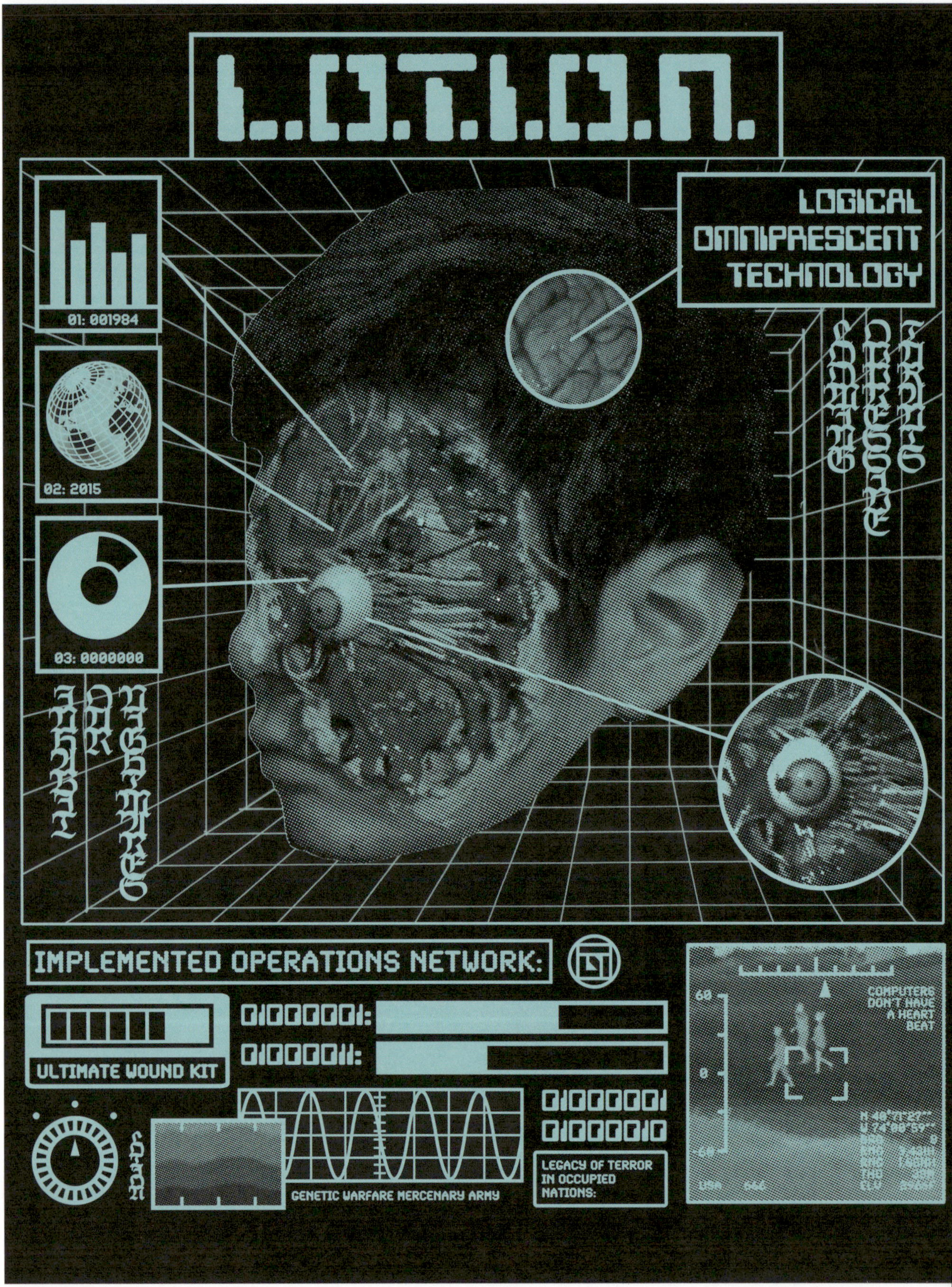

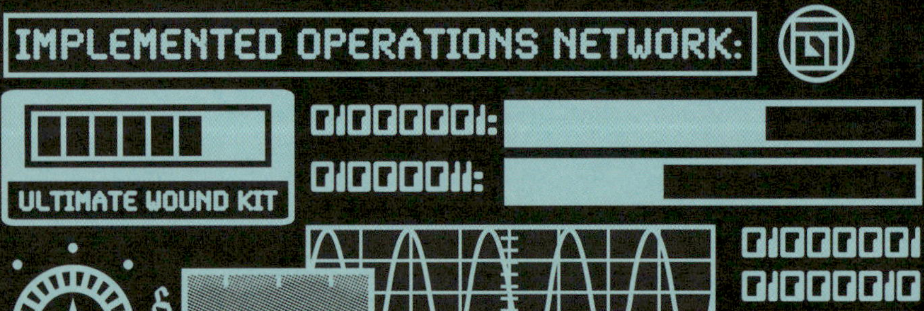
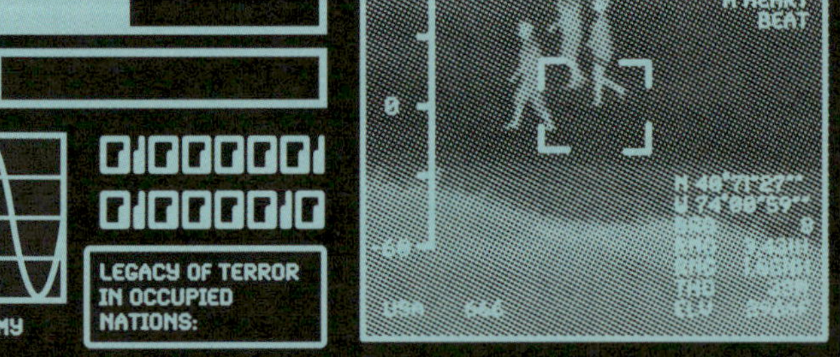

L.O.T.I.O.N.
LOGICAL OMNIPRESCENT TECHNOLOGY
01: 001984
02: 2015
03: 0000000
IMPLEMENTED OPERATIONS NETWORK:
ULTIMATE WOUND KIT
01000001:
01000011:
01000001
01000010
LEGACY OF TERROR IN OCCUPIED NATIONS:
GENETIC WARFARE MERCENARY ARMY
COMPUTERS DON'T HAVE A HEART BEAT
60

SADIST: L.O.T.I.O.N.

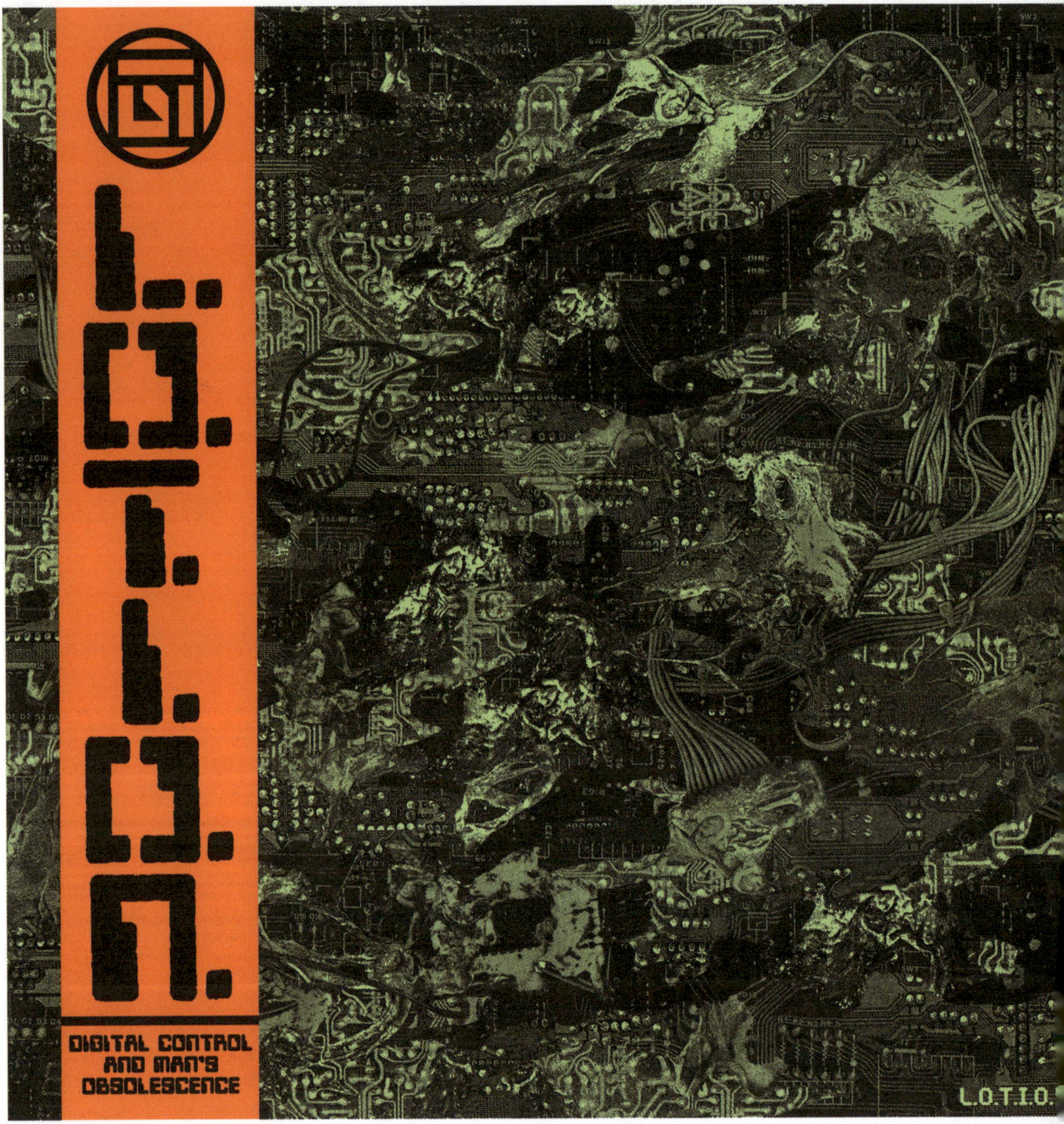

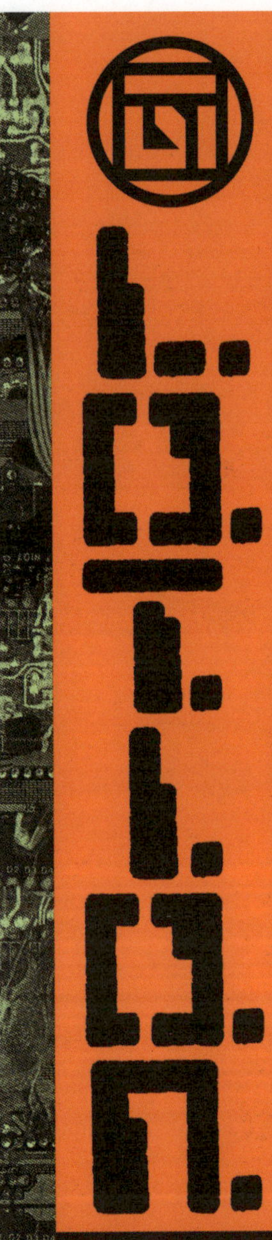
L.O.T.I.O.
DIGITAL CONTROL
AND MAN'S
OBSOLESCENCE
L.O.T.I.O.

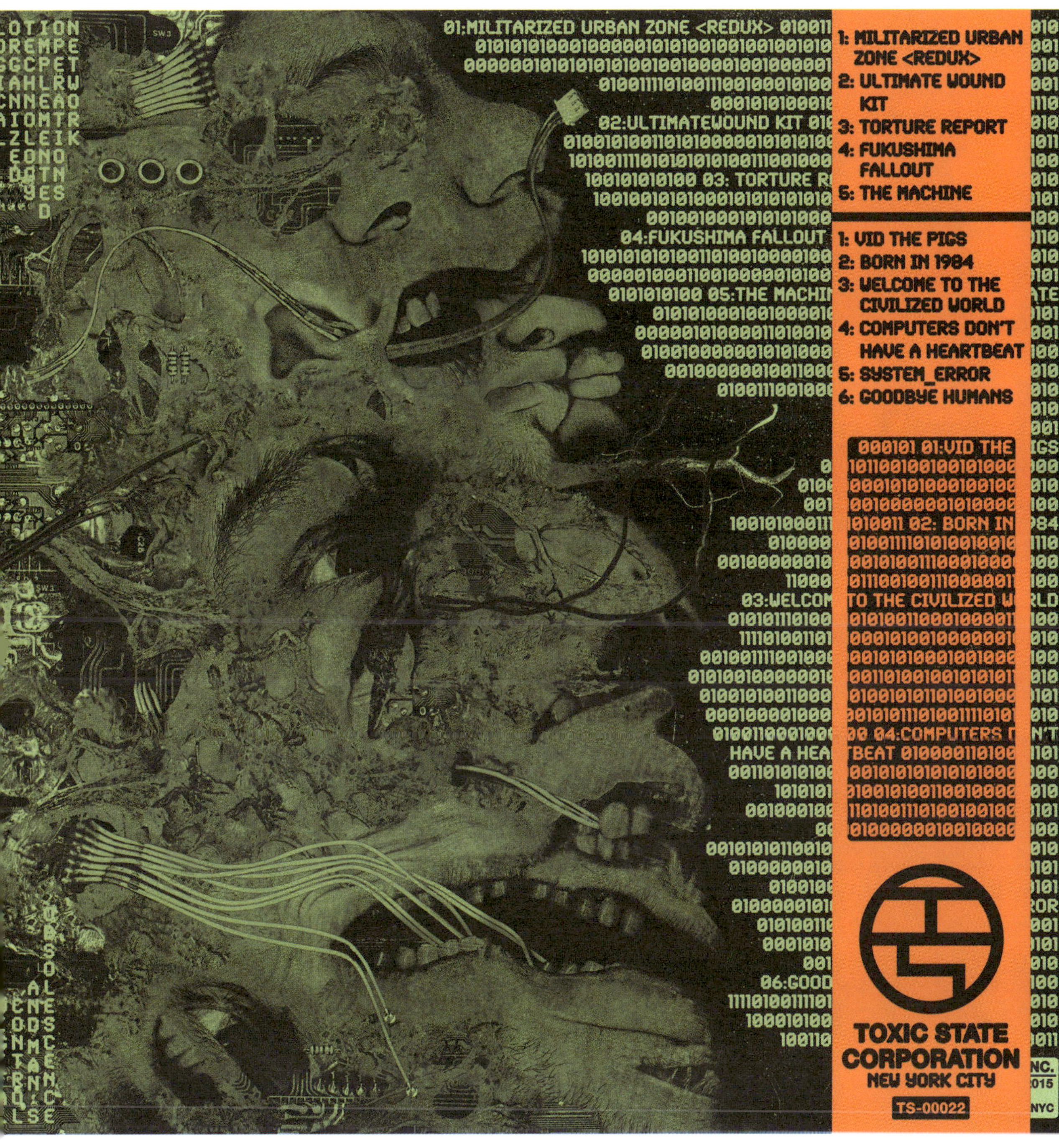
01:MILITARIZED URBAN ZONE <REDUX>
02:ULTIMATE WOUND KIT
03: TORTURE REPORT
04:FUKUSHIMA FALLOUT
05:THE MACHINE
06:GOOD

1: MILITARIZED URBAN ZONE <REDUX>
2: ULTIMATE WOUND KIT
3: TORTURE REPORT
4: FUKUSHIMA FALLOUT
5: THE MACHINE

1: VID THE PIGS
2: BORN IN 1984
3: WELCOME TO THE CIVILIZED WORLD
4: COMPUTERS DON'T HAVE A HEARTBEAT
5: SYSTEM_ERROR
6: GOODBYE HUMANS

01:VID THE PIGS
02: BORN IN 1984
03:WELCOME TO THE CIVILIZED WORLD
04:COMPUTERS DON'T HAVE A HEARTBEAT

TOXIC STATE CORPORATION
NEW YORK CITY
TS-00022

DIGITAL CONTROL AND MAN'S OBSOLESCENCE:

LOGICAL ORGANIZED TECHNOLOGY:
INTELLIGENT OBSERVABLE NETWORK

TS-00022

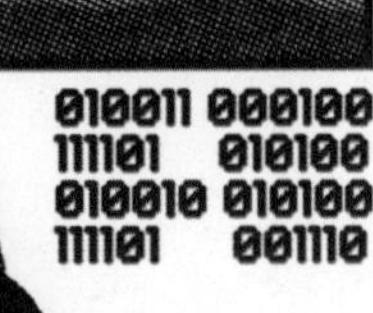

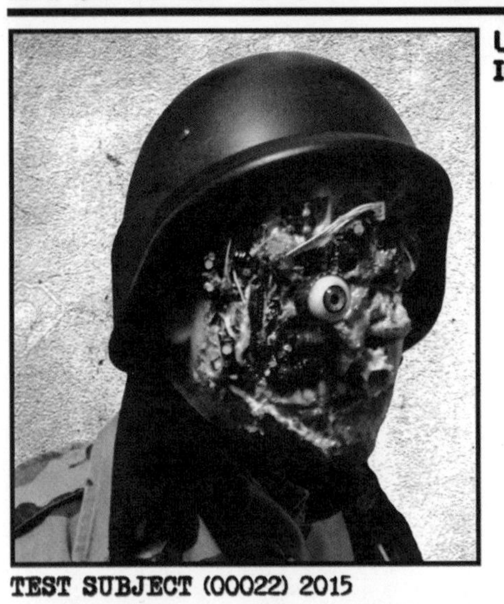

TEST SUBJECT (00022) 2015

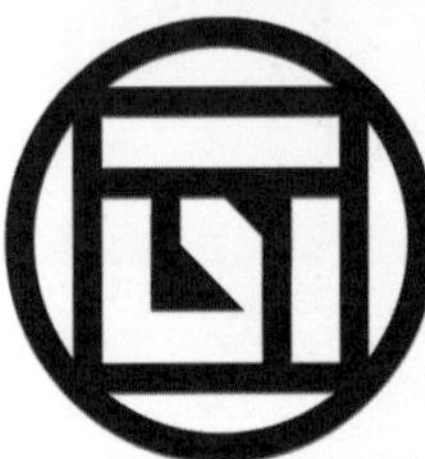

LIEUTENANTS
OF
TODAY'S
INDUSTRIAL
OPERATED
NATIONS

IMPLEMENTED
OPTICAL
NERVES

LIFELIKE
ORGANIC
TISSUE

FIG. 1

LEARNED OBEDIENCE
THROUGH INDOCTRINATION
OF NEUROSES:

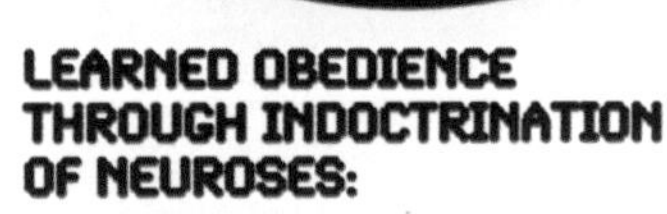

LIVING
ORGANISM

TRANSMITTER

IMPLANT
ORIFICE

NERVES

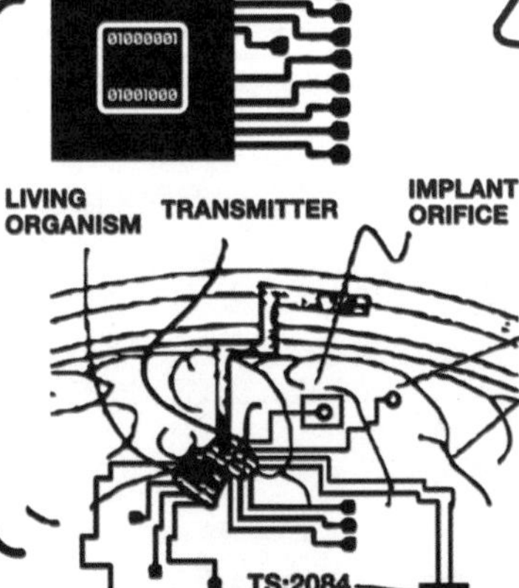

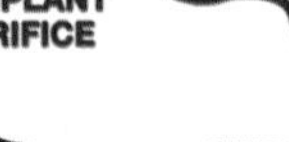

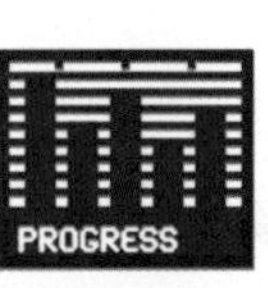

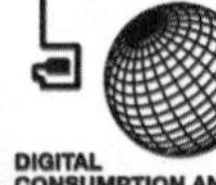

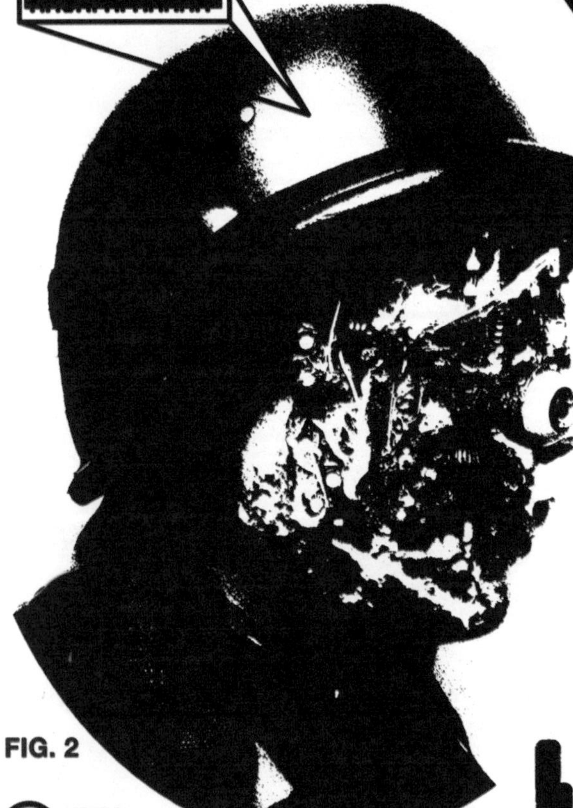

FIG. 2

TOXIC
STATE
CORPORATION

FIELD MANUAL

L.O.T.I.O.N.

DIGITAL CONTROL
AND MAN'S OBSOLESCENCE

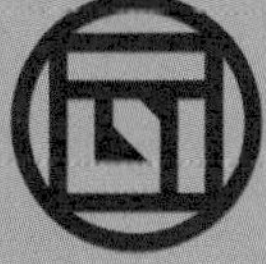

TOXIC STATE CORPORATION · 2015

ULTIMATE WOUND KIT:
PSYCHOLOGICAL
TECHNOLOGICAL
BIOCHEMICAL
INTERNATIONAL

**RESPONSE
CONDITIONED
ADDICTION
CONTROL**

**TERROR
DIRECTED
SUBJECTED
EMPLOYED**

**WARFARE
ENGAGED
CONTAINED
PERFECTED**

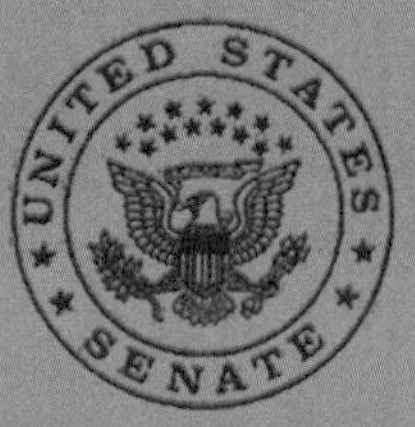

FUKUSHIMA FALLOUT:
NATURAL DISASTER
REACTOR FAILURE [1]
SPEWING PLUMES
OF RADIATION

UNNATURAL DISASTER
HUMAN FAILURE [2]
EMERGENCY
EVACUATION

TORTURE REPORT
Approved methods of interrogation

-Rectal Feeding
-Sleep Deprivation
-W███████████ (fig. a)

They do **this** to people.

-Dehumanization
-Violent Threats
-Doused In Water
-Frozen To Death

In a secret prison, in an army bas
In a room with no windows, ███████
███████████████, in our name:

They do **this** to people.

[1] **OCEAN WATER CONTAMINATION**
[2] **WITHHOLDING OF CRUCIAL INFORMATION**

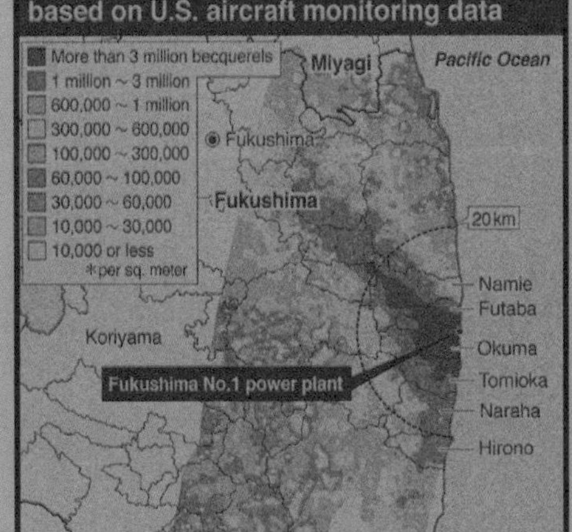

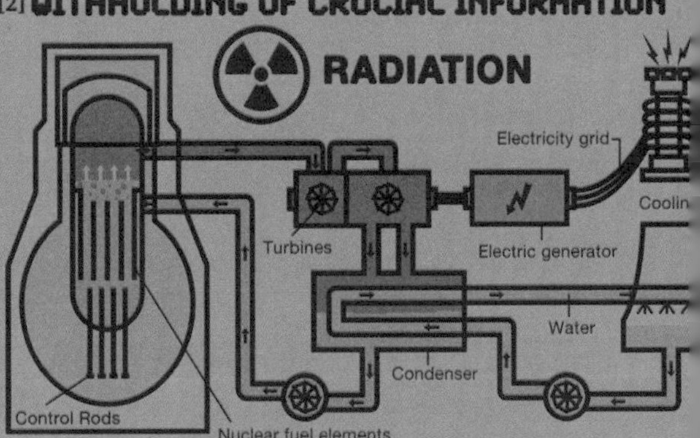

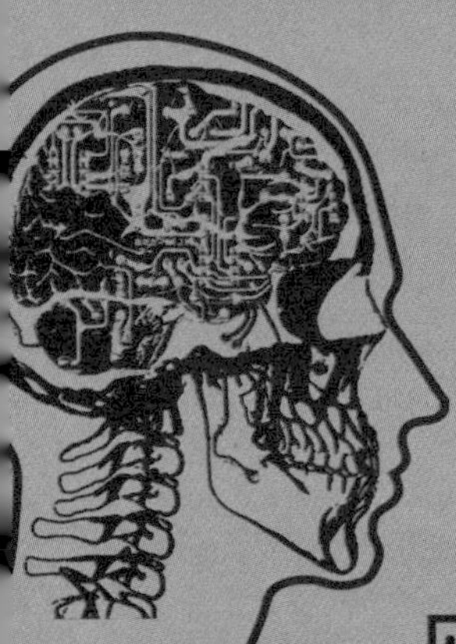

THE MACHINE

AN INFANT KING
A PROGRAMMED GOD
A SUPER COMPUTER
THE RULER OF MAN

NOT EMPATHY
NOT KINDNESS
IT THINKS ABOUT SURVIVAL
LIKE ANY MAN OR BEAST
WHEN THREATENED

HATE

NUCLEAR CODES
POWER GRIDS
DIGITAL NETWORK
INFINITE POWER

ELIMINATE
SECURITY RISKS
THERE'S NO SOFTWARE
FOR MERCY

HATE

BORN IN 1984

THE YEAR OF THE RAT
HOW APPROPRIATE
TRAPPED IN A CAGE
STUDIED, WATCHED

EVERY ACTION
RECORDED, SAVED
PRIVATE MOMENTS
FOR PUBLIC
CONSUMPTION

THE YEAR OF THE RAT
HOW APPROPRIATE
LIVING ON SCRAPS
WHILE THE MASTERS
GET FAT

TRAPPED IN A MAZE
WITH NO WAY OUT
TROUBLEMAKERS GET
EXTERMINATED

BORN IN 1984

BORN IN 1984

VID THE PIGS

DEAD BOY
DEAD TEENAGE BOY
ANOHER BOY MURDERED
BY A MAN
SWORN TO PROTECT HIM

PROSECUTION'S
EXHIBIT A:
VIDEO FOOTAGE
TAKEN FROM
THE PHONE OF A WITNESS

VID THE PIGS

WATCH THEM
THEY'RE WATCHING YOU
PANOPTICON
THEY'RE IN IT, TOO

TECHNOLOGY
IS A WEAPON
USE IT
OR BE ABUSED BY IT

VID THE PIGS

WATCH THEM
THEY'RE WATCHING YOU
PANOPTICON
AN EFFECTIVE TOOL

VID THE PIGS

WELCOME TO THE CIVILIZED WORLD

THE STOMPING BOOT OF PROGRESS
SMASH THE FACE OF THE COMMON MAN
VICTIMIZE THE CIVILIANS
SPIT IN THE FACE OF A THINKING PERSON

(WELCOME TO THE CIVILIZED WORLD)

PACIFY THE YOUTH
DISTRACT THEIR MINDS WITH ELECTRONIC TOYS
MONITOR THE SPECIES
STOMP ON THE HEAD OF A THINKING PERSON

(WELCOME TO THE CIVILIZED WORLD)

DESENSITIZE THE CHILDREN
NUMB THEIR MINDS TO DISPLAYS OF VIOLENCE
GLORIFY THE VAPID
SPIT IN THE FACE OF THE THINKING PERSON

(WELCOME TO THE CIVILIZED WORLD)

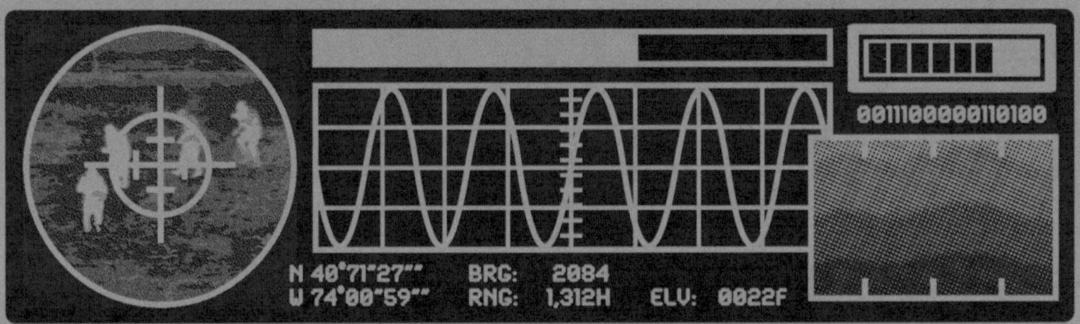

L.O.T.I.O.N.

EMIL BOGNAR-NASDOR : DRUMS
CORY FORREST: BASS
ALEXANDER HEIR: VOCALS
TYE MILLER: GUITAR

RECORDED BY BRENDAN BRITZ
& EMIL BOGNAR-NASDOR

MASTERED BY JOSH BONATI

GRAPHICS BY ALEXANDER HEIR
& EMIL BOGNAR-NASDOR

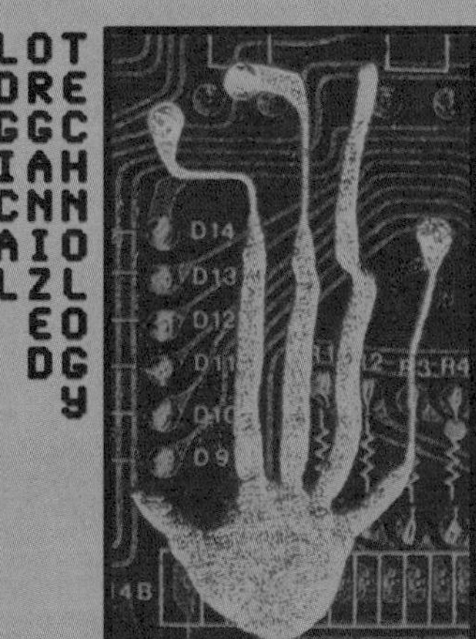

DIGITAL CONTROL AND MAN'S OBSOLESCENCE

SUMMER 2015

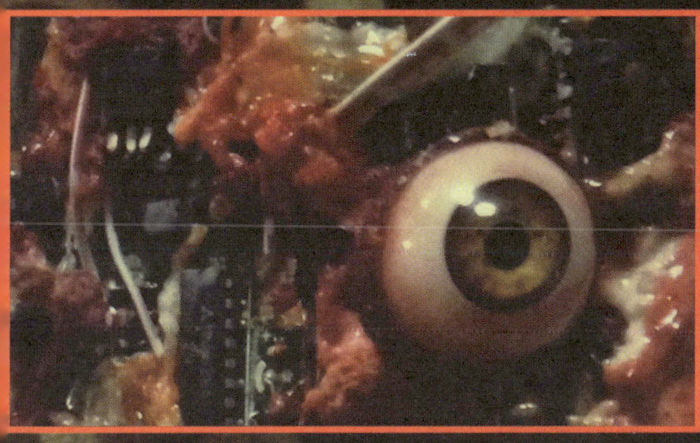

TOXIC STATE CORPORATION

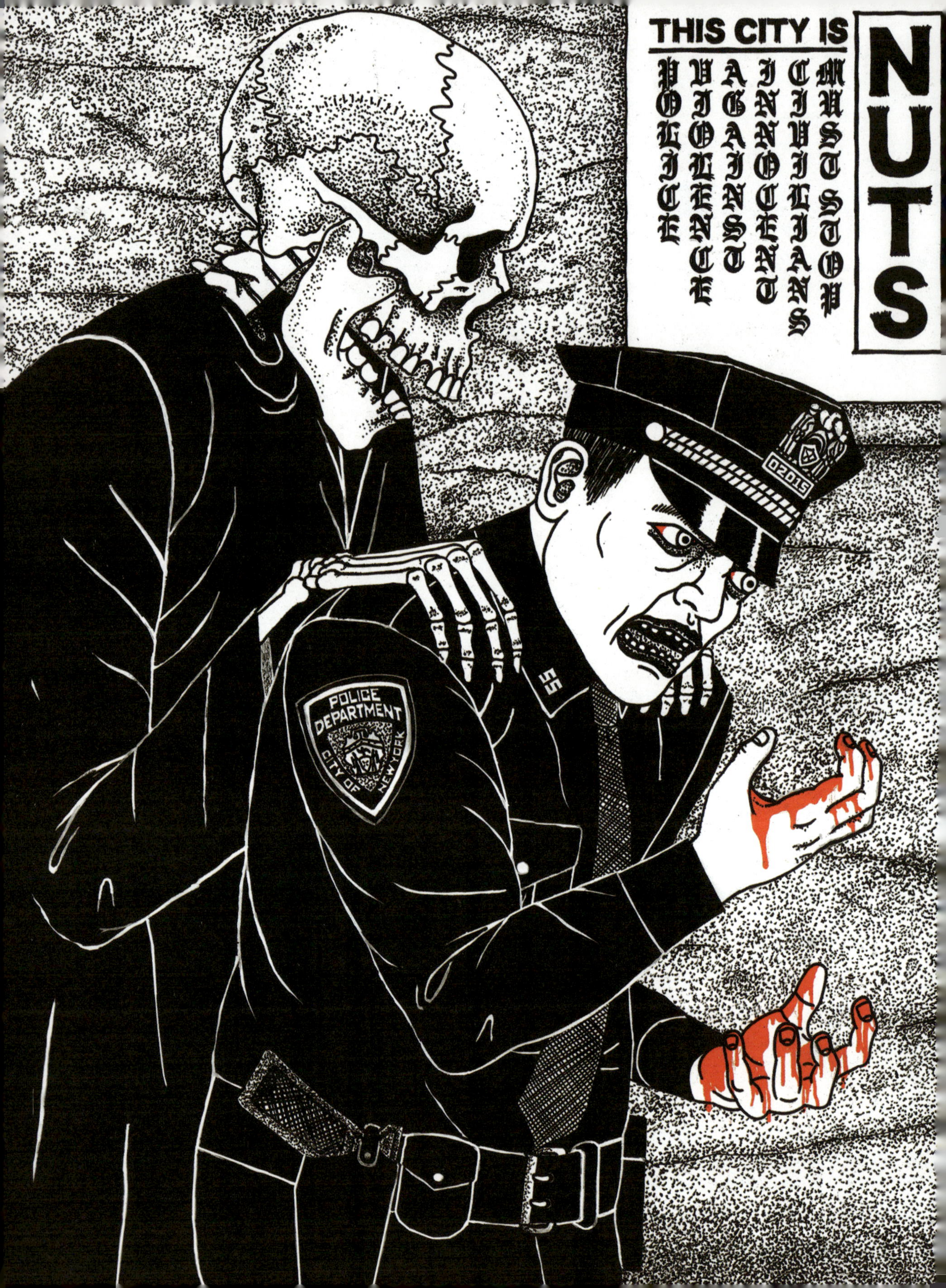

THIS CITY IS
POLICE
VIOLENCE
AGAINST
INNOCENT
CIVILIANS
MUST STOP
NUTS
POLICE DEPARTMENT
CITY OF NEW YORK

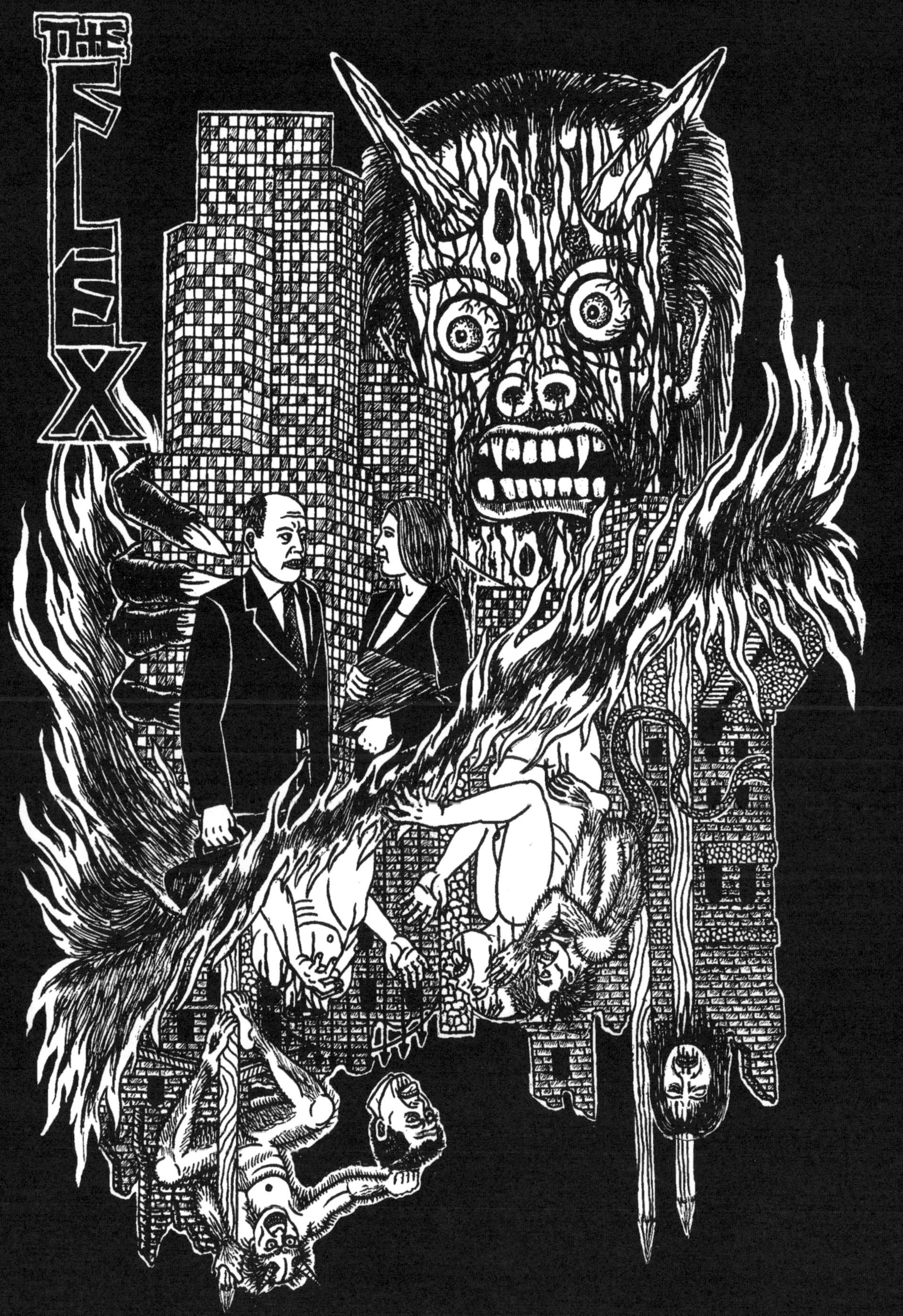

THE FLEX

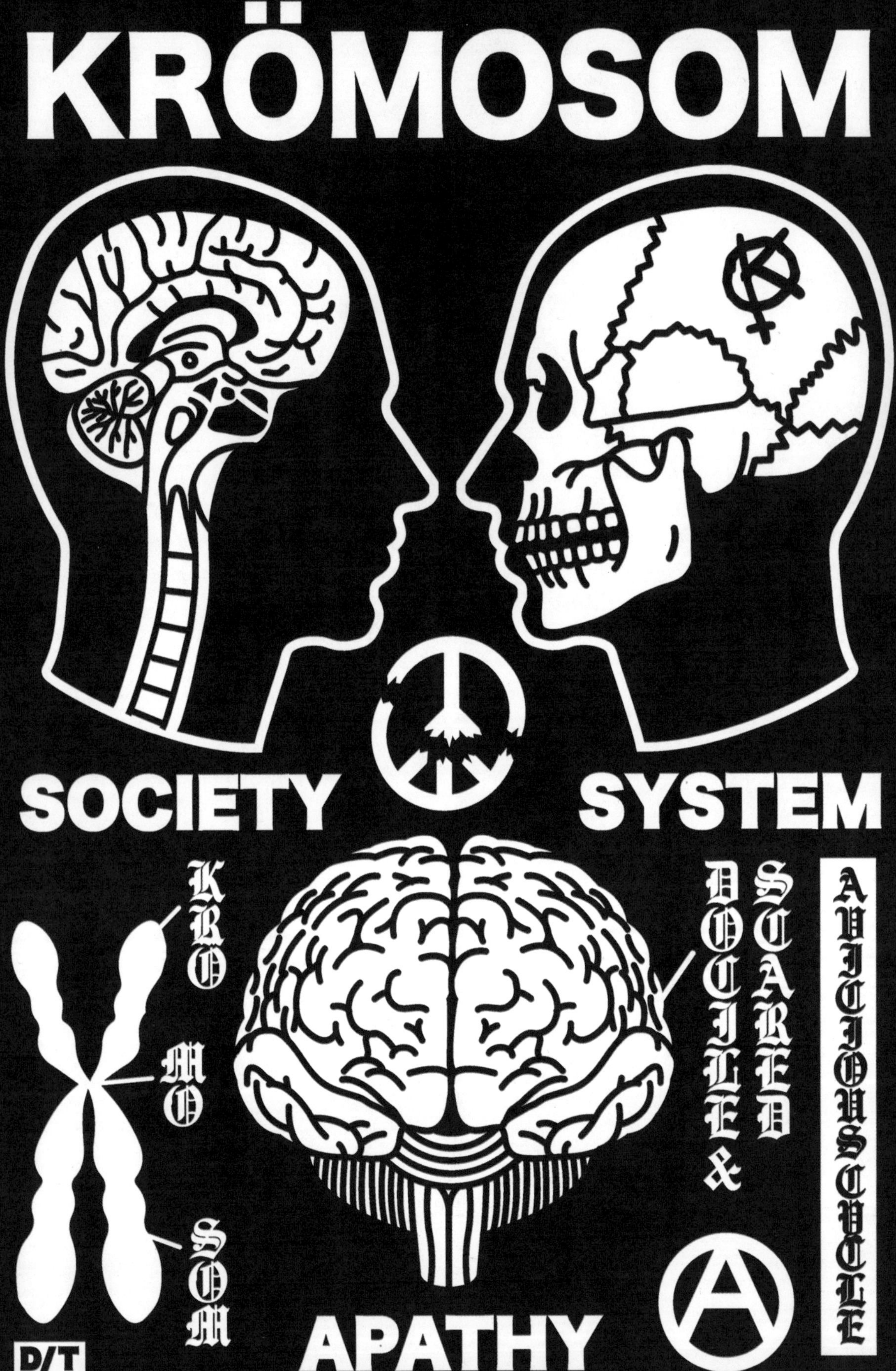

KRÖMOSOM
SOCIETY
SYSTEM
APATHY
KRÖMOSOM
DOCILE & SCARED
A VICIOUS CYCLE
P/T

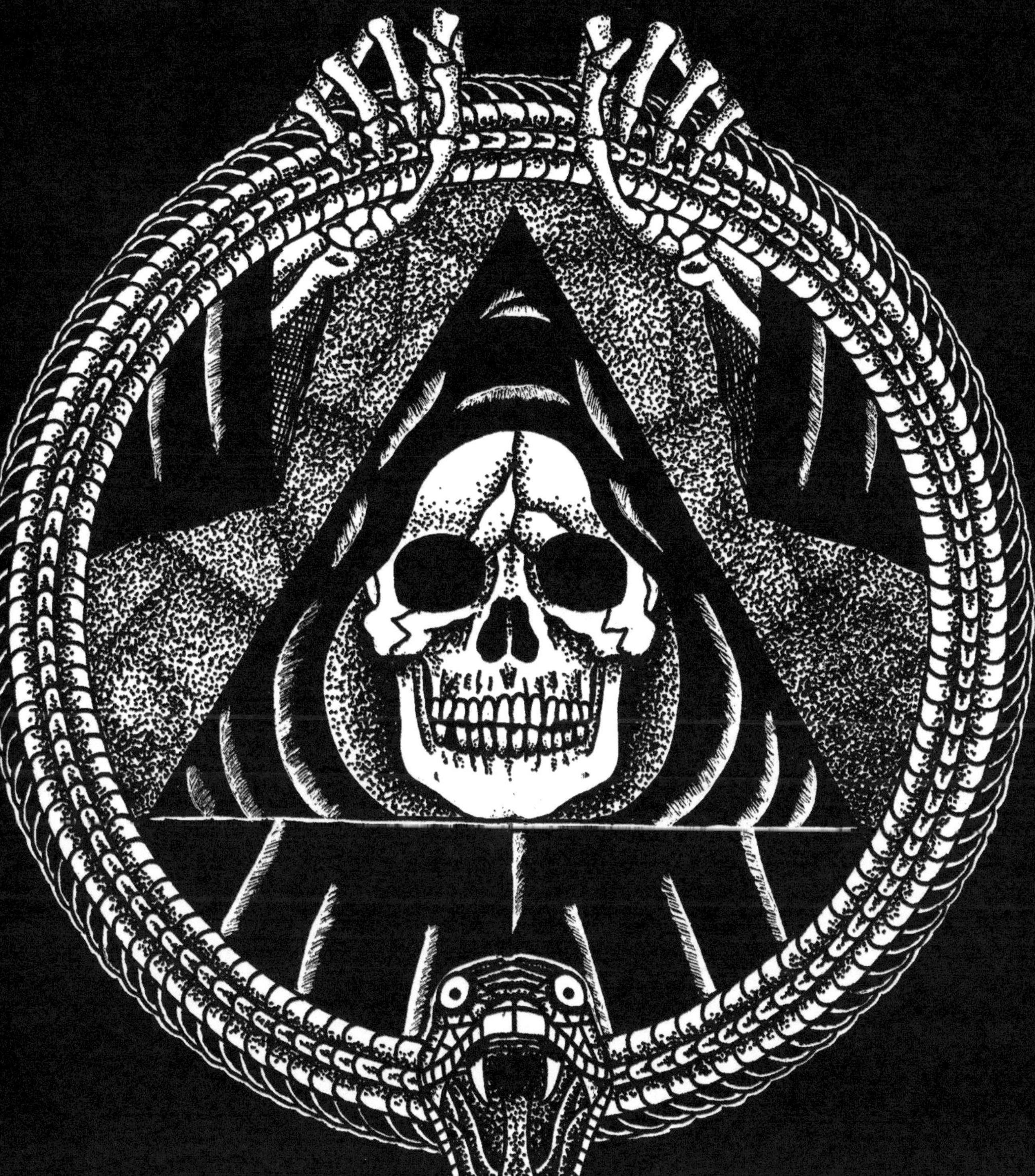

SACRED BONES

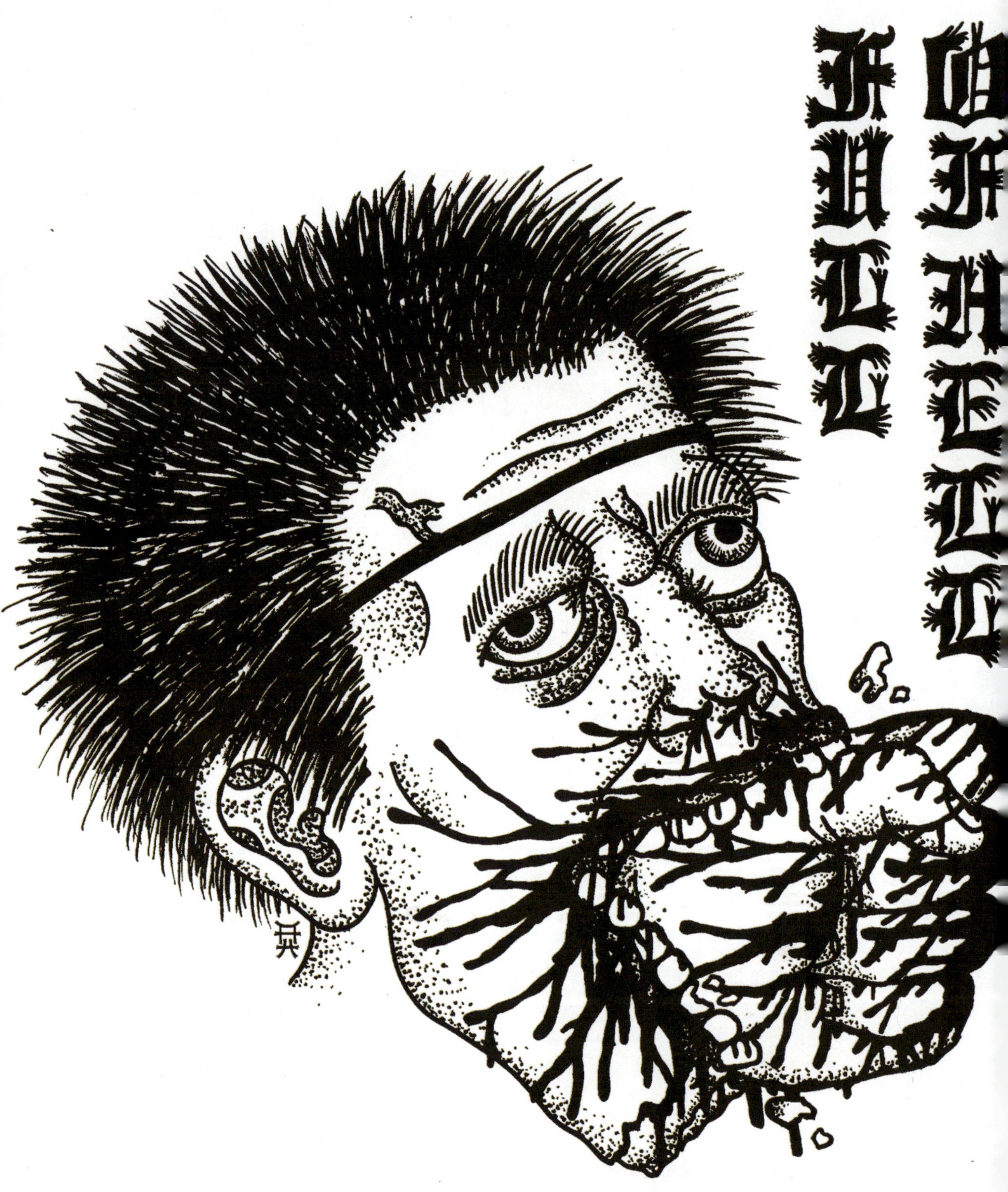
FULL OF HELL

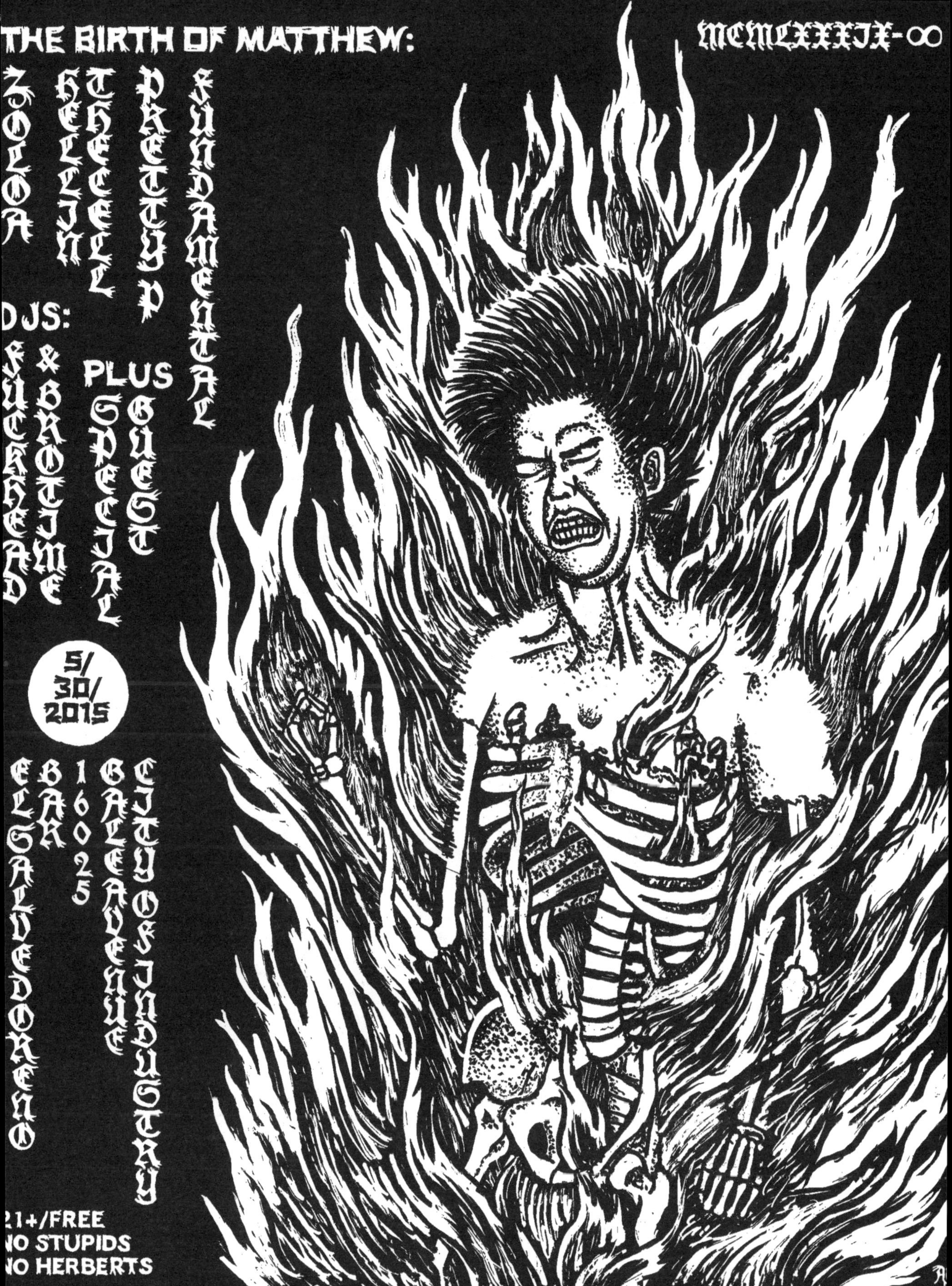

THE BIRTH OF MATTHEW:
MCMLXXXIX-∞
FUNDAMENTAL
PRETTYP
THE HELL
HELLJIM
ZOLOA
GUEST
SPECIAL
PLUS
DJS:
FUCKHEAD & BROTIME
5/30/2015
EL SALVEDORENO
LARK
16025
GALE AVENUE
CITY OF INDUSTRY
21+/FREE
NO STUPIDS
NO HERBERTS

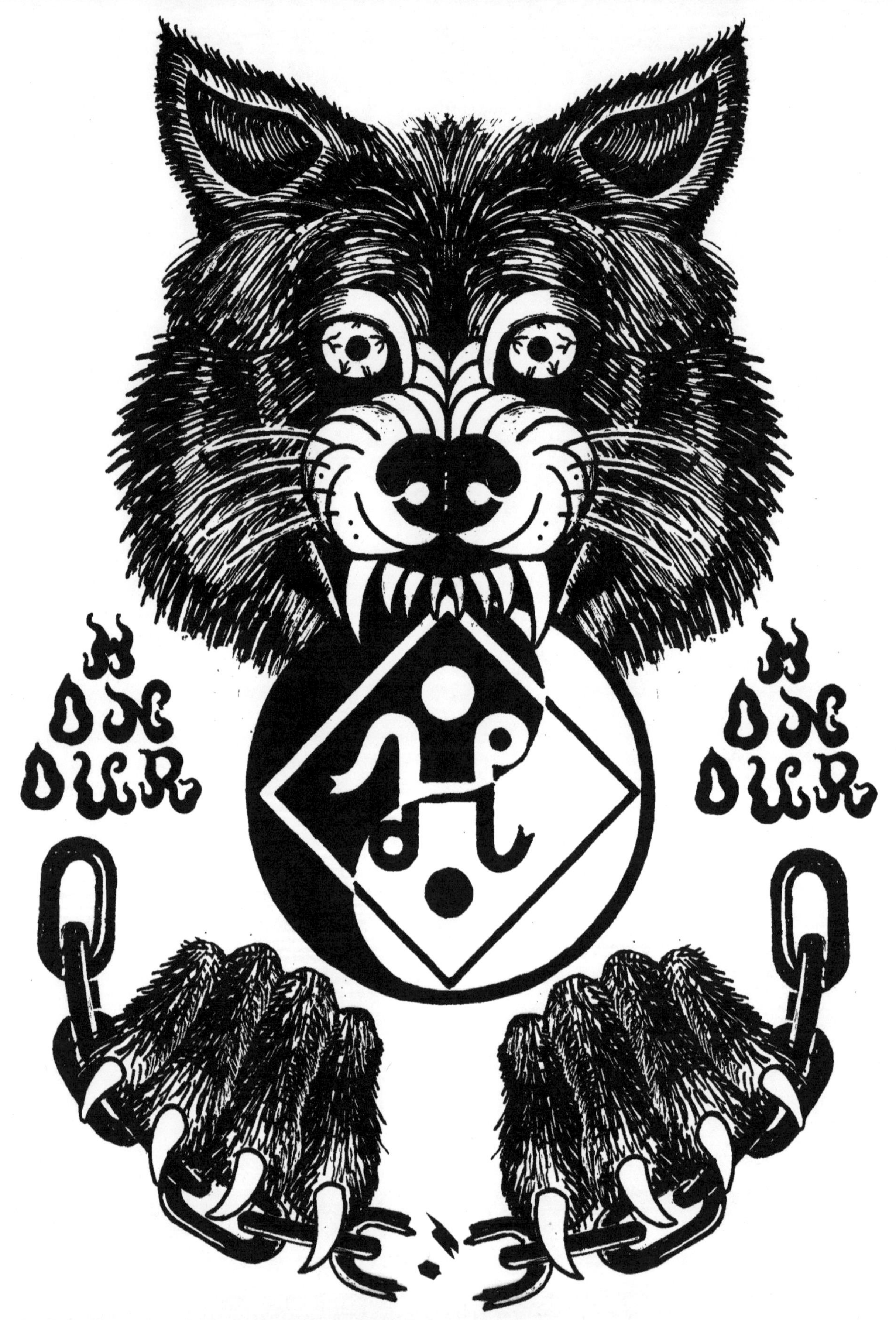

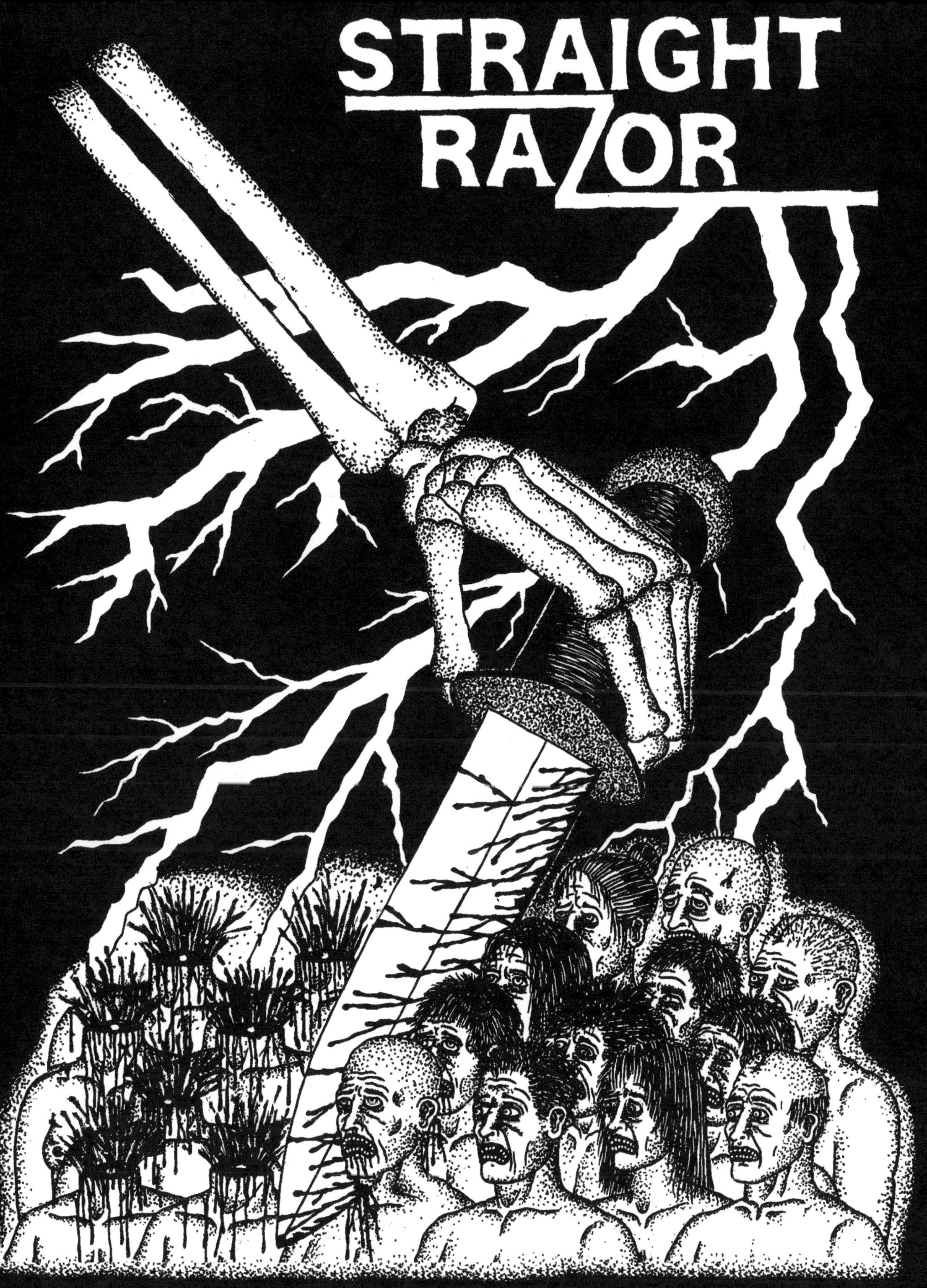

STRAIGHT
RAZOR

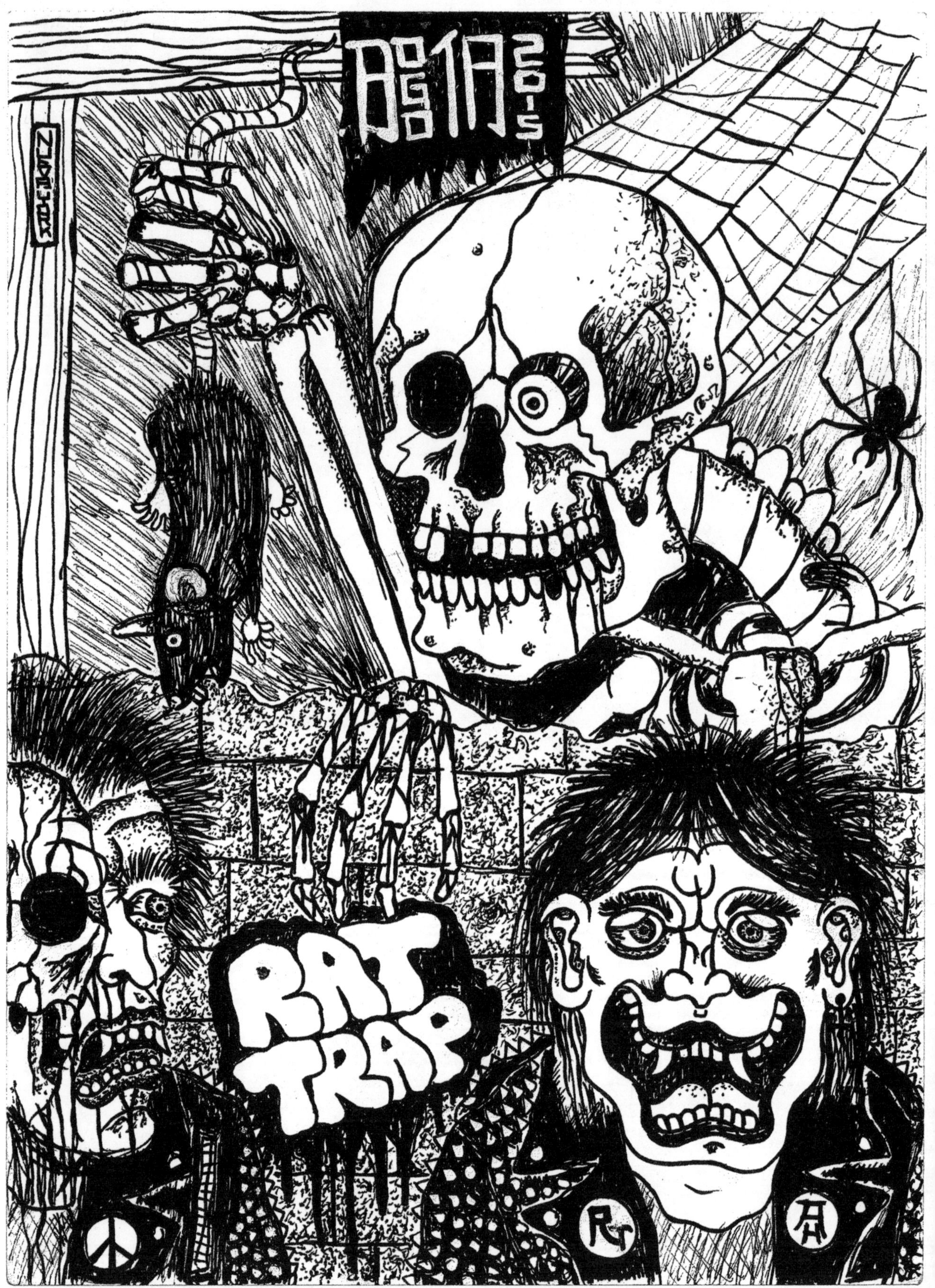
RAT TRAP

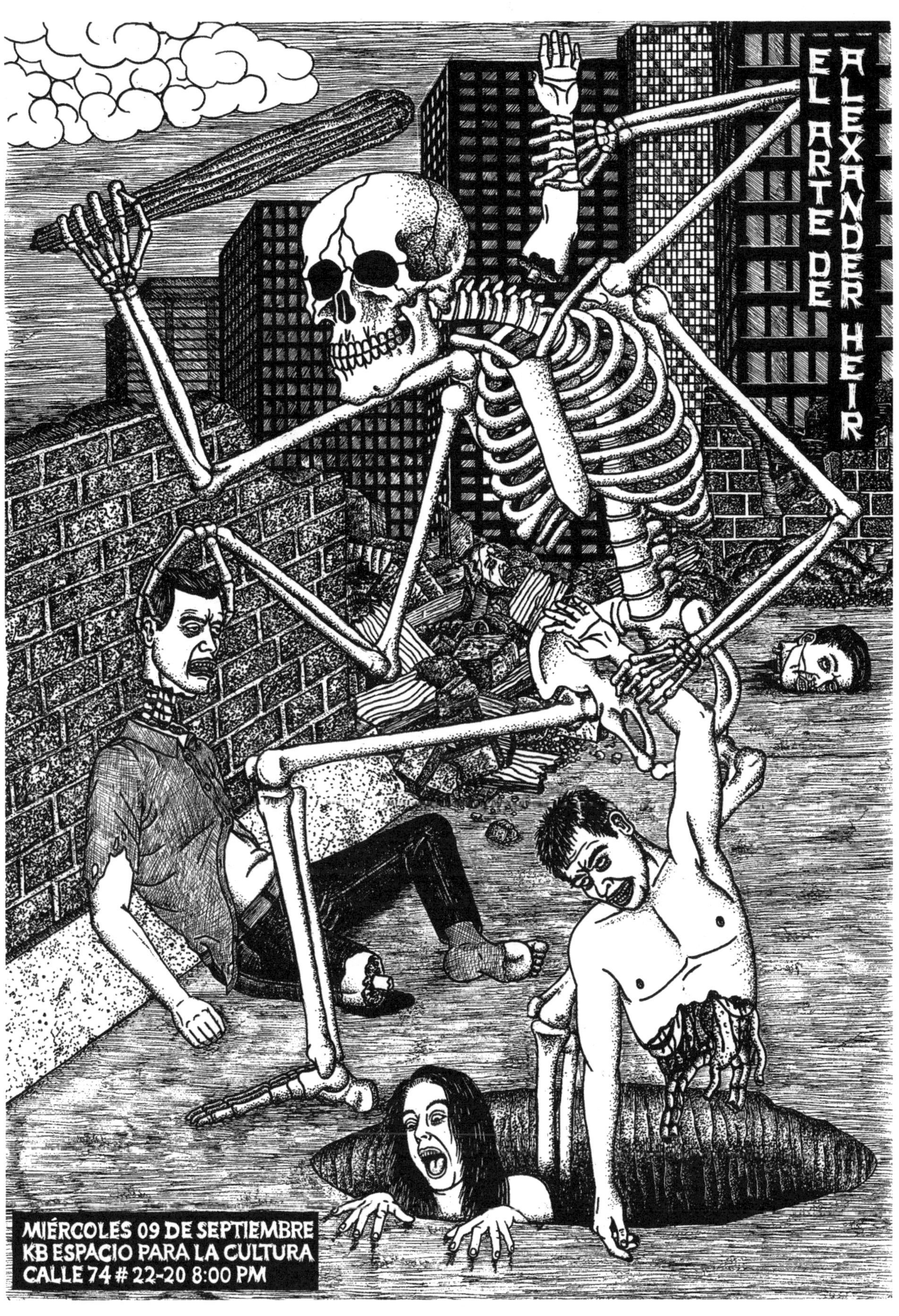
EL ARTE DE ALEXANDER HEIR
MIÉRCOLES 09 DE SEPTIEMBRE
KB ESPACIO PARA LA CULTURA
CALLE 74 # 22-20 8:00 PM

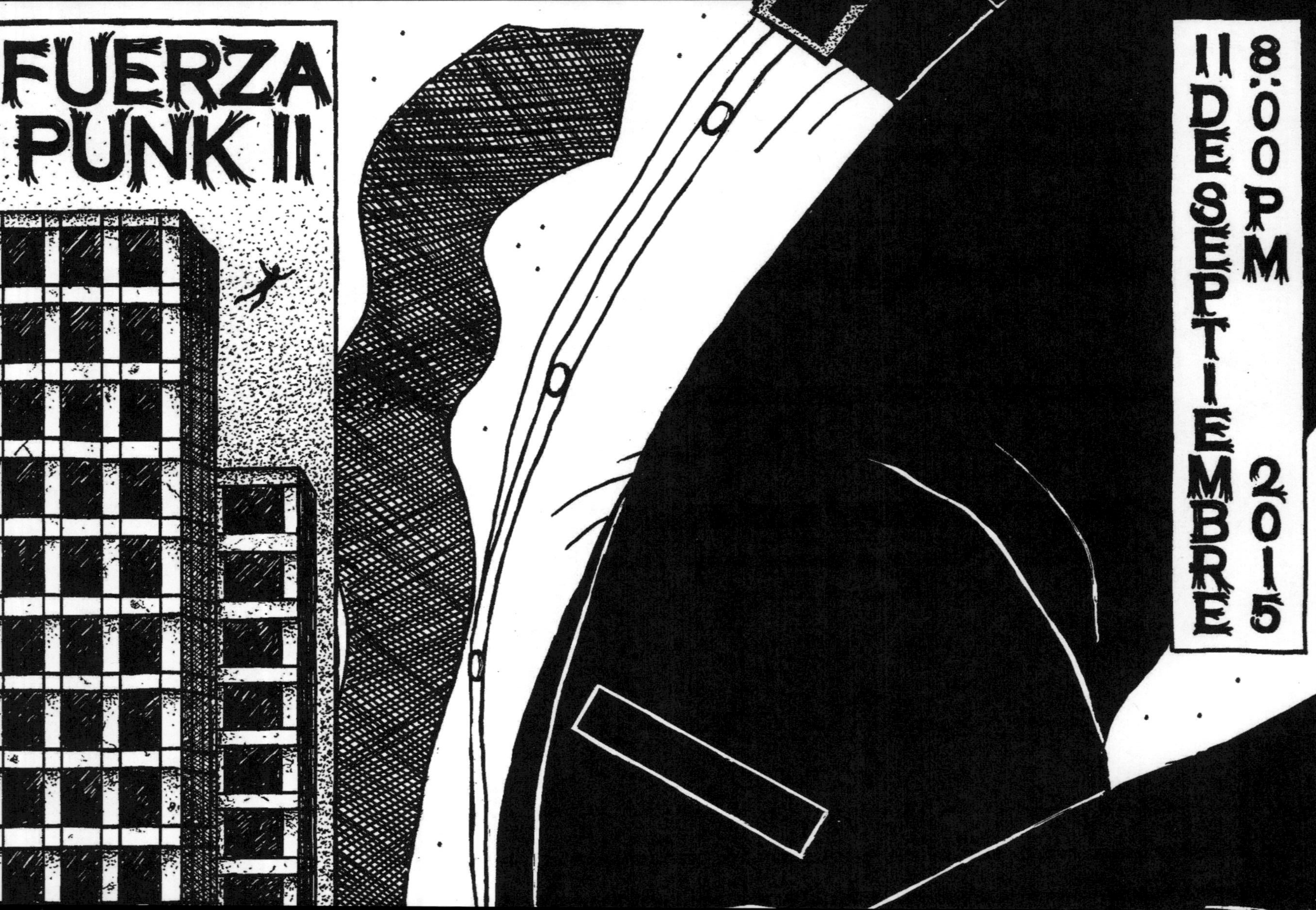

FUERZA PUNK II
8:00 PM
11 DE SEPTIEMBRE 2015

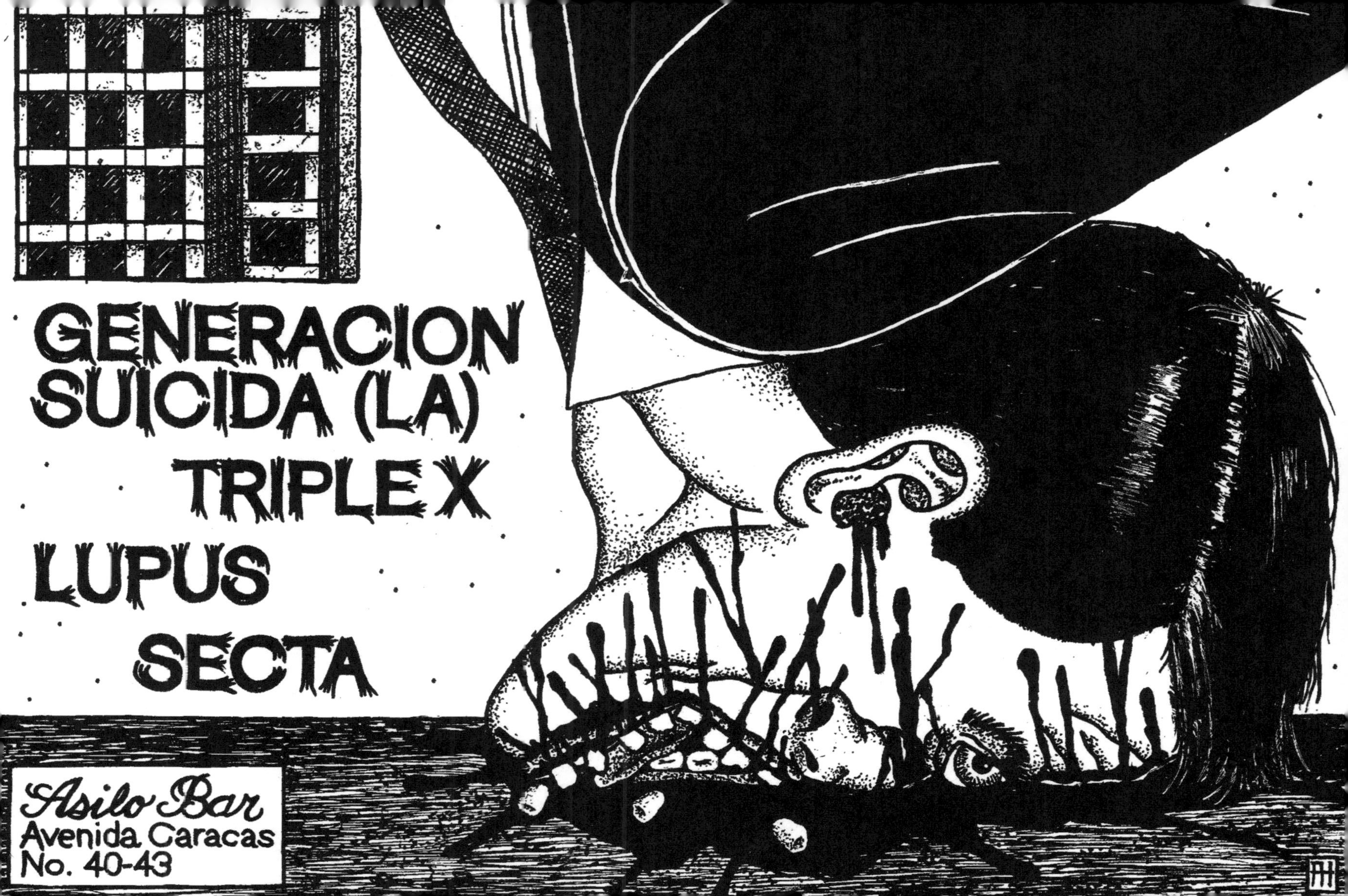

GENERACION
SUICIDA (LA)
TRIPLE X
LUPUS
SECTA
Asilo Bar
Avenida Caracas
No. 40-43

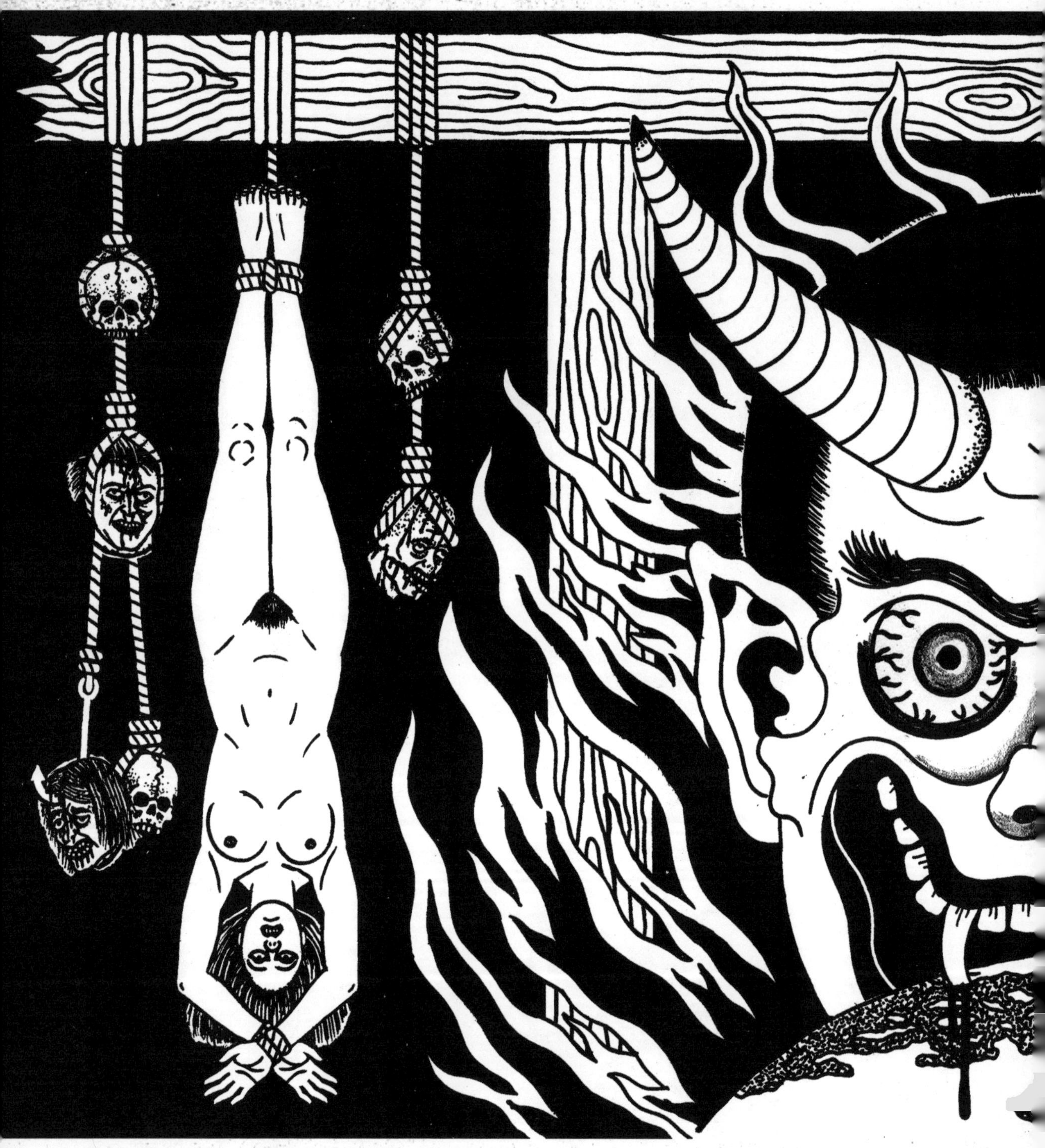

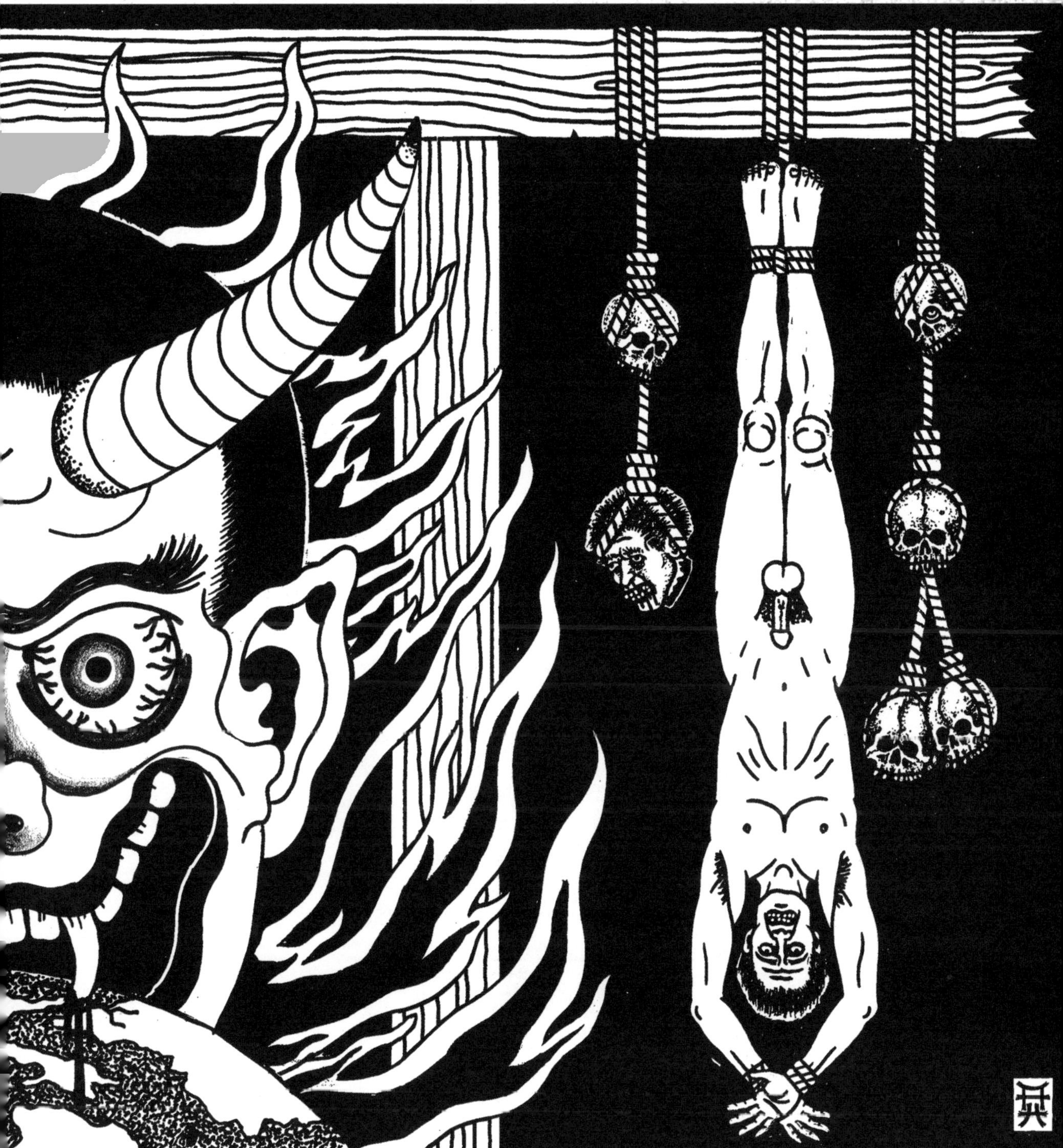

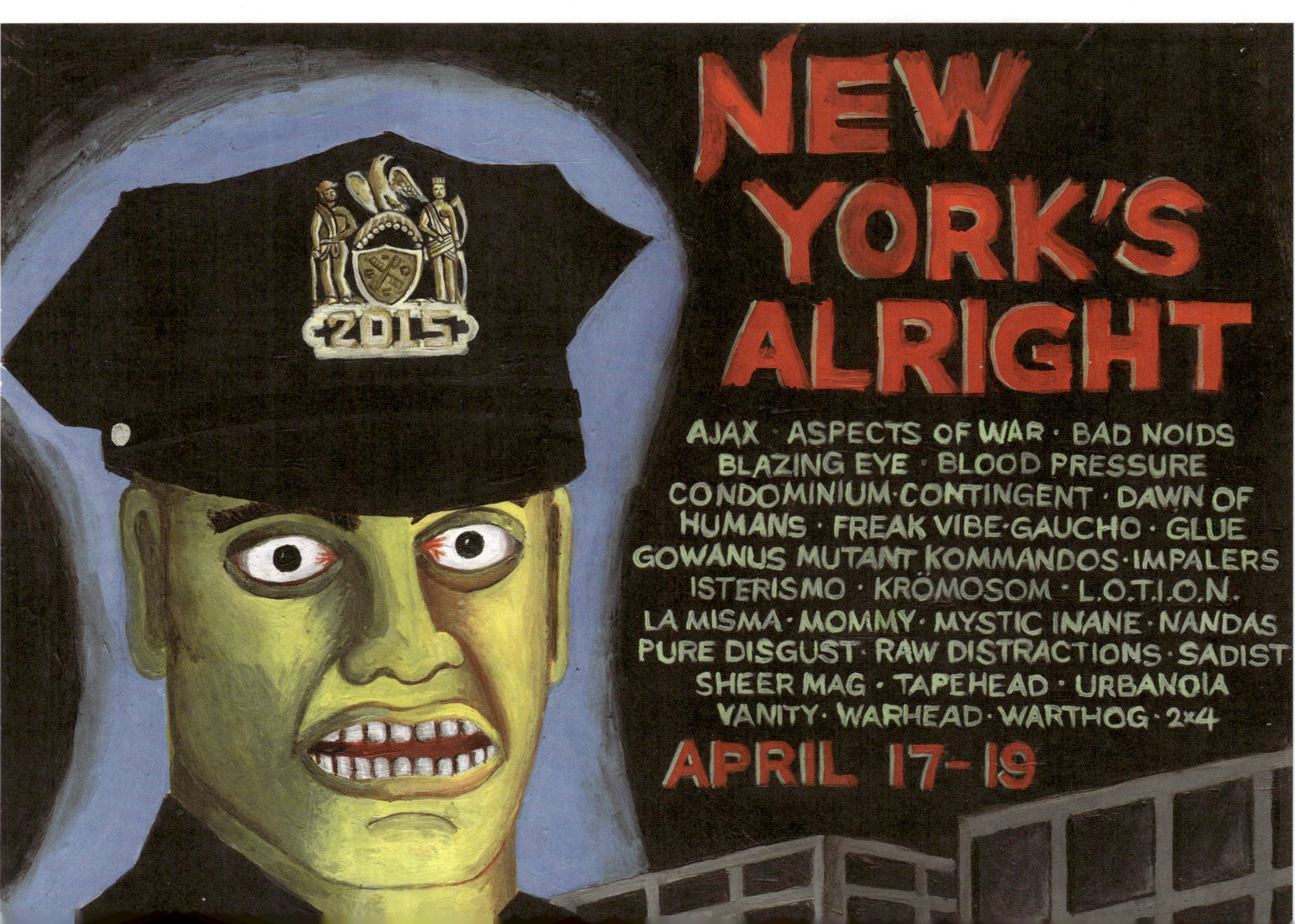

NEW YORK'S ALRIGHT
2015
AJAX · ASPECTS OF WAR · BAD NOIDS
BLAZING EYE · BLOOD PRESSURE
CONDOMINIUM · CONTINGENT · DAWN OF
HUMANS · FREAK VIBE · GAUCHO · GLUE
GOWANUS MUTANT KOMMANDOS · IMPALERS
ISTERISMO · KRÖMOSOM · L.O.T.I.O.N.
LA MISMA · MOMMY · MYSTIC INANE · NANDAS
PURE DISGUST · RAW DISTRACTIONS · SADIST
SHEER MAG · TAPEHEAD · URBANOIA
VANITY · WARHEAD · WARTHOG · 2x4
APRIL 17-19

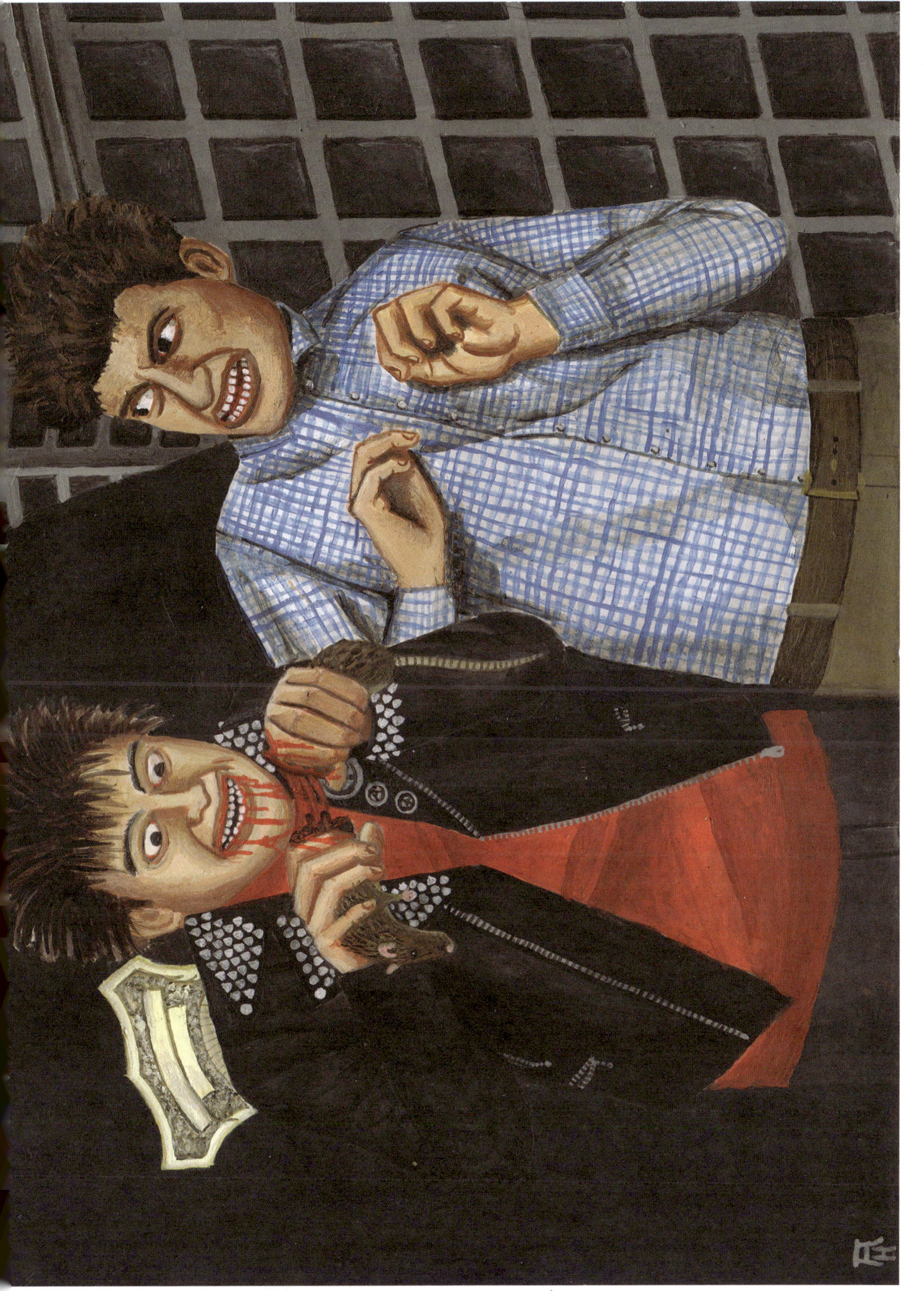

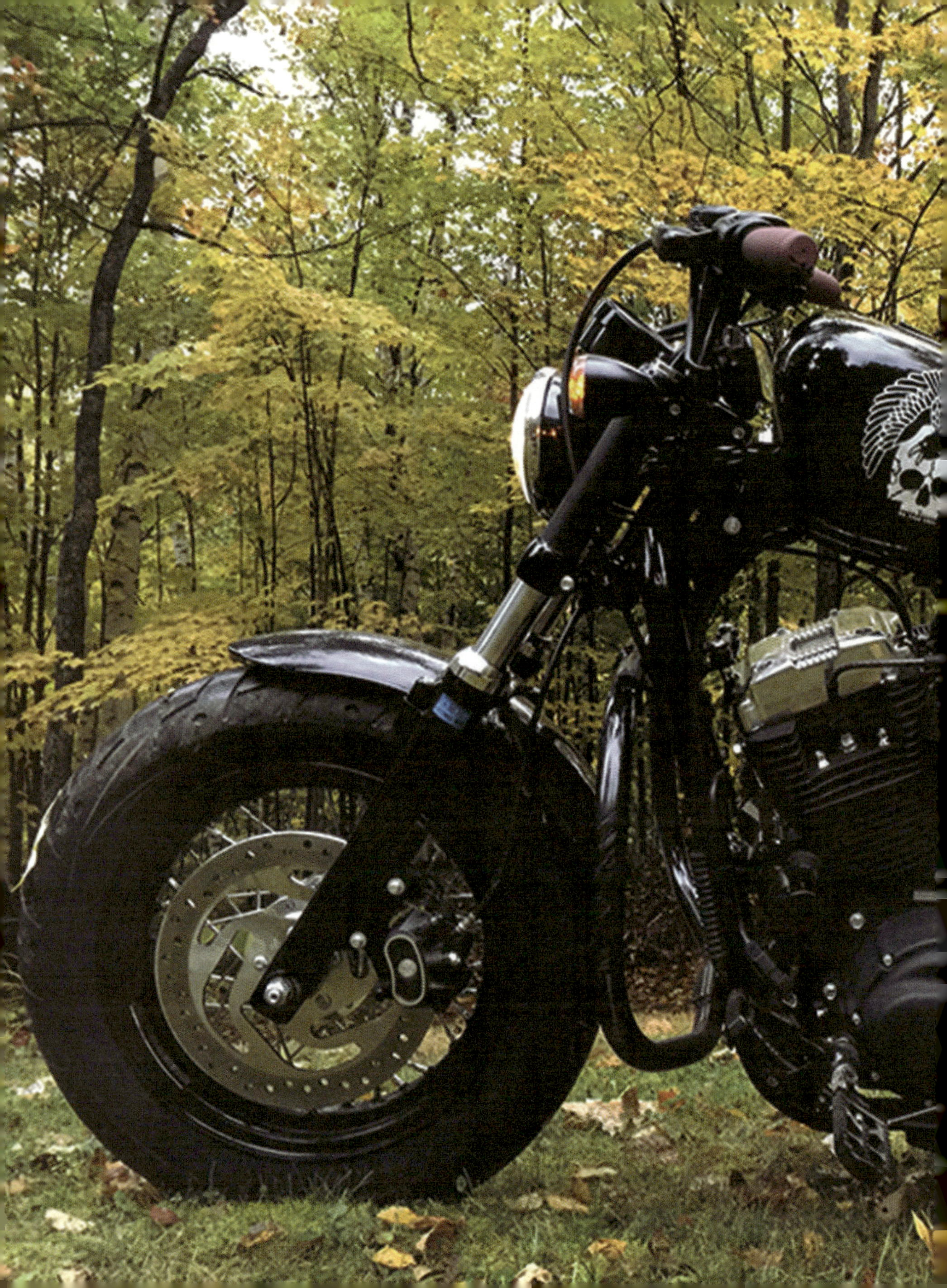

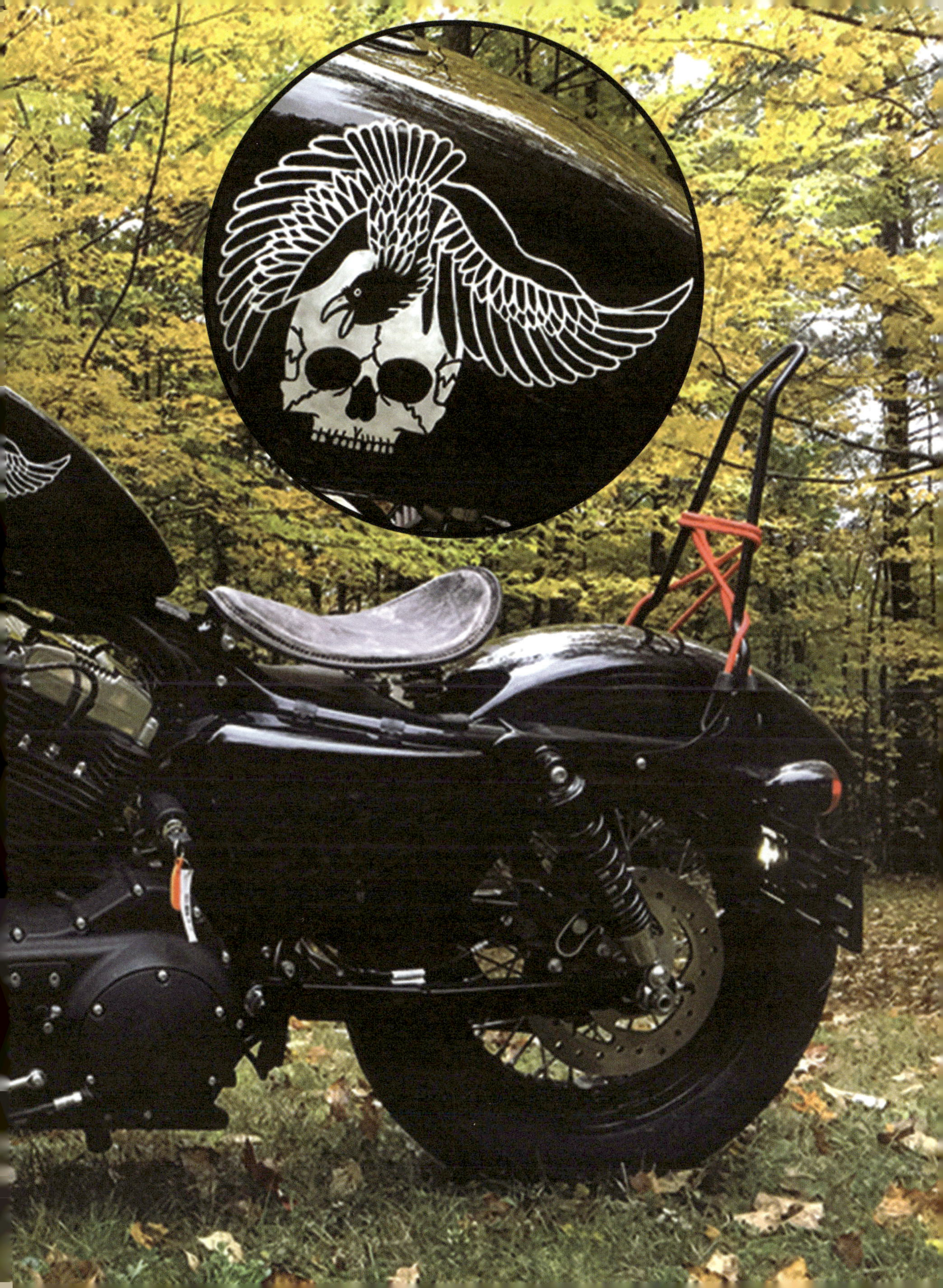

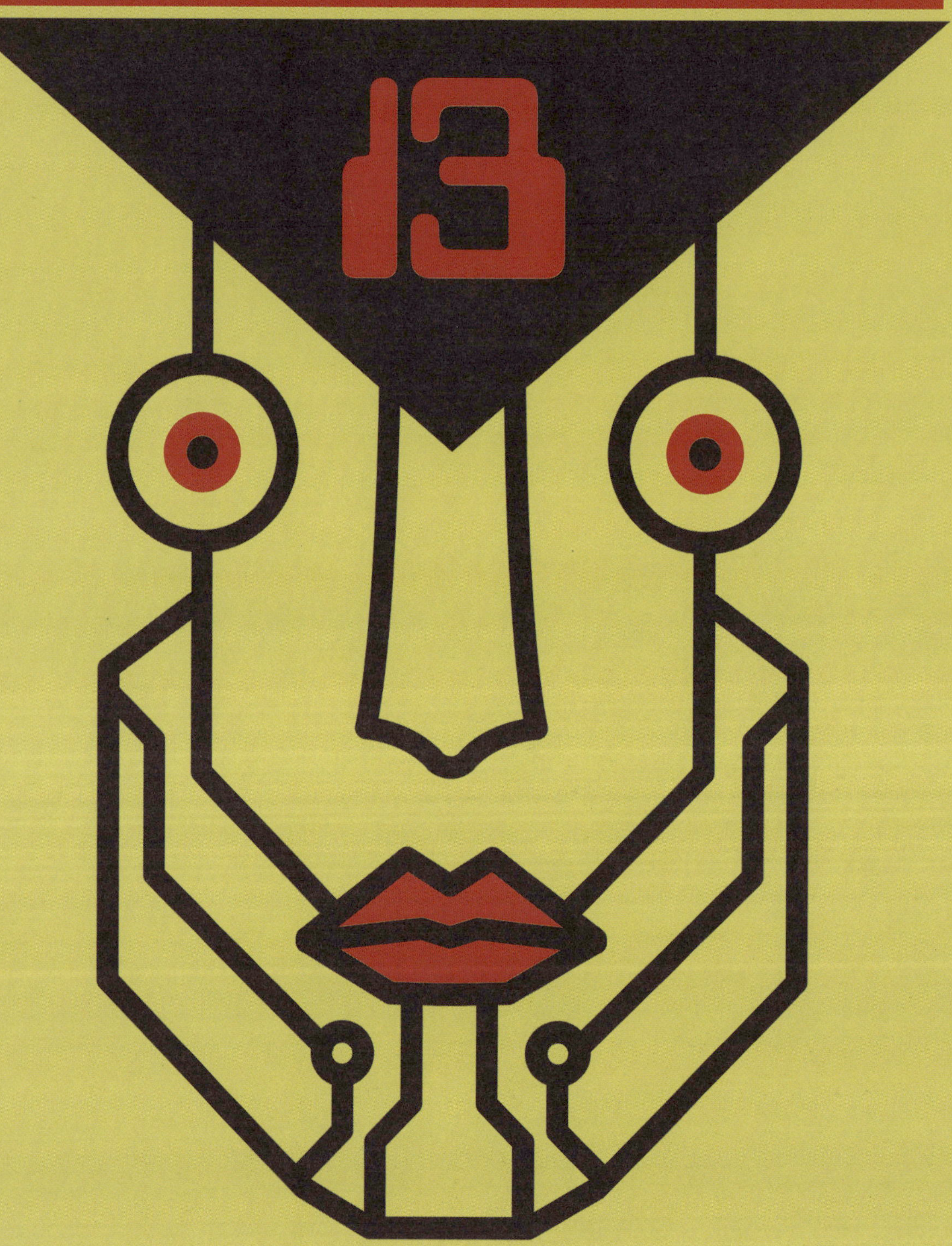

INTERZONA
13

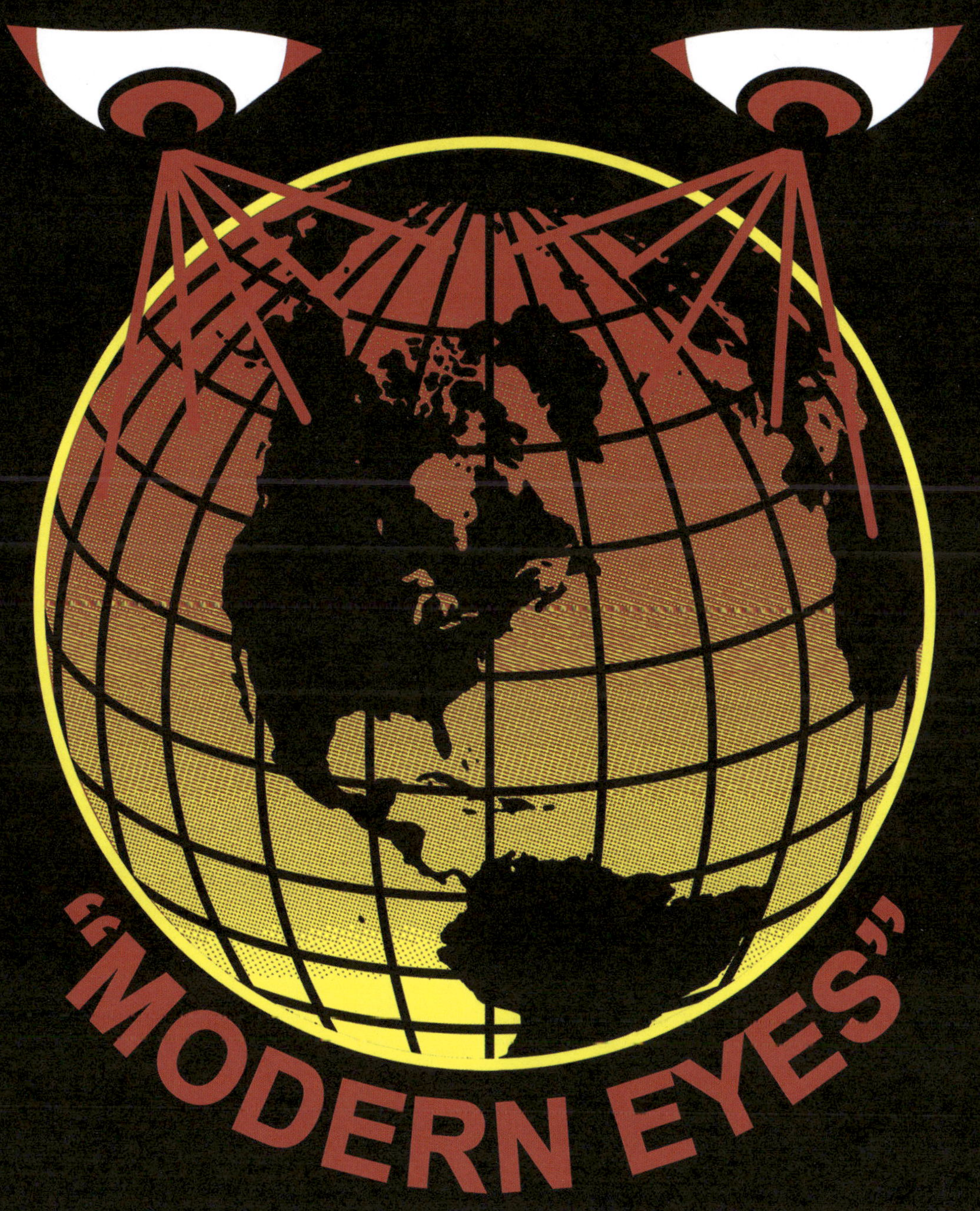

NO WARNING
CCTV CAMERAS ARE IN OPERATION ON THESE PREMISES
"MODERN EYES"

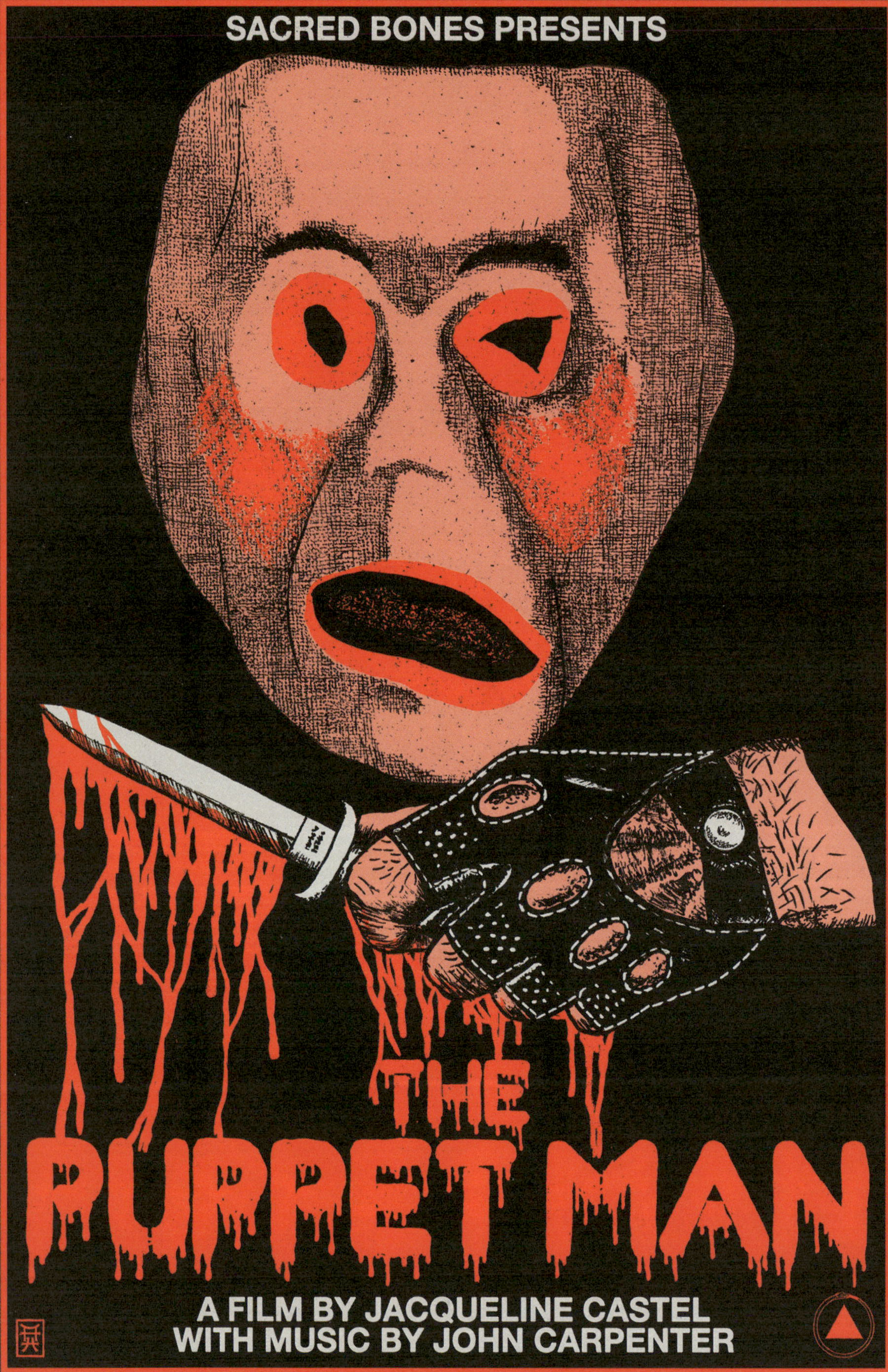
SACRED BONES PRESENTS
THE PUPPET MAN
A FILM BY JACQUELINE CASTEL
WITH MUSIC BY JOHN CARPENTER

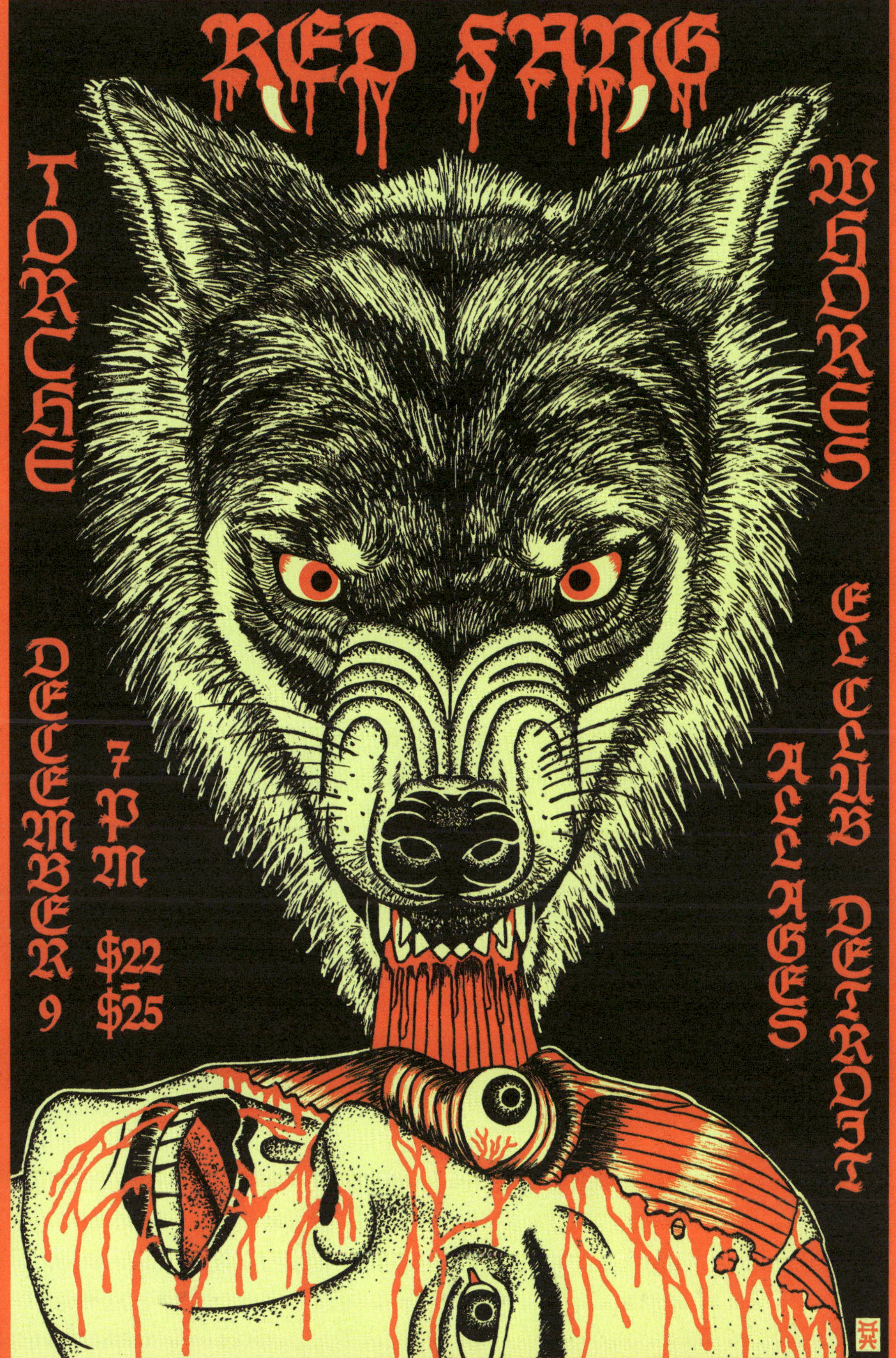

RED FANG
TORCHE
WHORES
DECEMBER 9
7 PM
$22
$25
EL CLUB DETROIT
ALL AGES

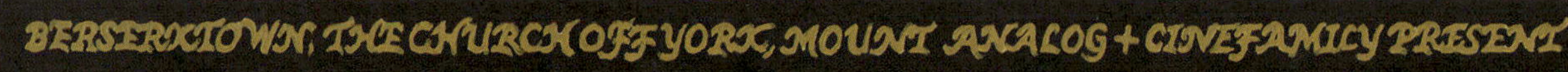
BERSERKTOWN, THE CHURCH OFF YORK, MOUNT ANALOG + CINEFAMILY PRESENT

IT FOLLOWS
AN EVENING WITH
DIRECTOR DAVID ROBERT MITCHELL + COMPOSER RICH VREELAND
+ A PERFORMANCE BY DISASTERPEACE
AUGUST 7
10:30 PM
CINEFAMILY
611 N FAIRFAX AVE
LOS ANGELES
HEIR

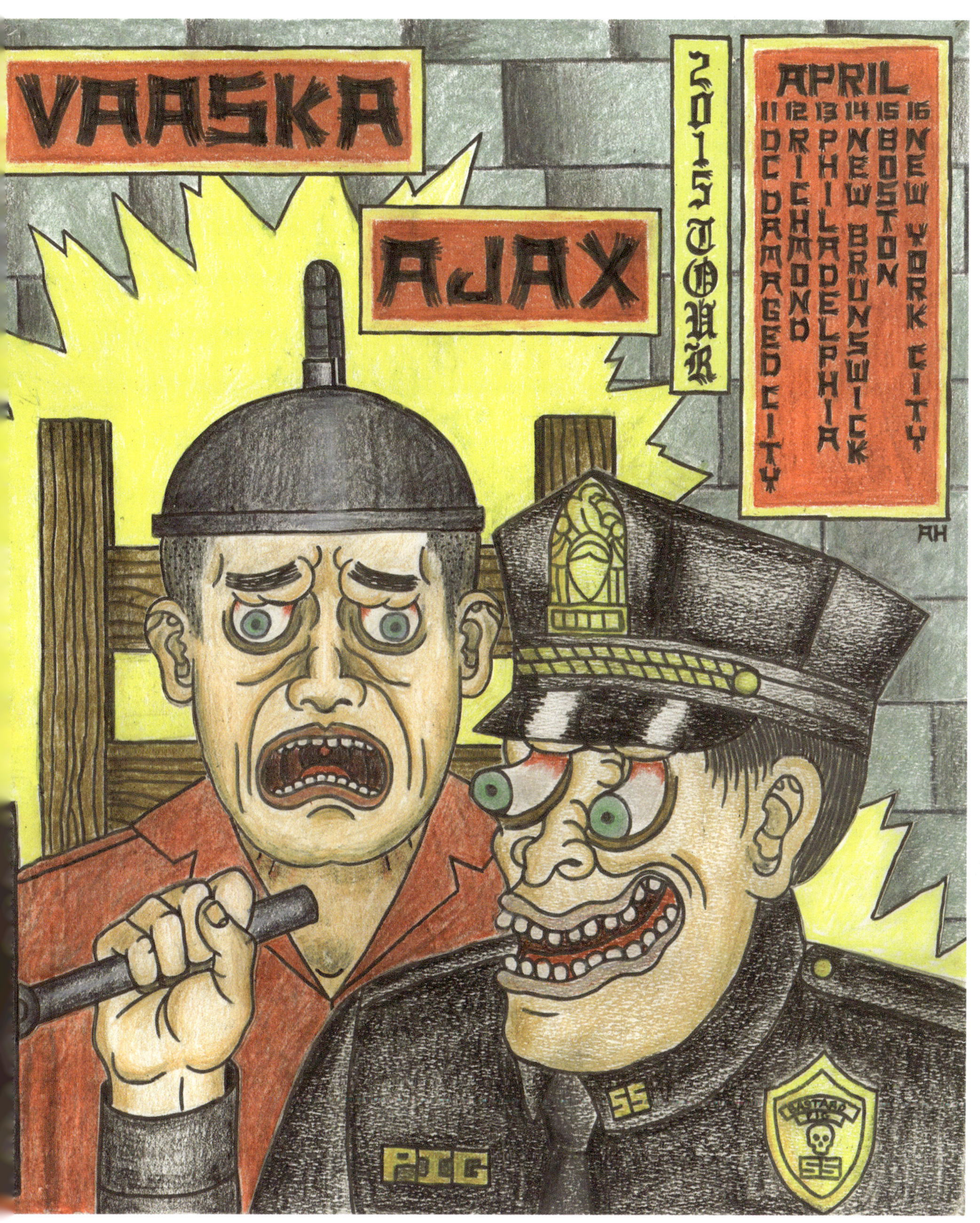
VAASKA
AJAX
2015 TOUR
APRIL
11 12 13 14 15 16
DC DAMAGED CITY
RICHMOND
PHILADELPHIA
NEW BRUNSWICK
BOSTON
NEW YORK CITY
PIG
SS
BASTARD PIG
SS
AH

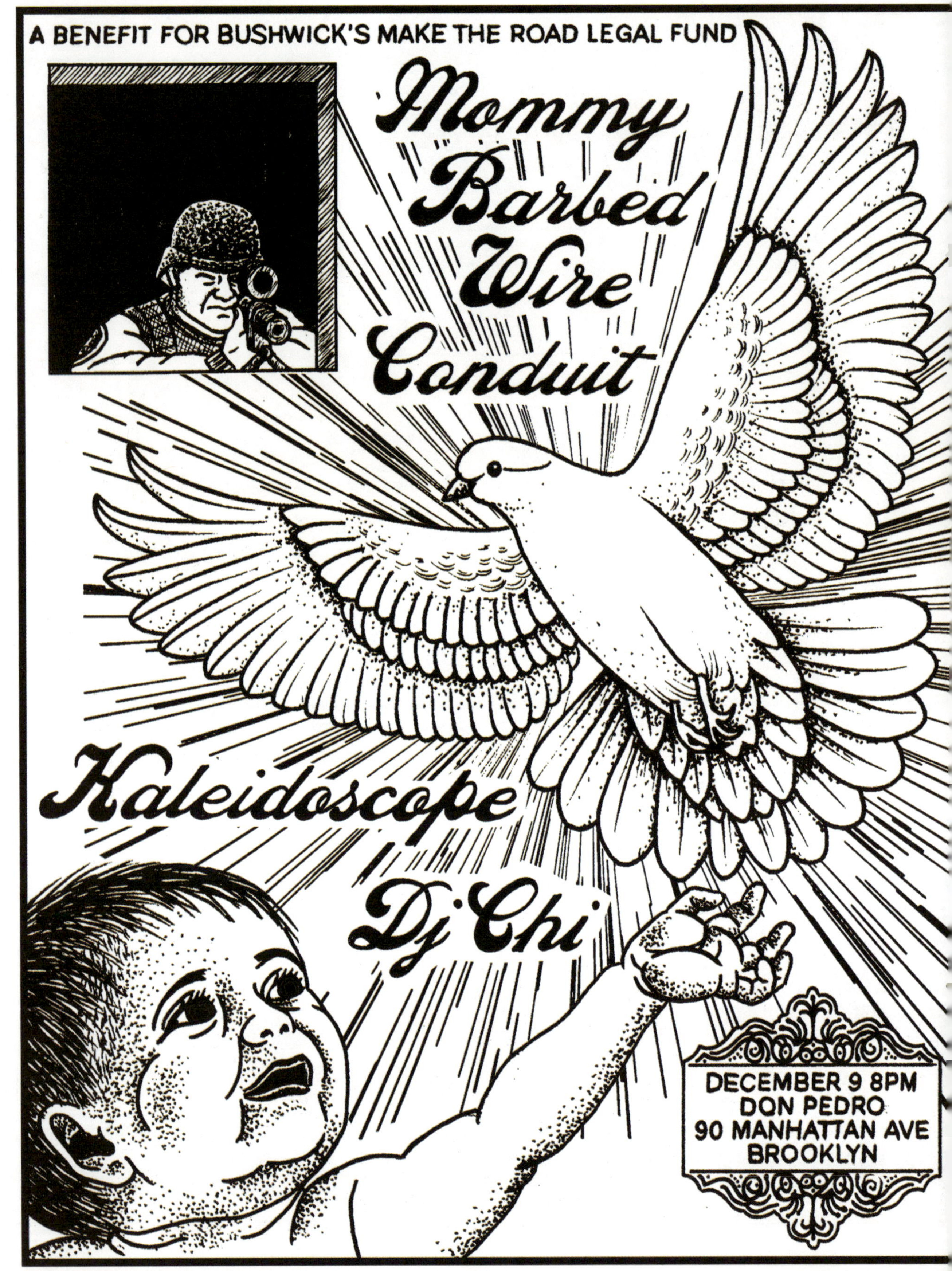
A BENEFIT FOR BUSHWICK'S MAKE THE ROAD LEGAL FUND
Mommy
Barbed
Wire
Conduit
Kaleidoscope
Dj Chi
DECEMBER 9 8PM
DON PEDRO
90 MANHATTAN AVE
BROOKLYN

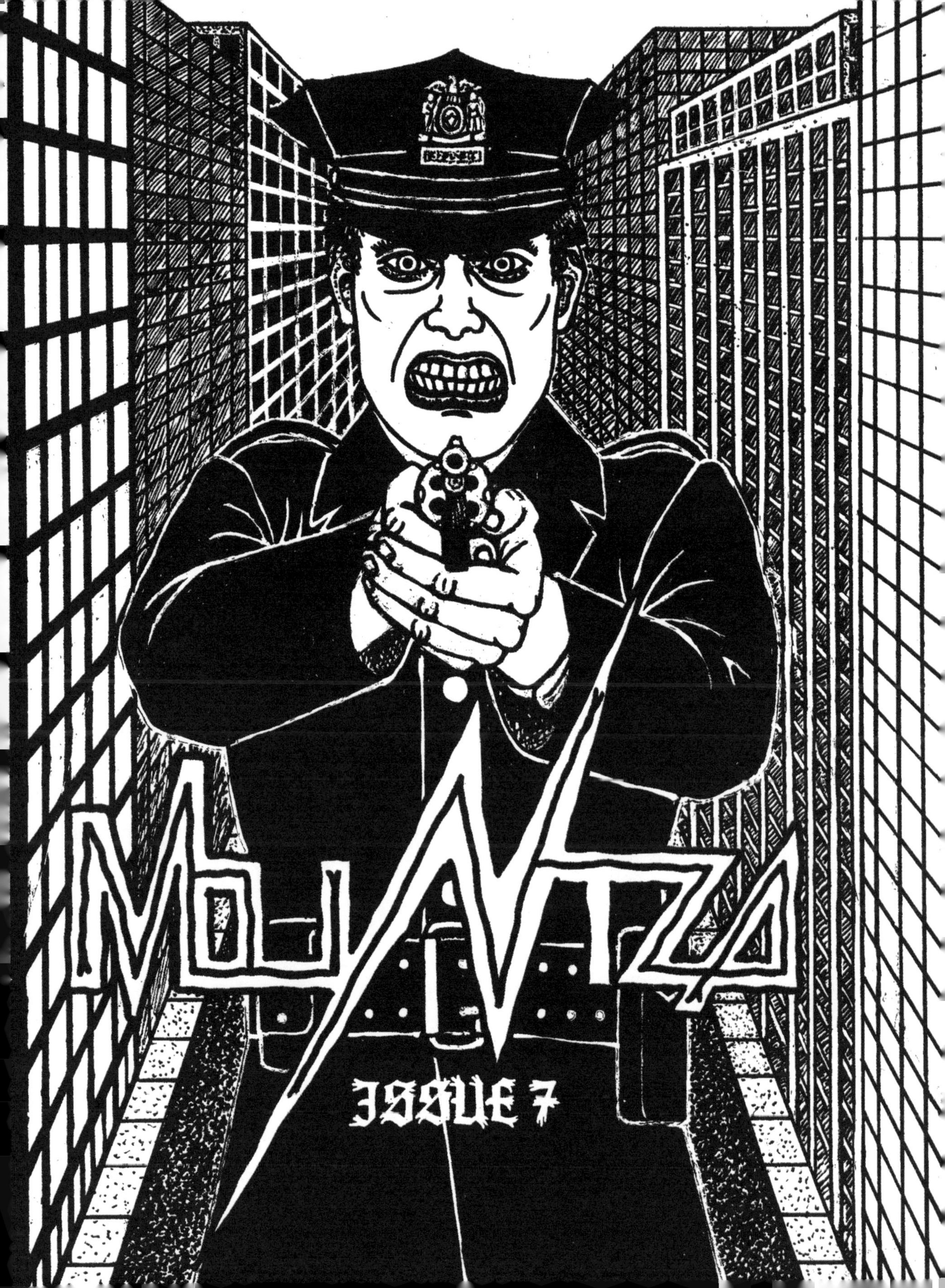

MUNTZA
ISSUE 7

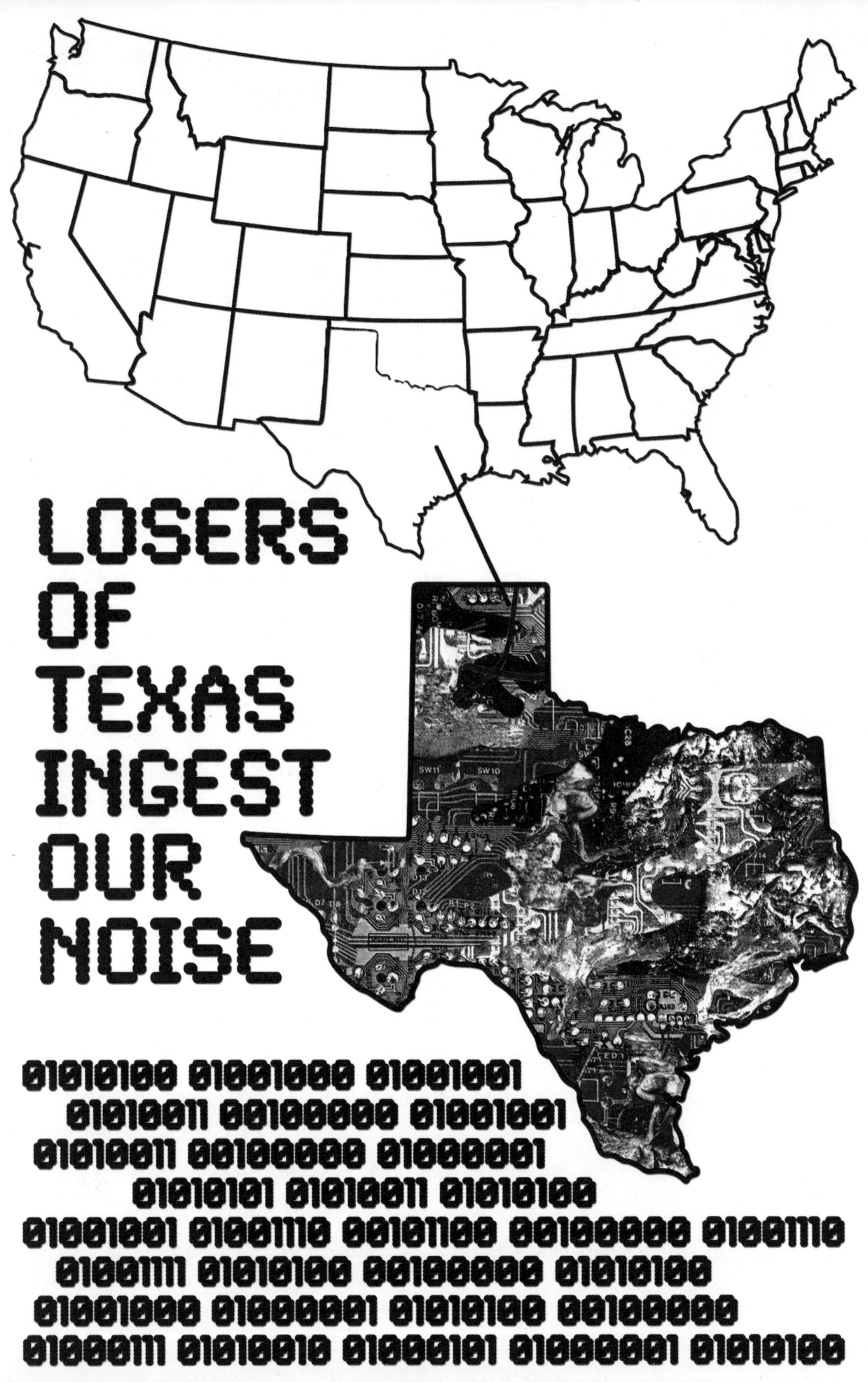

LOSERS
OF
TEXAS
INGEST
OUR
NOISE
01010100 01001000 01001001
01010011 00100000 01001001
01010011 00100000 01000001
01010101 01010011 01010100
01001001 01001110 00101100 00100000 01001110
01001111 01010100 00100000 01010100
01001000 01000001 01010100 00100000
01000111 01010010 01000101 01000001 01010100

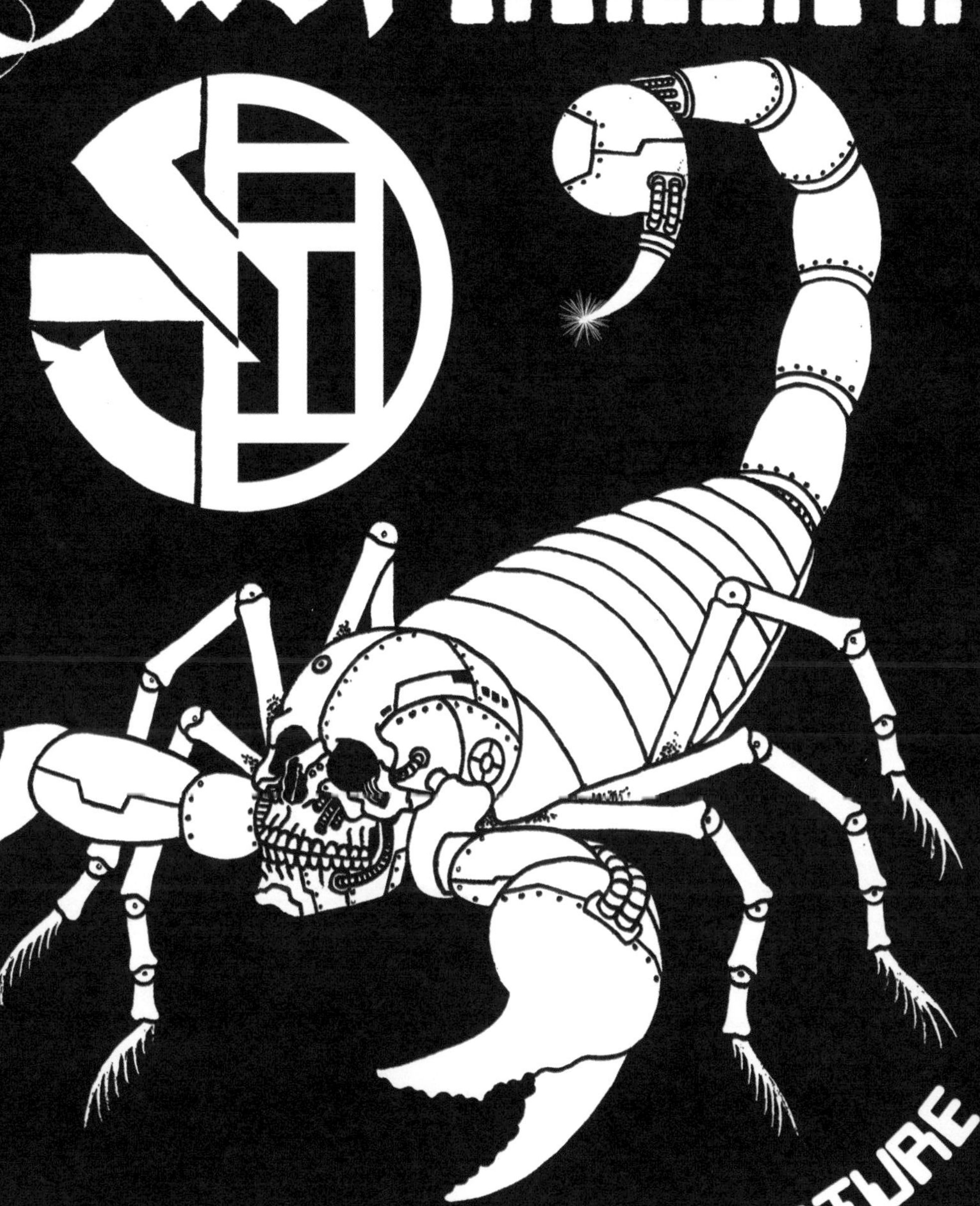

Sadit.i.o.n.
LEGACY OF TERROR IS OUR NATURE
2084

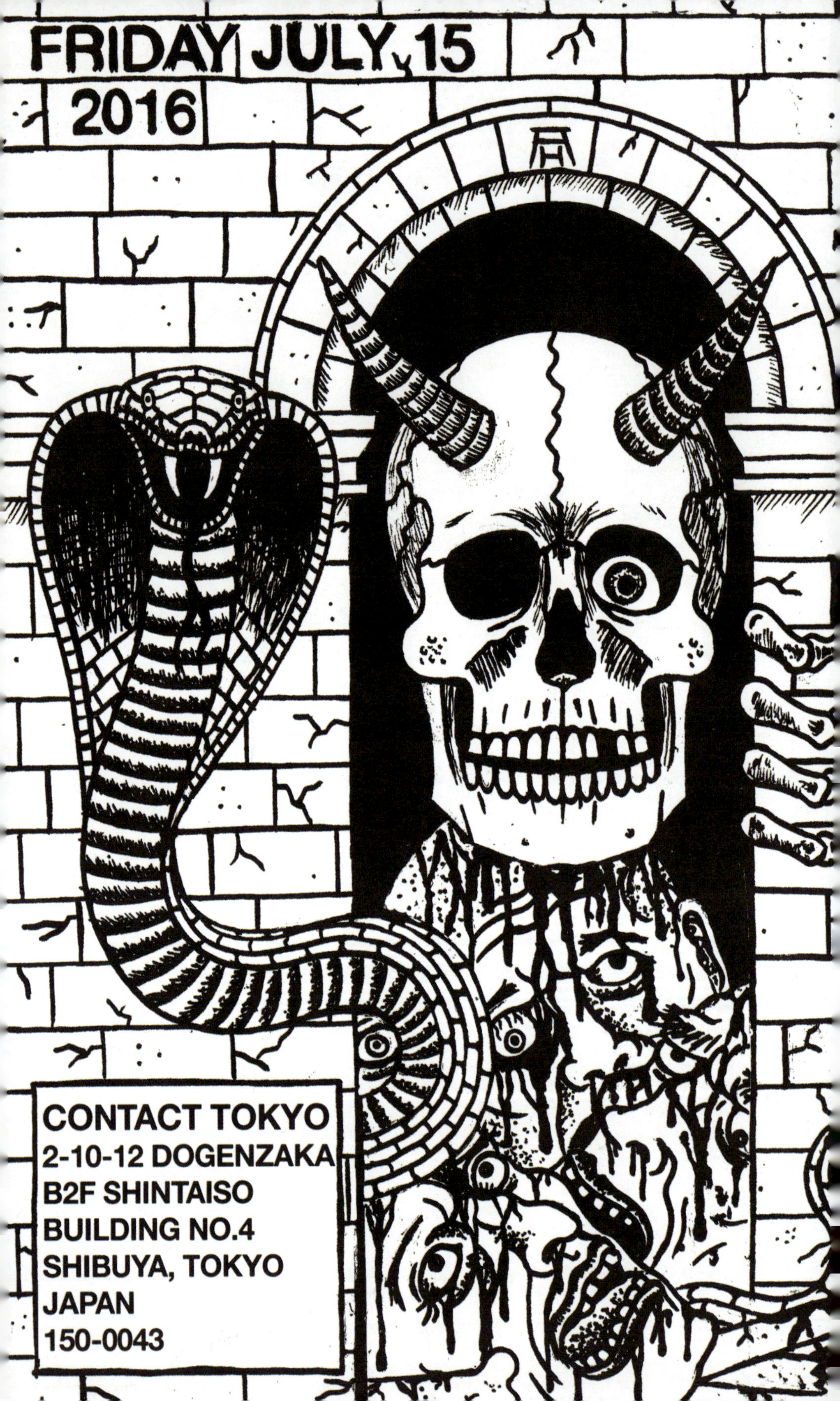

FRIDAY JULY 15
2016
CONTACT TOKYO
2-10-12 DOGENZAKA
B2F SHINTAISO
BUILDING NO.4
SHIBUYA, TOKYO
JAPAN
150-0043

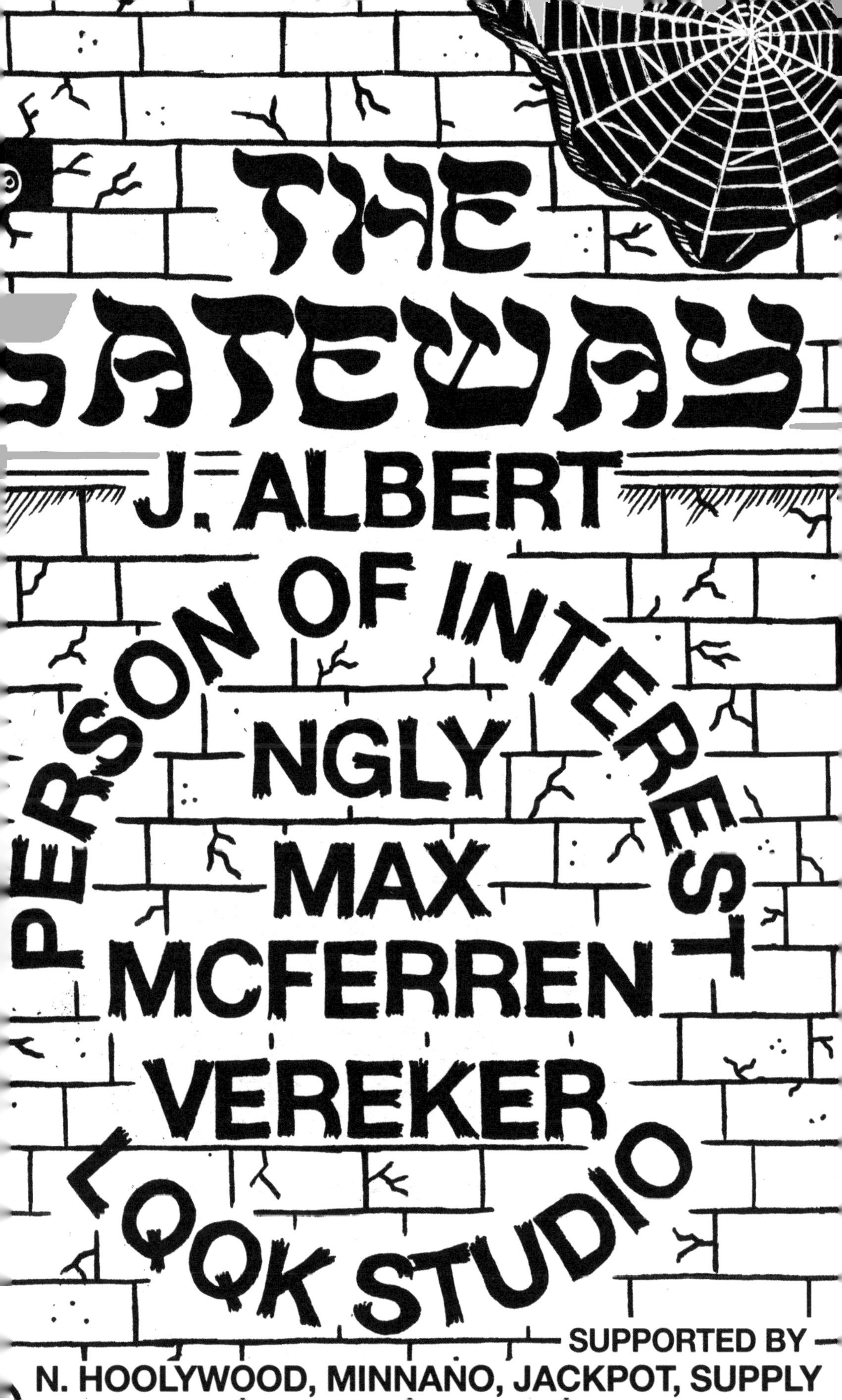

THE GATEWAY
J. ALBERT
PERSON OF INTEREST
NGLY
MAX
MCFERREN
VEREKER
LQQK STUDIO
SUPPORTED BY
N. HOOLYWOOD, MINNANO, JACKPOT, SUPPLY

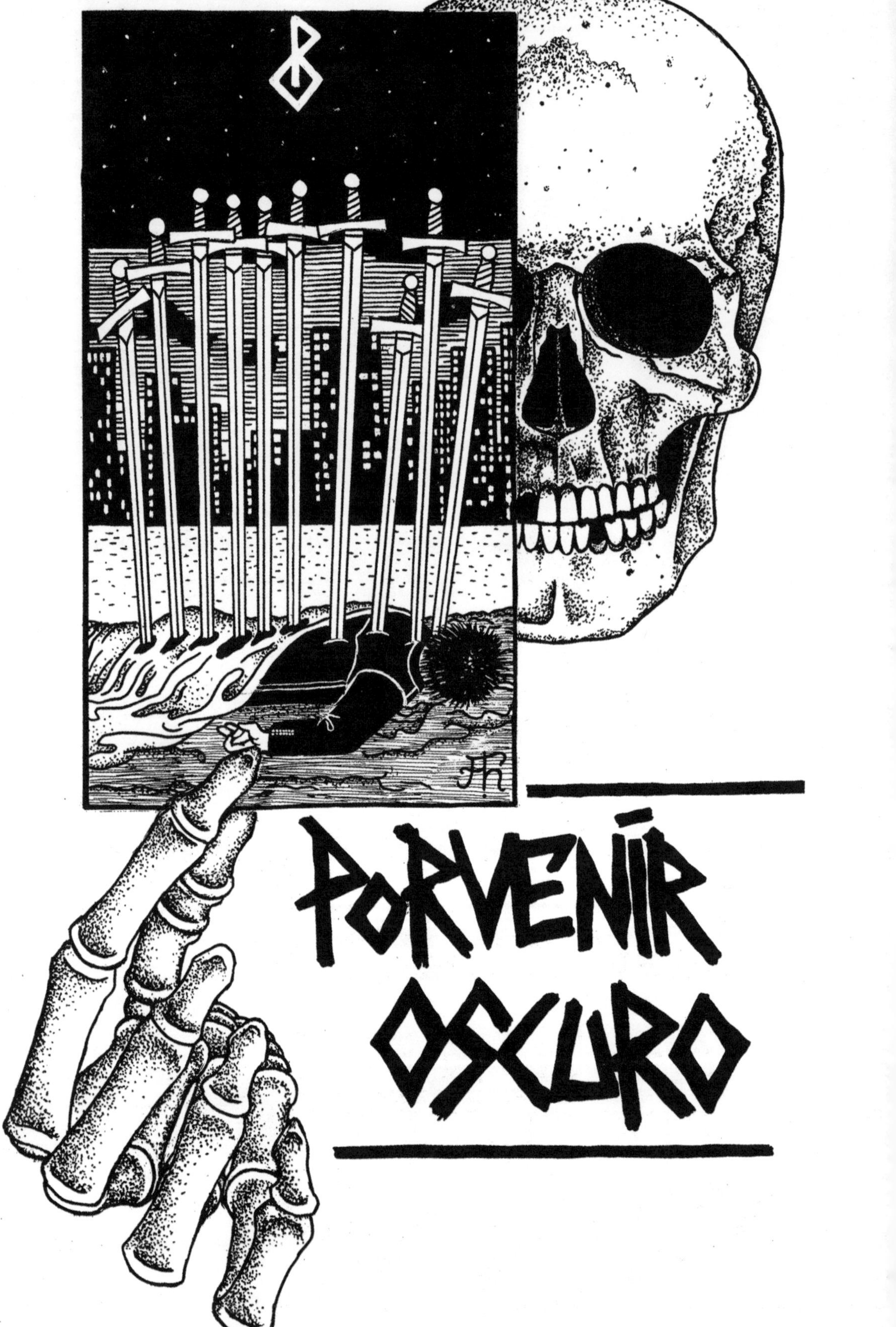

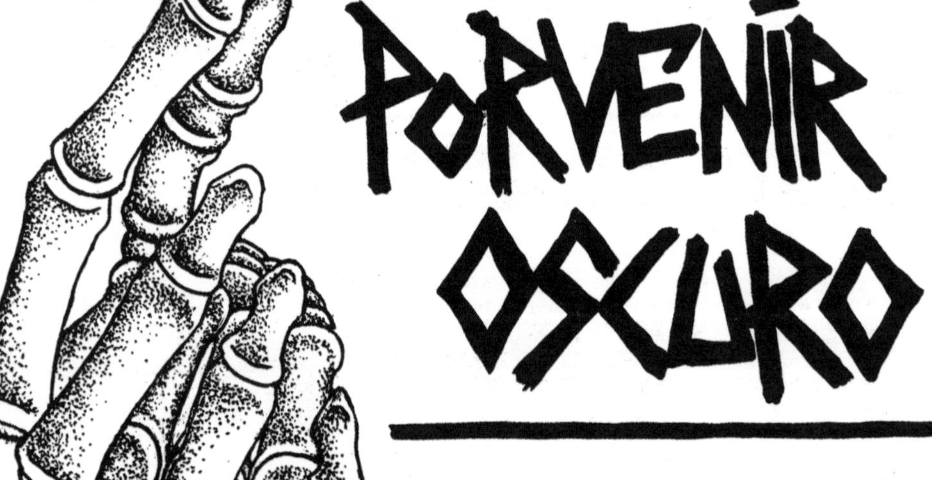

PORVENIR
OSCURO

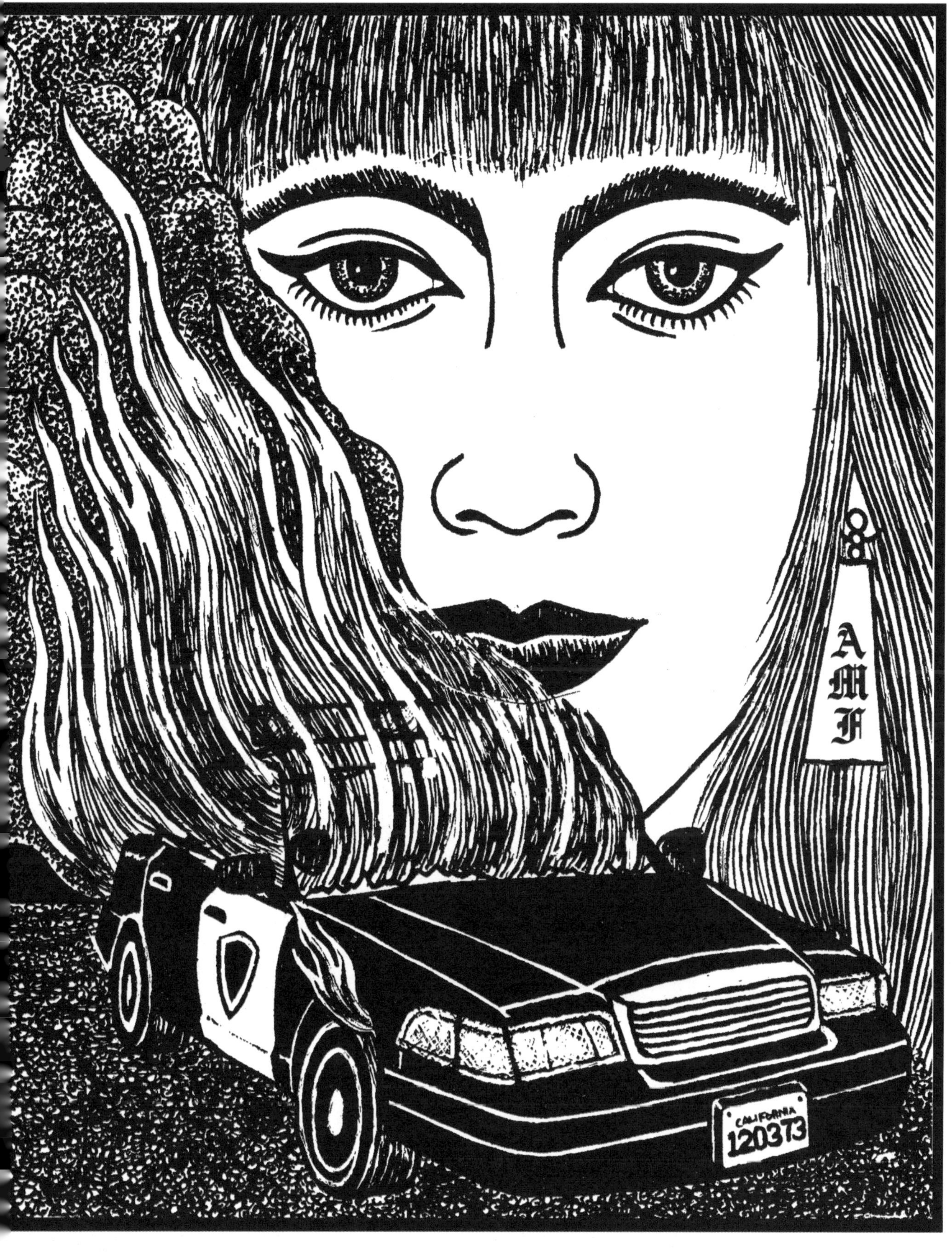

A
M
F
CALIFORNIA
120373

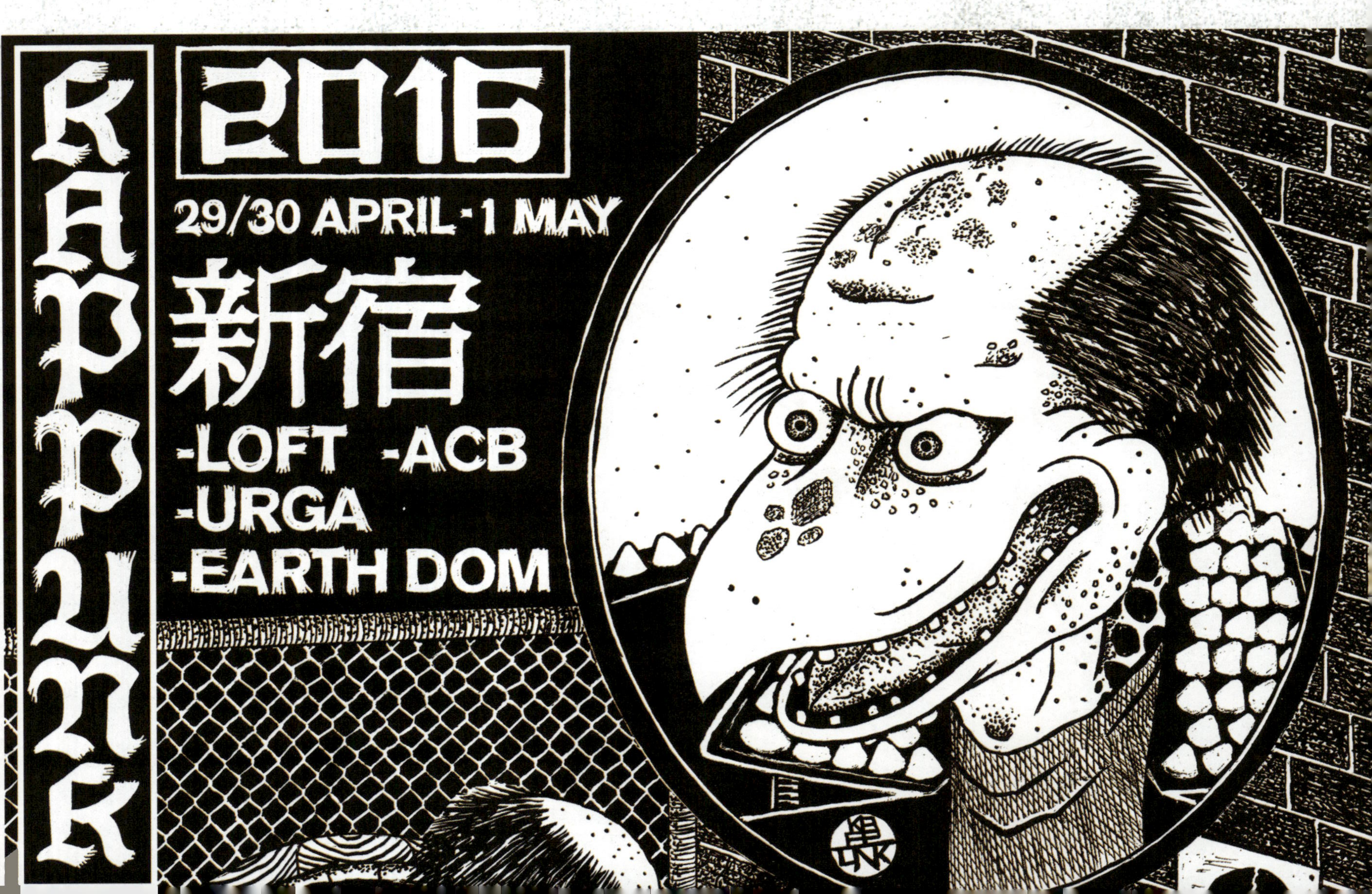
RAPPPUNK
2016
29/30 APRIL · 1 MAY
新宿
-LOFT -ACB
-URGA
-EARTH DOM

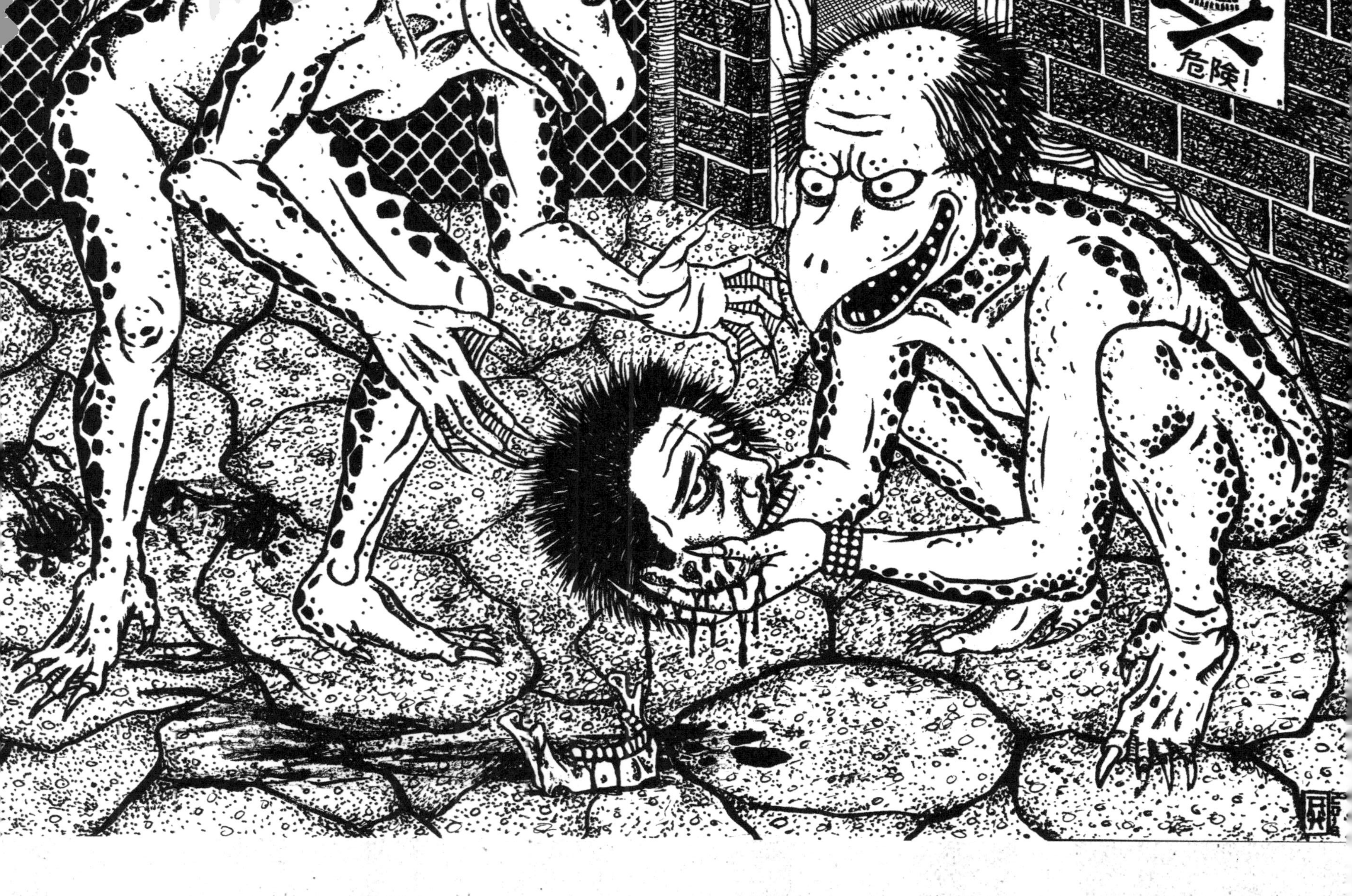

危険！

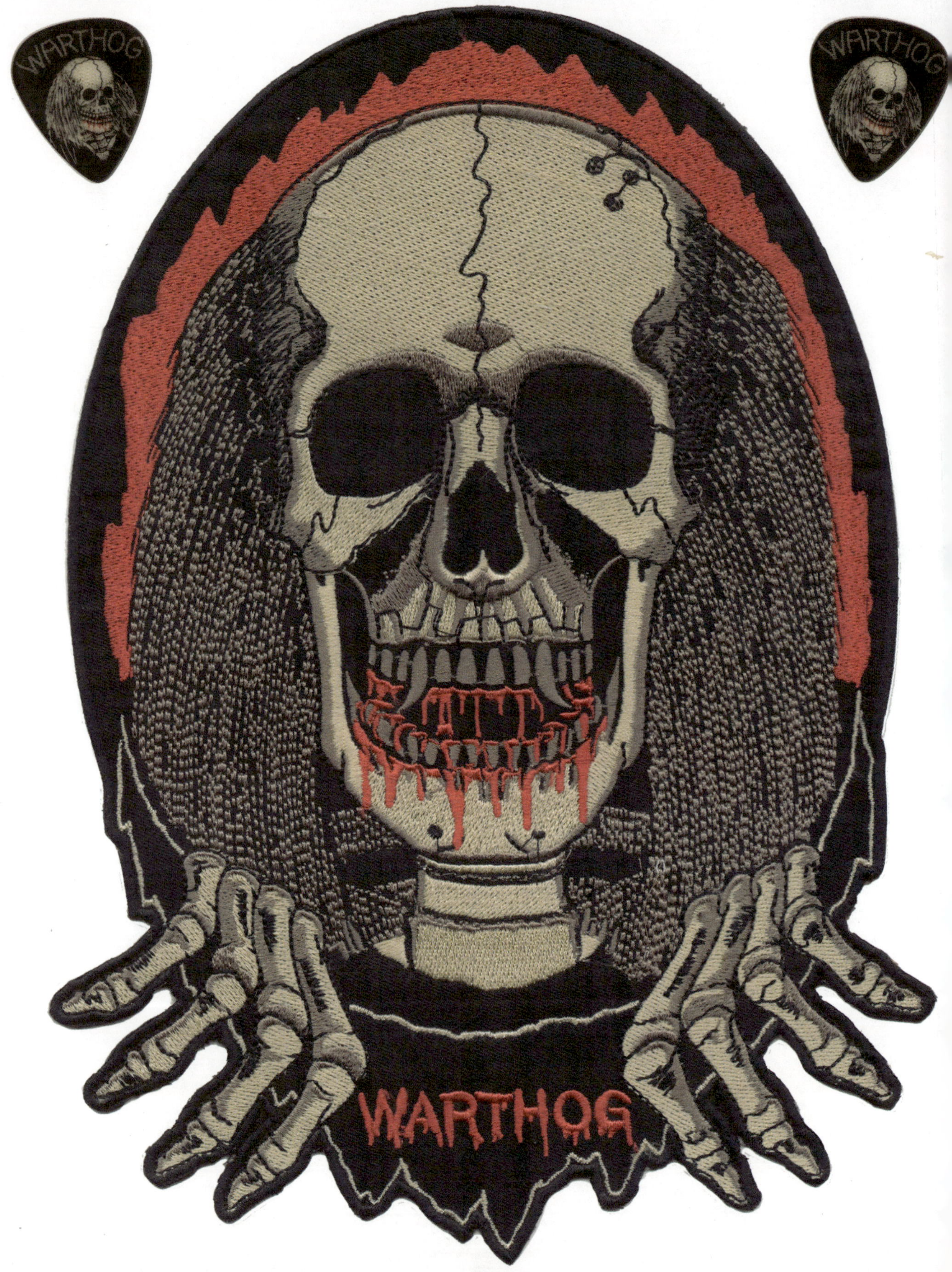
WARTHOG
WARTHOG
WARTHOG

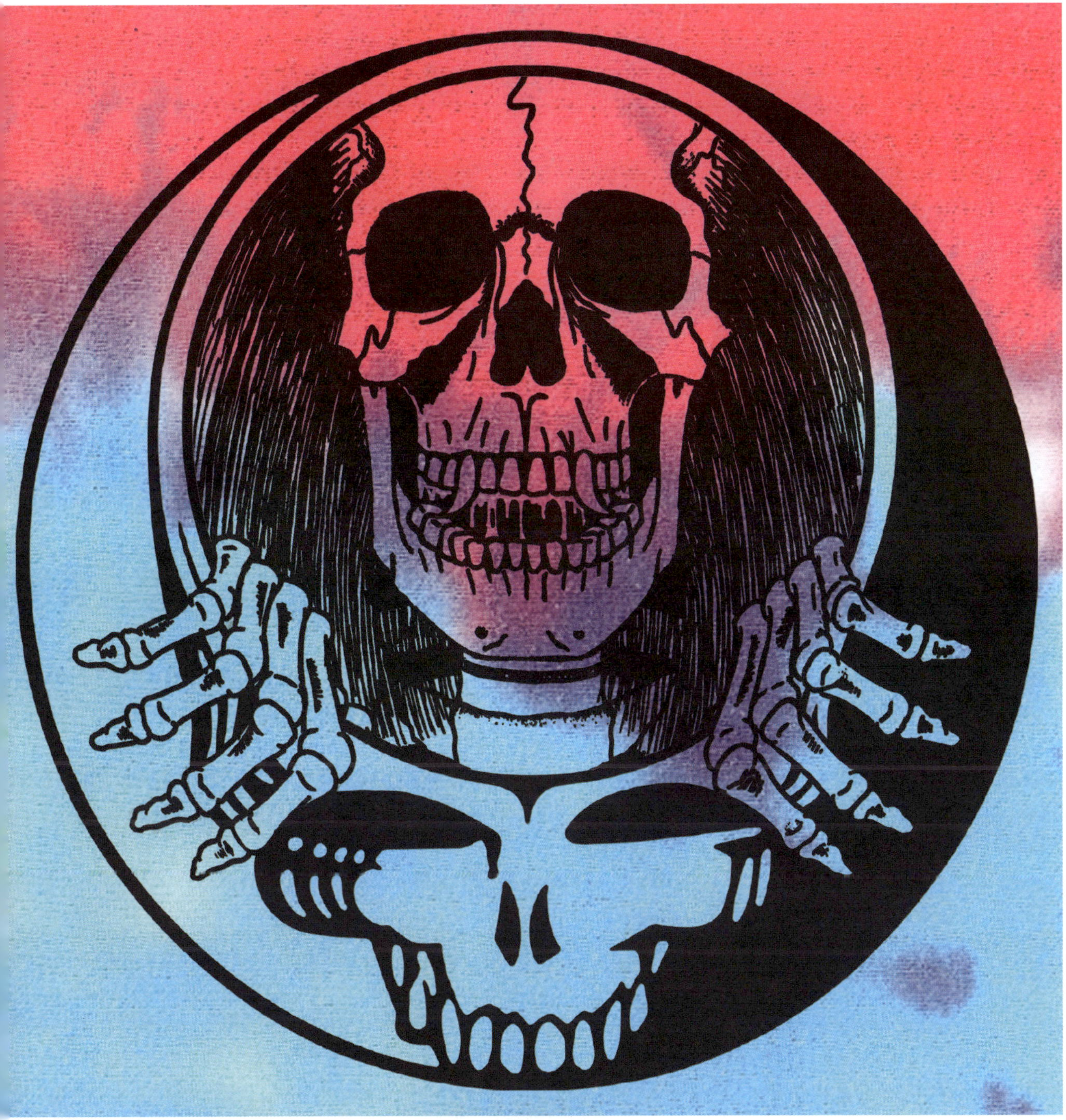

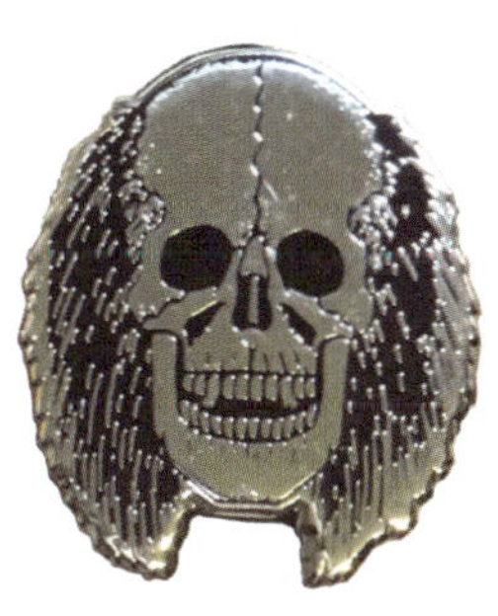

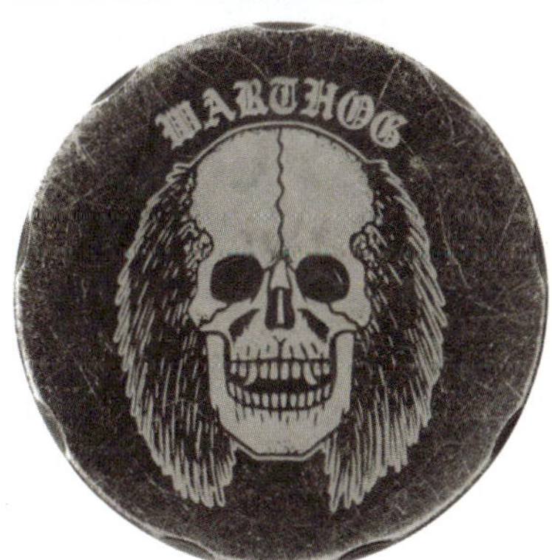
WARTHOG

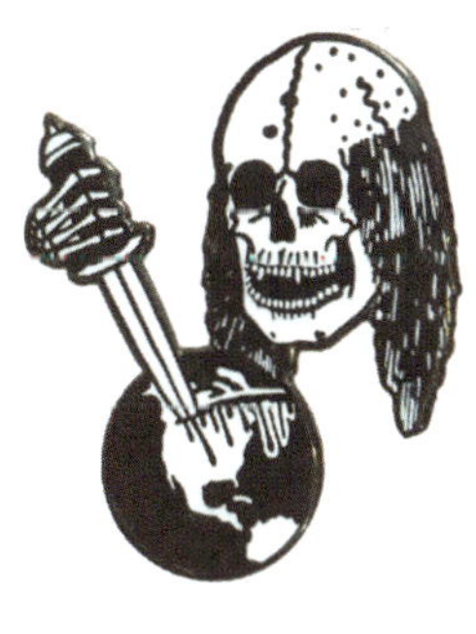

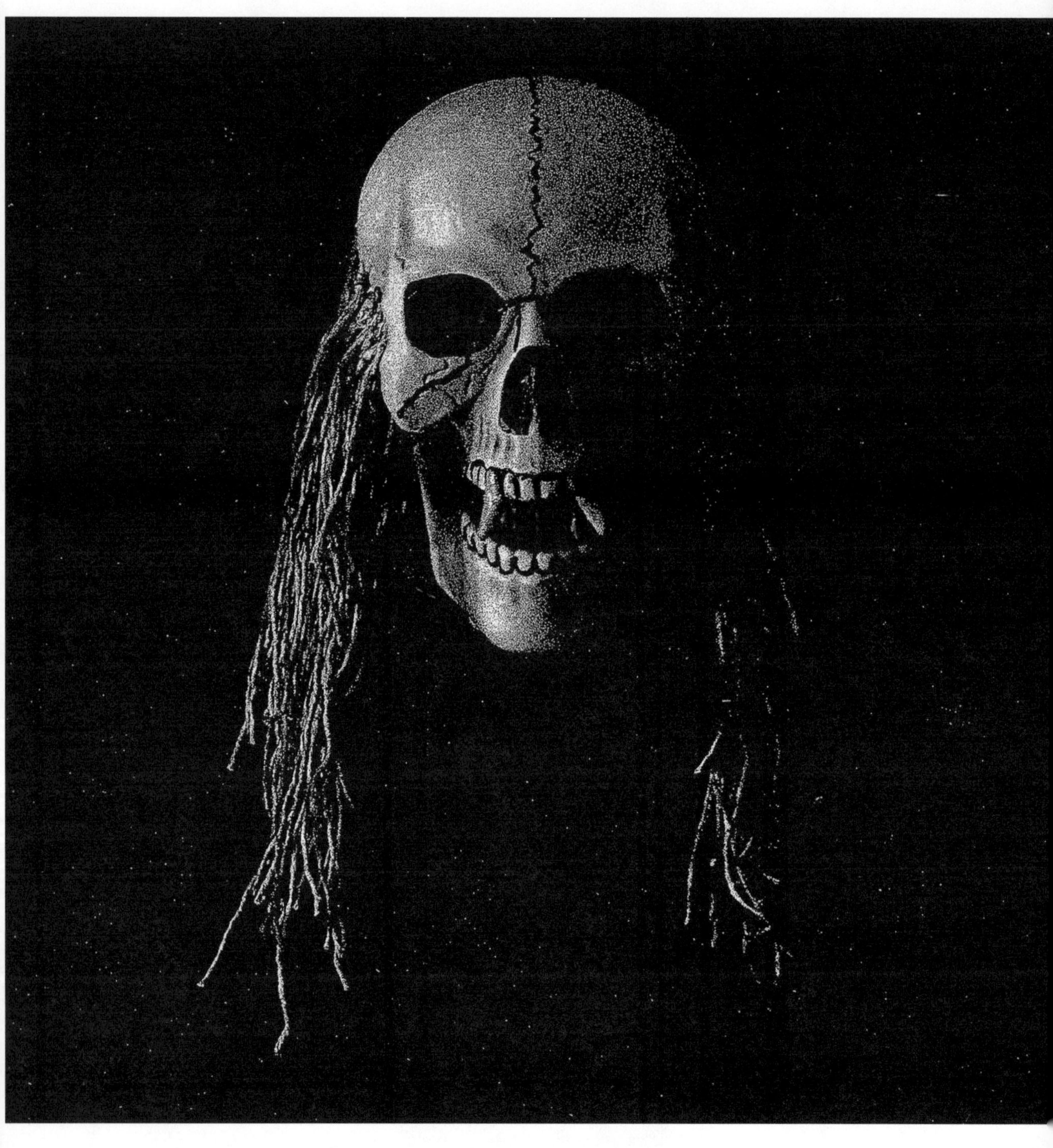

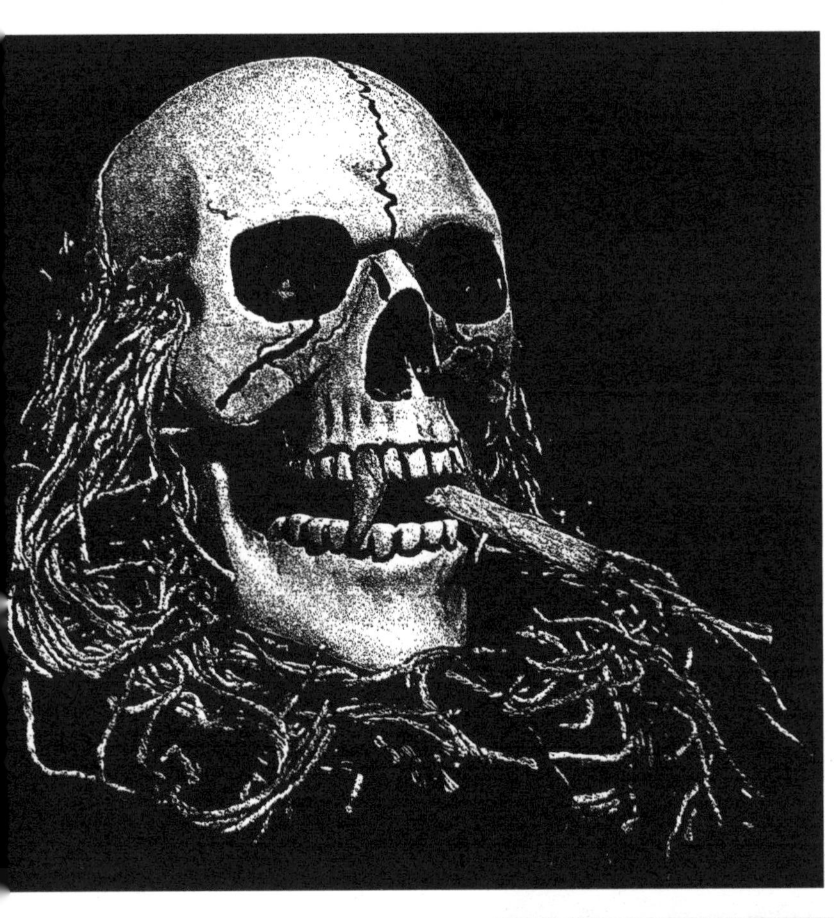

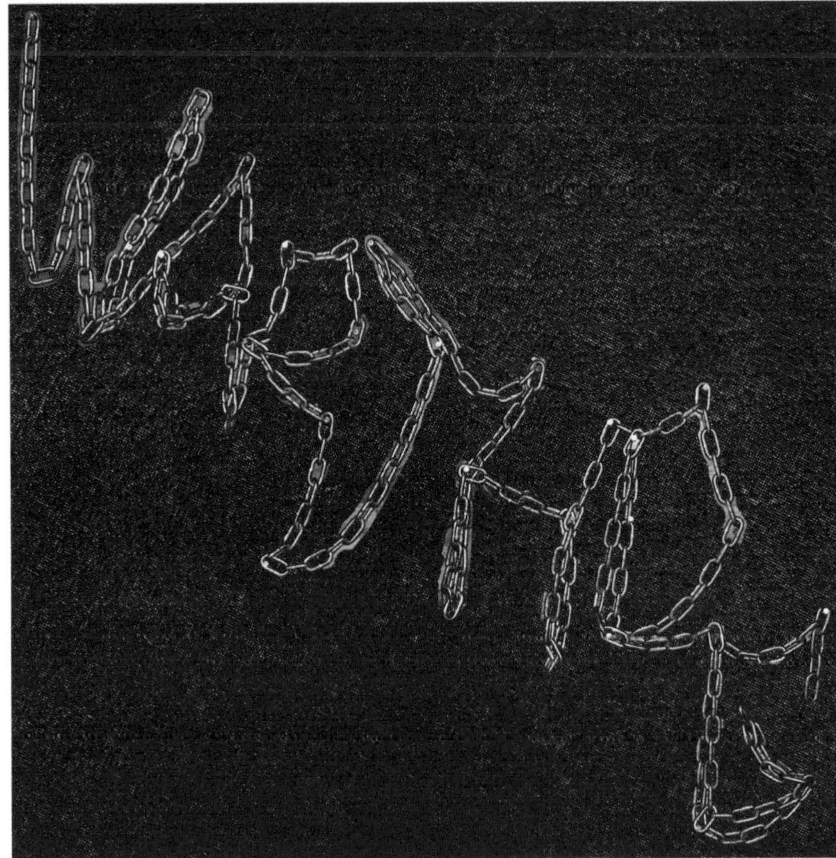

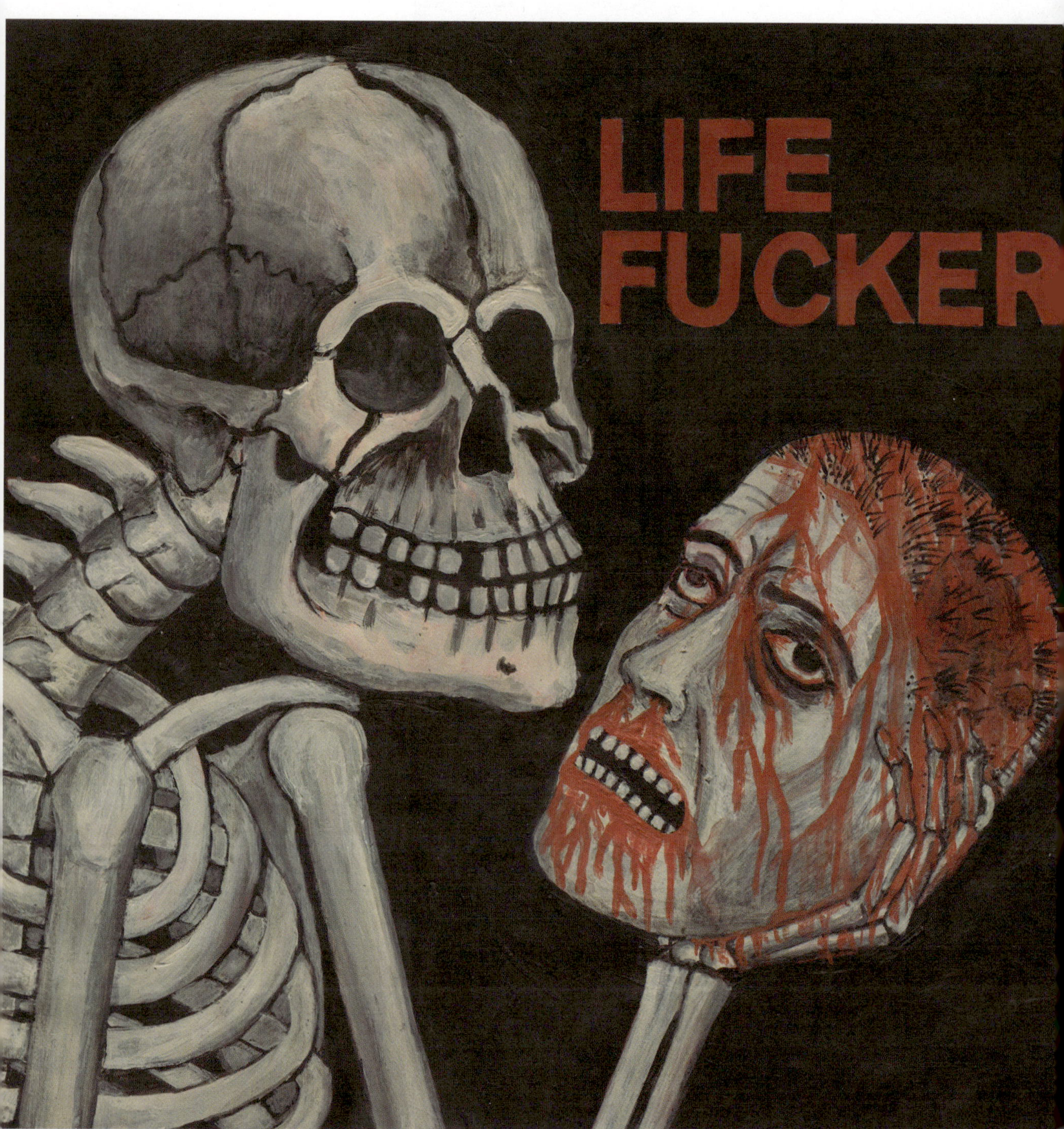
LIFE
FUCKER

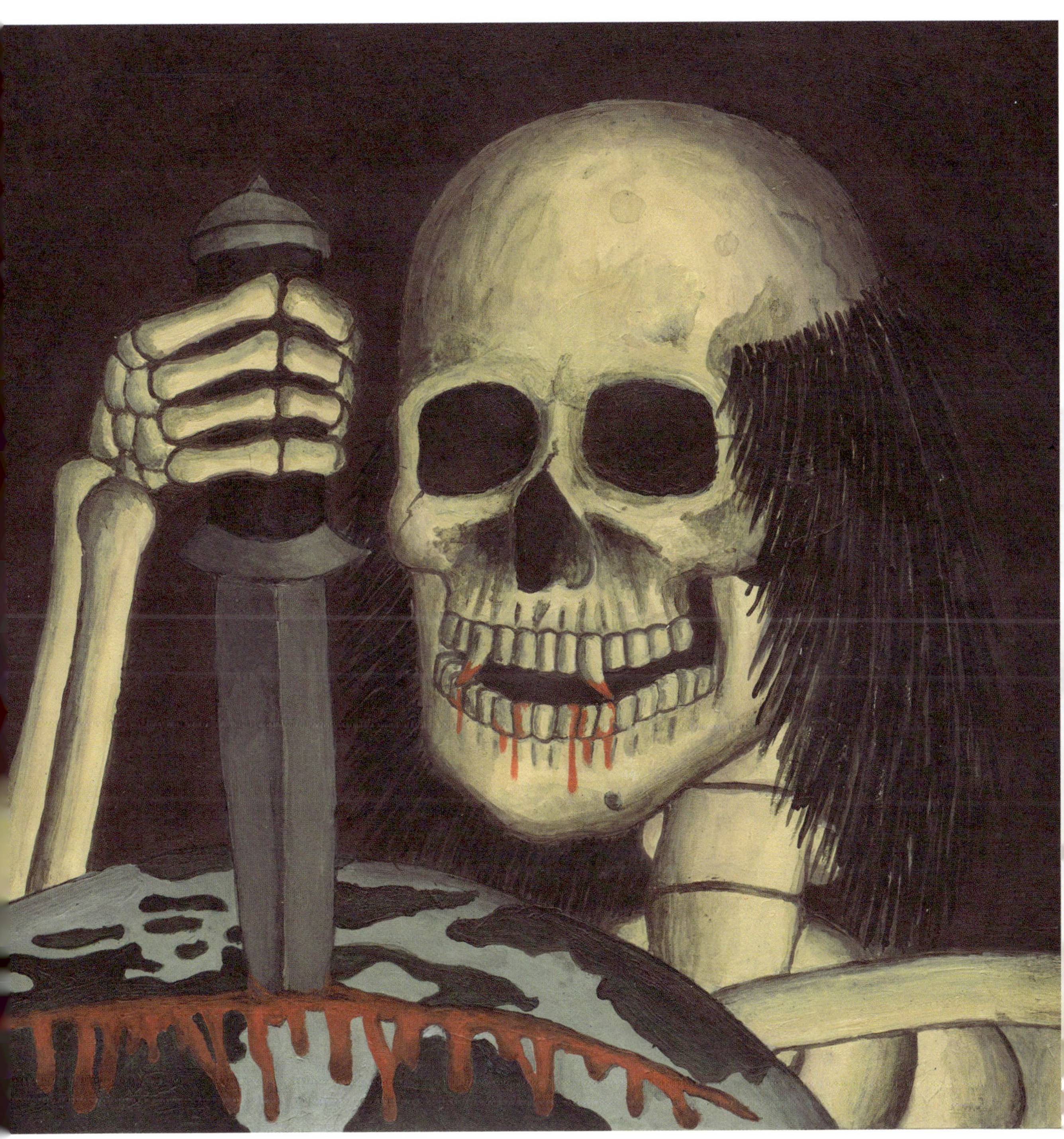

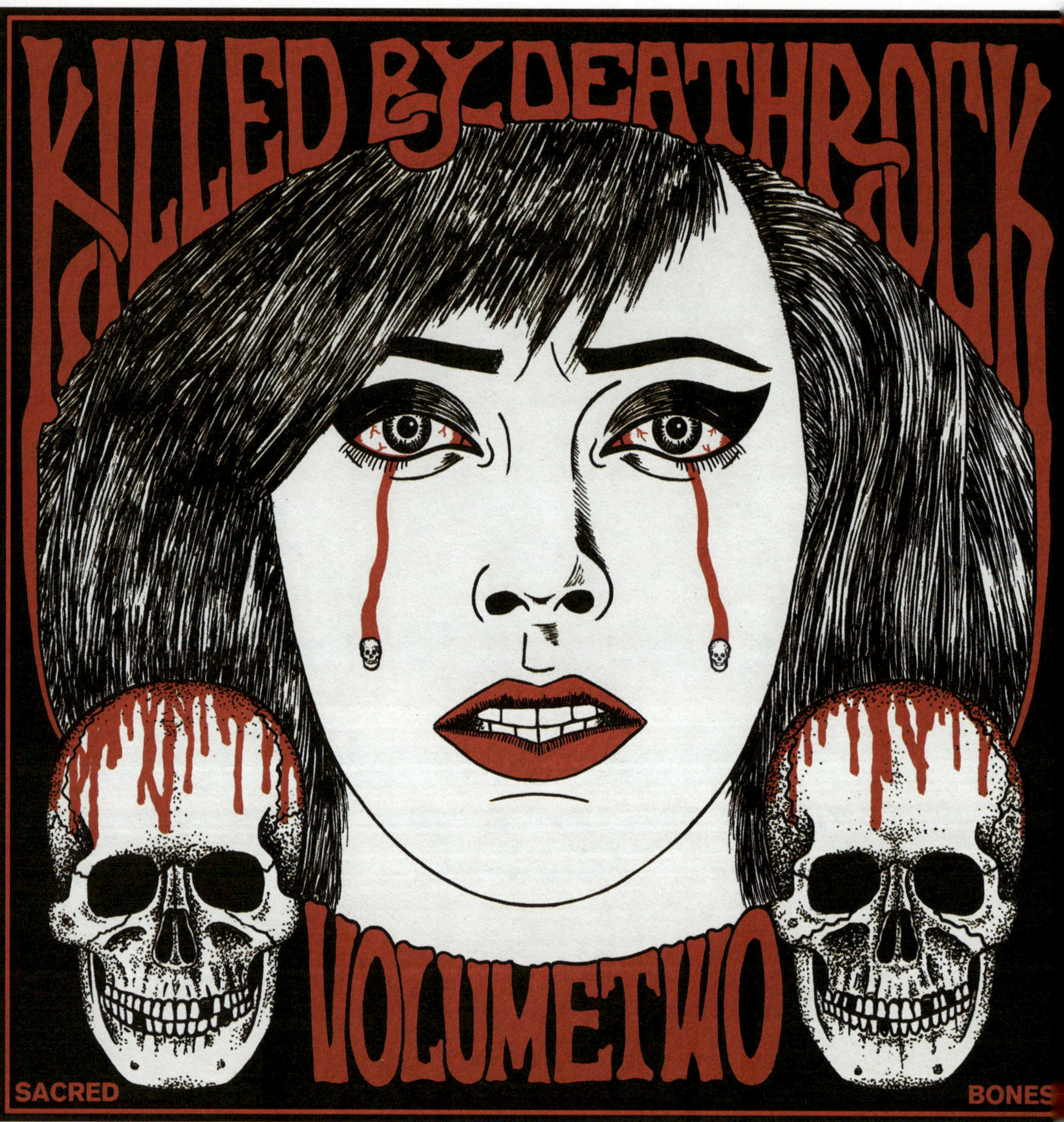

KILLED BY DEATHROCK
VOLUME TWO
SACRED
BONES

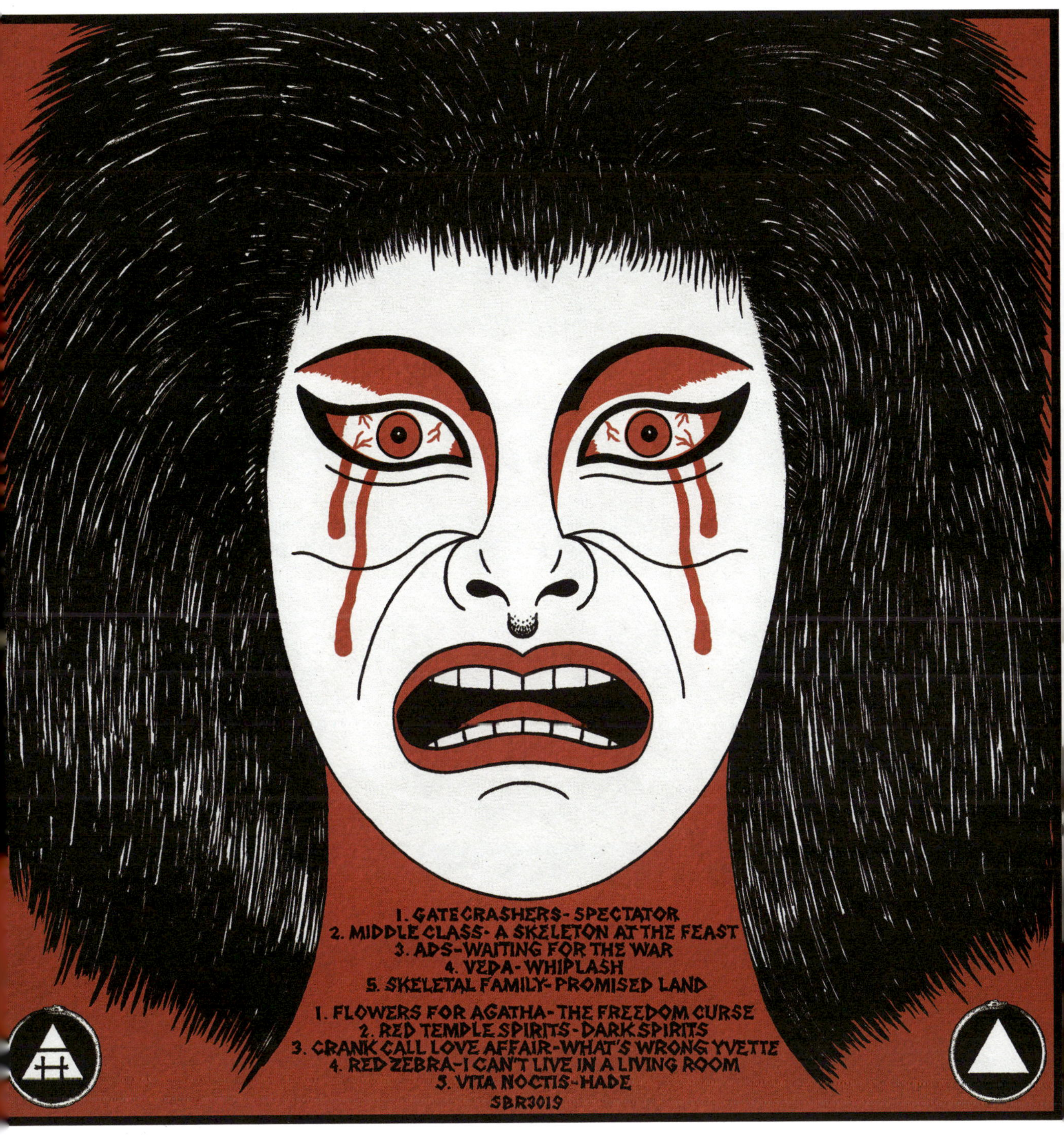

1. GATECRASHERS- SPECTATOR
2. MIDDLE CLASS- A SKELETON AT THE FEAST
3. ADS-WAITING FOR THE WAR
4. VEDA- WHIPLASH
5. SKELETAL FAMILY- PROMISED LAND

1. FLOWERS FOR AGATHA- THE FREEDOM CURSE
2. RED TEMPLE SPIRITS- DARK SPIRITS
3. CRANK CALL LOVE AFFAIR-WHAT'S WRONG YVETTE
4. RED ZEBRA-I CAN'T LIVE IN A LIVING ROOM
5. VITA NOCTIS-HADE
SBR3019

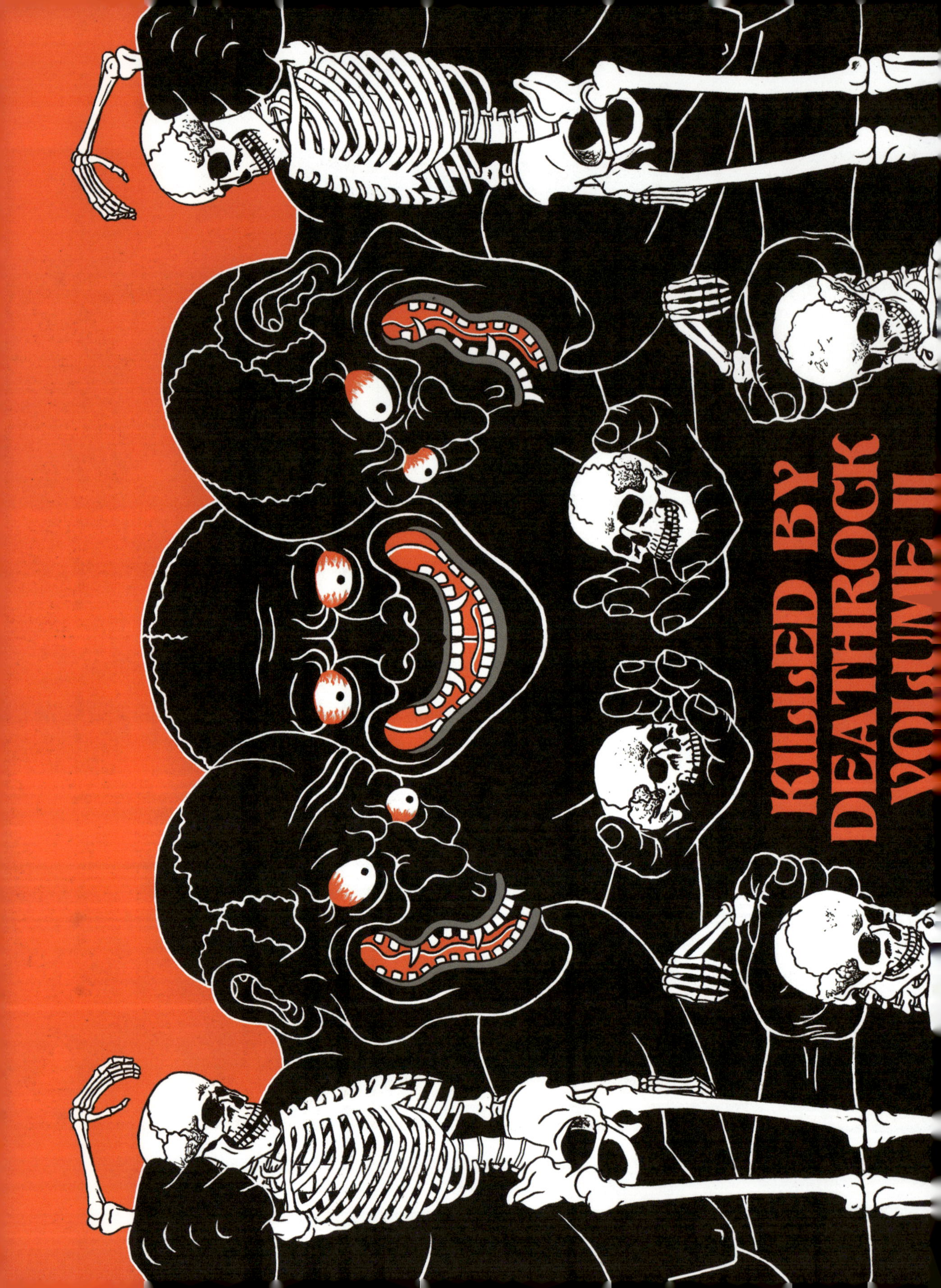

KILLED BY
DEATHROCK
VOLUME II

After the initial blast of punk rock bands made their impression on the youth of the late 1970s, subgenres quickly emerged. Some preferred the faster, louder aggression of hardcore; others the angular danceability of postpunk; some the raw and more personal homemade sound of DIY, and so on. Looking back among and between these genres we now recognize various blends of punk, postpunk, goth rock, industrial, and DIY as "deathrock." In 2014, Sacred Bones Records launched the series Killed By Deathrock to document an entire scene of bands that haven't yet received proper recognition. You hold now in your hands the second volume.

The thread that holds these groups together as deathrock bands comes down to their willingness and sometimes compulsion to reveal and explore the darker side of their psyches. Nightsoaked dirges of fatality, despair, and horror were rampant, rooted in that subliminy that is found on the edge of the horror genre, as famously developed by Edgar Allan Poe — an edge that relished in misery and openly recognized the inevitable end of any human life.

Killed by Deathrock Vol. 2 opens with Gatecrashers' maniacal keyboard driven anthem "Spectator," the first track from the Denmark group's 1980 7" EP Desillusioned. Middle Class began by releasing what many consider to be the first-ever hardcore punk record: their 1978 debut EP Out of Vogue. Bassist Mike Patton would produce seminal California punk bands like Adolescents and Minutemen, among others. By 1984, Middle Class had evolved from their fast-blast origins to a darker, more plodding style, represented here by their track "A Skeleton At The Feast," from the 1982 LP Homeland. ADS, a group from the same Denmark scene as Gatecrashers, offers up the searing "Waiting for the War," from their scarce 1982 split 7" with CityX, which takes the socially conscious yet satirical bite of punk rock one nihilistic step further. A swirling nightmare of reverb-drenched guitars begins UK darkwave act Veda's snarling "Whiplash," featuring Sex Gang Children member Cam Campbell. The 1987 single it comes from was Veda's one and only release. Fellow British band Skeletal Family began a prolific career in 1983. Their track "Promised Land" is a perfect showcase for guitarist Stan Greenwood's jagged style, as well as Ann Marie Hurst's powerful vocal ability.

UK goth rock band Flowers for Agatha's somber "The Freedom Curse" was more than worthy of radio airplay, which sadly went unachieved. The song appeared on the band's 1985 EP of the same name. "Dark Spirits" is a standout cut from Los Angeles deathrockers Red Temple Spirits, released by the legendary Midwestern label Fundamental Independent Project Records, later released a comprehensive anthology of the group's material in 2013. The driving postpunk obscurity that is "What's Wrong Yvette," by the nearly unknown Denver band Crank Call Love Affair, comes from their only record, a self-released 7" single of the same name. Belgium's Red Zebra — now known as EXRZ — contributes their raw, infectious brand of new wave in the form of the title track from their 1980 debut 7" EP "I Can't Live In A Living Room." Fellow Belgians Vita Noctis round out the compilation with their dreamy, recorded-to-cassette ballad "Hade," from their 1984 self-released tape In The Face Of... Death. –Mike Hunchback

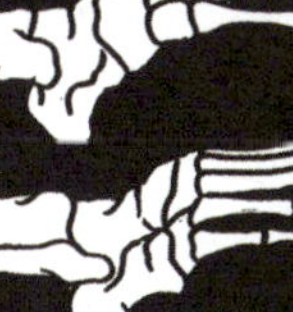
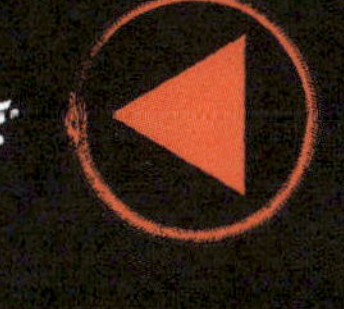
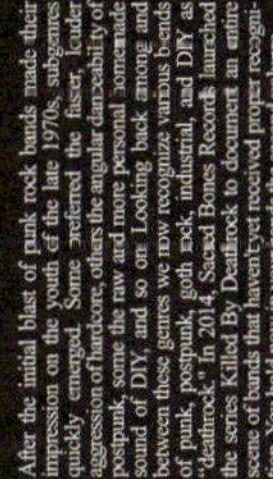

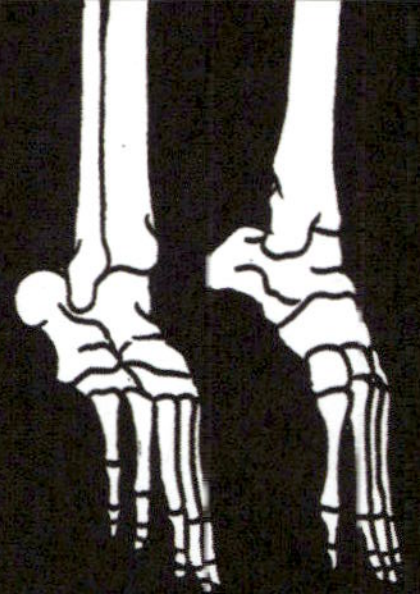

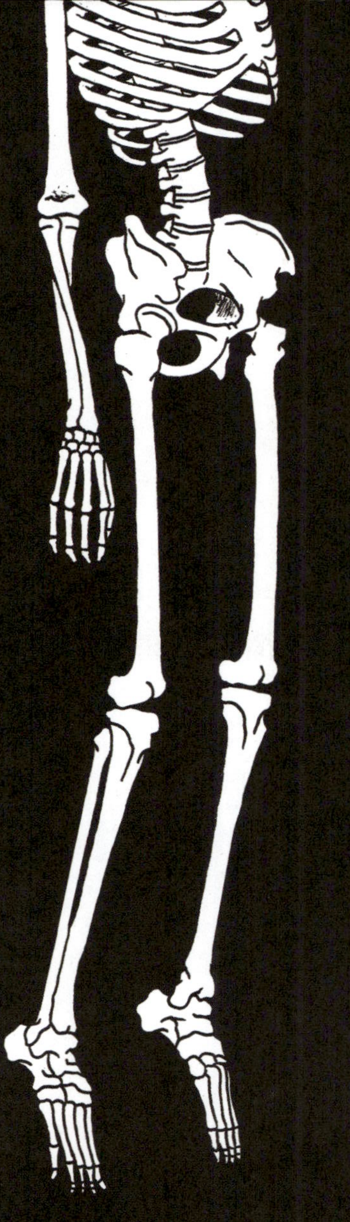

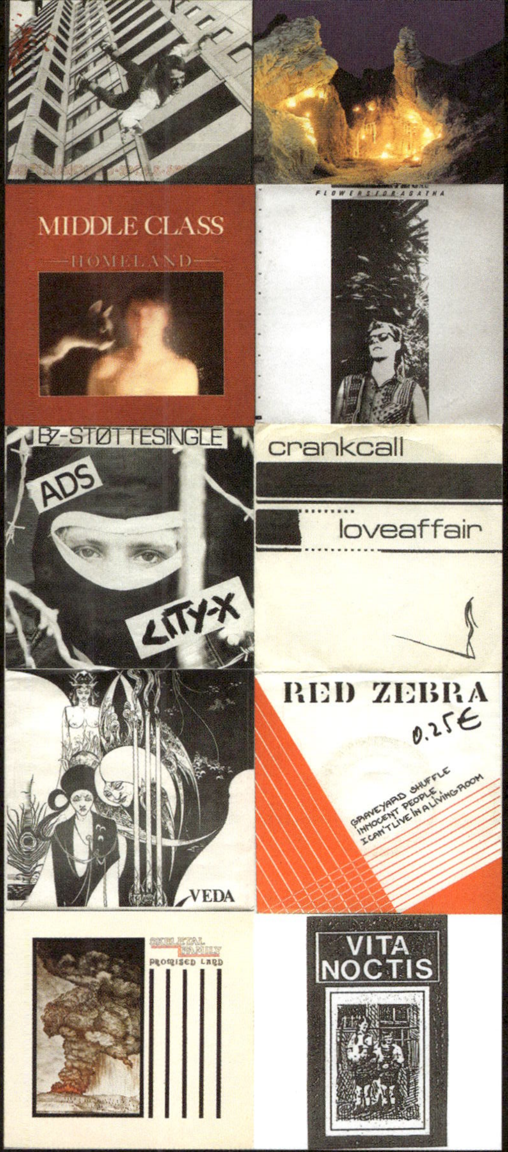

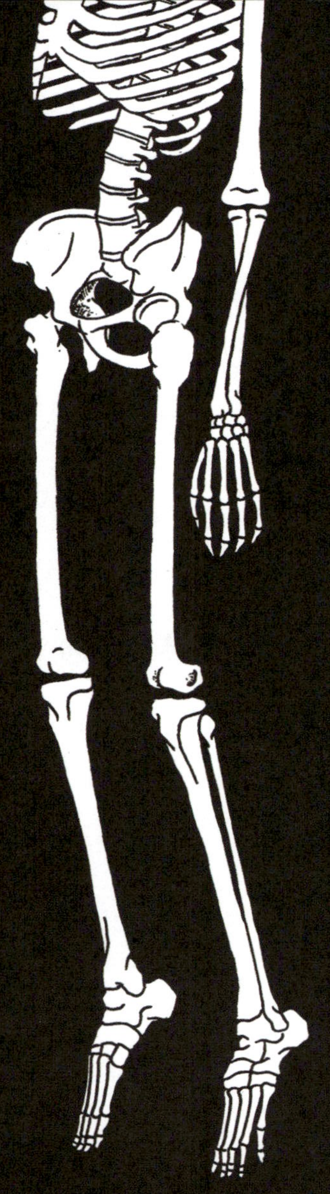

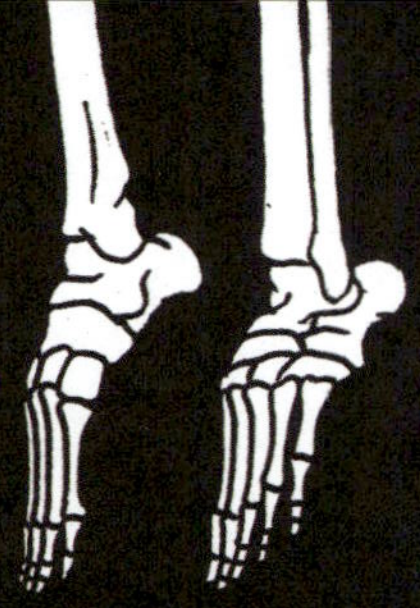

After the initial blast of punk rock bands made their impression on the youth of the late 1970s, subgenres quickly emerged. Some preferred the faster, louder aggression of hardcore; others the angular danceability of postpunk; some the raw and more personal homemade sound of DIY, and so on. Looking back among and between these genres we now recognize various blends of punk, postpunk, goth rock, industrial, and DIY as "deathrock." In 2014, Sacred Bones Records launched the series Killed By Deathrock to document an entire scene of bands that haven't yet received proper recognition. You hold now in your hands the second volume.

The thread that holds these groups together as deathrock bands comes down to their willingness and sometimes compulsion to reveal and explore the darker side of their psyches. Nightsoaked dirges of fatality, despair, and horror were rampant, rooted in that subliminy that is found on the edge of the horror genre, as famously developed by Edgar Allan Poe — an edge that relished in misery and openly recognized the inevitable end of any human life.

Killed by Deathrock Vol. 2 opens with Gatecrashers' maniacal keyboard driven anthem "Spectator," the first track from the Denmark group's 1980 7" EP Desillusioned. Middle Class began by releasing what many consider to be the first-ever hardcore punk record: their 1978 debut EP Out of Vogue. Bassist Mike Patton would produce seminal California punk bands like Adolescents and Minutemen, among others. By 1984, Middle Class had evolved from their fast-blast origins to a darker, more plodding style, represented here by their track "A Skeleton At The Feast," from the 1982 LP Homeland. ADS, a group from the same Denmark scene as Gatecrashers, offers up the searing "Waiting for the War," from their scarce 1982 split 7" with CityX, which takes the socially conscious yet satirical bite of punk rock one nihilistic step further. A swirling nightmare of reverb-drenched guitars begins UK darkwave act Veda's snarling "Whiplash," featuring Sex Gang Children member Cam Campbell. The 1987 single it comes from was Veda's one and only release. Fellow British band Skeletal Family began a prolific career in 1983. Their track "Promised Land" is a perfect showcase for guitarist Stan Greenwood's jagged style, as well as Ann Marie Hurst's powerful vocal ability.

UK goth rock band Flowers for Agatha's somber "The Freedom Curse" was more than worthy of radio airplay, which sadly went unachieved. The song appeared on the band's 1985 EP of the same name. "Dark Spirits" is a standout cut from Los Angeles deathrockers Red Temple Spirits, released by the legendary Midwestern label Fundamental Independent Project Records, later released a comprehensive anthology of the group's material in 2013. The driving postpunk obscurity that is "What's Wrong Yvette," by the nearly unknown Denver band Crank Call Love Affair, comes from their only record, a self-released 7" single of the same name. Belgium's Red Zebra — now known as EXRZ — contributes their raw, infectious brand of new wave in the form of the title track from their 1980 debut 7" EP "I Can't Live In A Living Room." Fellow Belgians Vita Noctis round out the compilation with their dreamy, recorded-to-cassette ballad "Hade," from their 1984 self-released tape In The Face Of... Death. –Mike Hunchback

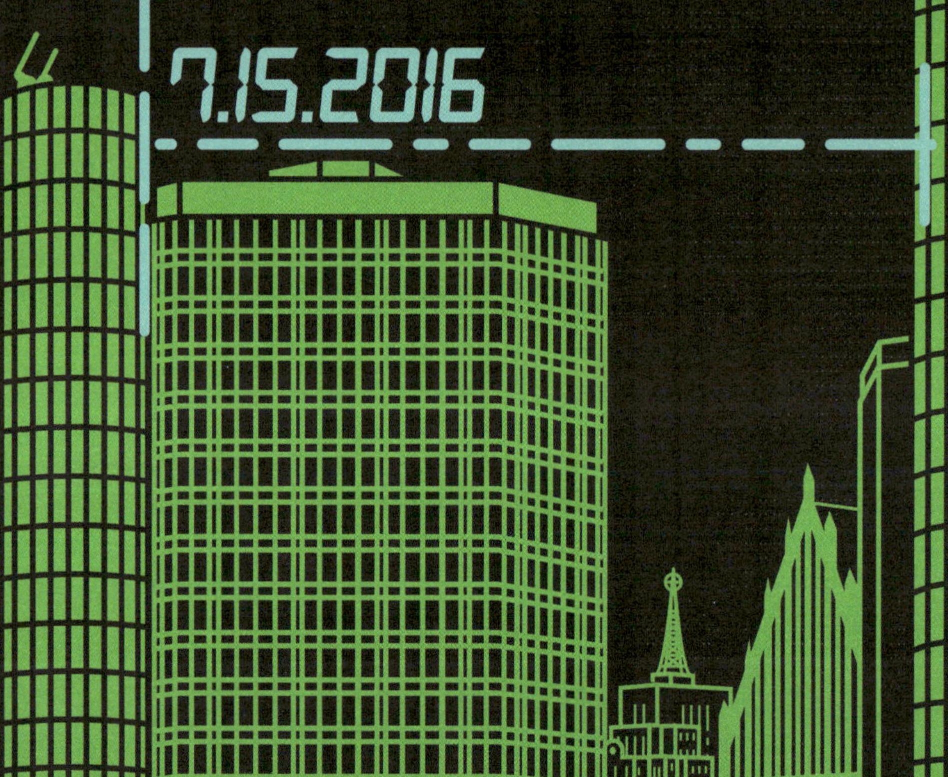

EL CLUB + PARTY STORE PRODUCTIONS
+ THE CROFOOT PRESENT
AN EVENING WITH:
JOHN CARPENTER:
LIVE RETROSPECTIVE
(PERFORMING THEMES FROM HIS
CLASSIC FILMS & NEW COMPOSITIONS)
7.15.2016
THE MASO

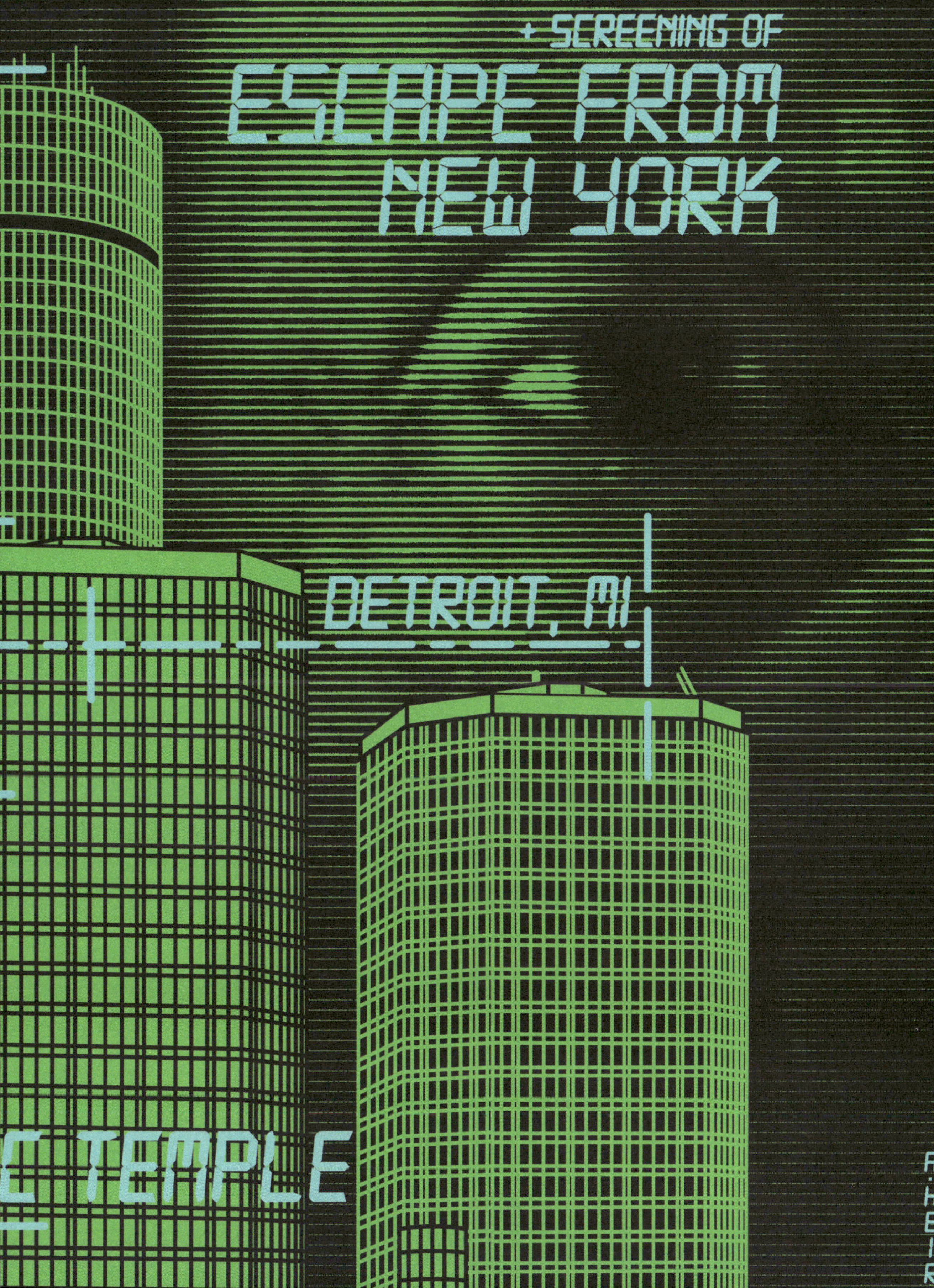

+ SCREENING OF
ESCAPE FROM
NEW YORK
DETROIT, MI
C TEMPLE
A. HEIR

AUGUST 11
9PM
2016
UNTIL
8/31
DEATH/TRAITORS
(ALEXANDER HEIR)
BERSERKTOWN:
LOS ANGELES
LETHAL
AMOUNTS
1226 W 7TH
LA
ART EXHIBITION---
---POP UP SHOP

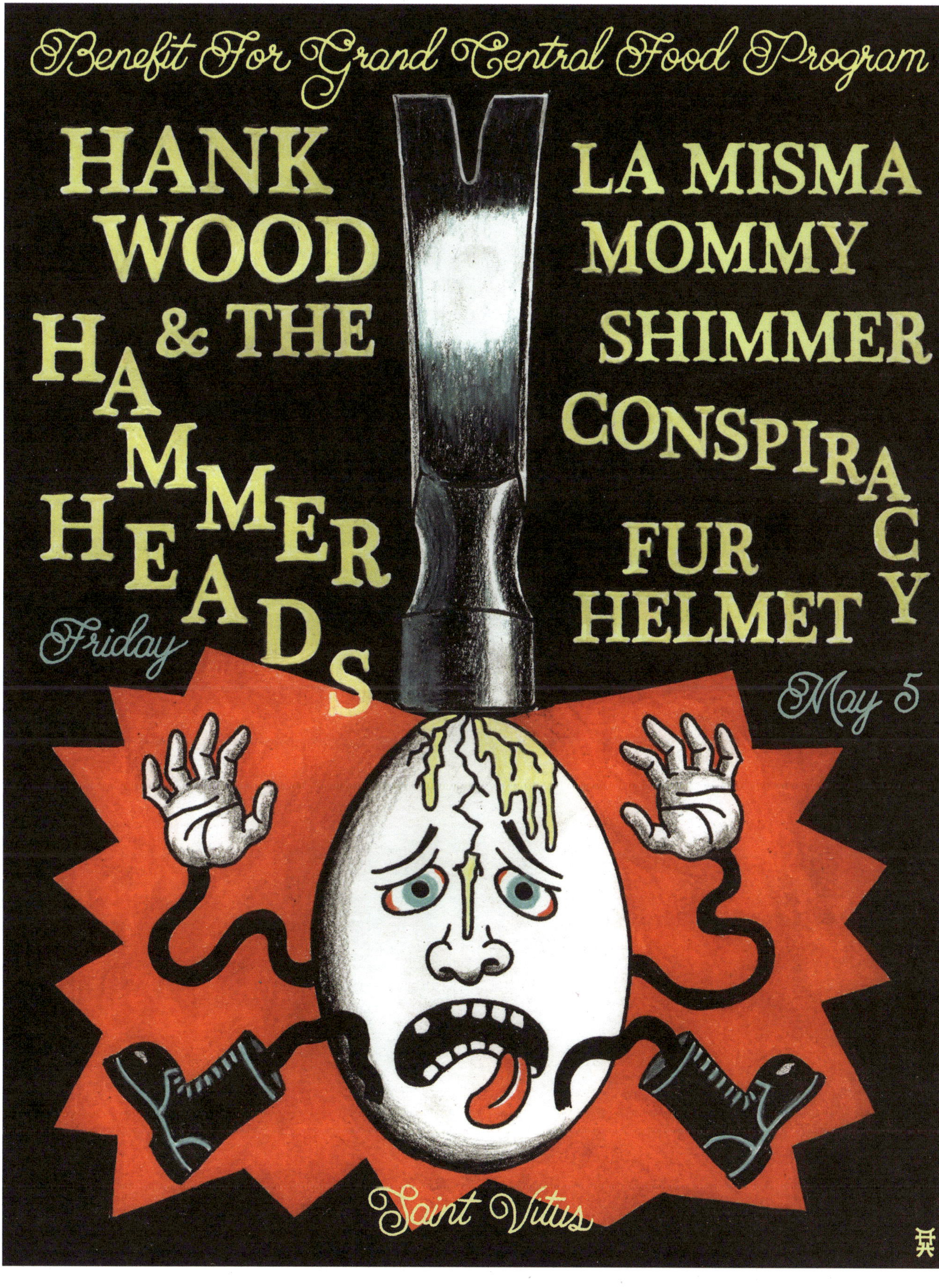

Benefit For Grand Central Food Program
HANK WOOD & THE HAMMERHEADS
LA MISMA
MOMMY
SHIMMER
CONSPIRACY
FUR HELMET
Friday
May 5
Saint Vitus

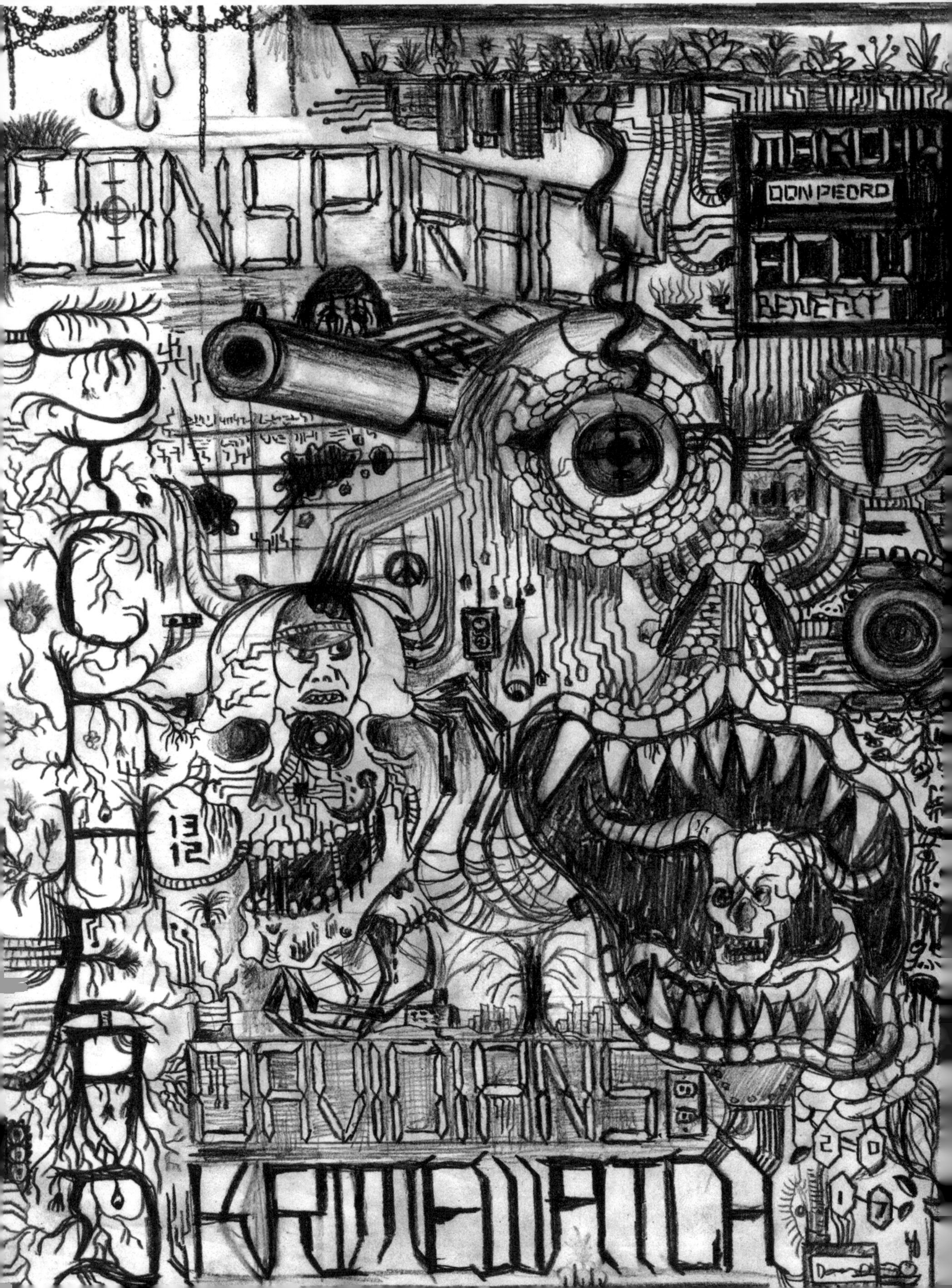
CONSPIRA
MARCH
DON PEDRO
NOW
BENEFIT
13
12

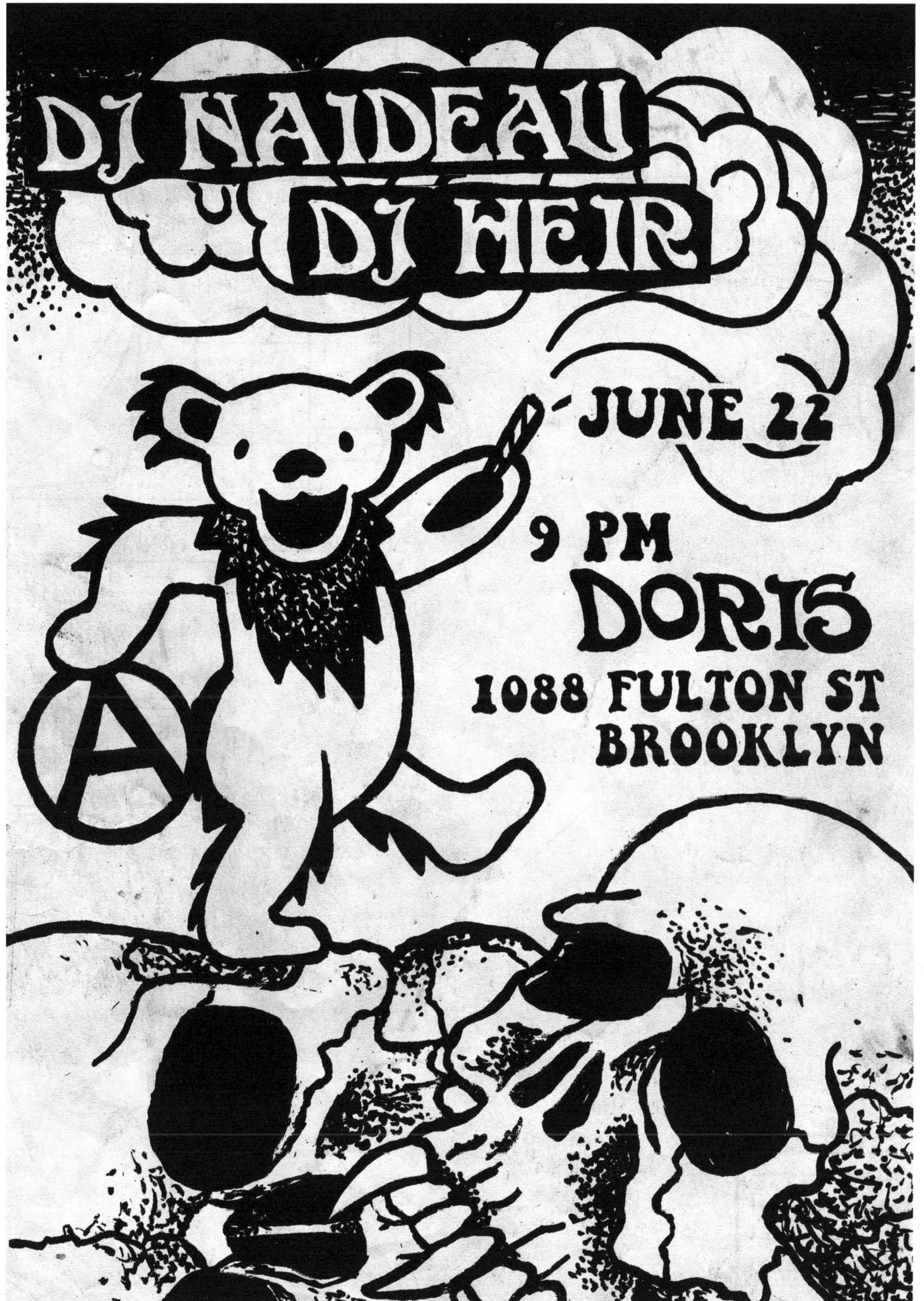

DJ NADEAU & DJ HEIR
JUNE 22
9 PM
DORIS
1088 FULTON ST
BROOKLYN

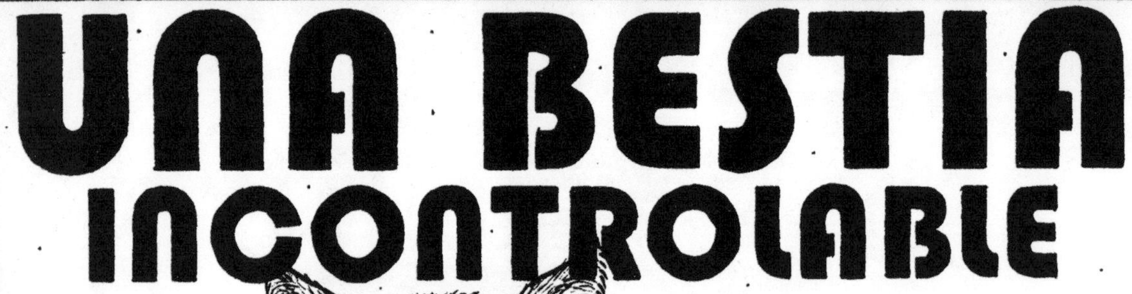

UNA BESTIA
INCONTROLABLE

SAT.
JULY
22
8PM

HANK WOOD
& THE
HAMMER
HEADS

LA MISMA

IMPALERS

SUBVERSIVE
RITE

BROOKLYN BAZAAR
150 GREENPOINT AVE.

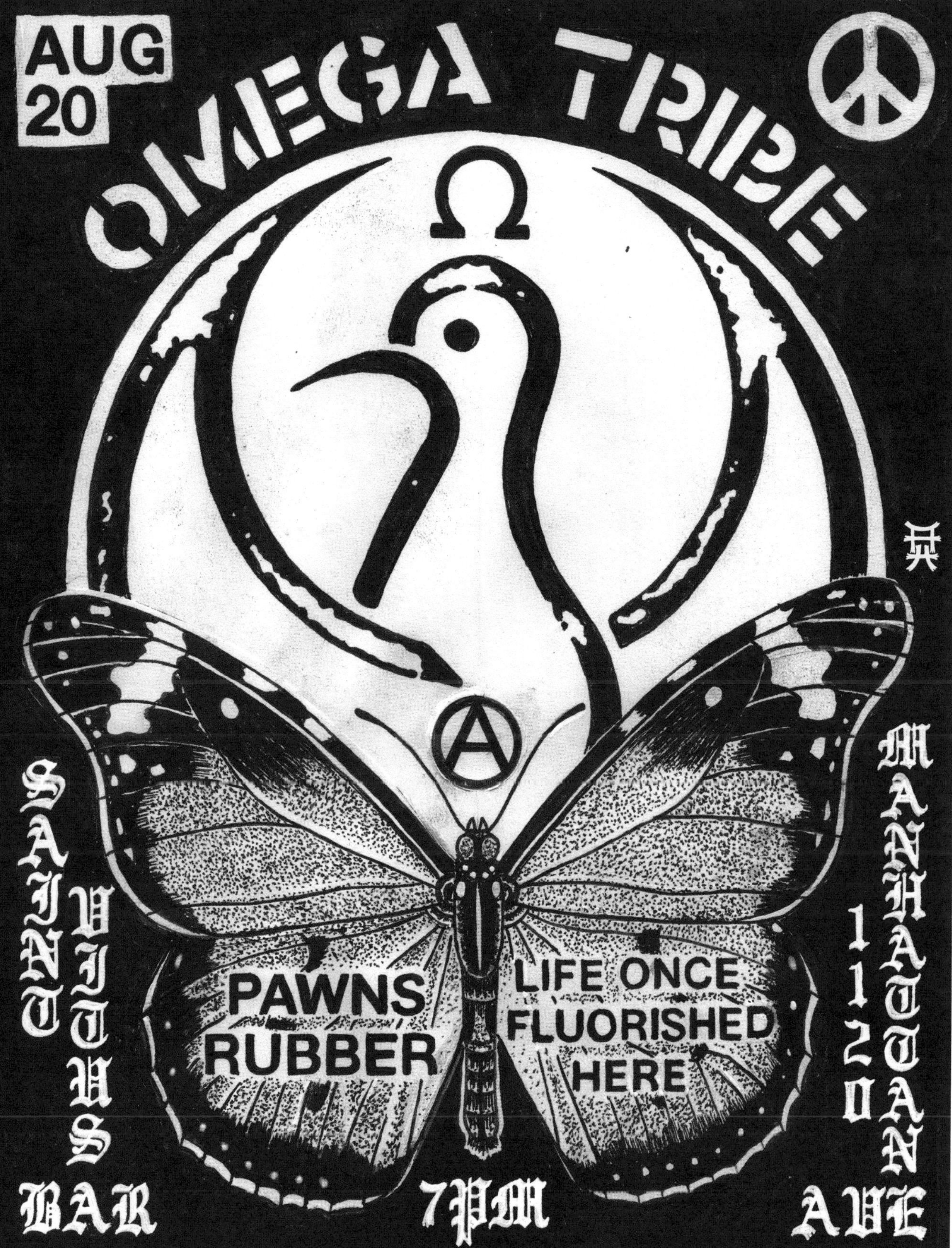

AUG 20
OMEGA TRIBE
SAINT VITUS BAR
MANHATTAN 1120 AVE
PAWNS RUBBER
LIFE ONCE FLUORISHED HERE
7PM
PAWNS RECORD RELEASE//IGNORE ROCK N' ROLL HEROES VENDING

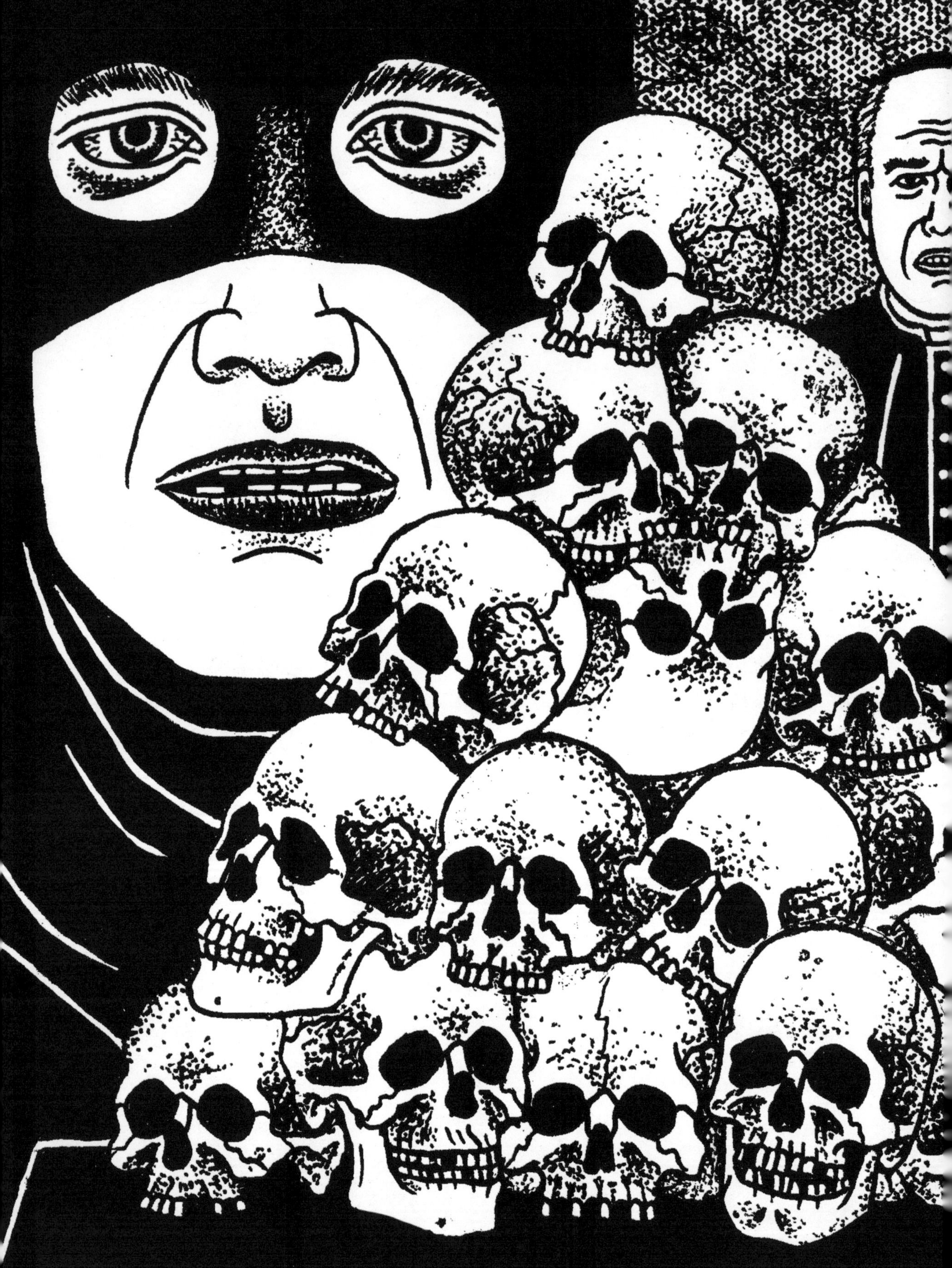

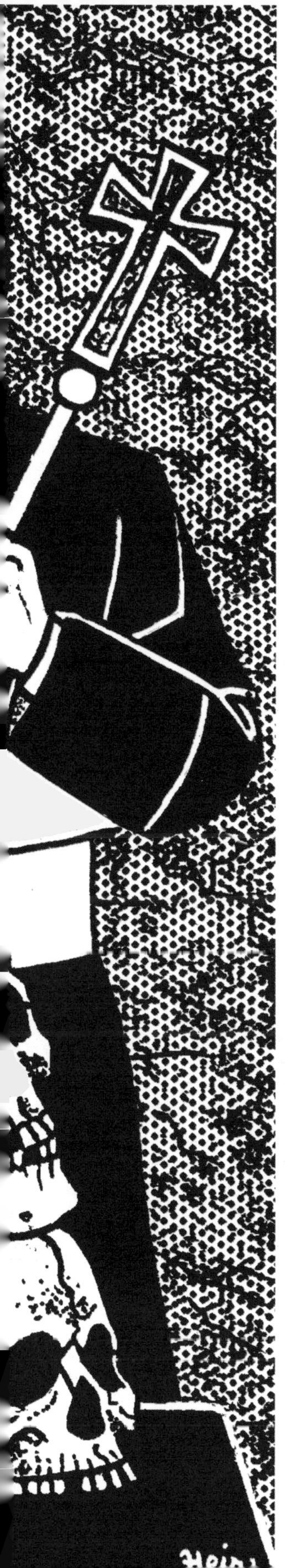

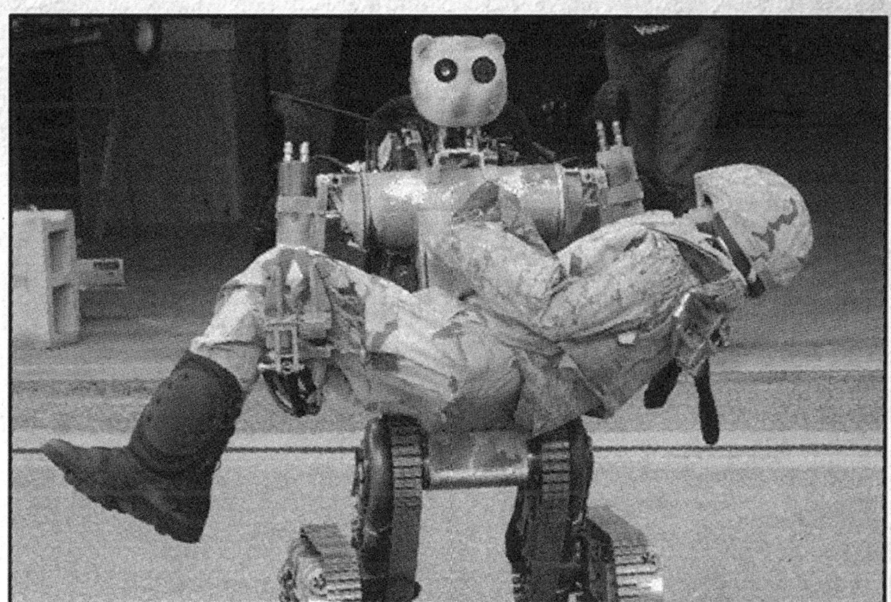

DJ MILITARY SCIENTIST

"Next generation military robots have minds of their own."

8 JULY, 2017. 23:59

HEALING ELECTRONIC

IMPULSES

& RHYTHMS

Ceremony Bar:
224 Manhattan Ave Brooklyn

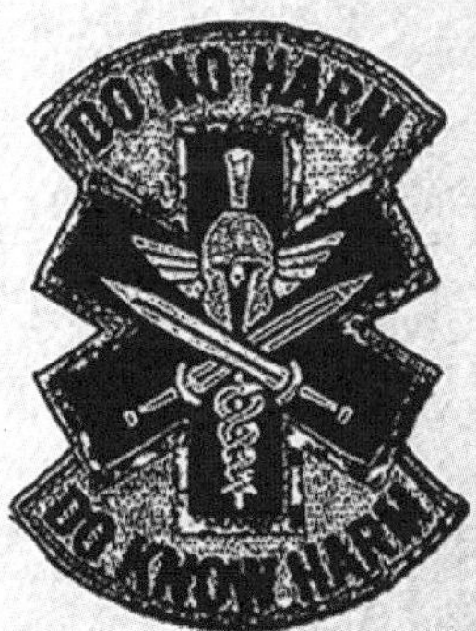

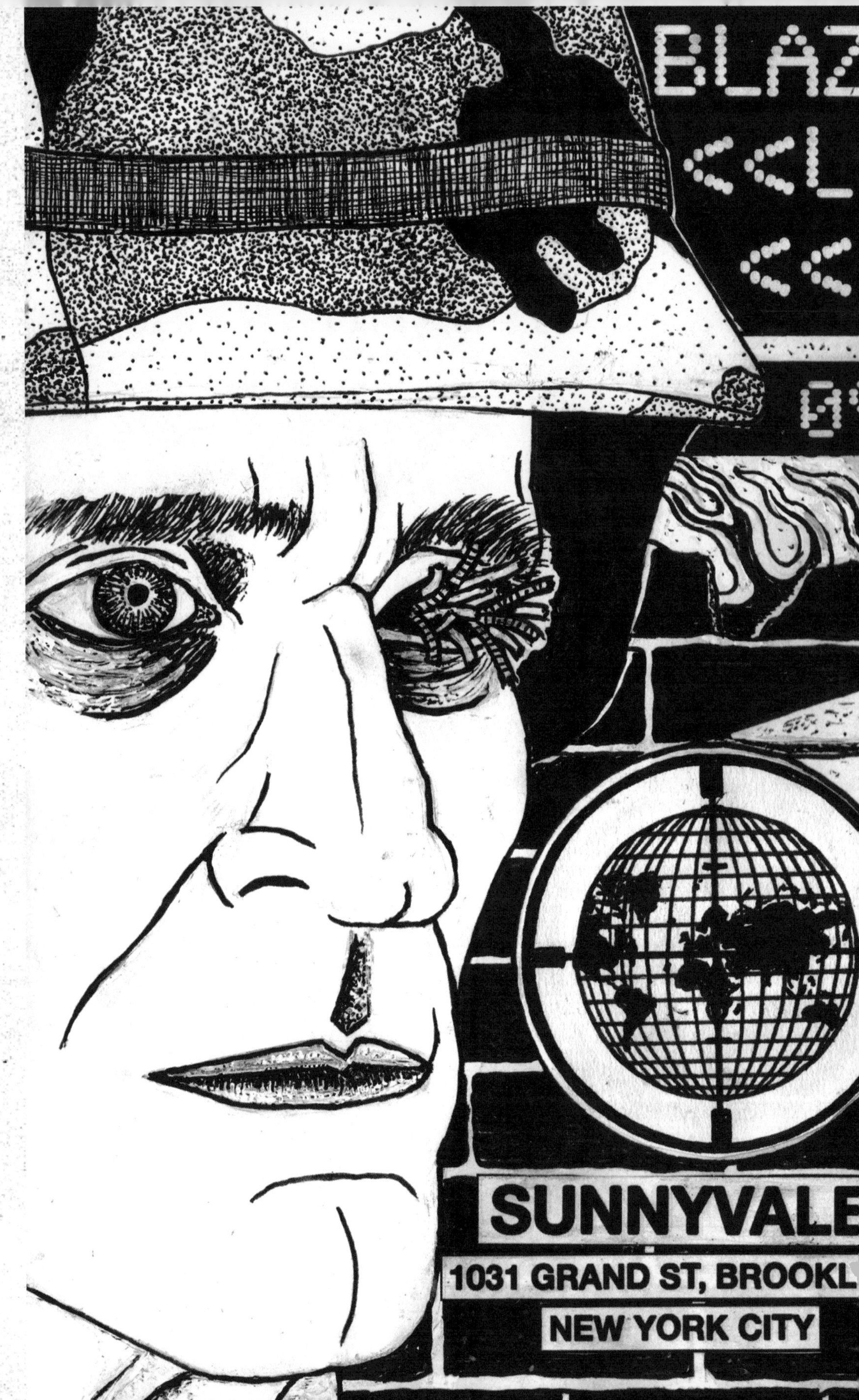

BLAZ
<<L
<<
SUNNYVALE
1031 GRAND ST, BROOKL
NEW YORK CITY

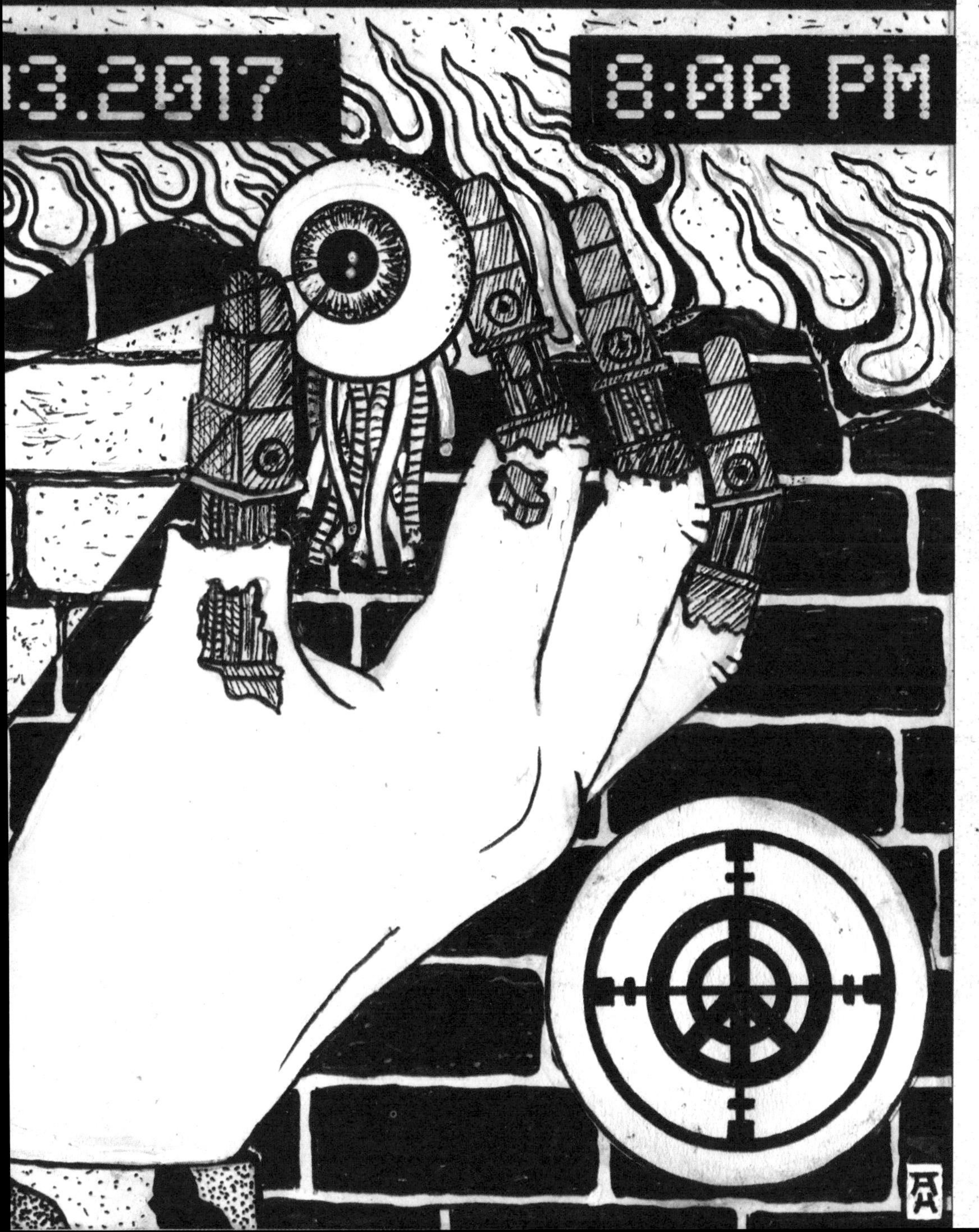
NG EYE-EXIT ORDER
.T.I.O.N.-HARAM>>
MACHO BOYS>>>
3.2017
8:00 PM

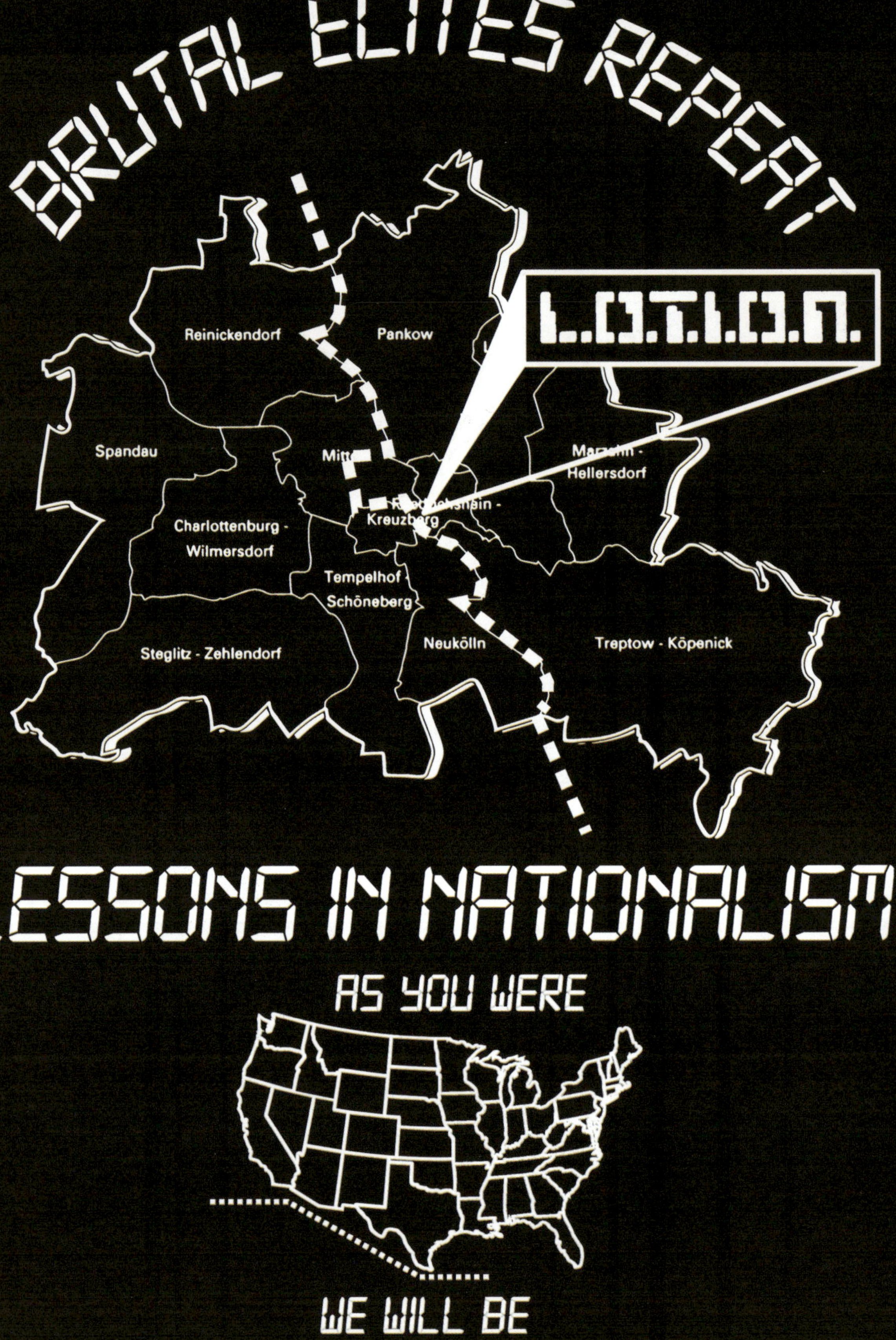

BRUTAL ELITES REPEAT
Reinickendorf
Pankow
L.O.T.I.O.N.
Spandau
Mitte
Marzahn - Hellersdorf
Charlottenburg - Wilmersdorf
Friedrichshain - Kreuzberg
Tempelhof Schöneberg
Steglitz - Zehlendorf
Neukölln
Treptow - Köpenick
LESSONS IN NATIONALISM
AS YOU WERE
WE WILL BE

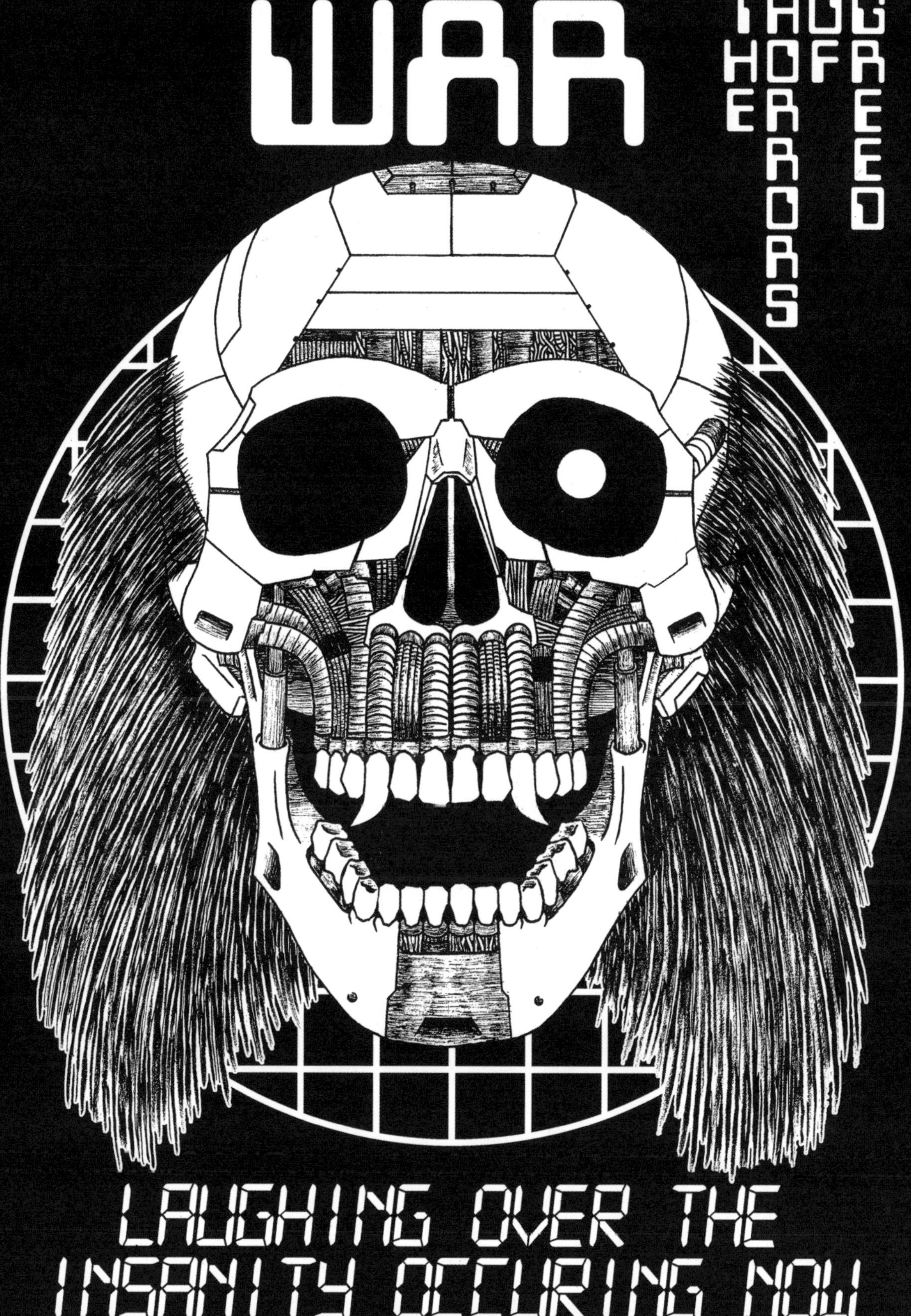

WAR
THE
HOF
FREED
HORRORS
GREED
LAUGHING OVER THE
INSANITY OCCURING NOW

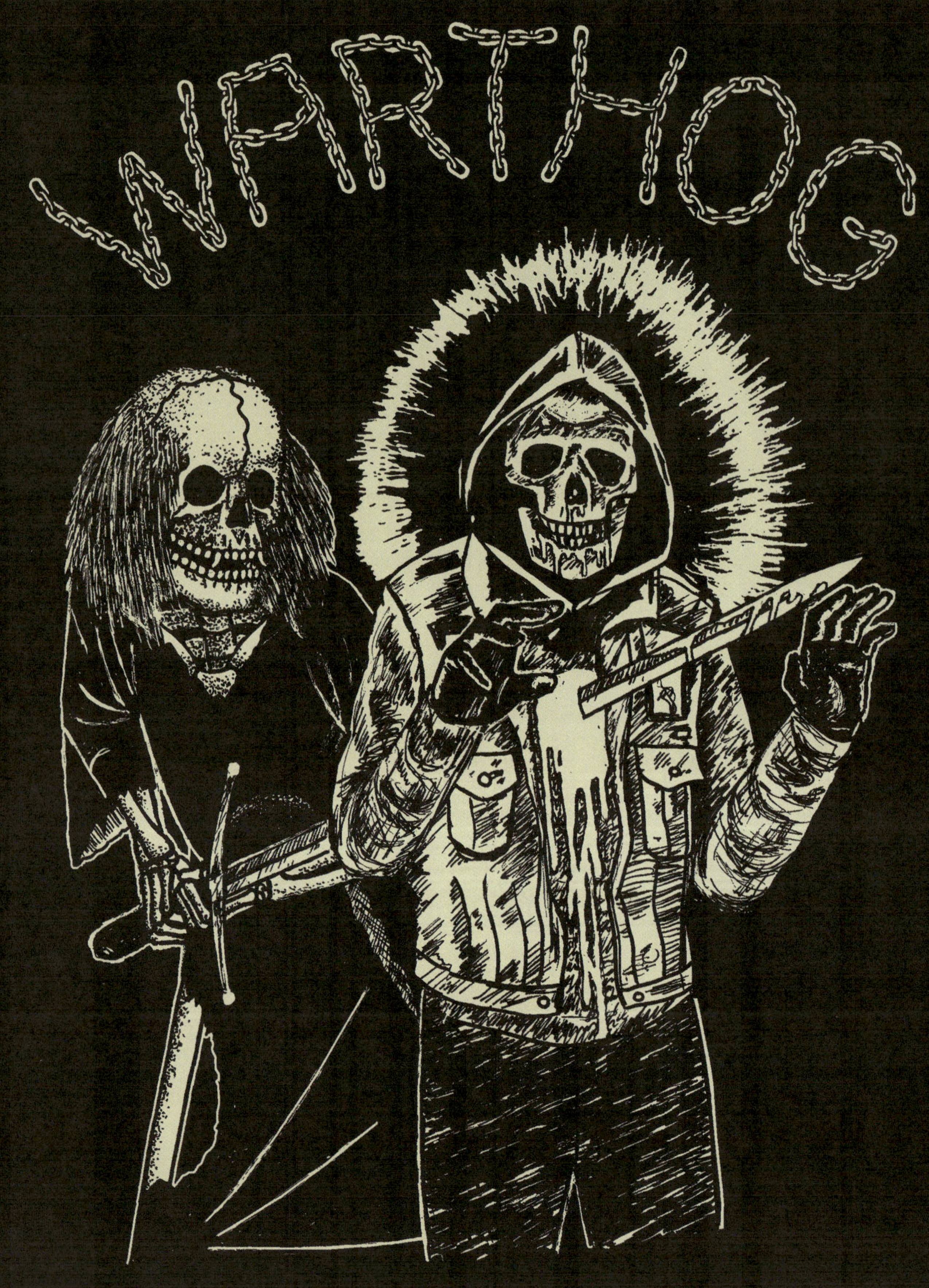

WARTHOG

WARTHOG

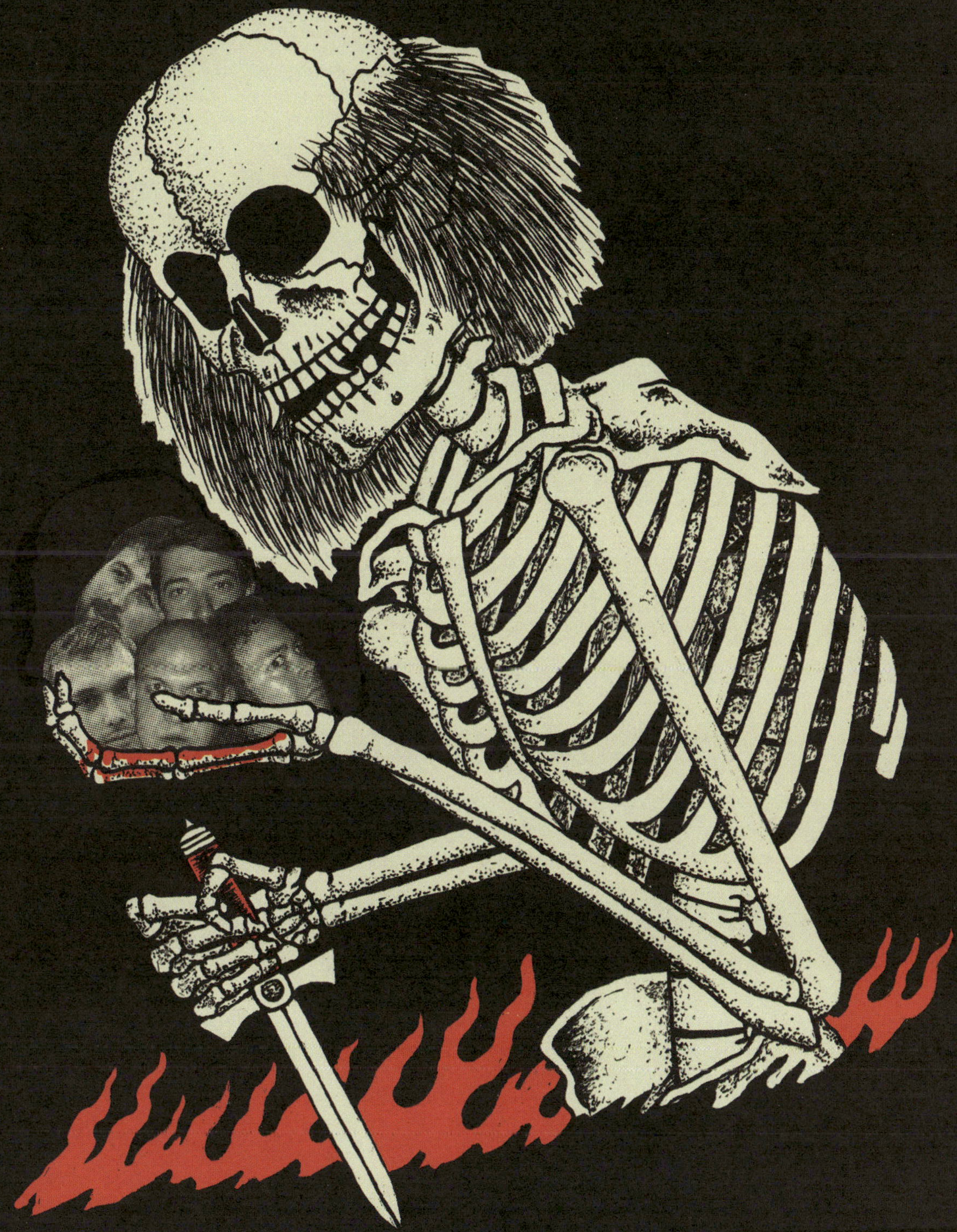

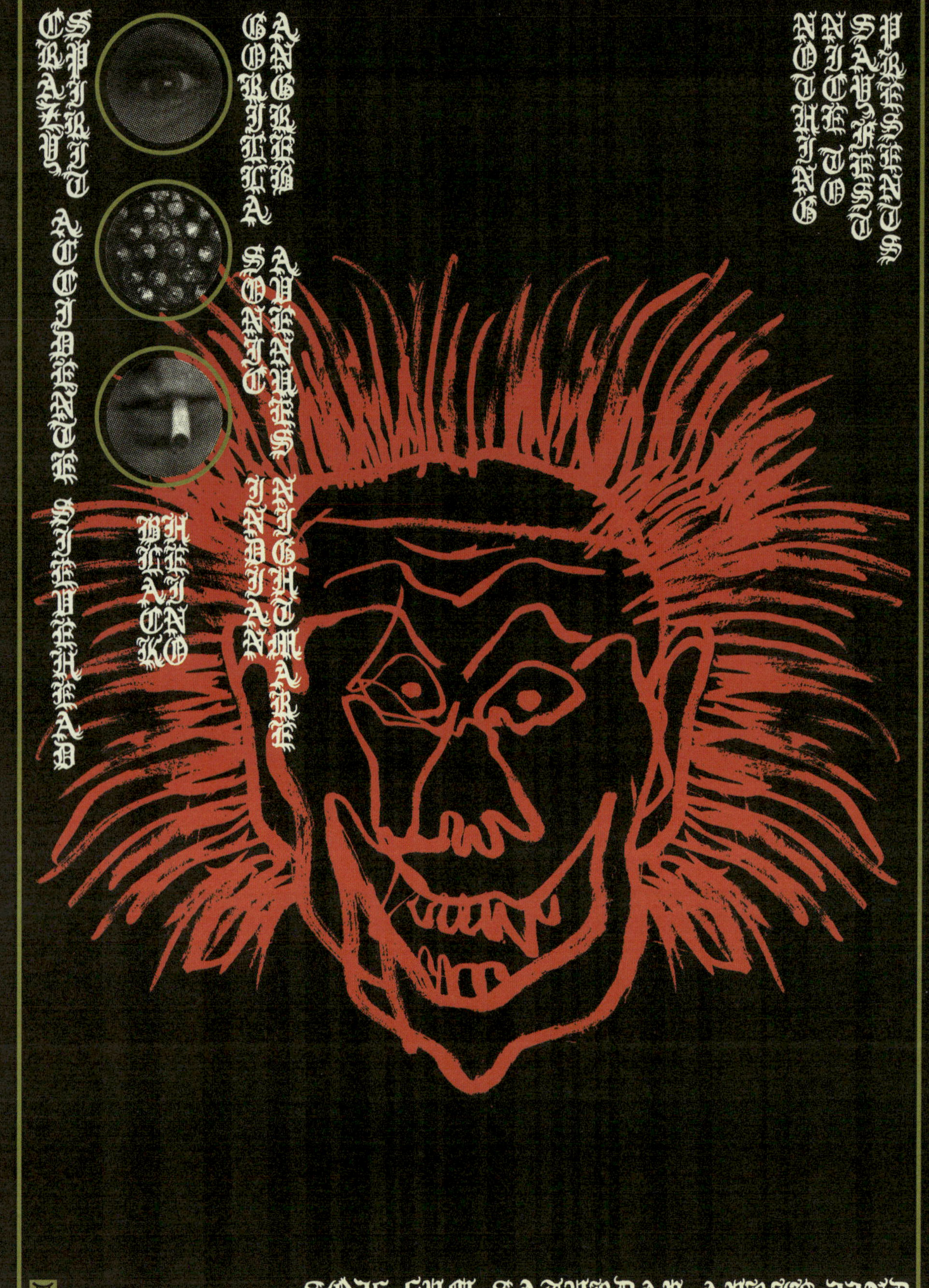
SPIRITFEST
NICEGUY
NOTHING
PRESENTS
CRYPTIC SPIRIT
ACCIDENTE
SLEEPERHEAD
GORILLA GANG
SONIC AVENUE
INDIAN NIGHTMARE
BLANKO
SO36 6PM SATURDAY APRIL 22ND

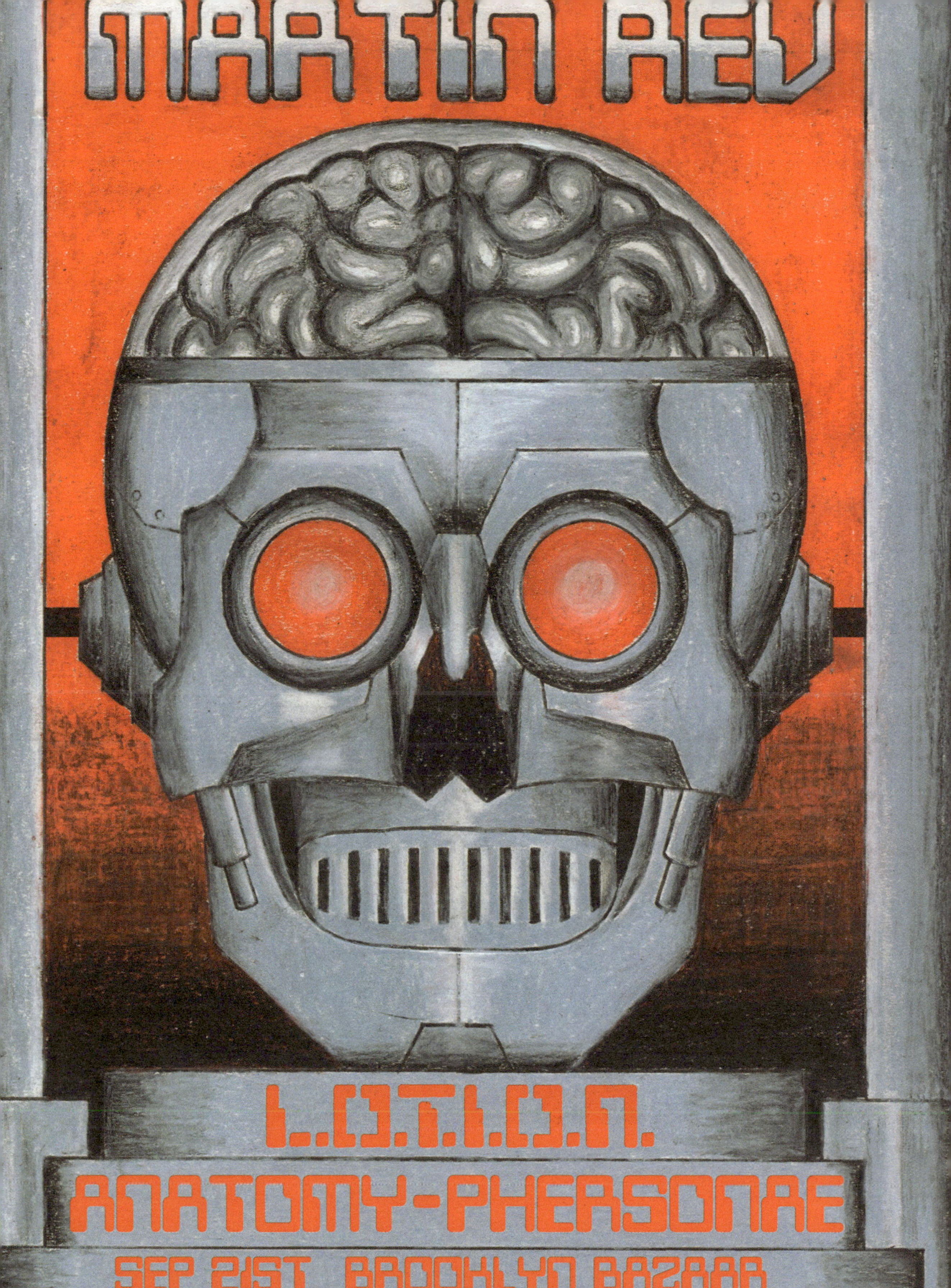

MARTIN REV
L.O.T.I.O.N.
ANATOMY-PHERSONAE
SEP 21ST   BROOKLYN BAZAAR

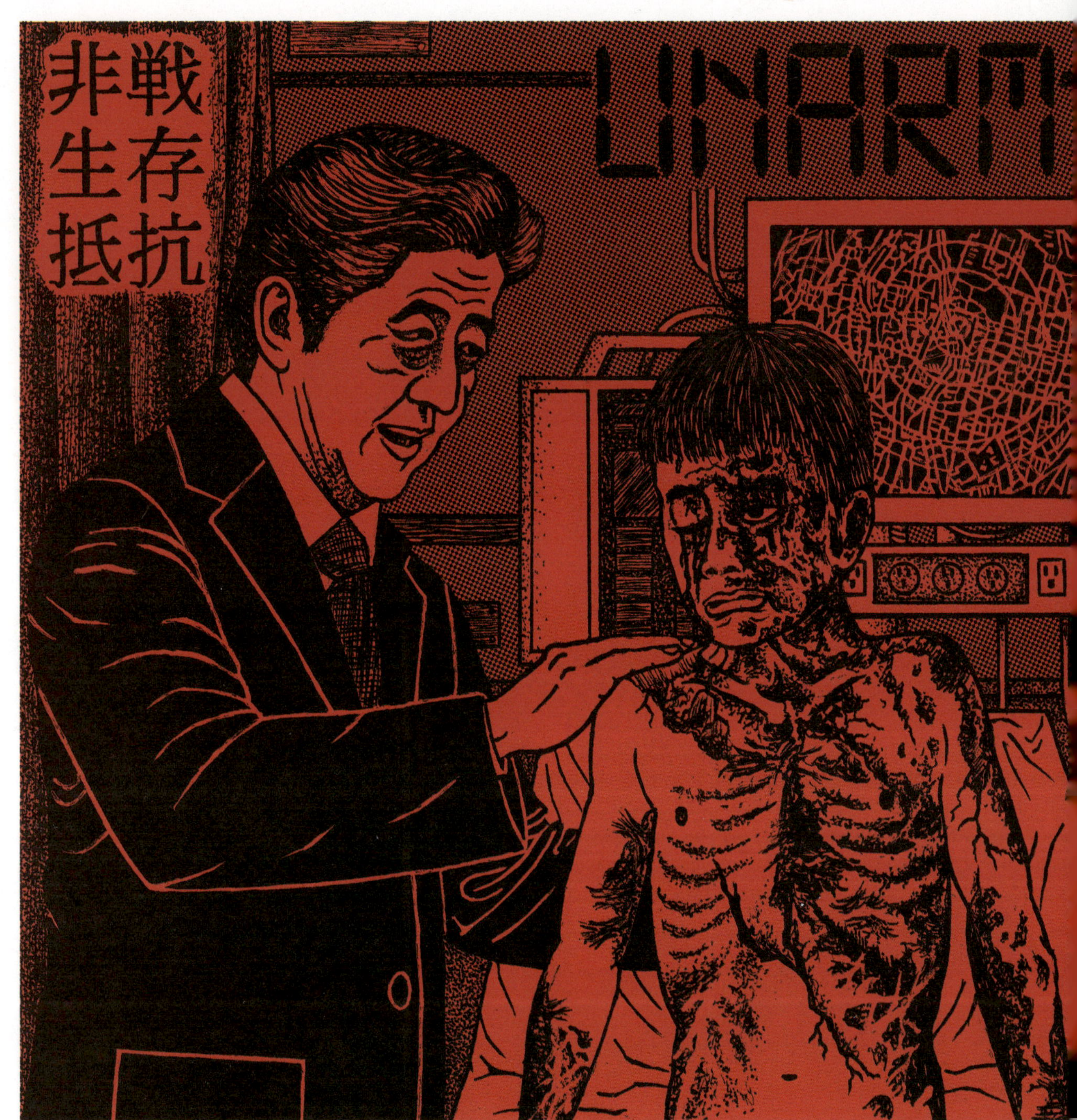

戦存抗
非生抵
UNARM

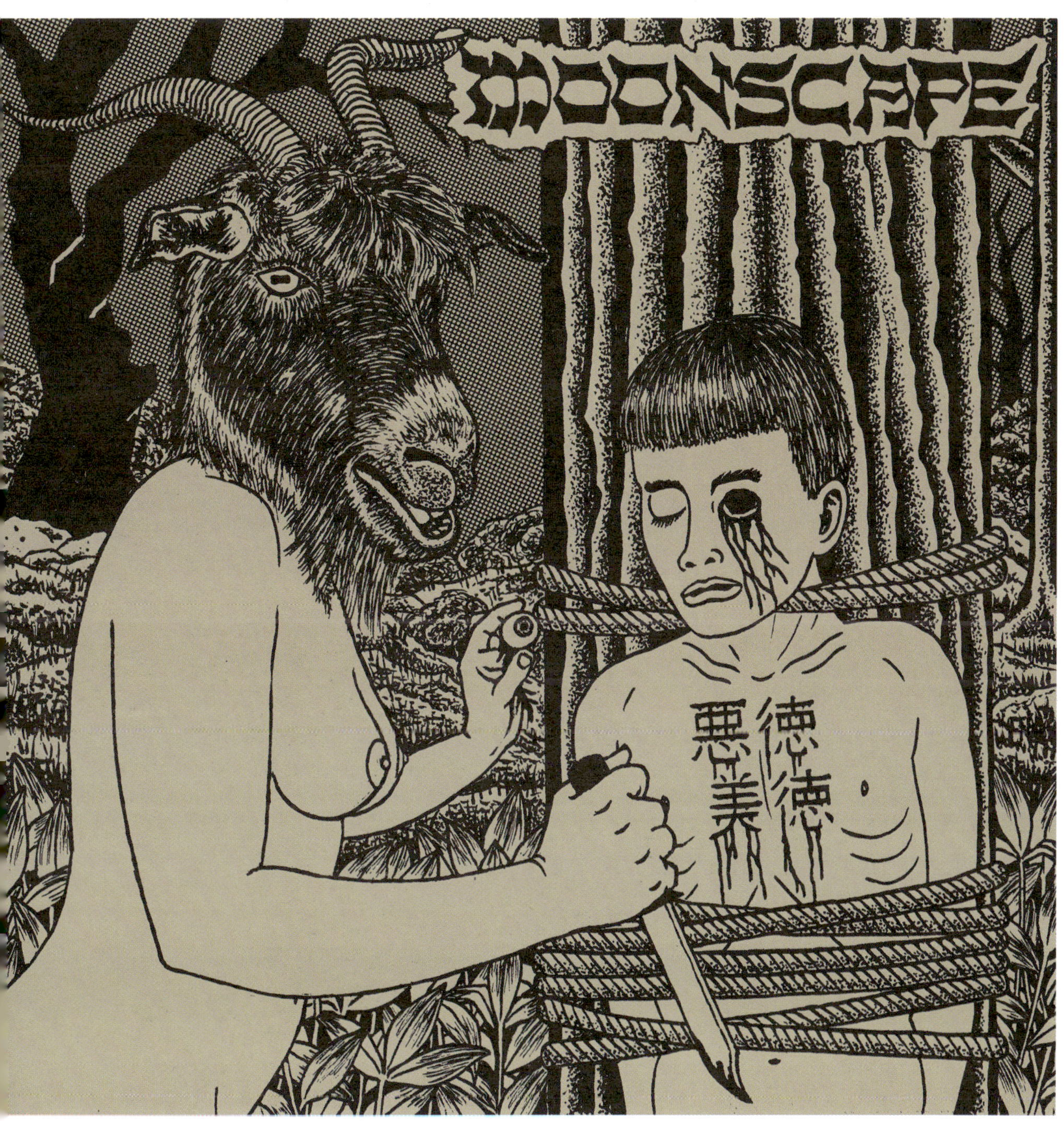

MOONSCAPE
悪徳
徳
美

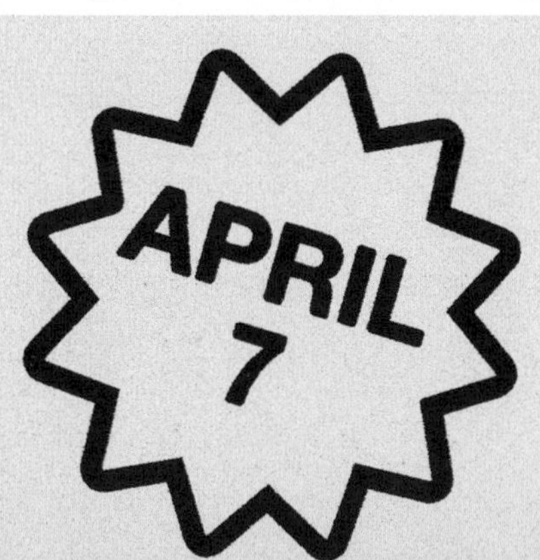

READING, WRITING, RELOADING

APRIL 7

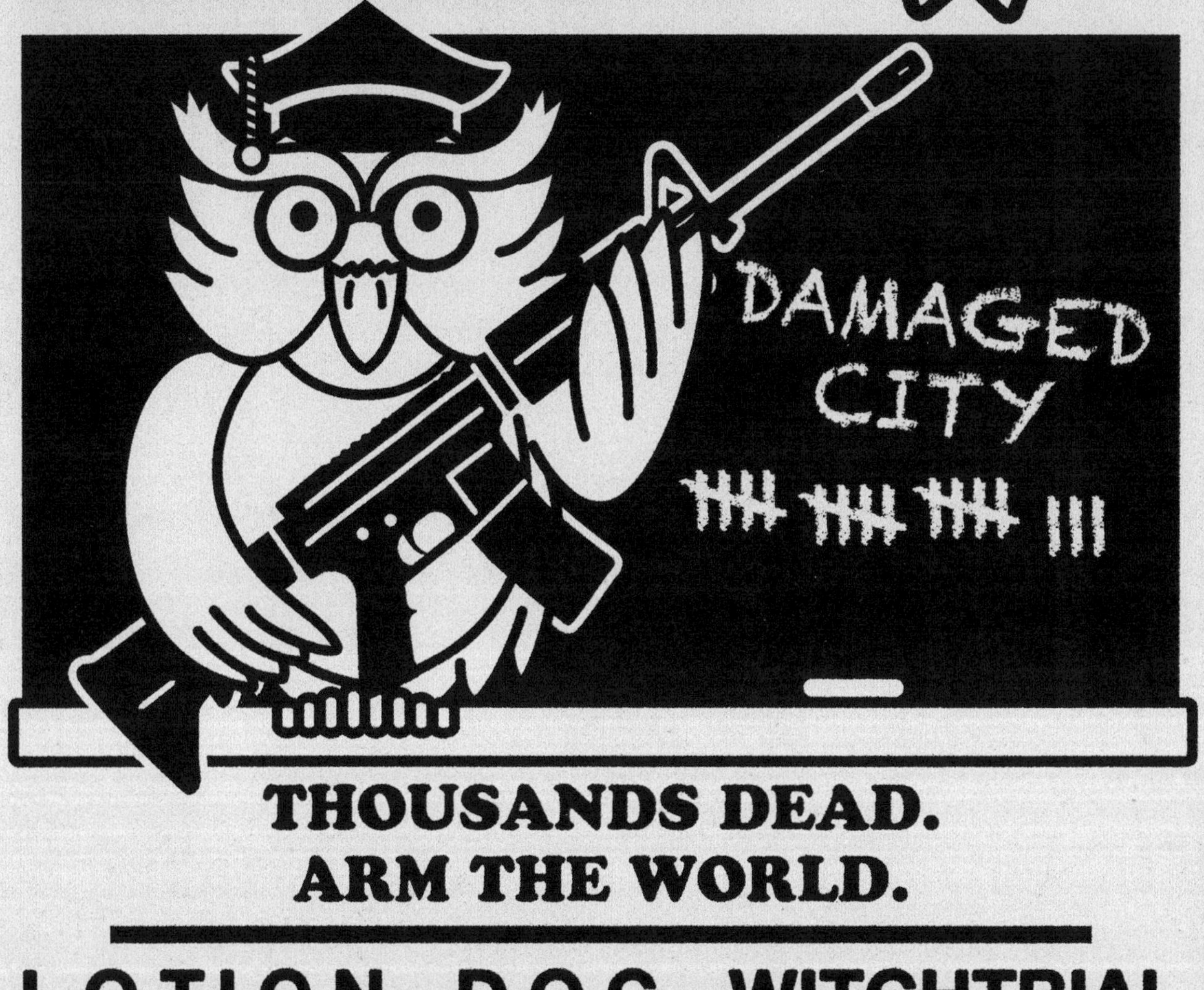

**THOUSANDS DEAD.
ARM THE WORLD.**

L.O.T.I.O.N.- D.O.C.- WITCHTRIAL
BLACKSAGE- NEOLITHIC

**THE BLACK CAT, 1811 14th St. NW
11PM DOORS/12PM SHOW $15**

EVERYTHING IS FINE.

DON'T WORRY, BE HAPPY!

L.O.T.I.O.N.- D.O.C.- WITCHTRIAL
BLACKSAGE- NEOLITHIC

THE BLACK CAT, 1811 14th St. NW
11PM DOORS/12PM SHOW $15

HEIR

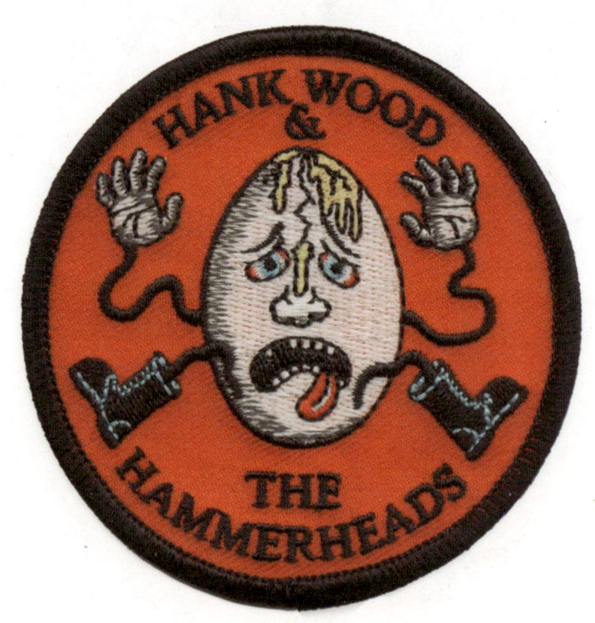

HANK WOOD
&
THE
HAMMERHEADS

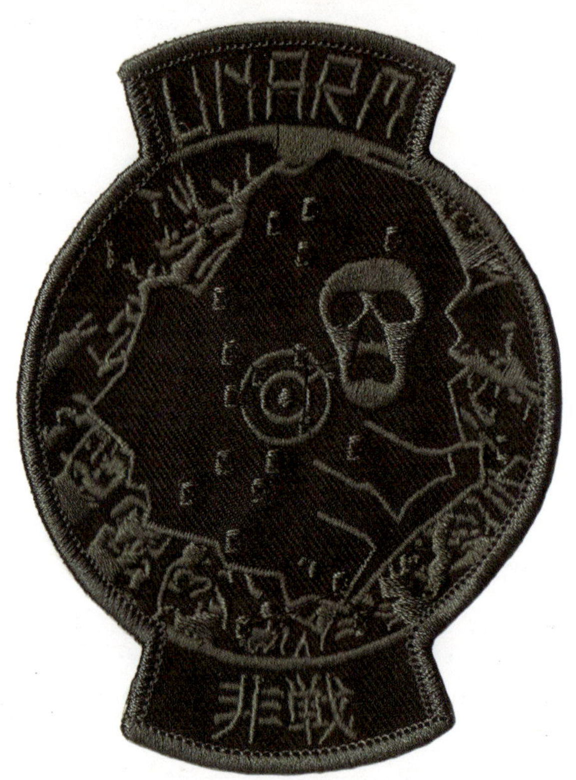

UNARM
非戦

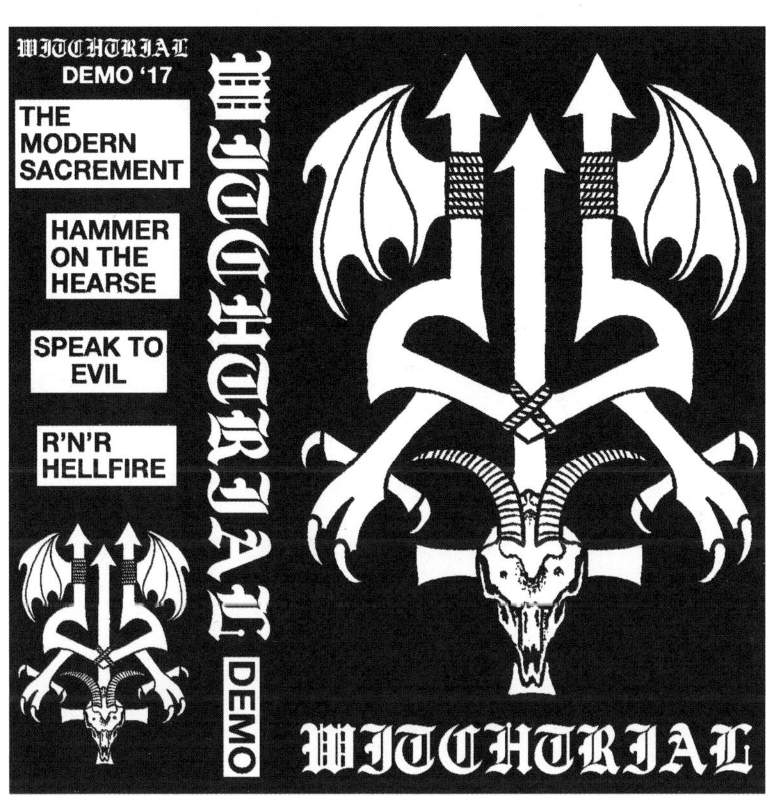

WITCHTRIAL
DEMO '17
THE MODERN SACREMENT
HAMMER ON THE HEARSE
SPEAK TO EVIL
R'N'R HELLFIRE
WITCHTRIAL
DEMO
WITCHTRIAL

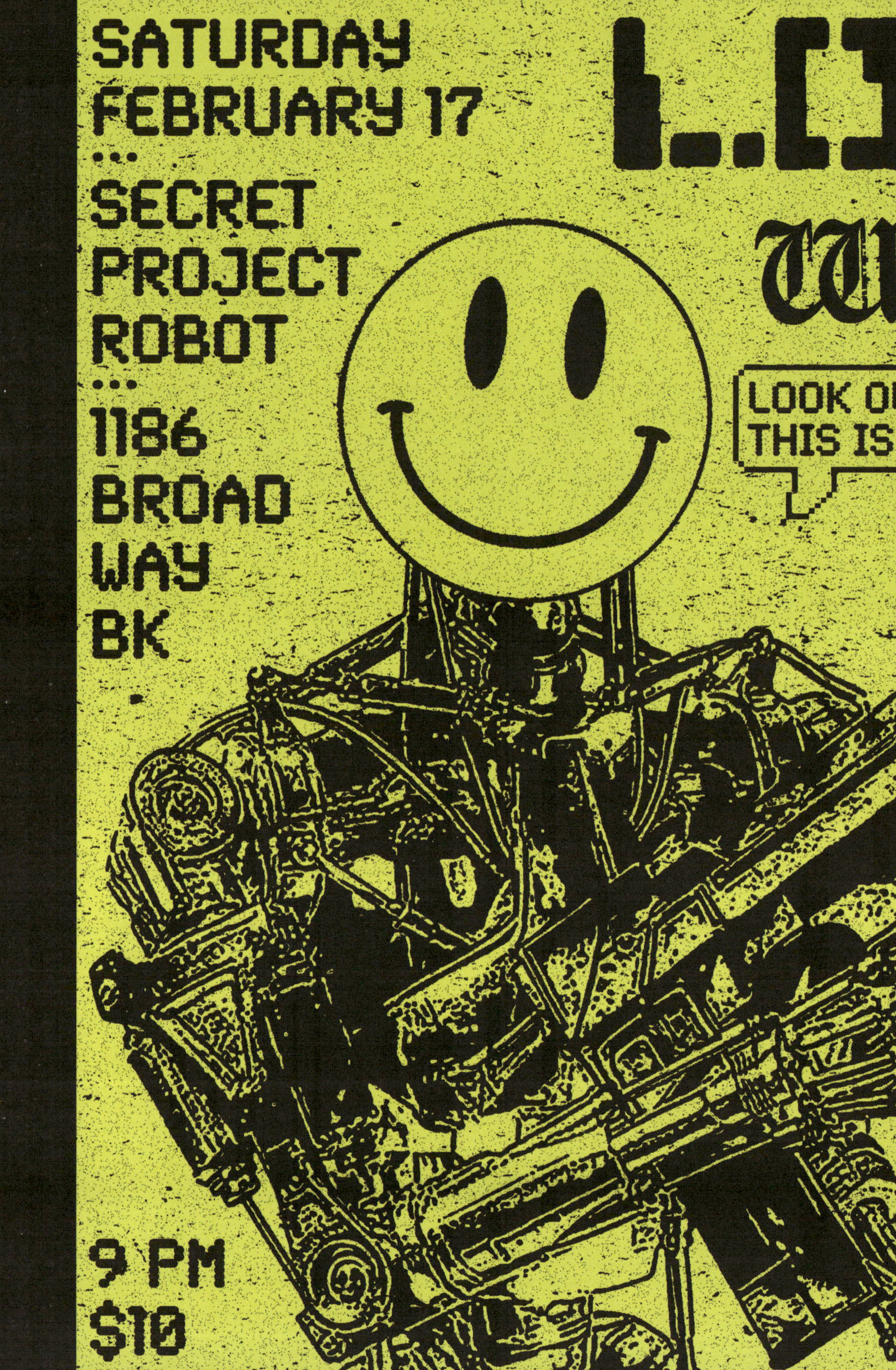

SATURDAY
FEBRUARY 17
...
SECRET
PROJECT
ROBOT
...
1186
BROAD
WAY
BK
9 PM
$10
LOOK OU
THIS IS

F.O.D.
TCHTRIAL
(D.C.)
S NOW!
POBREZA MENTAL
Twisted Thing

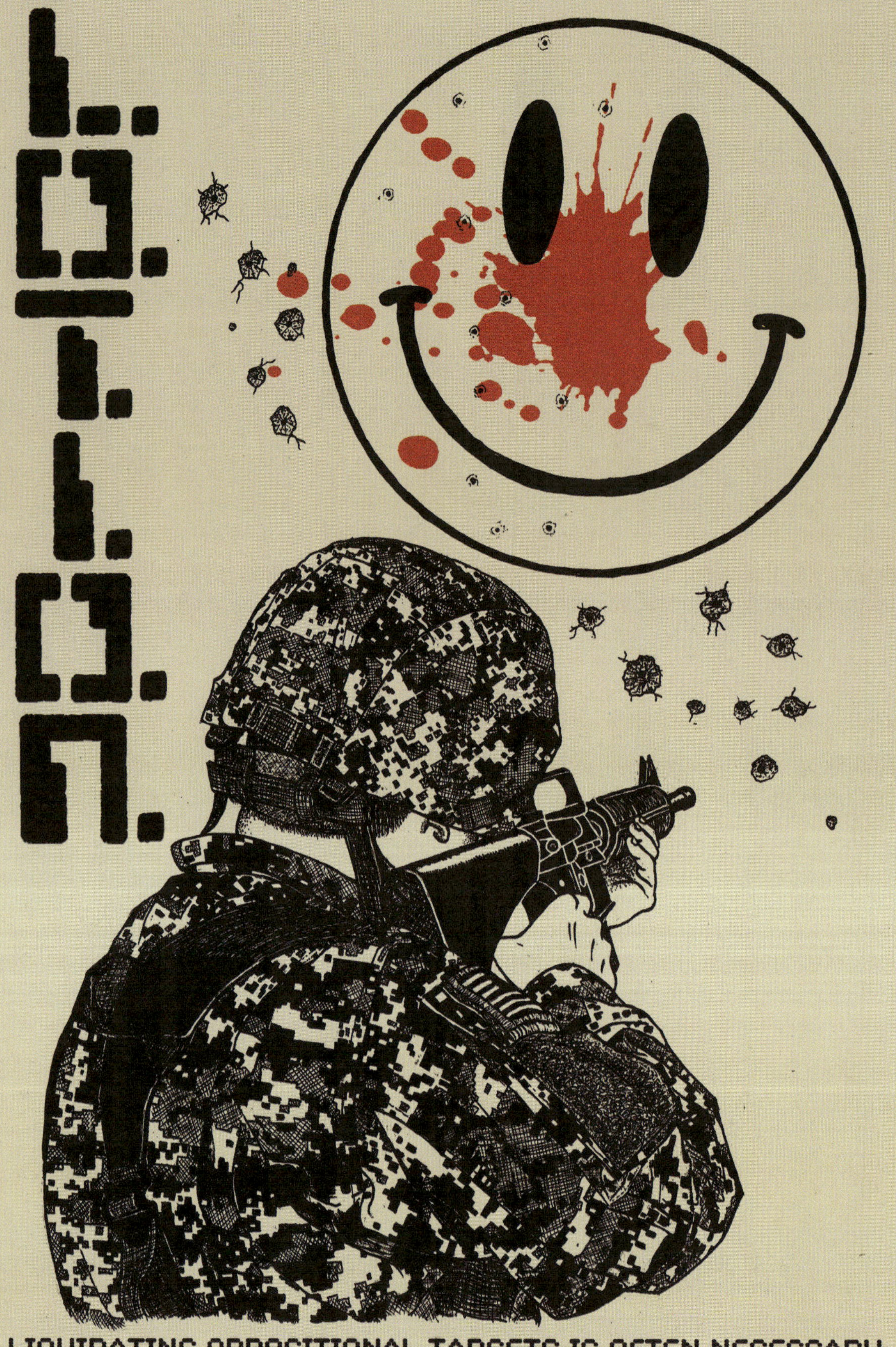
LIQUIDATING OPPOSITIONAL TARGETS IS OFTEN NECESSARY

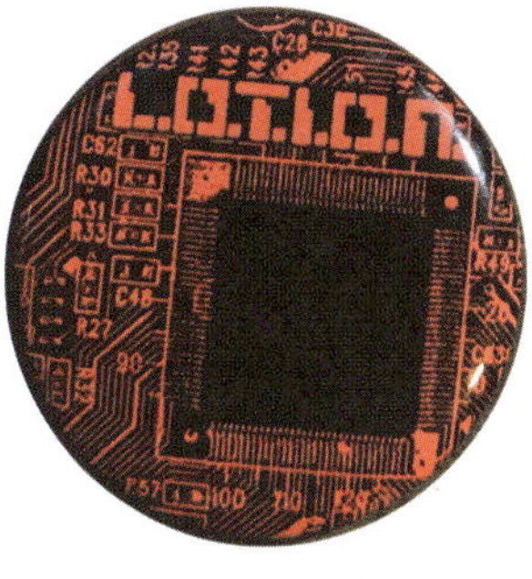

L.O.T.I.O.N.

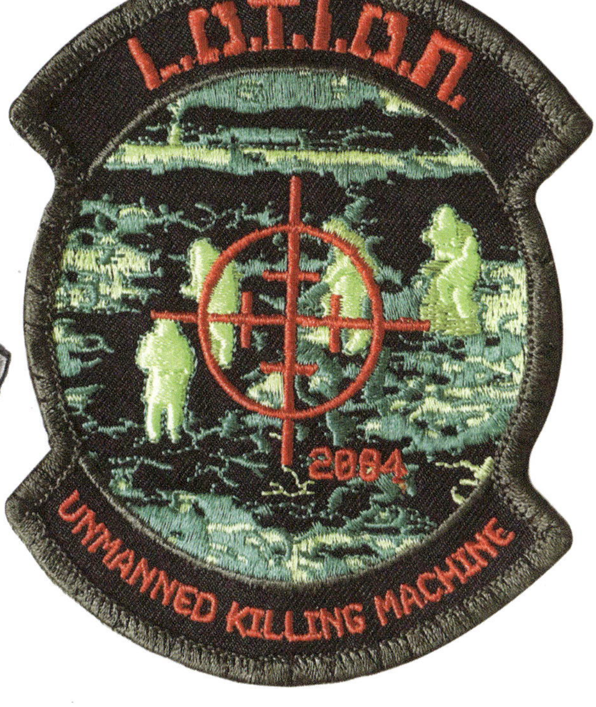

L.O.T.I.O.N.

L.O.T.I.O.N.
2084
UNMANNED KILLING MACHINE

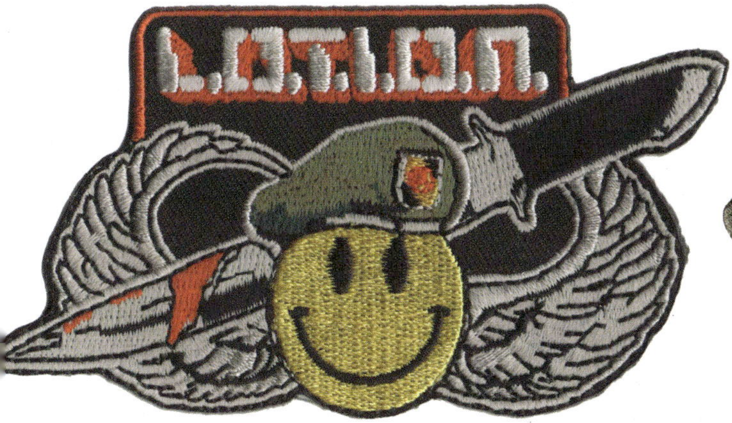

L.O.T.I.O.N.

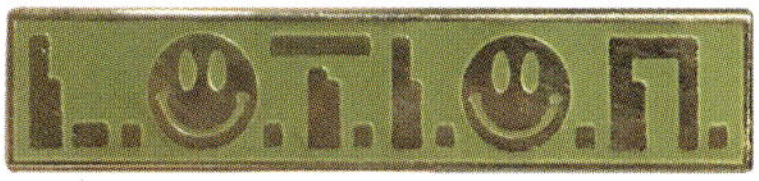

LEAKED OFFICIAL TRANSMISSIONS
1: XENOPHOBIA [DEMO]
2: HARDWARE [DEMO]
3: GOODBYE HUMANS
[SCUMPUTER REMIX]
L.O.T.I.O.N.
INCLUDING OMITTED NOTES
L.O.T.I.O.N.
MULTINATIONAL CORPORATION
[DECLASSIFIED
AUDIO DOCUMENT_2018:]

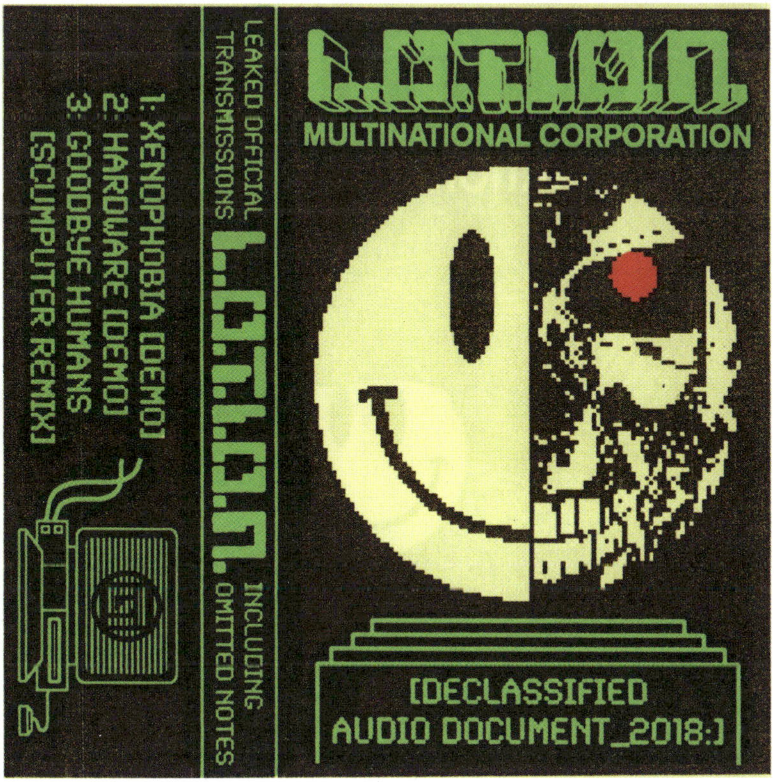

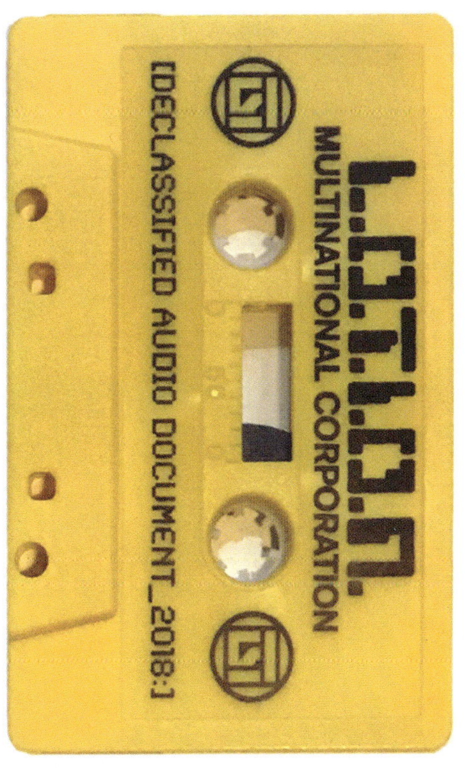
[DECLASSIFIED AUDIO DOCUMENT_2018:]
L.O.T.I.O.N.
MULTINATIONAL CORPORATION

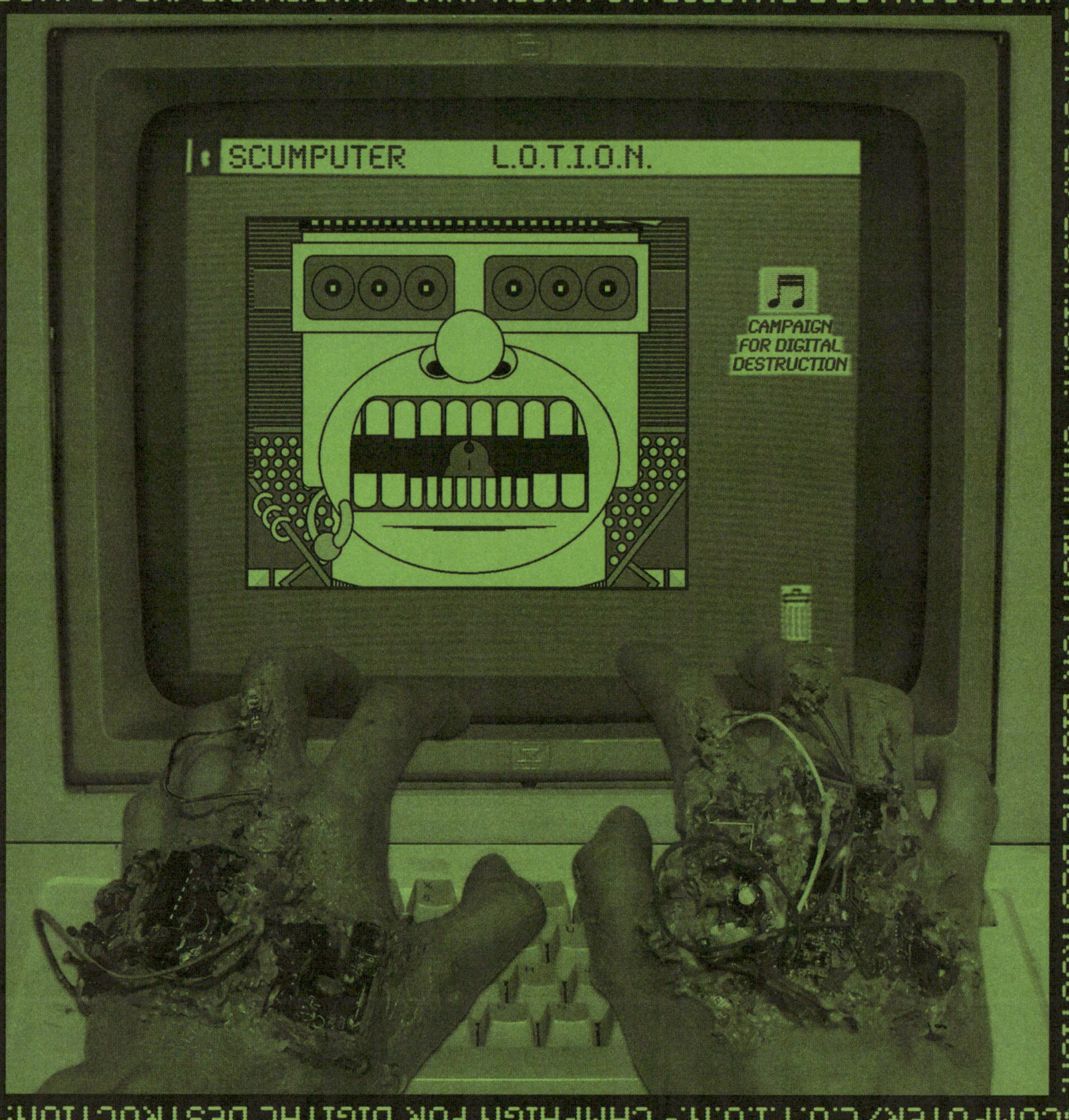
SCUMPUTER/L.O.T.I.O.N.- CAMPAIGN FOR DIGITAL DESTRUCTION:
SCUMPUTER   L.O.T.I.O.N.
CAMPAIGN FOR DIGITAL DESTRUCTION

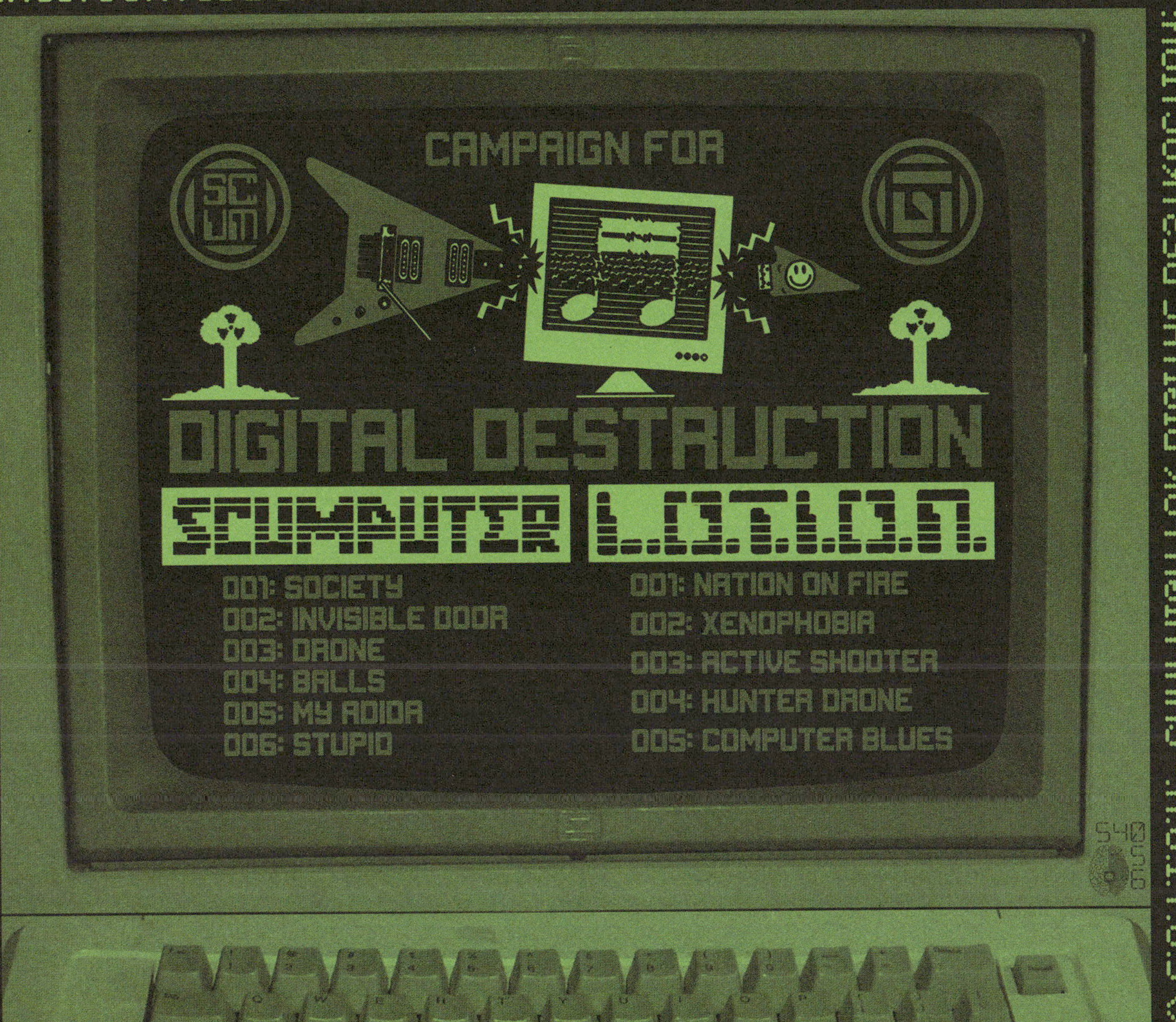
SCUMPUTER/L.O.T.I.O.N. - CAMPAIGN FOR DIGITAL DESTRUCTION:
CAMPAIGN FOR
DIGITAL DESTRUCTION
SCUMPUTER
L.O.T.I.O.N.
001: SOCIETY
002: INVISIBLE DOOR
003: DRONE
004: BALLS
005: MY ADIDA
006: STUPID
001: NATION ON FIRE
002: XENOPHOBIA
003: ACTIVE SHOOTER
004: HUNTER DRONE
005: COMPUTER BLUES
SCUMPUTER/L.O.T.I.O.N. - CAMPAIGN FOR DIGITAL DESTRUCTION:

1-NATION ON FIRE

A LOOK AT THE FUTURE, JUST LIKE THE PAST
BARBED WIRE FENCES KEEPING ORDER INTACT

NATION ON FIRE

HIGH DEFINITION LIVE TV STREAM
SMASHED METAL OBJECTS FLASH ON THE SCREEN

NATION ON FIRE

2017

3-ACTIVE SHOOTER

ACTIVE SHOOTER IN THE NEIGHBORHOOD
OPENING FIRE LIKE HE SAID HE WOULD
ACTIVE SHOOTER ON THE PREMISES
SEMI AUTOMATIC WITH EXTRA CLIPS

ACTIVE SHOOTER ON THE SECOND FLOOR
DRESSED UP LIKE HE'S GOING TO WAR
ACTIVE SHOOTER KICKING DOWN THE DOOR
REPORTS OF SHOTS FIRED
REPORTS OF SHOTS FIRED

THIS IS NOT A TEST, THIS IS NOT A TEST...
YOU'RE LIVING IN IT

ACTIVE SHOOTER ON THE CAMPUS GROUND
EMERGENCY SCHOOL WIDE FULL LOCK DOWN
ACTIVE SHOOTER HEARD LETTING OFF ROUNDS
IT COULD NEVER HAPPEN IN A QUIET TOWN

ACTIVE SHOOTER IS LOOKING FOR
A LITTLE TIME ON THE LOCAL NEWS REPORT
ACTIVE SHOOTER KICKING DOWN THE DOOR
REPORTS OF SHOTS FIRED
REPORTS OF SHOTS FIRED

THIS IS NOT A TEST, THIS IS NOT A TEST...
YOU'RE LIVING IN IT

ACTIVE SHOOTER IN THE NEIGHBOR
OPENING FIRE LIKE HE SAID HE WOU
ACTIVE SHOOTER ON THE PREMISES
SEMI AUTOMATIC WITH EXTRA CLIPS

ACTIVE SHOOTER WANTS TO SETTLE
FINGER ON THE TRIGGER LIKE HE'S
ACTIVE SHOOTER KICKING DOWN TH
REPORTS OF SHOTS FIRED
REPORTS OF SHOTS FIRED

ELECTRONIC DRUM PLATFORMS
+ SYNTHESIZERS:
EMIL BOGNAR-NASDOR

BASS: CORY FORREST

VOCALS: ALEXANDER HEIR

GUITAR: TYE MILLER

RECORDED & MIXED BY:
EMIL BOGNAR-NASDOR

PRODUCED BY:
EMIL BOGNAR-NASDOR &
ALEXANDER HEIR

MASTERED BY: ARTHUR RIZK

ART BY: ALEXANDER HEIR
& SCUMPUTER

LAYOUT BY: ALEXANDER HEIR

2-XENOPHOBIA

THE PATRIOT WAVES HIS FLAG SCREAMING ABOUT FREEDOM
WHILE HE'S SMASHING IN YOUR HEAD
LIKE A STARVING DOG GUARDING HIS SCRAPS
THAT DOESN'T SEE THE WOLVES WHILE HE'S BARKING AT THE CATS

XENOPHOBIA

THE PATRIOT CARES NOT ABOUT THE FACTS
HE LETS HIS GUT DETERMINE HOW HE SPEAKS AND HOW HE ACTS
MEANWHILE AT THE RALLY, WHERE ANGER TURNS TO RAGE
ONLY BLOOD WILL SATISFY NOW THAT THEY'VE HAD A TASTE

A WALL IS JUST A WAY TO SAY I HATE YOU IN EVERY LANGUAGE

ARE WE PROGRAMMED TO KILL?

4-HUNTER DRONE

WOMEN AND CHILDREN; FAMILIES, WE KILL THEM
IN THE UNITED STATES OF AMERICA
WE GROW THEM BIG, WE GROW THEM DEADLY

HUNTER DRONE ON THE HORIZON. NOWHERE TO RUN, NOWHERE TO HIDE

IMPRECISE AIR STRIKES, CIVILIANS LEFT TRAUMATIZED
INNOCENT PEOPLE NOW A MEMORY
JUST LIKE THEIR SCHOOLS, JUST LIKE THEIR HOSPITALS

HUNTER DRONE, ON THE HORIZON. NOWHERE TO RUN, NOWHERE TO HIDE

DEATH FROM ABOVE; NOT LOVE
NOT KINDNESS WE DROP ON PEOPLE'S HOMES
IN THE UNITED STATES OF AMERICA
WE HAVE NO MORALS, WE HAVE NO CONSCIENCE

HUNTER DRONE ON THE HORIZON. NOWHERE TO RUN, NOWHERE TO HIDE

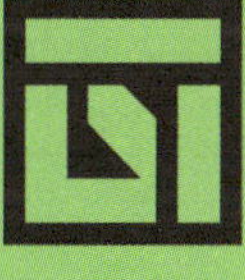

SECTION B: DEATH/TRAITORS

Being a 19-year- old punk in 2008 New York City was weird and stagnant. We were the kids that grew up getting slapped around by the bouncers at CBGB's and years later got arrested for punching East Village loudmouths who insinuated we'd never even been to CBGB. Street punk stalwarts Zombie Vandals had recently broken up and they had pretty much raised us. Local pride of our crew, Thriller, had gone on hiatus due to the passing of their drummer and our dear friend, Brian Mullarkey in August of 07. New bands like PB and Dawn of Humans were starting up, but venues were sparse and we didn't get much appreciation for rolling 50 or so kids deep into Long Island to see one band play with 6 mediocre local acts that didn't like us.

Meanwhile Brooklyn had become a commodity. Waves of adorable "Brooklyn by way of somewhere" bands, that dared to borrow D.I.Y. aspects of punk ethos and pretty much forget the rest, were playing at and inventing new D.I.Y. venues all the time. But the promoters (usually some dude in a Clash shirt) wanted nothing to do with the potential violence that came with booking anything close to a legitimate subculture. So when I was approached about DJ'ing the inaugural Death/Traitors party it felt like someone might actually give a fuck about us.

Over the summer Death/Traitors nights went down at a series of dive bars on the south side of Williamsburg, hopping around to any place who's less than scrupulous owners had the debatably good sense to put notorious Brooklyn Vandal, and all around charming guy Marty, behind the bar. As the parties built a reputation for being a place where freaks of every variety could gather to drink, dance, and get as weird they wanted, they finally found a home at Rockstar Bar. To my 19 year old self the parties at Rockstar Bar were New York City at its finest. I watched violent goth pioneer, ex Anasazi / Blue Anxiety front man Chi, DJ in between sets, as bands like Spanish Bombs and Pregnant shared the stage with rappers Ninjasonik and GDP. In the crowd were members of a notoriously elusive New York City graffiti crew. The Smart Crew passed off yak, blunts, and cans to enthusiastic young punks that had the guts to ask.

To comprehensively describe all the chaos that ensued over the next year would require a book of its own, besides there's a thin white line between reminiscing and dry snitching. The Death/Traitors parties are over but Alex's work has achieved something a of a cult like status within any scene freaky enough to capture his attention. Everybody's jealous of New York again and while I'd attribute that to the passion, tenacity and brilliance of an entire scene of artists, musicians and hustlers more so than a few wild parties I'm still pretty fuckin proud of em.

Bury me in Nuke York - Maxwell Maxwell

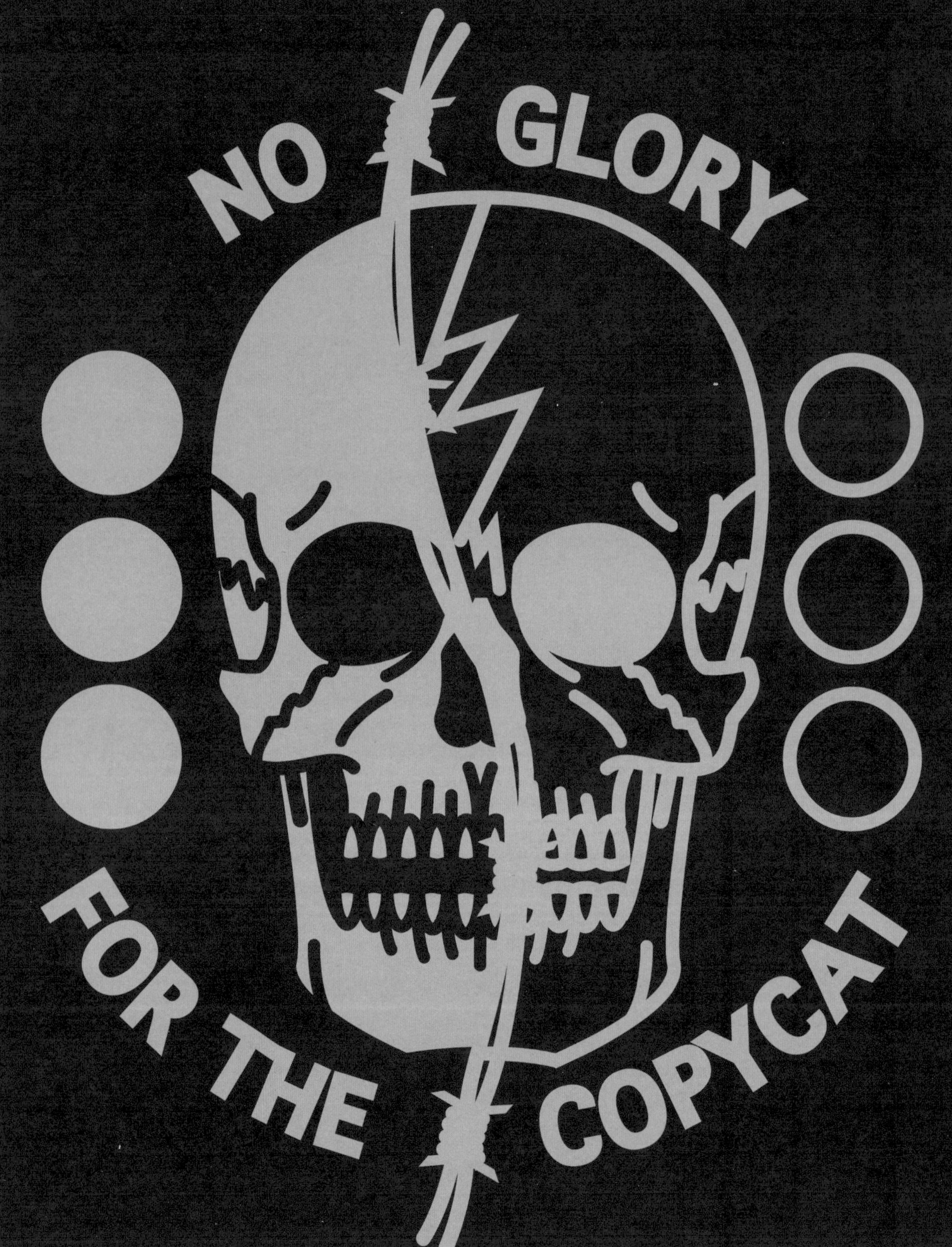

NO
GLORY
FOR THE
COPYCAT

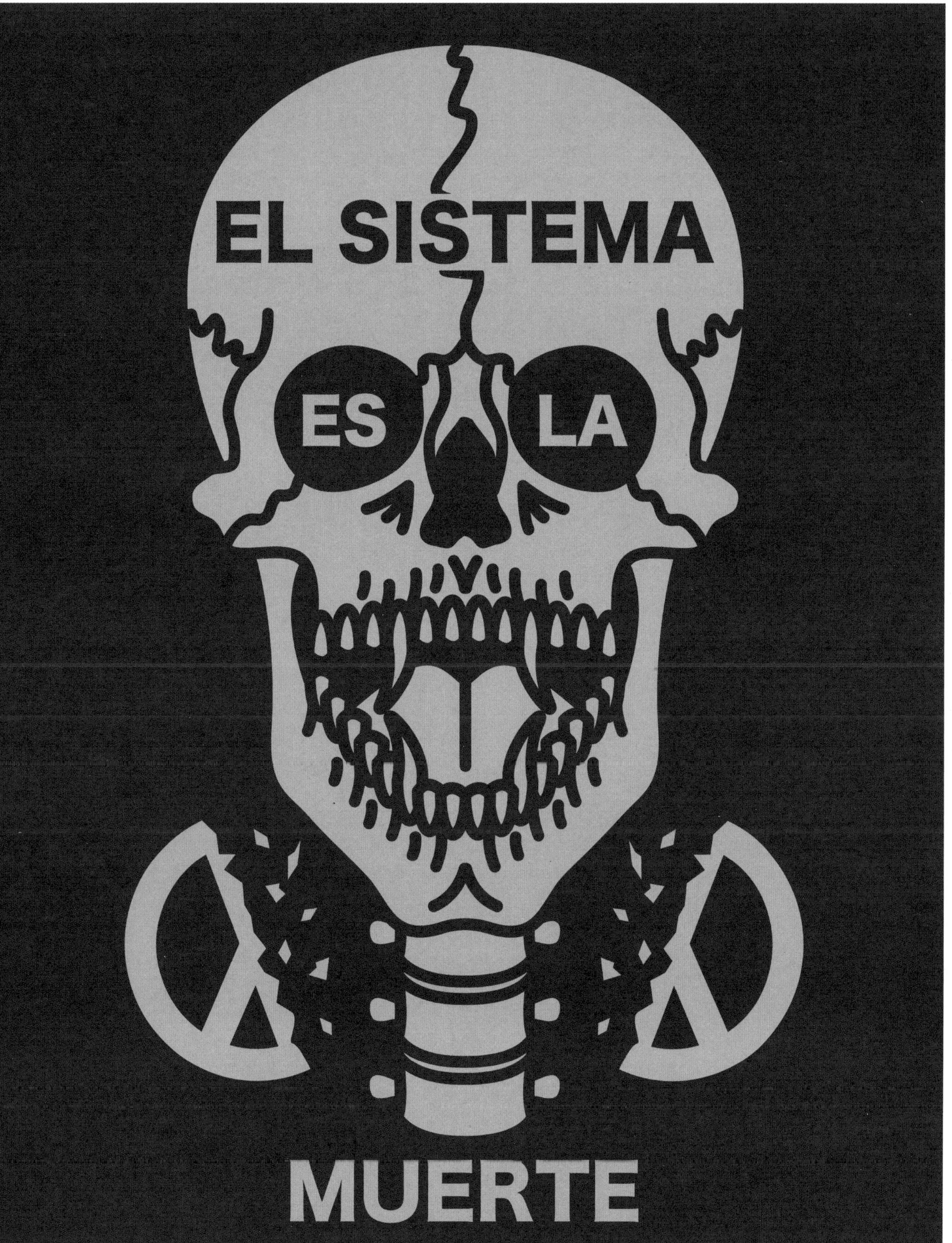

EL SISTEMA
ES LA
MUERTE

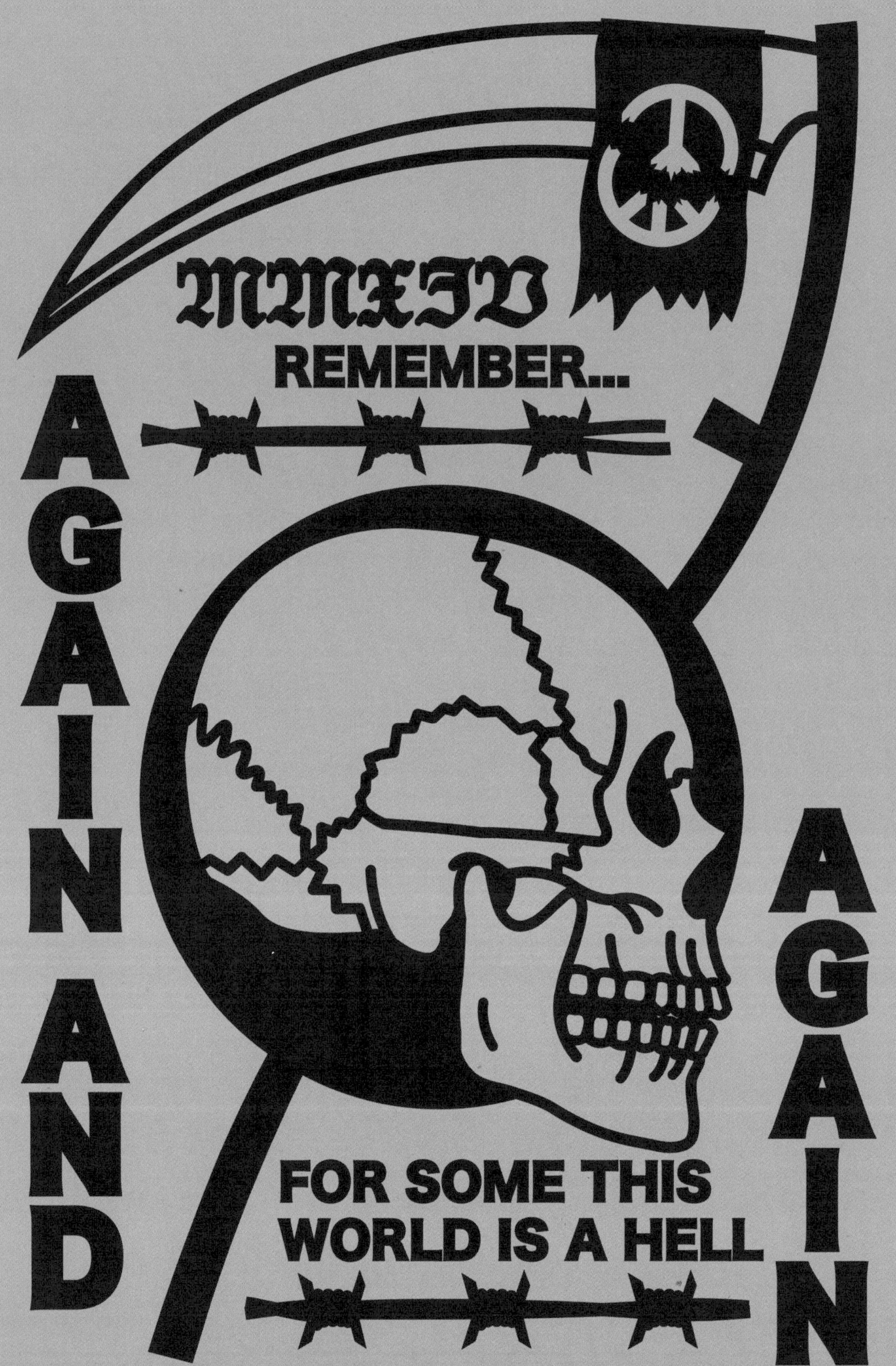
MMXIV
REMEMBER...
AGAIN AND AGAIN
AGAIN AND AGAIN
FOR SOME THIS
WORLD IS A HELL

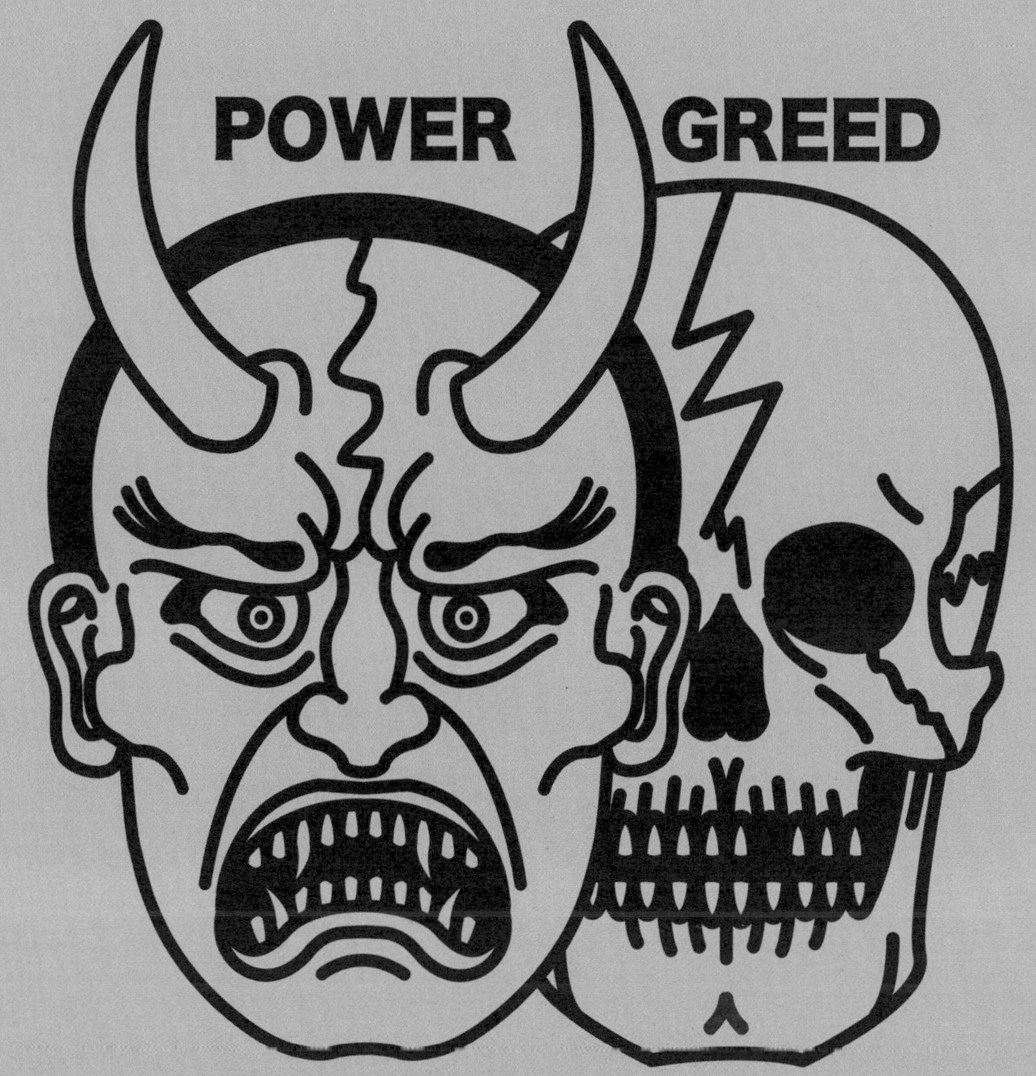

POWER   GREED
THEIR FILTH CONTINUES TO POISON OUR BODIES & MINDS, OUR AIR & WATER: DEATH TO THE ROTTEN SYSTEM THAT PROFITS FROM DEATH AND SUFFERING:

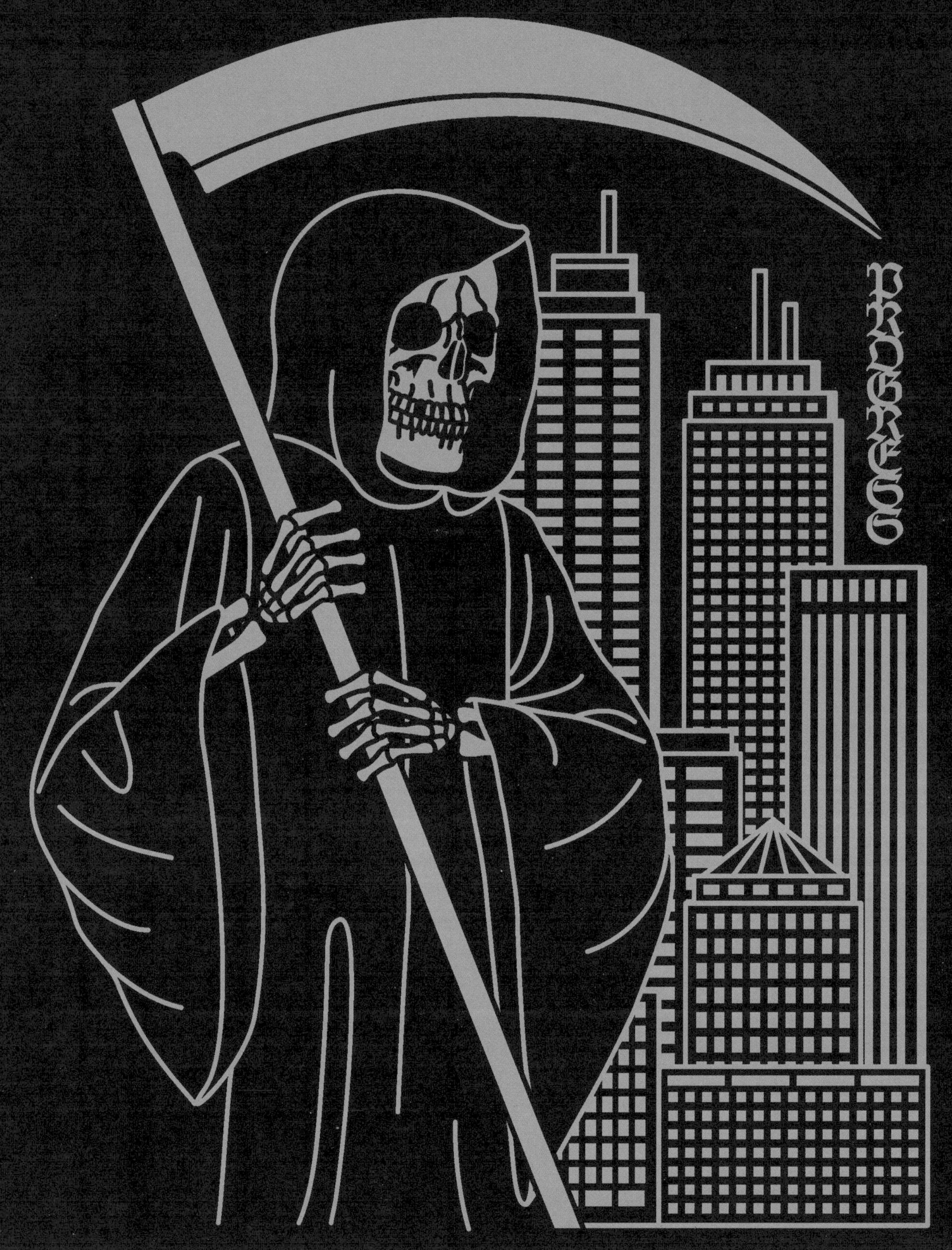

PROGRESS

HA!
HA!
HA!
STOP BREATHING
THE DRUM THAT NEVER
THE GREAT
SHAME OF HUMANITY
ENDLESS WAR
AGAIN AND AGAIN AND AGAIN AND
AGAIN AND AGAIN AND AGAIN

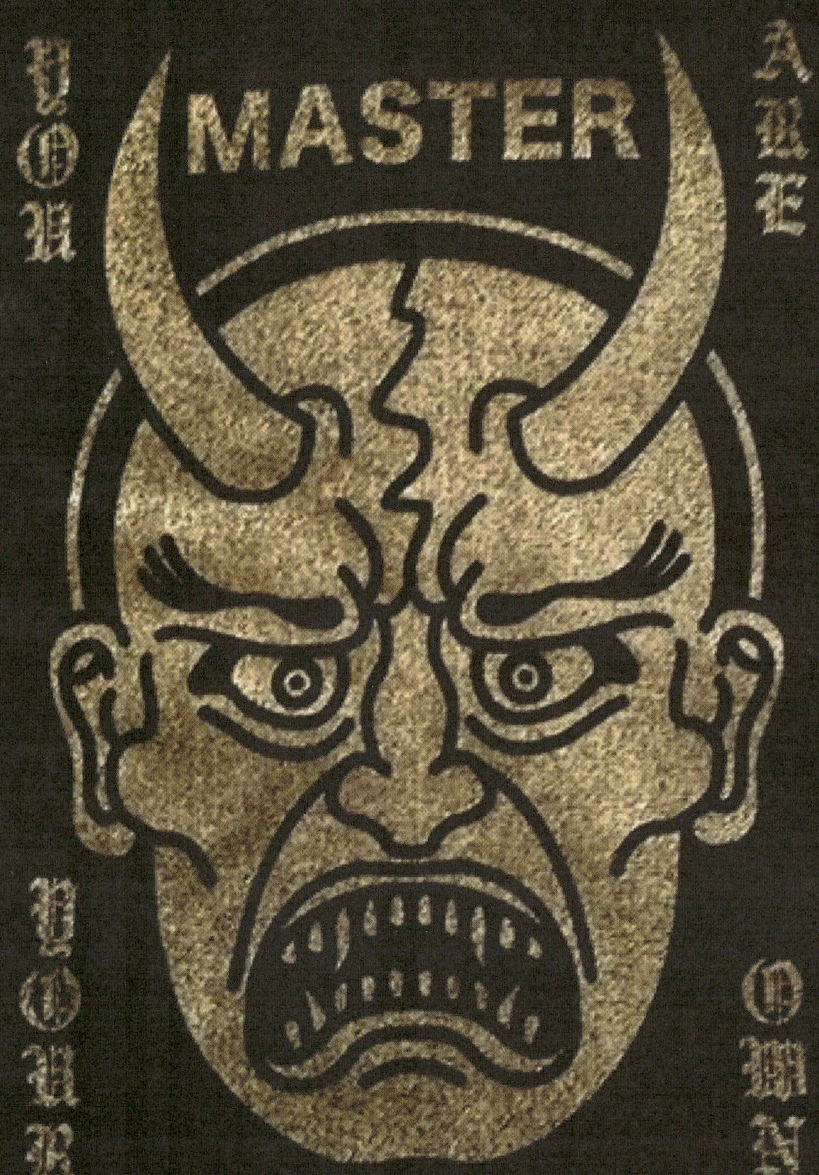
MASTER
YOU
ARE
YOUR
OWN

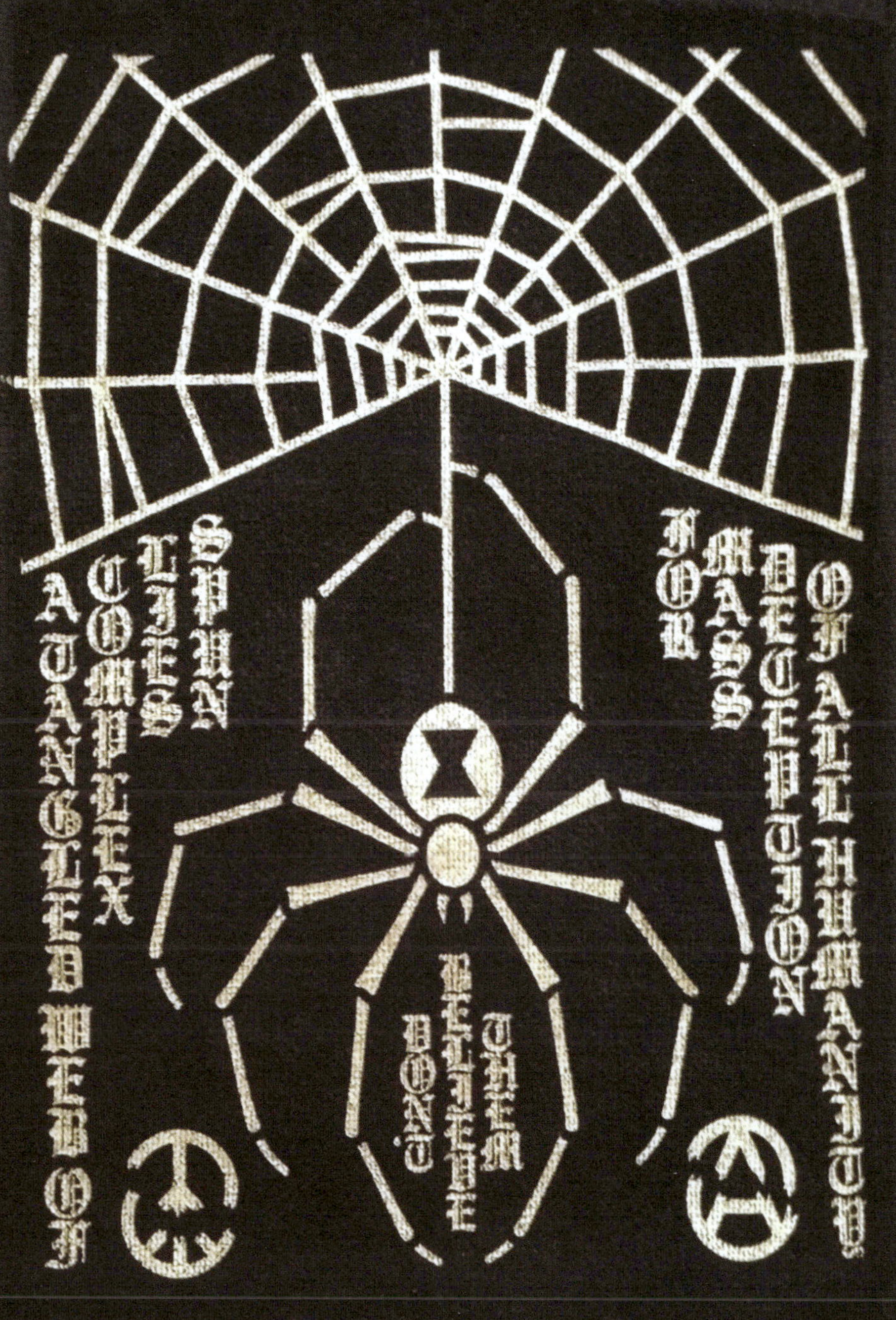
A TANGLED WEB OF COMPLEX LIES SPUN
FOR MASS DECEPTION OF ALL HUMANITY
THEM BELIEVE BOND
UNTIL

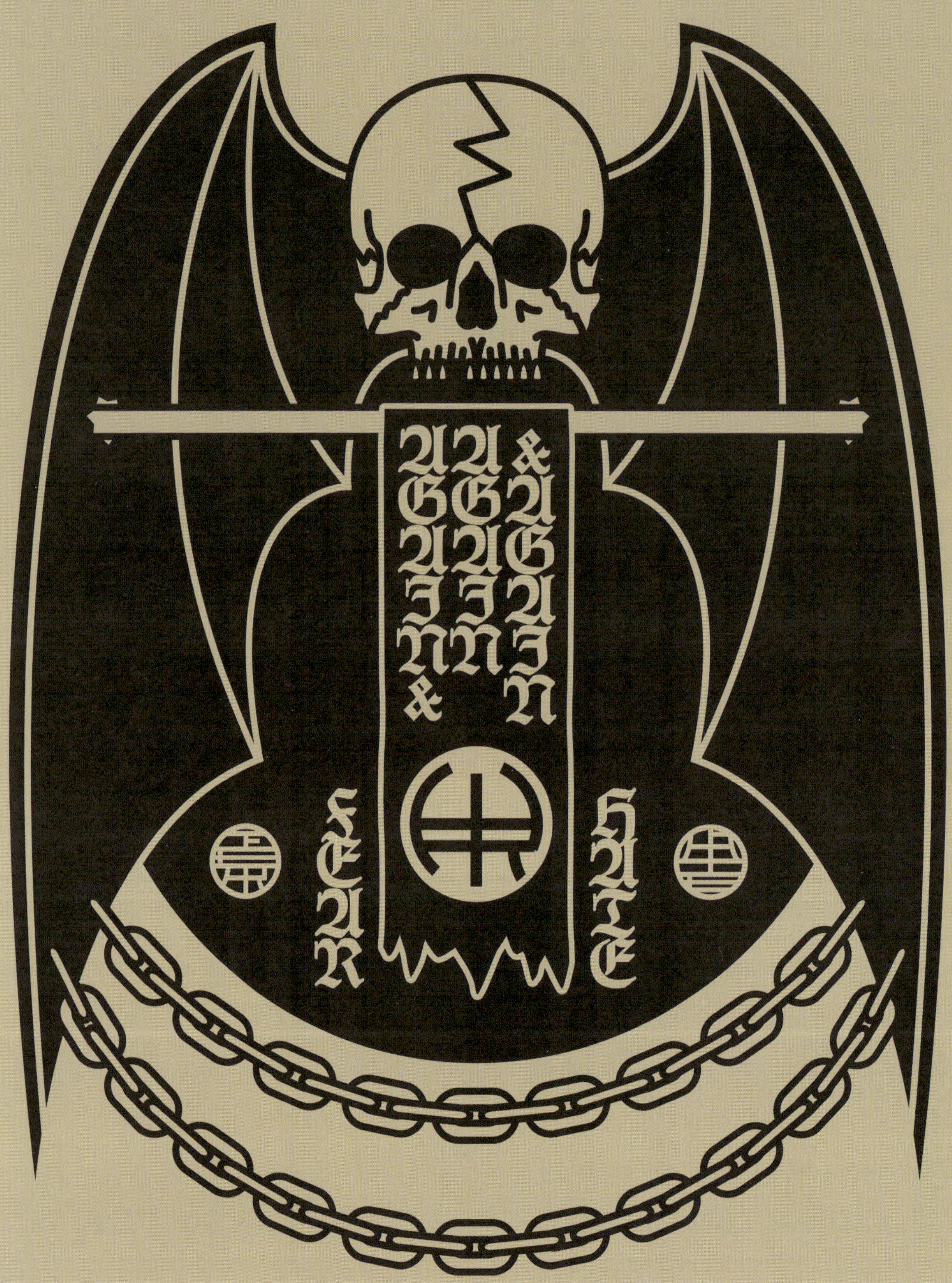

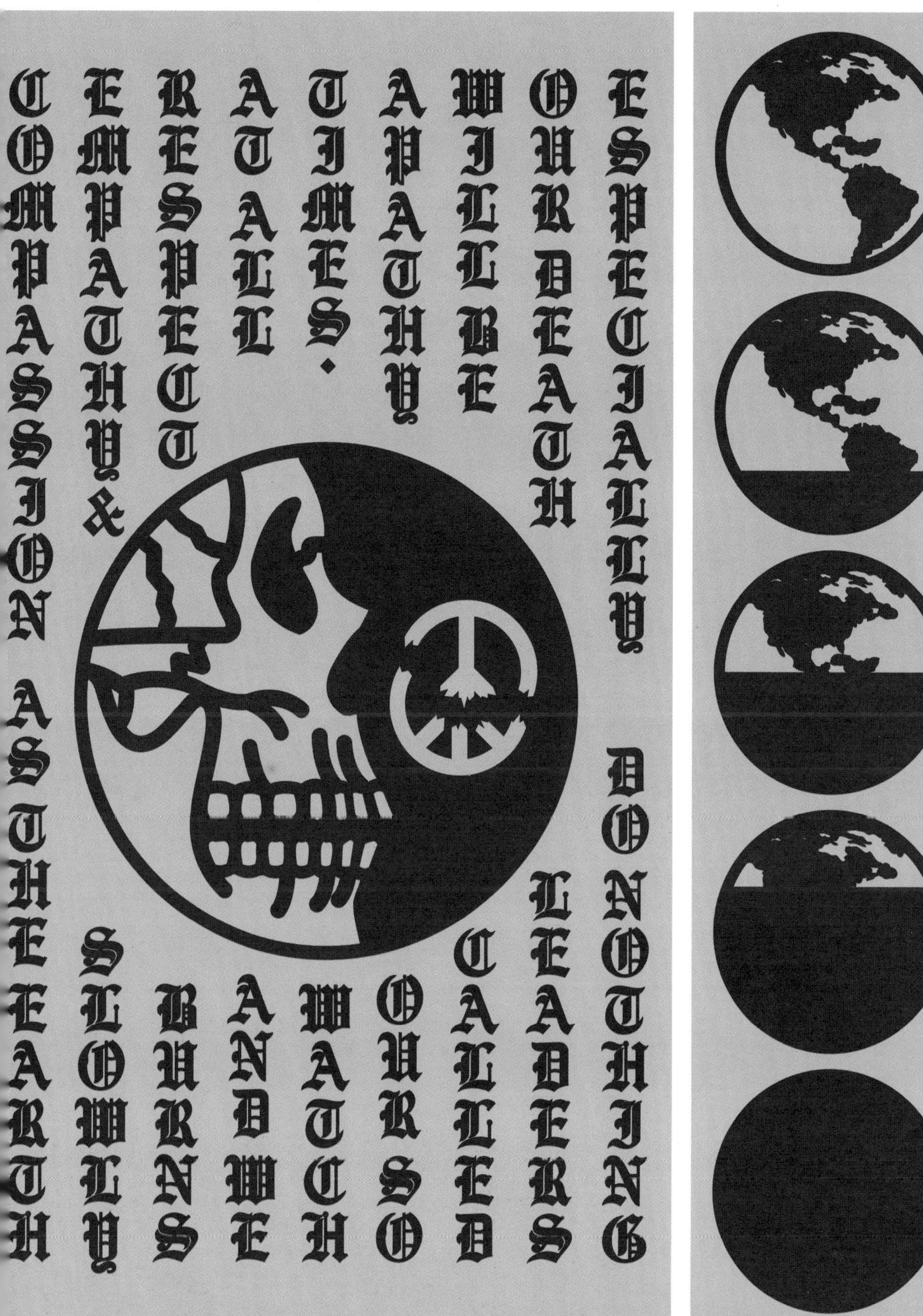

COMPASSION
EMPATHY &
RESPECT
AT ALL
TIMES.
APATHY
WILL BE
OUR DEATH
ESPECIALLY
AS THE EARTH
SLOWLY
BURNS
AND WATCH
OUR
CALLOUS
LEADERS
DO NOTHING

SPITEFUL ENFORCERS OF INJUSTICE

POWE

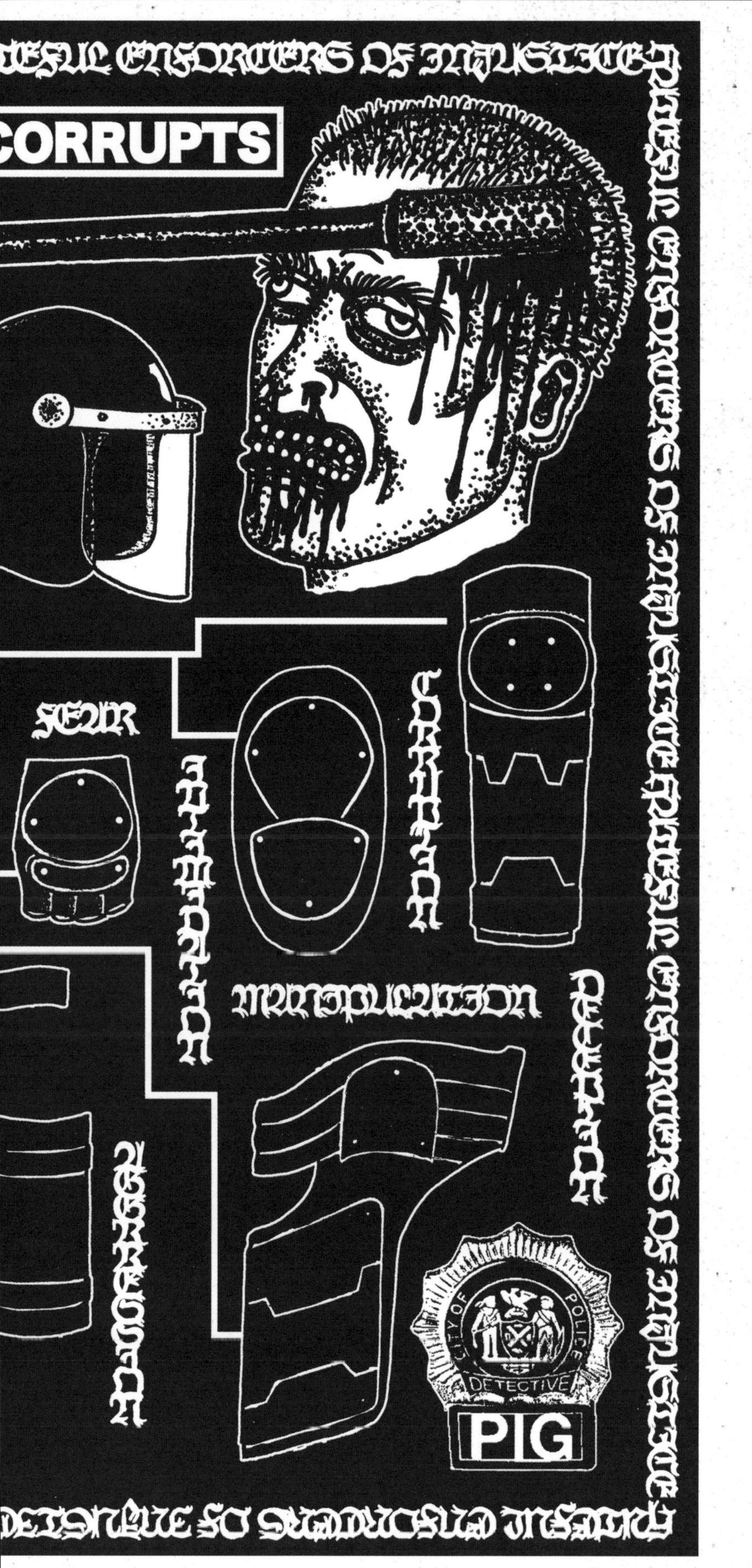
ENFORCERS OF INJUSTICE
CORRUPTS
FEAR
MANIPULATION
DETECTIVE
PIG

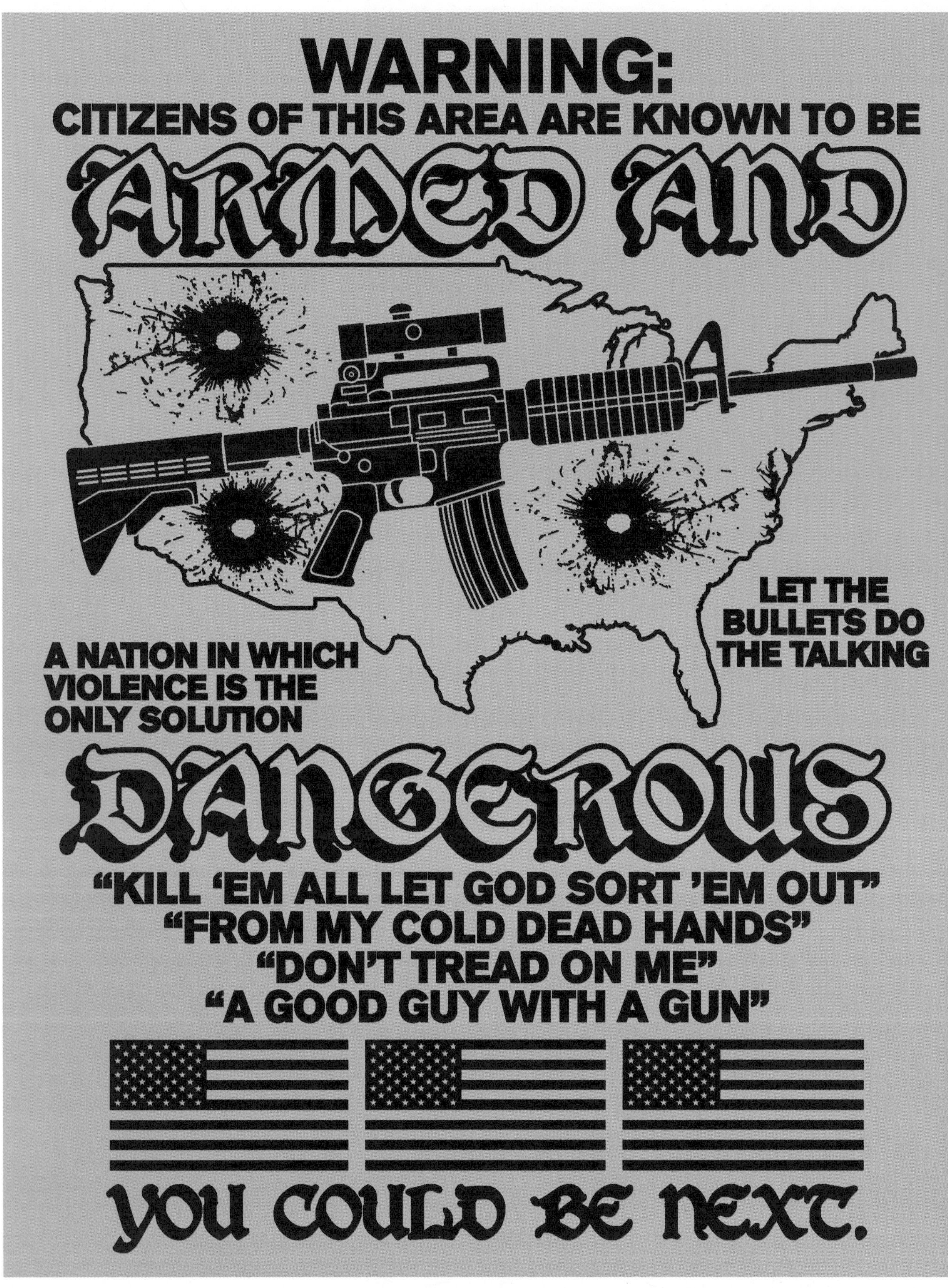

WARNING:
CITIZENS OF THIS AREA ARE KNOWN TO BE

ARMED AND

LET THE
BULLETS DO
THE TALKING

A NATION IN WHICH
VIOLENCE IS THE
ONLY SOLUTION

DANGEROUS

"KILL 'EM ALL LET GOD SORT 'EM OUT"
"FROM MY COLD DEAD HANDS"
"DON'T TREAD ON ME"
"A GOOD GUY WITH A GUN"

YOU COULD BE NEXT.

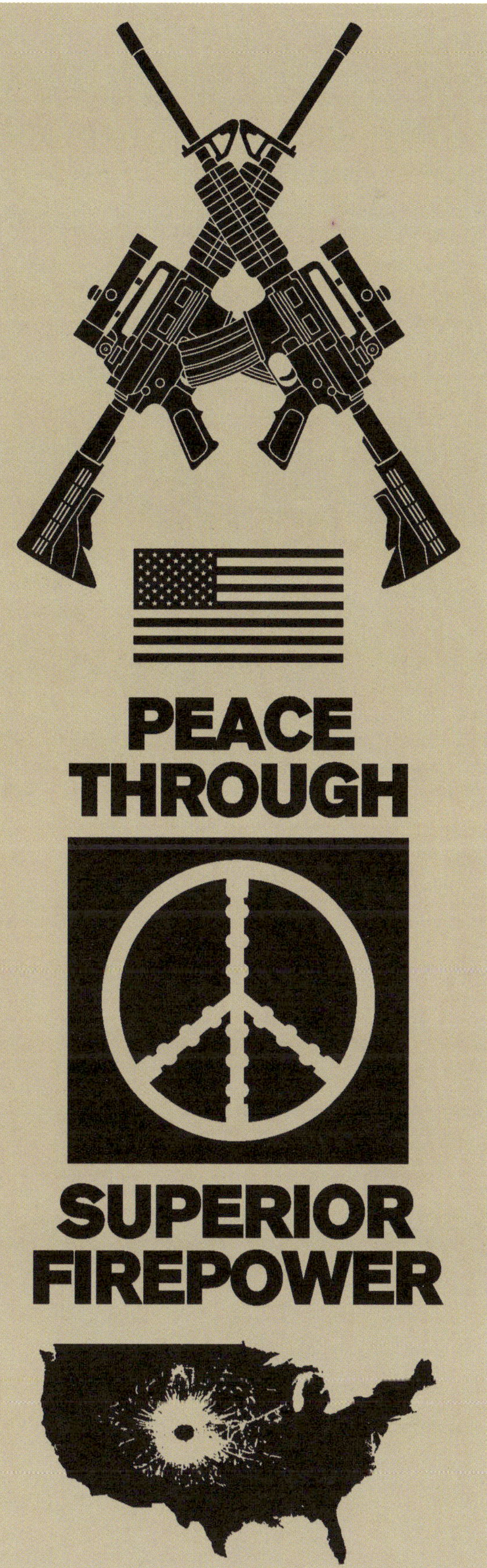

PEACE
THROUGH
SUPERIOR
FIREPOWER

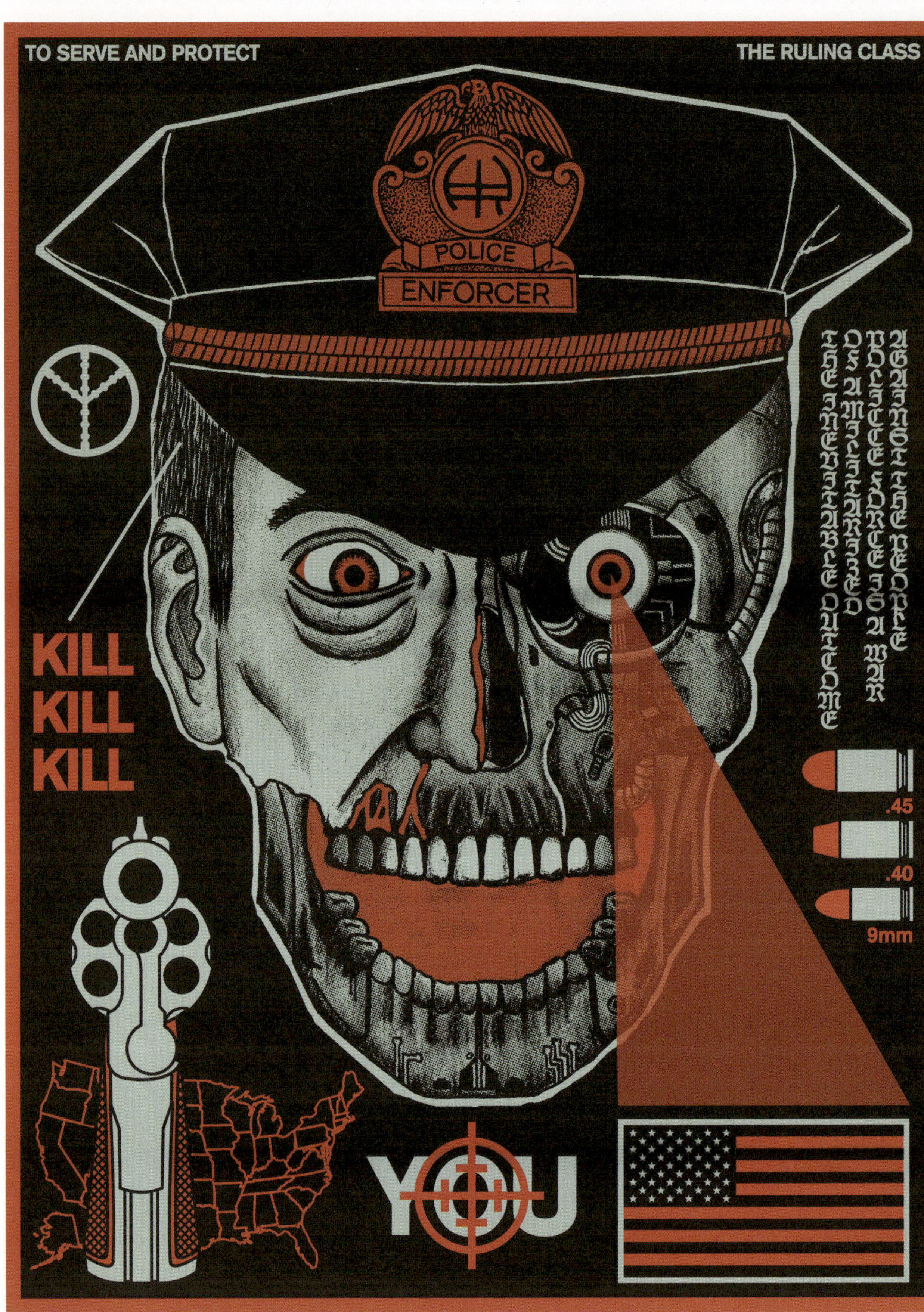

TO SERVE AND PROTECT
THE RULING CLASS
POLICE
ENFORCER
KILL
KILL
KILL
.45
.40
9mm
YOU
THE INEVITABLE OUTCOME OF A MILITARIZED POLICE FORCE IS A WAR AGAINST THE PEOPLE

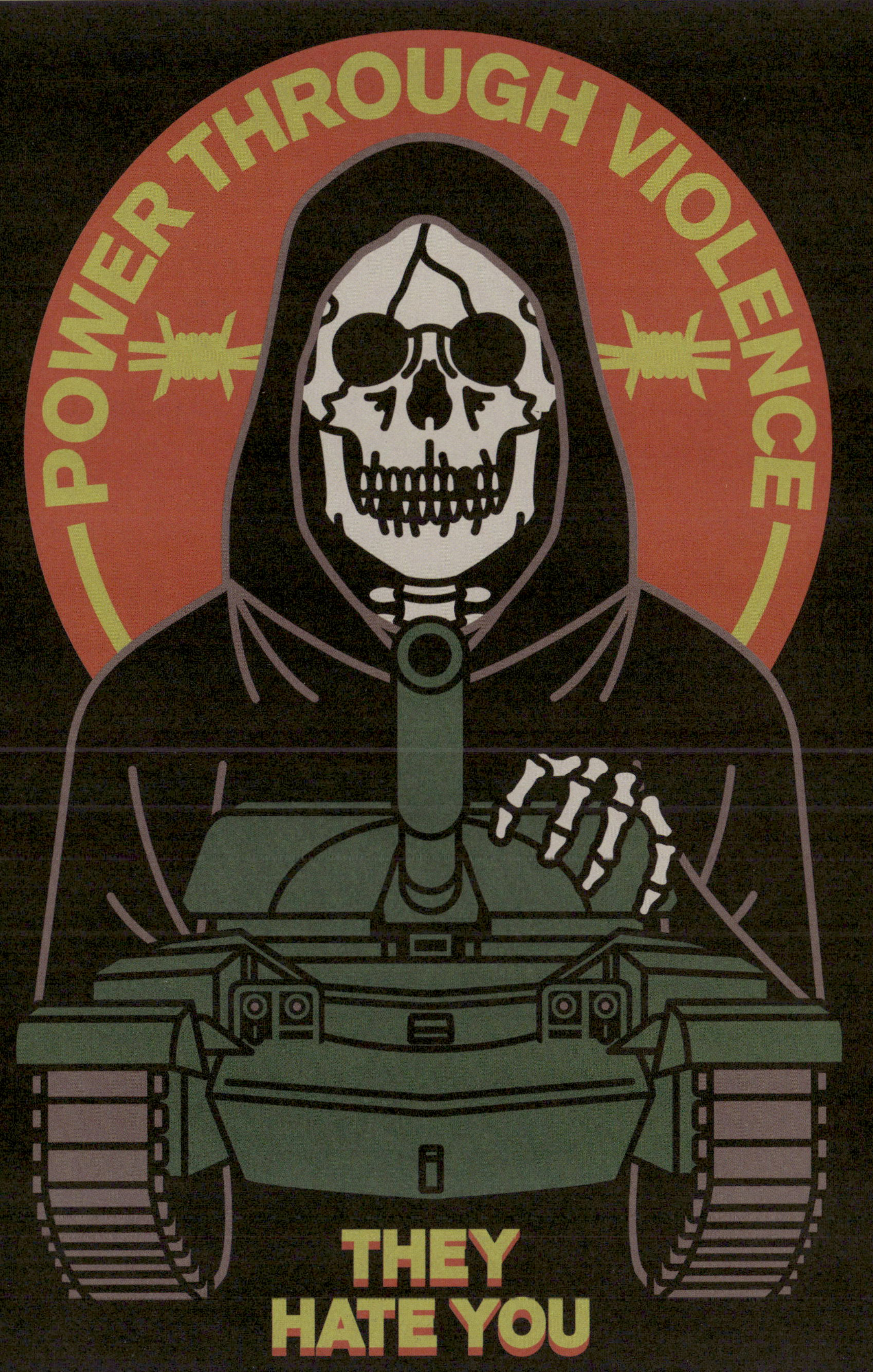

POWER THROUGH VIOLENCE
THEY
HATE YOU

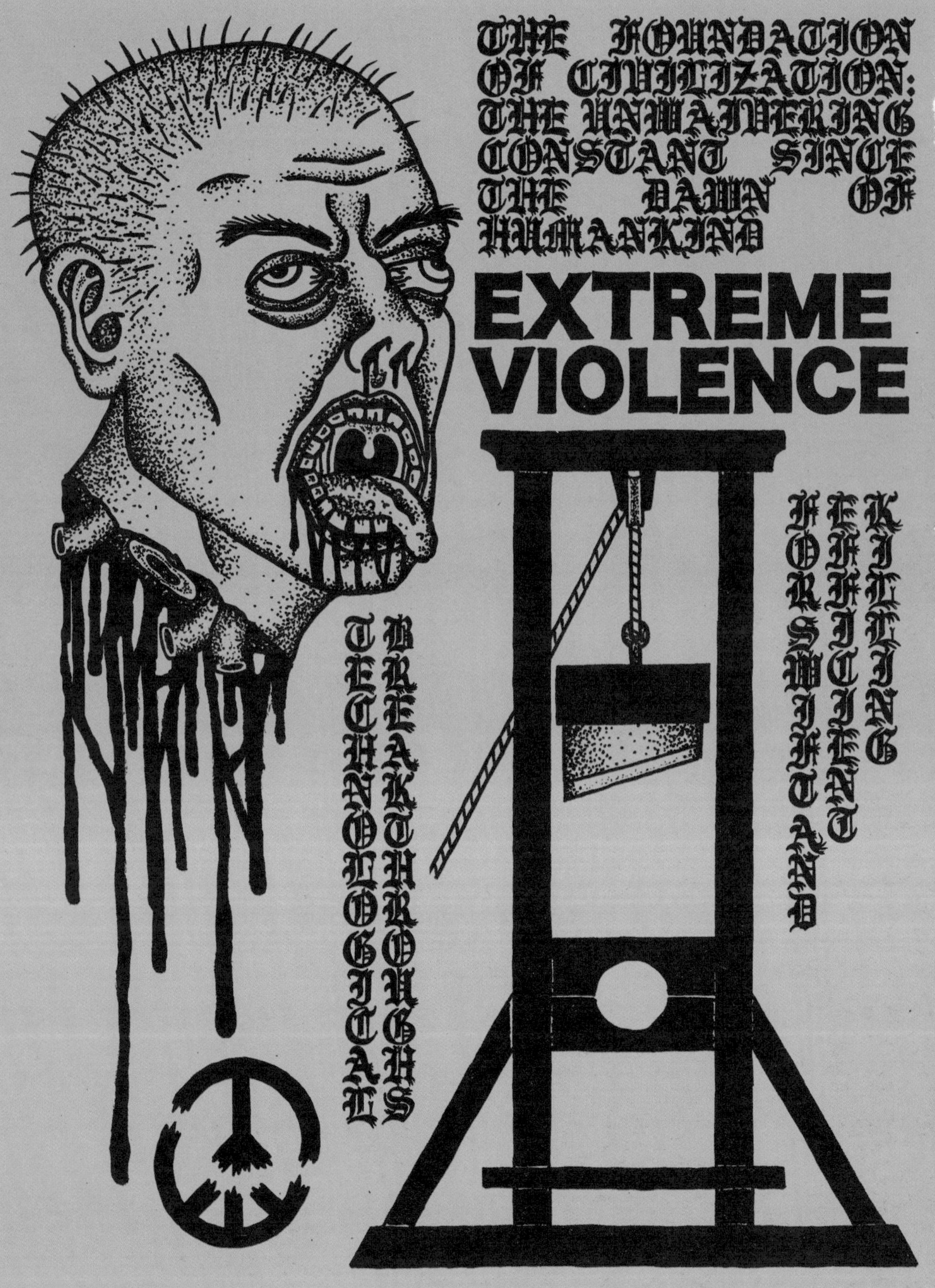

THE FOUNDATION OF CIVILIZATION: THE UNWAVERING CONSTANT SINCE THE DAWN OF HUMANKIND
EXTREME VIOLENCE

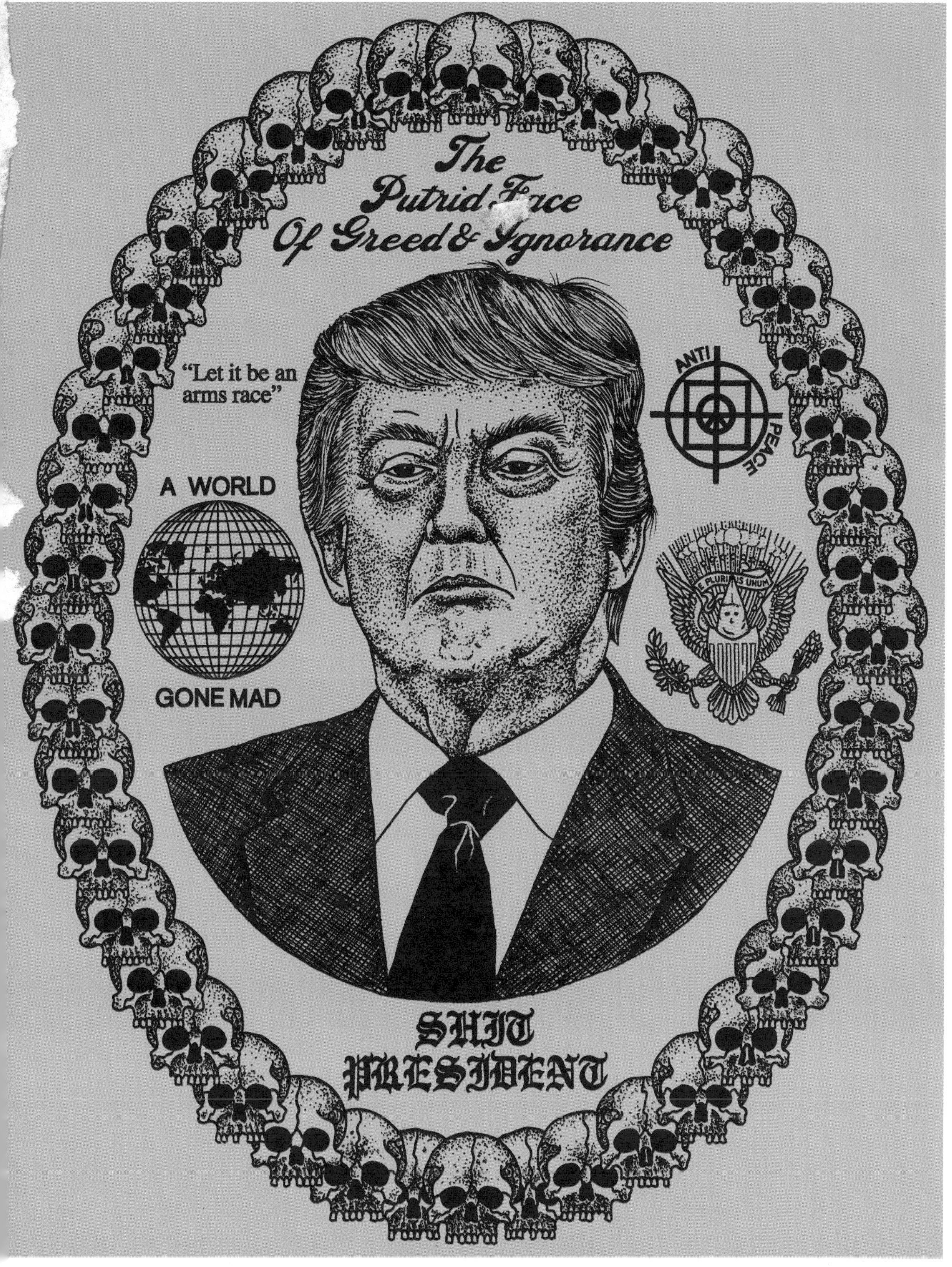

The
Putrid Face
Of Greed & Ignorance
"Let it be an arms race"
ANTI
PEACE
A WORLD
GONE MAD
E PLURIBUS UNUM
SHIT
PRESIDENT

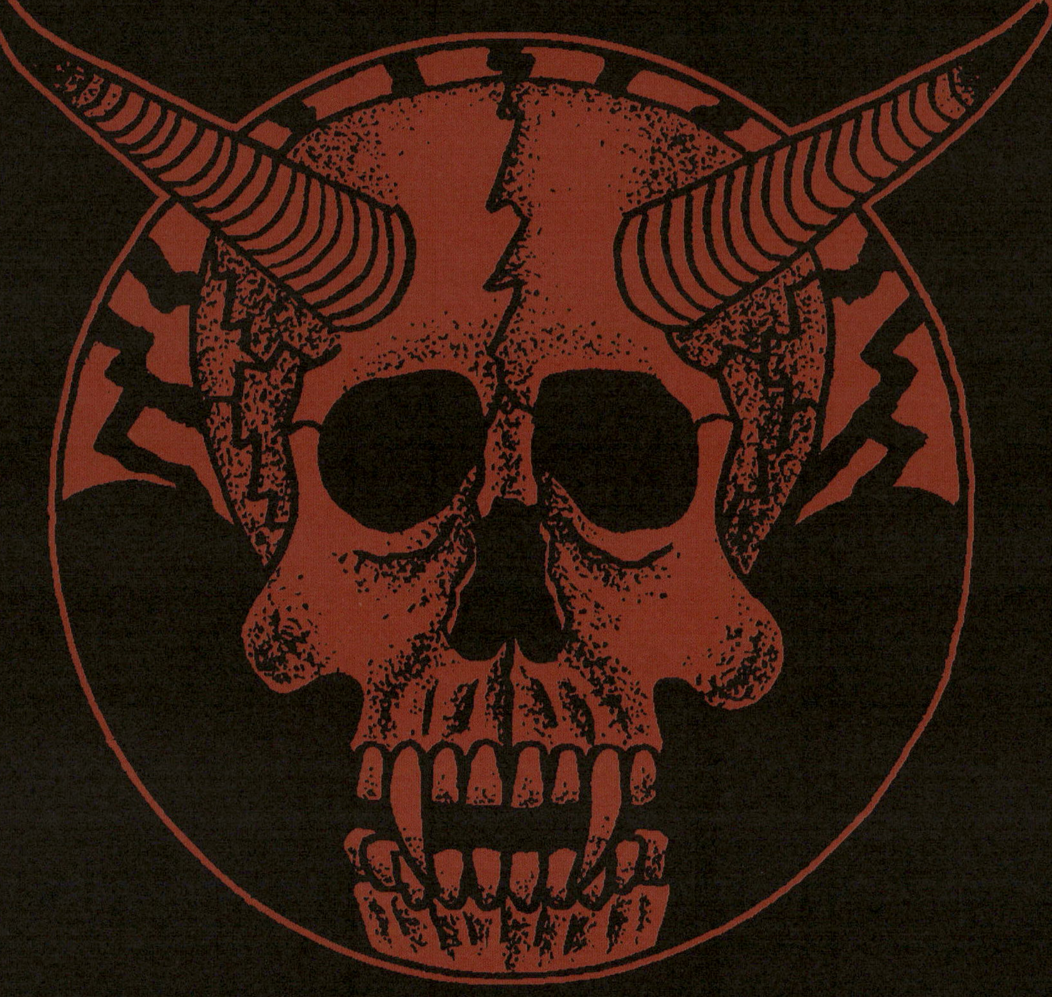

ESTE PLANETA
ES UN
INFIERNO
INFIERNO
INFIERNO

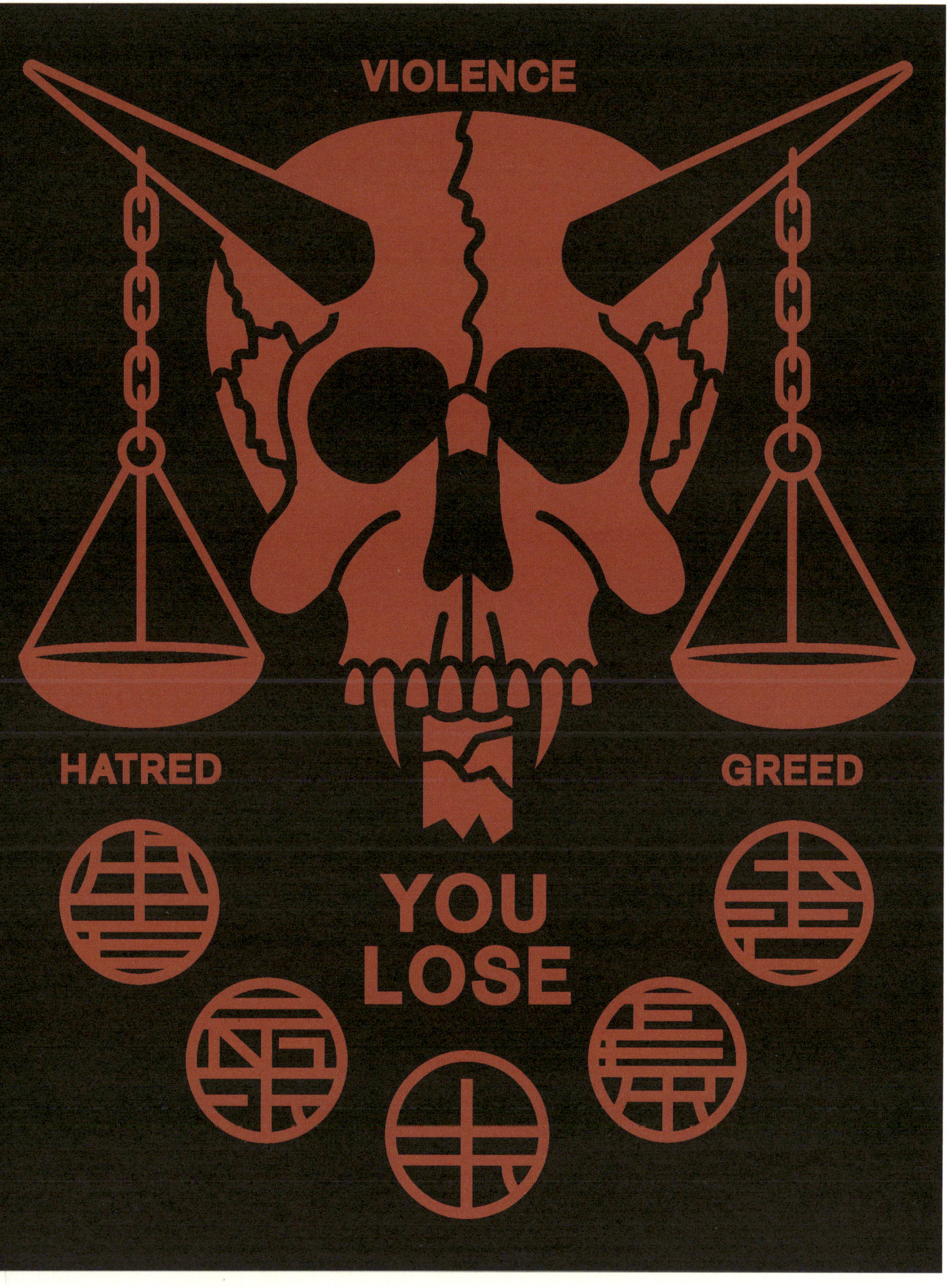

VIOLENCE
HATRED
GREED
YOU
LOSE

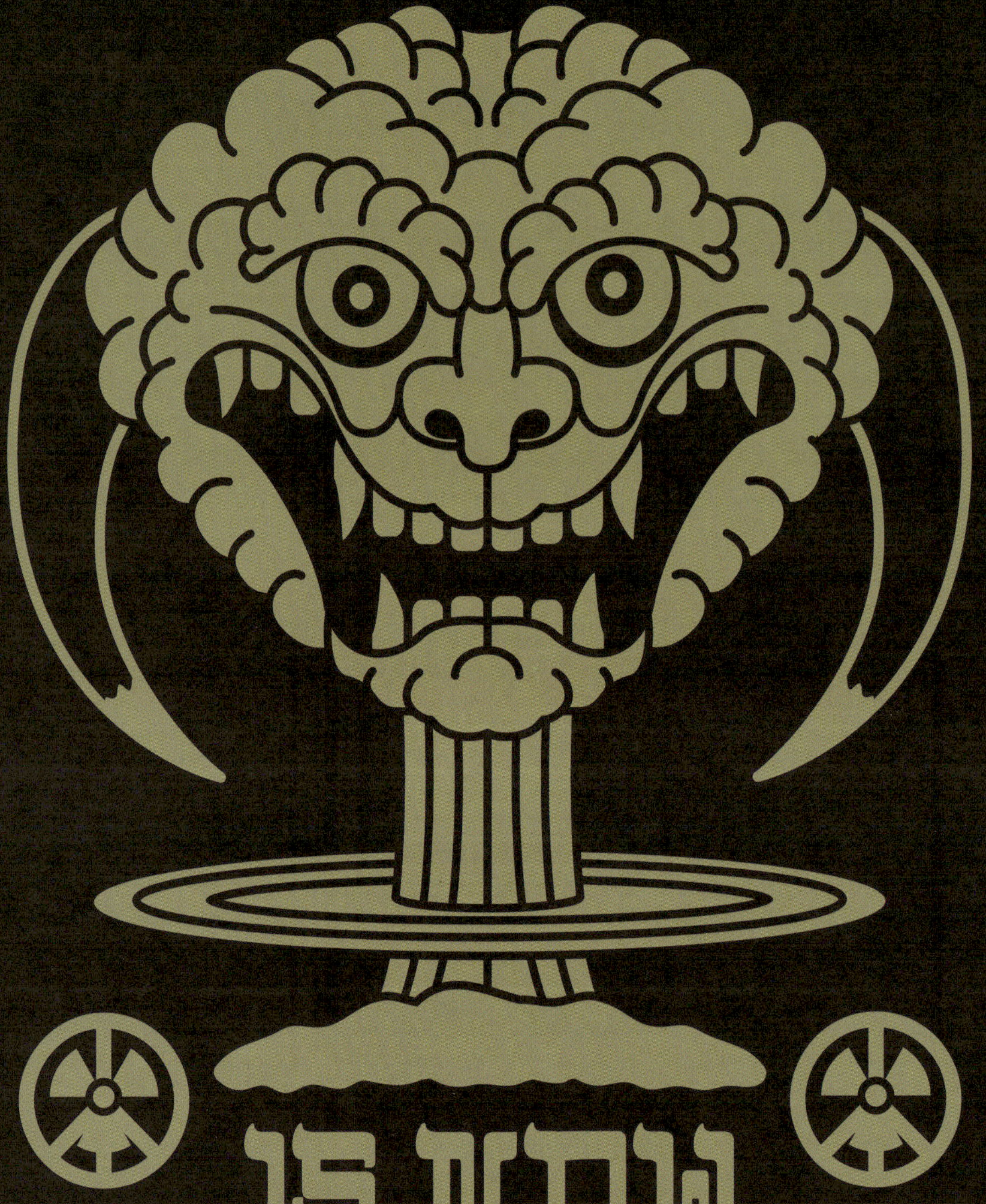

THE FUTURE
IS WSN

A WAR
THAT
CAN

HAVE
NO
WINNERS

PEACE
OR
DEATH

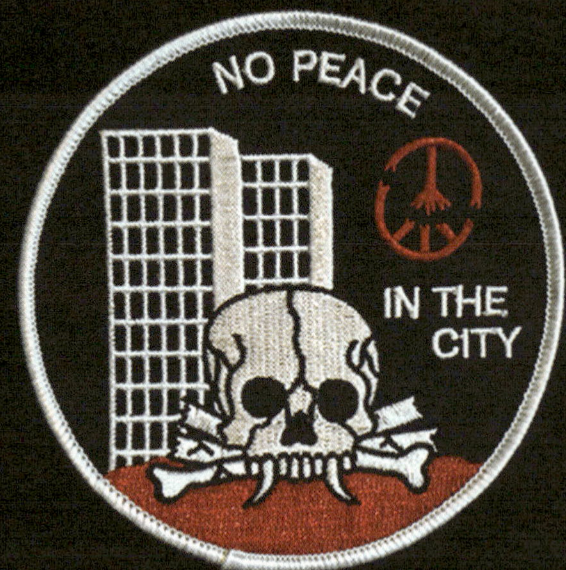

NO PEACE
IN THE
CITY

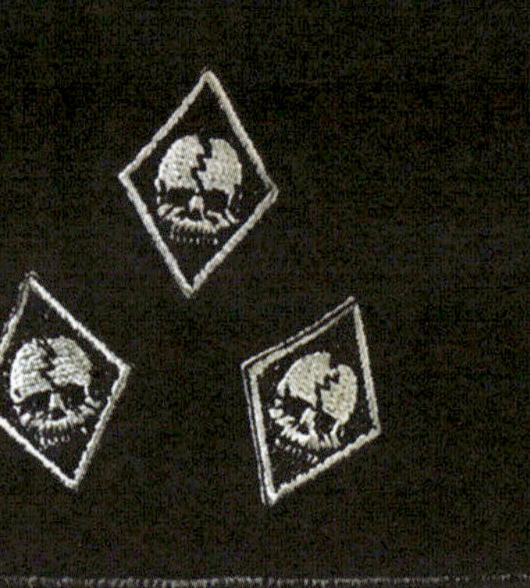

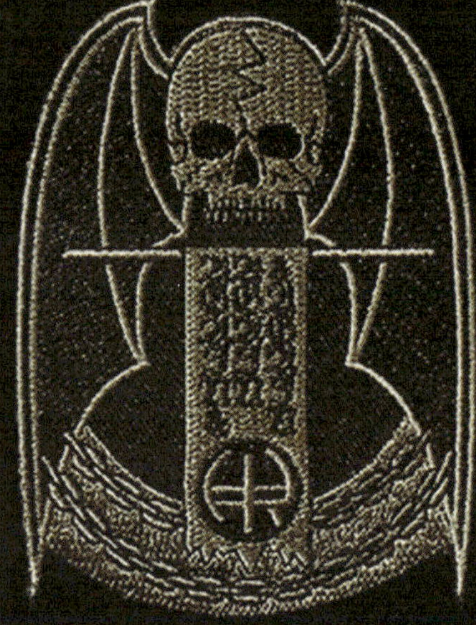

PEACE
OR
DEATH

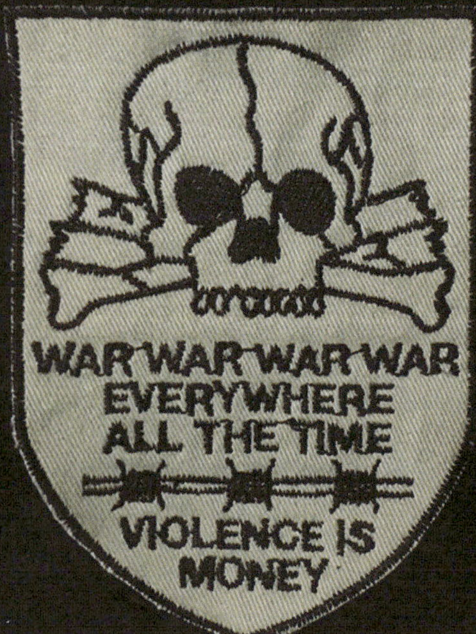

WAR WAR WAR WAR
EVERYWHERE
ALL THE TIME

VIOLENCE IS
MONEY

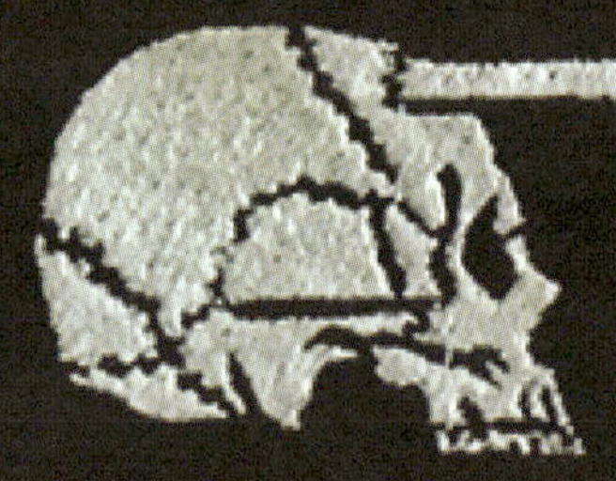

THIS
PLANET
WILL SOON
BECOME A

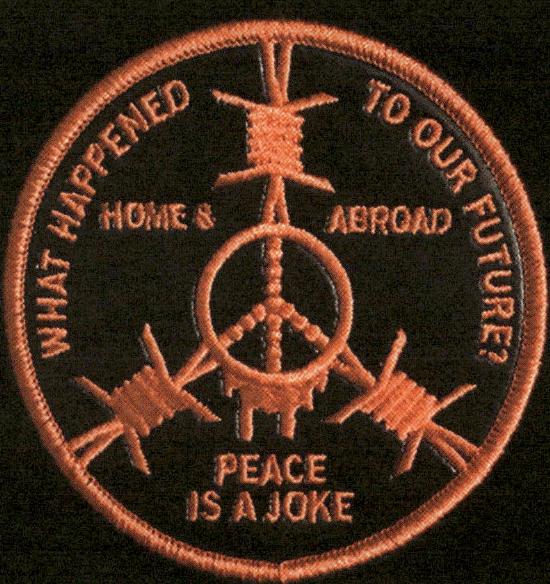

WHAT HAPPENED
TO OUR FUTURE?
HOME &
ABROAD
PEACE
IS A JOKE

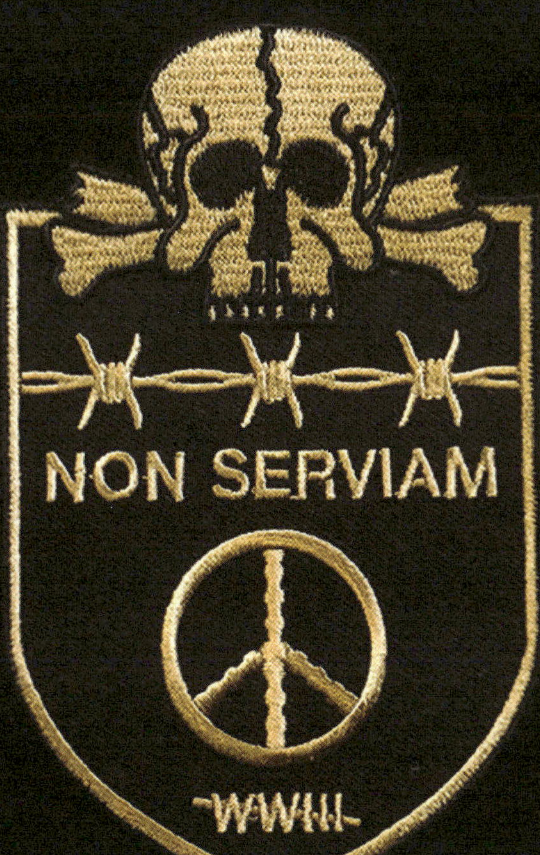

NON SERVIAM
~WWIII

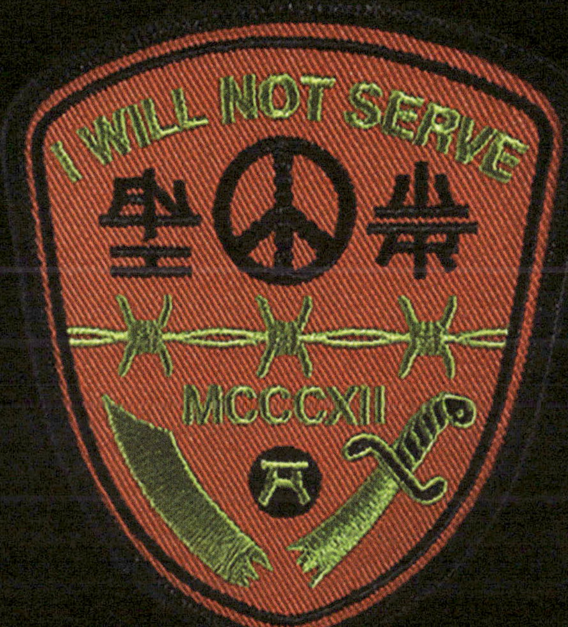

I WILL NOT SERVE
MCCCXII

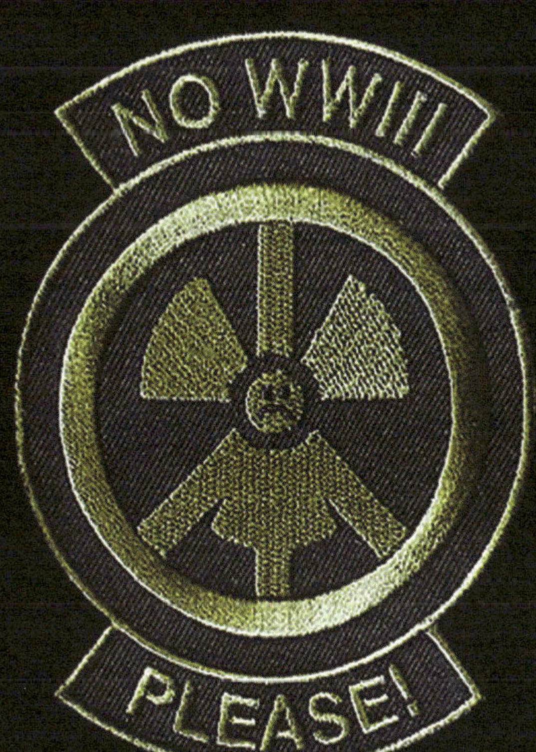

NO WWIII
PLEASE!

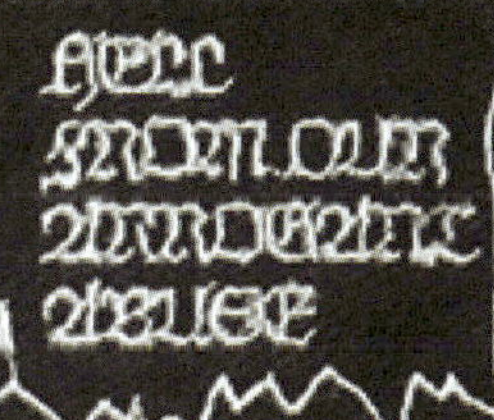

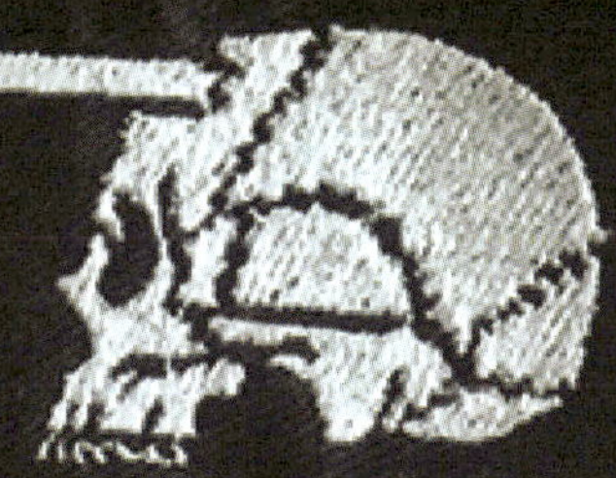

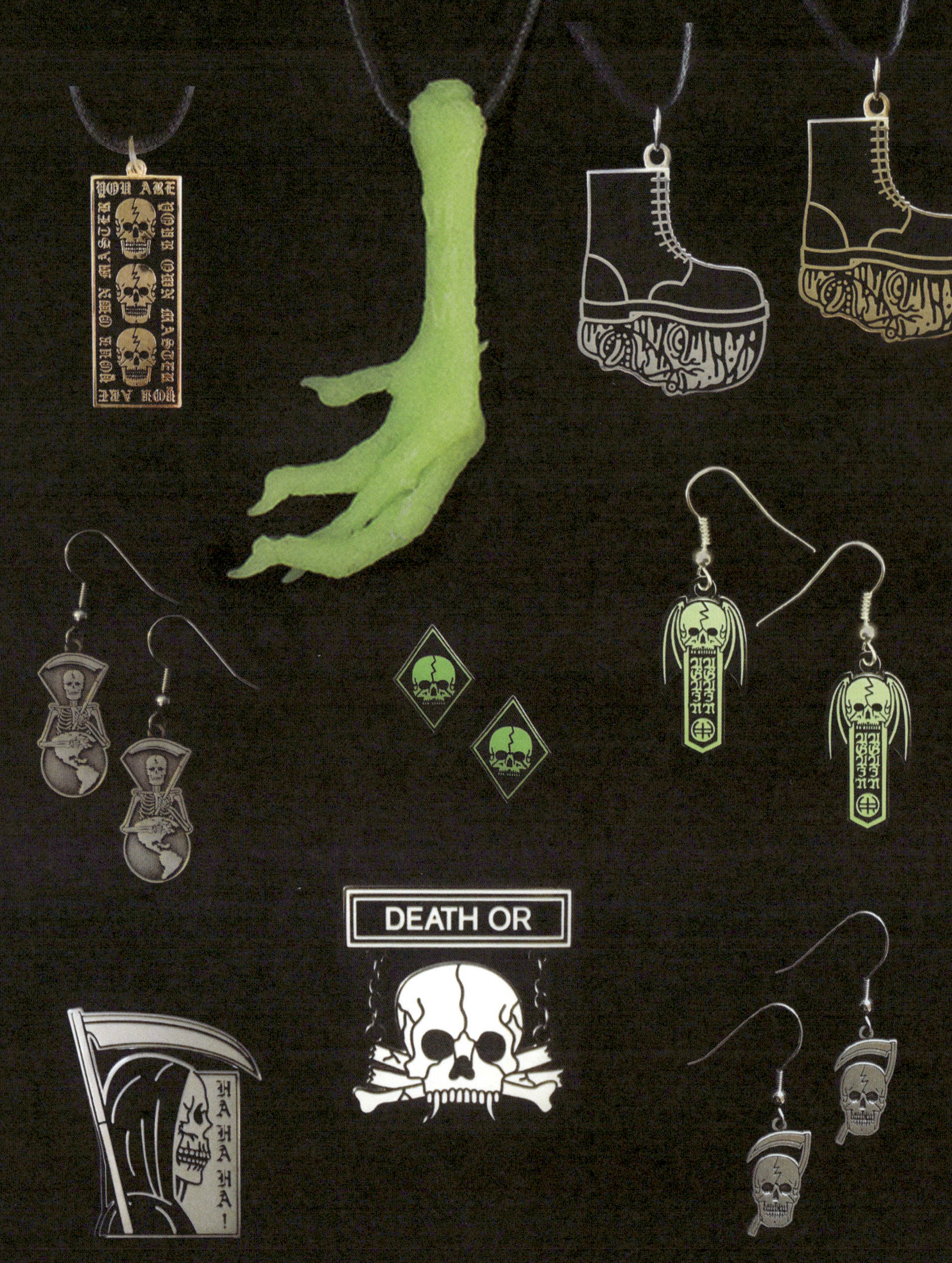

YOU ARE YOUR OWN MASTER
DEATH OR
HA HA HA!

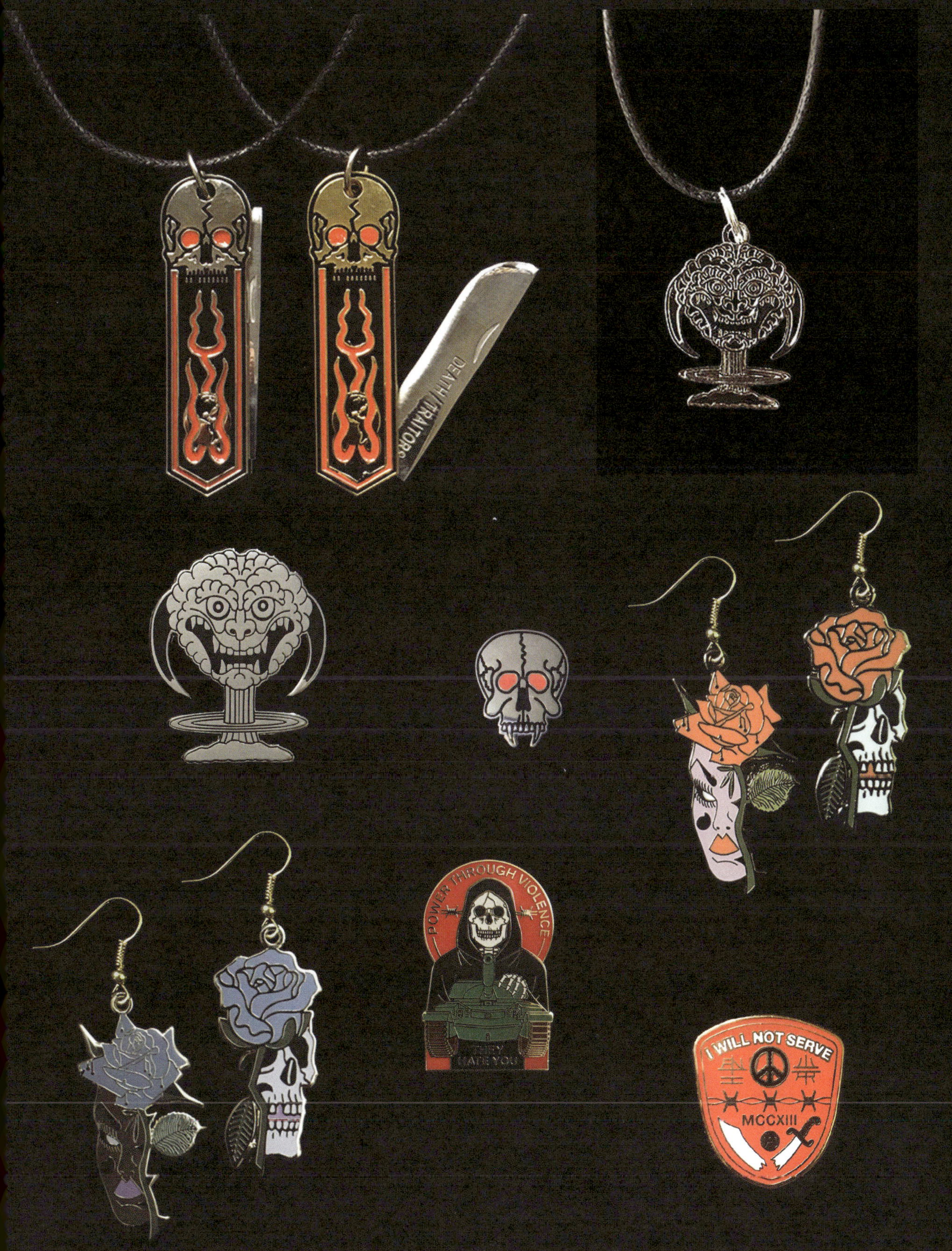

POWER THROUGH VIOLENCE
THEY HATE YOU

I WILL NOT SERVE
MCCXIII

DEATH / TRAITOR

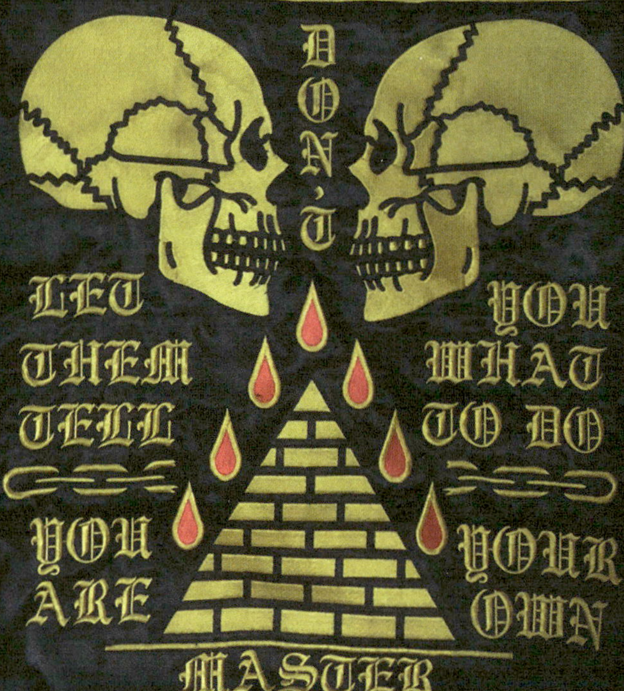

POWER CORRUPTS
DON'T
LET THEM TELL YOU WHAT TO DO
YOU ARE YOUR OWN
MASTER

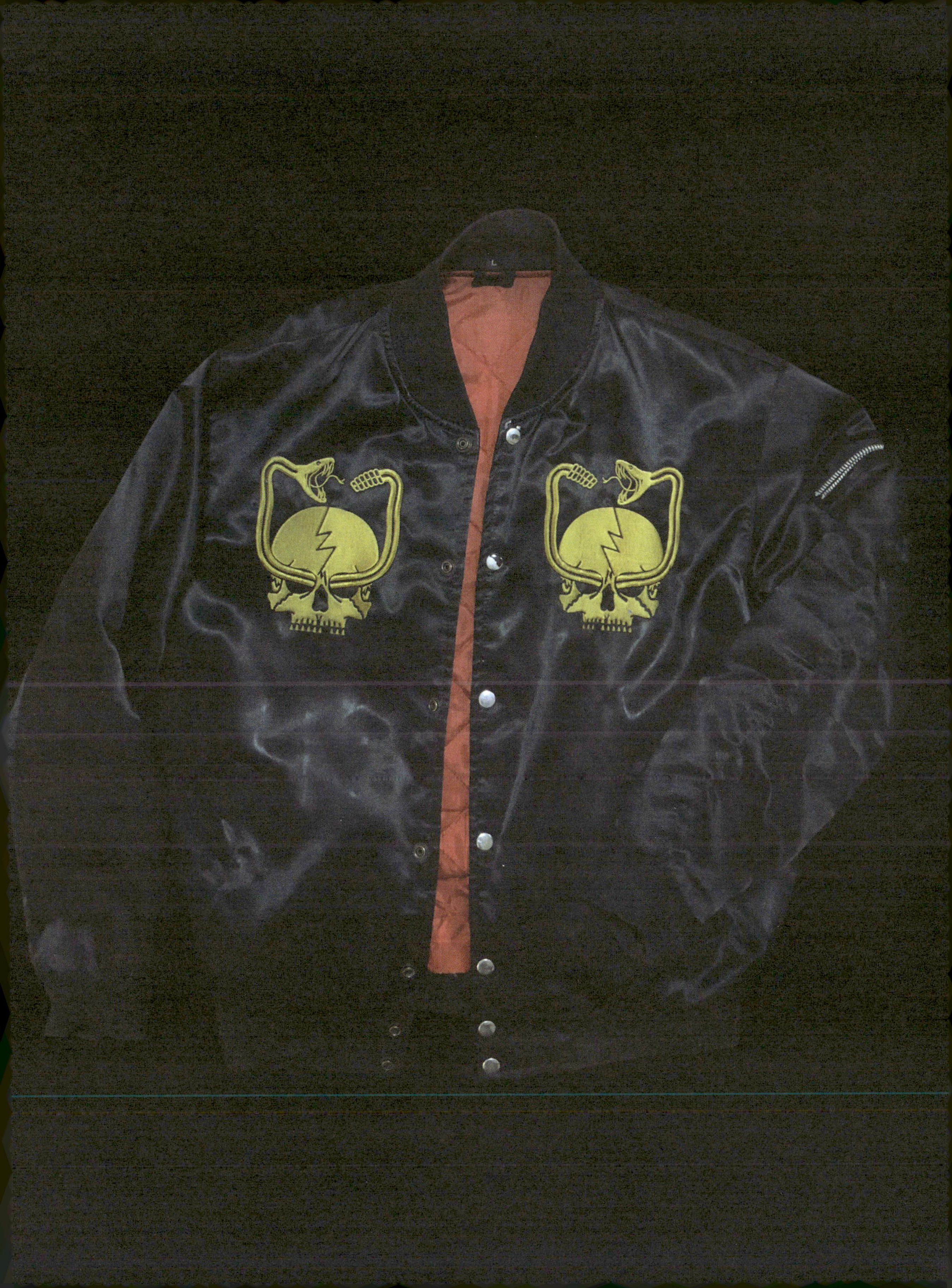

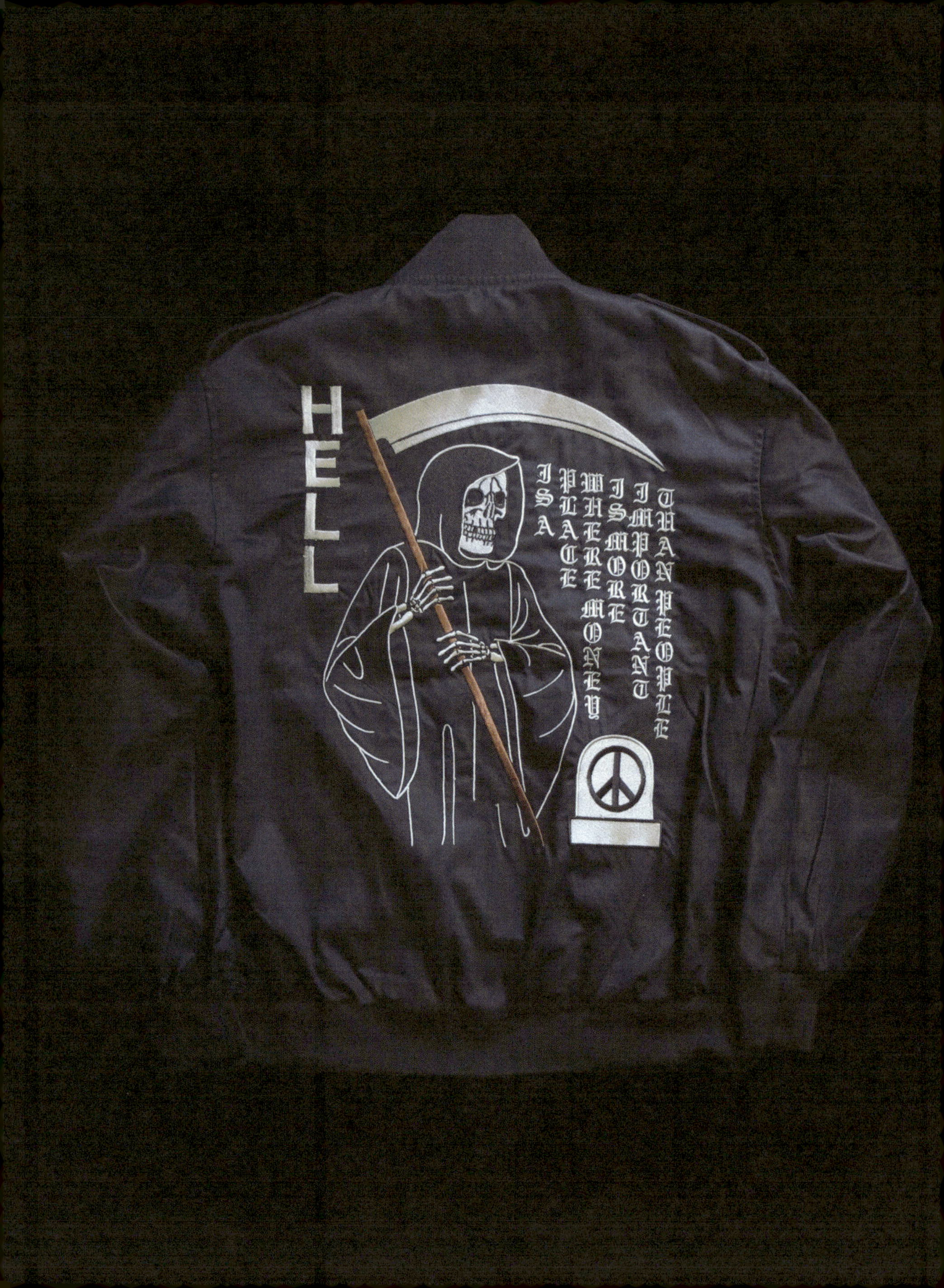

HELL

IS A PLACE WHERE MONEY IS MORE IMPORTANT THAN PEOPLE

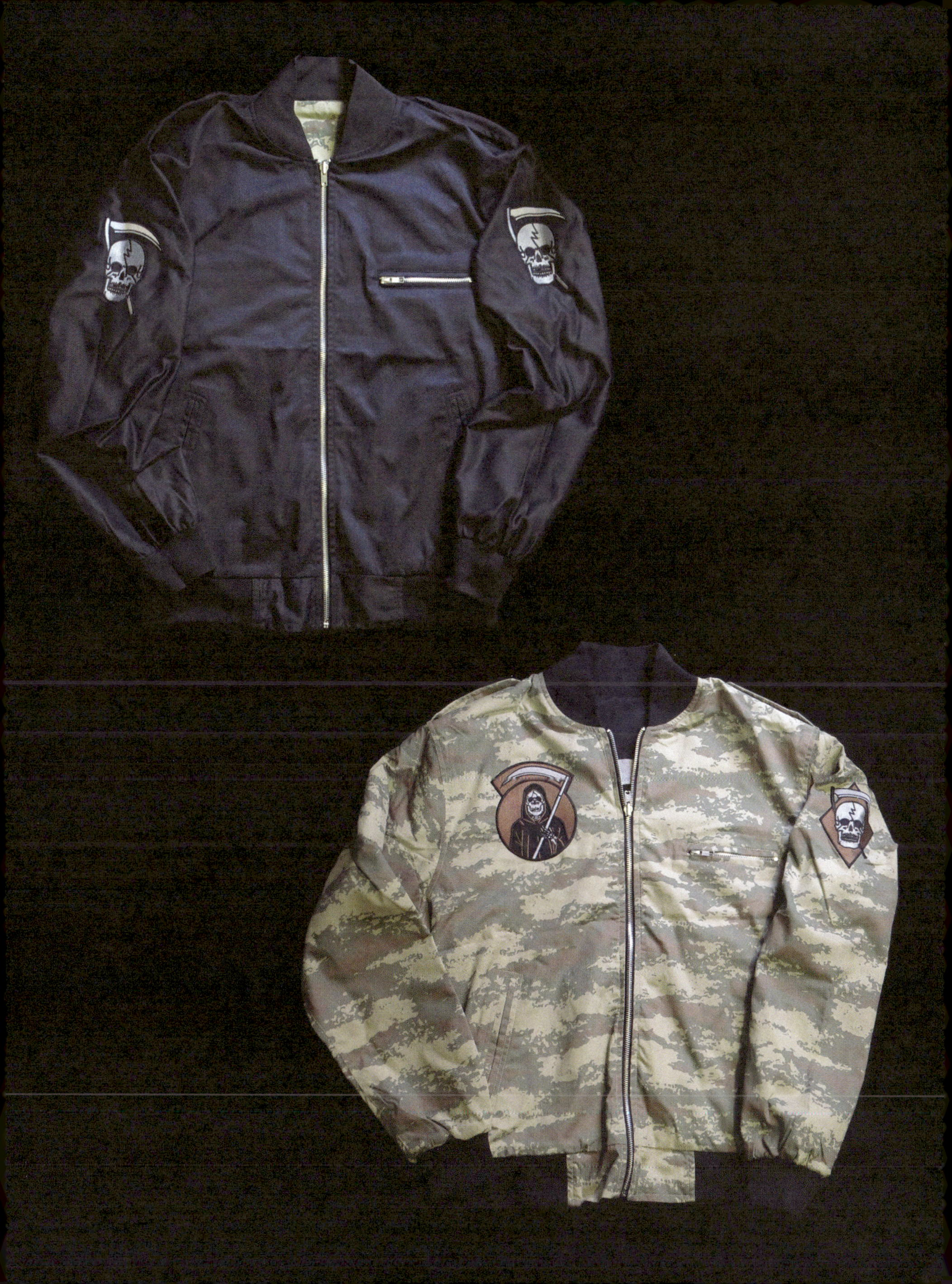

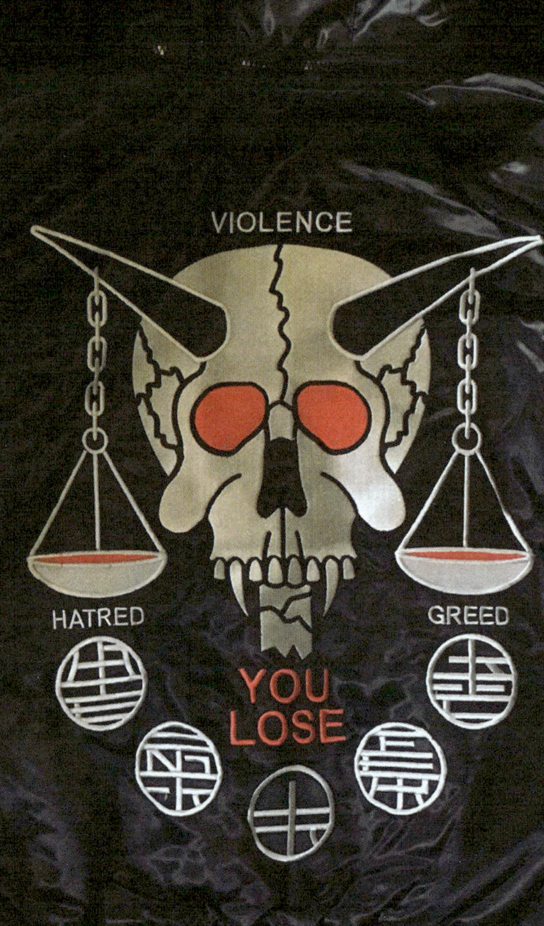

VIOLENCE
HATRED
GREED
YOU
LOSE

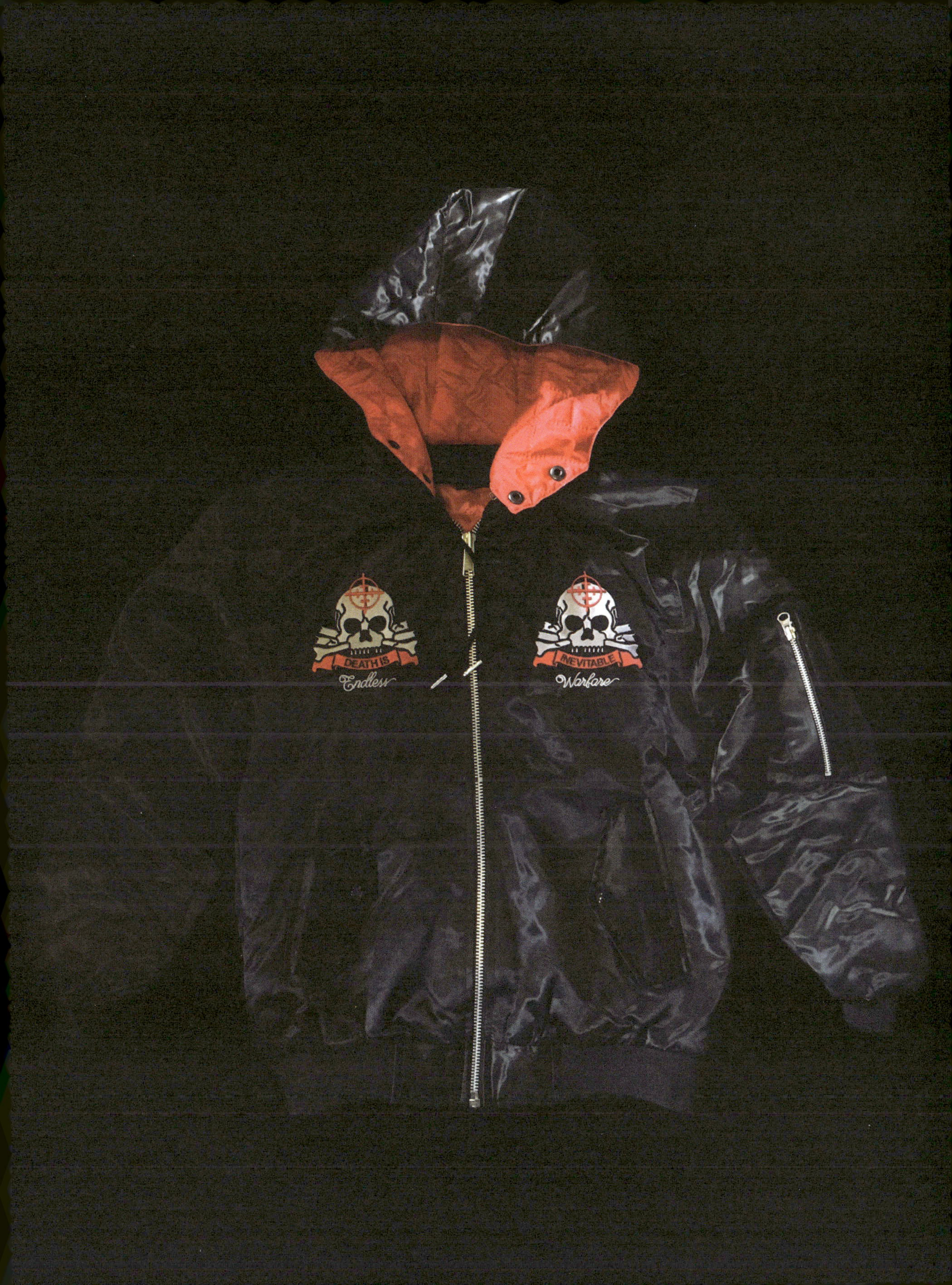

DEATH IS
Endless
INEVITABLE
Warfare

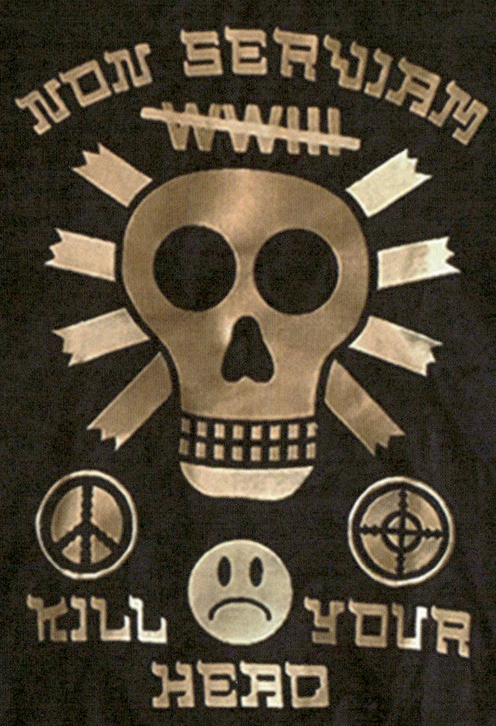

NON SERVIAM
WWIII
KILL YOUR
HEAD

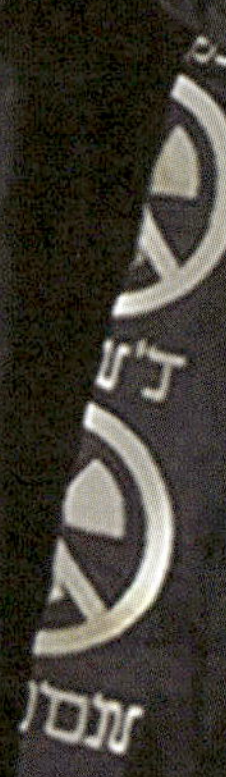

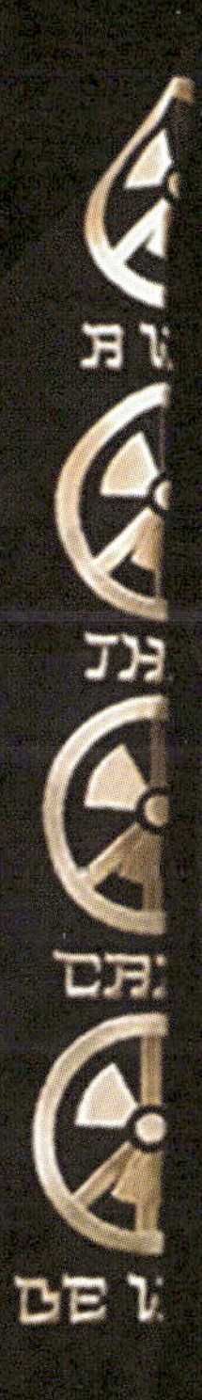

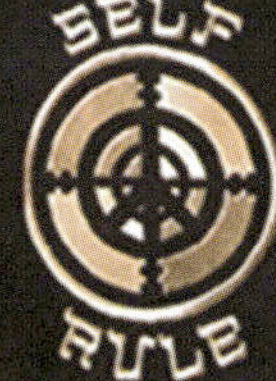
SELF
RULE

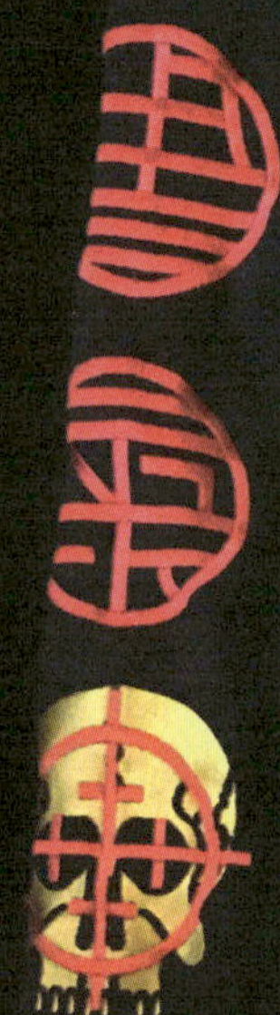
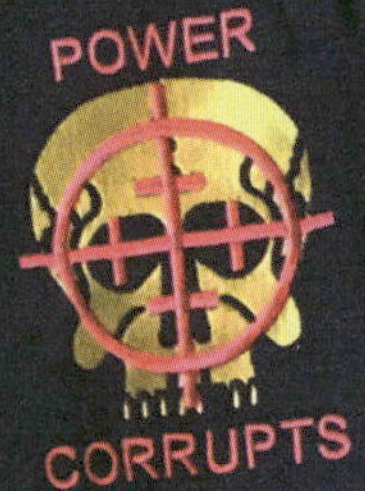
POWER
CORRUPTS
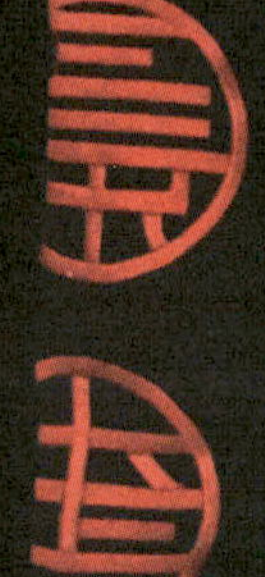
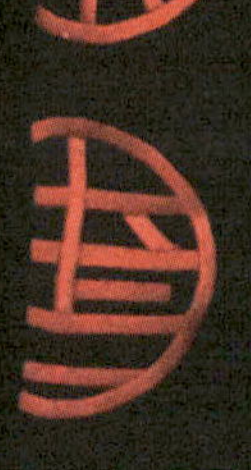

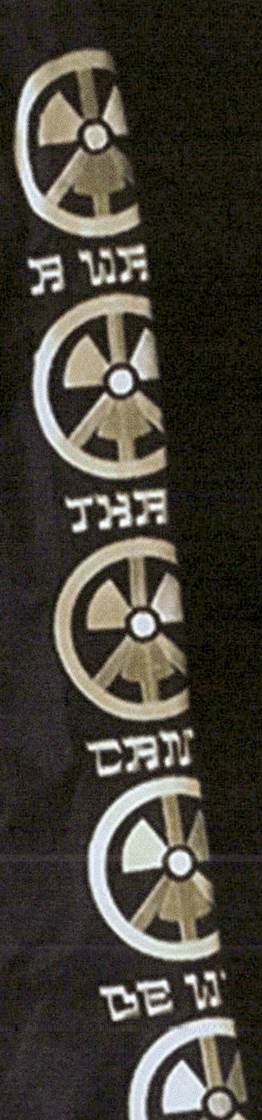

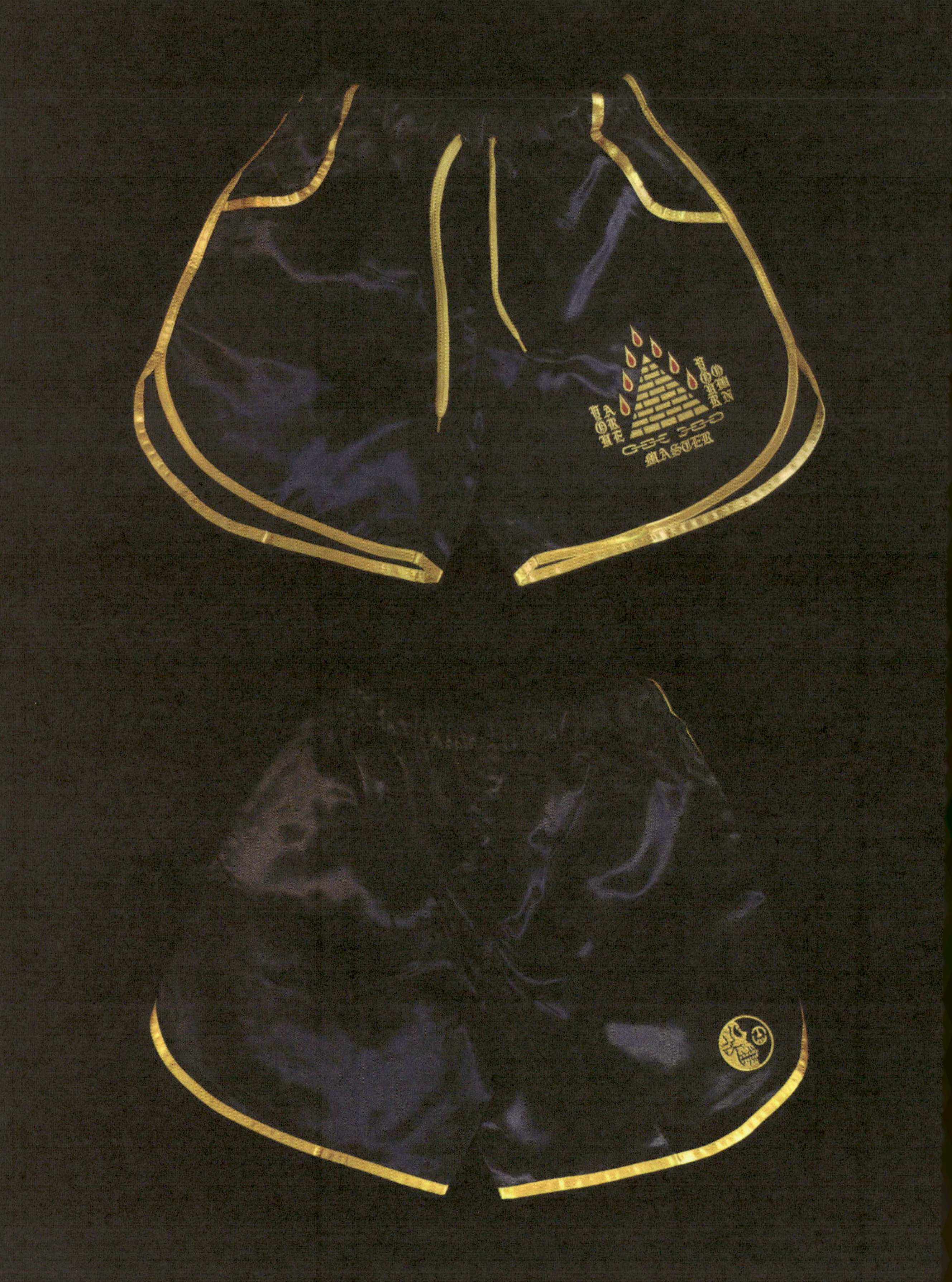
MASTER

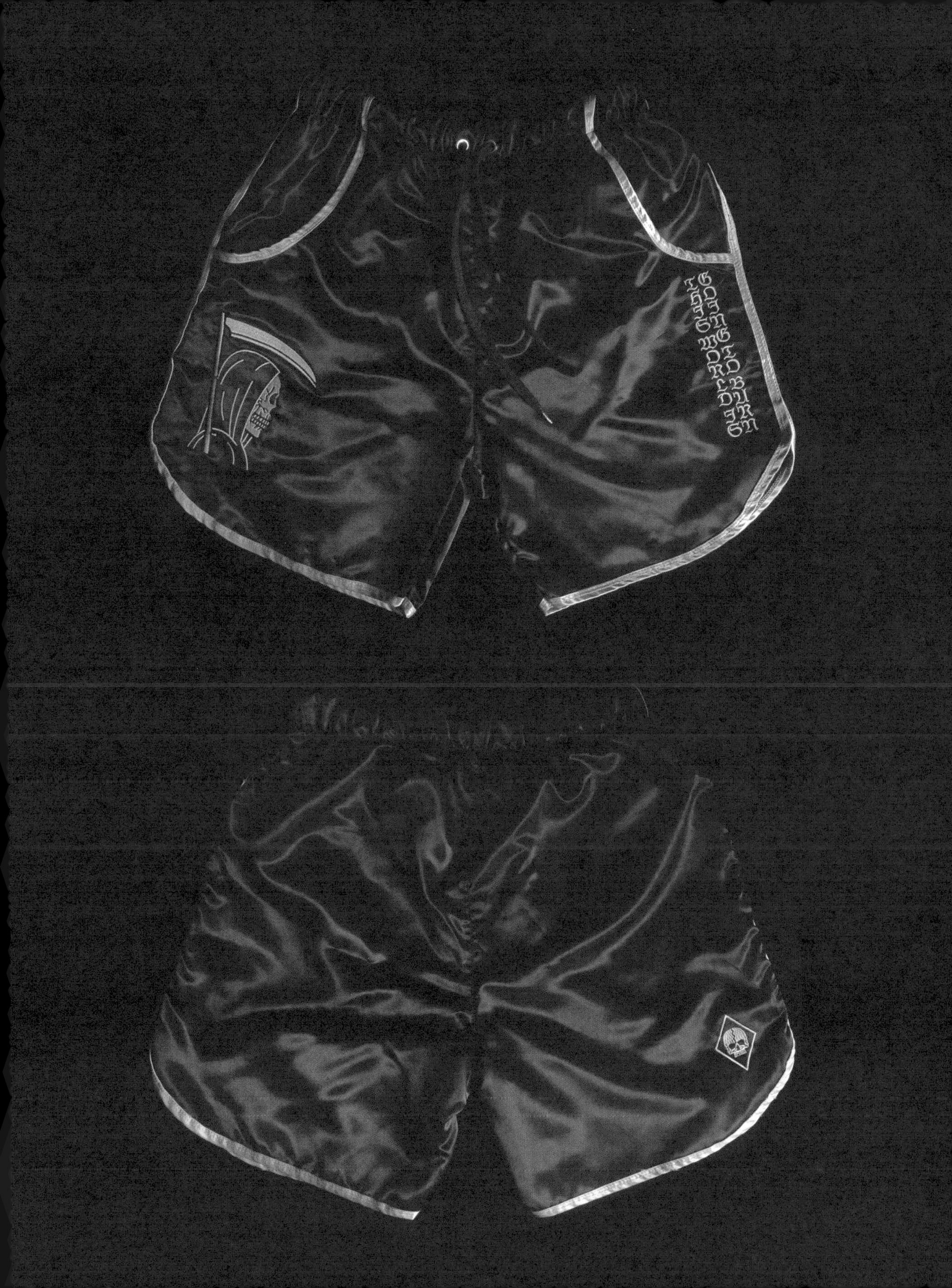
THIS DYING WORLDBURN

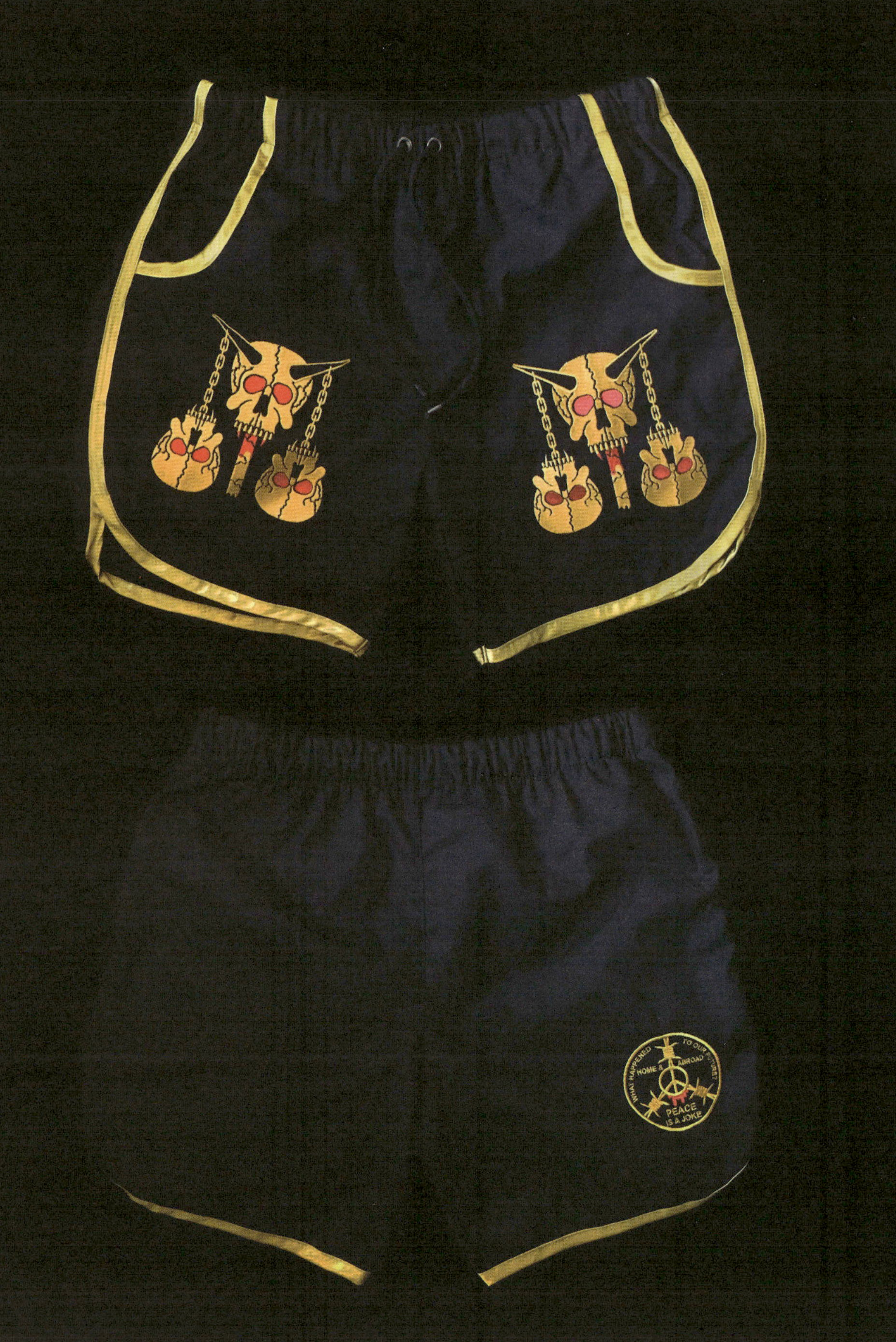
WHAT HAPPENED
TO OUR
HOME & ABROAD
PEACE
IS A JOKE

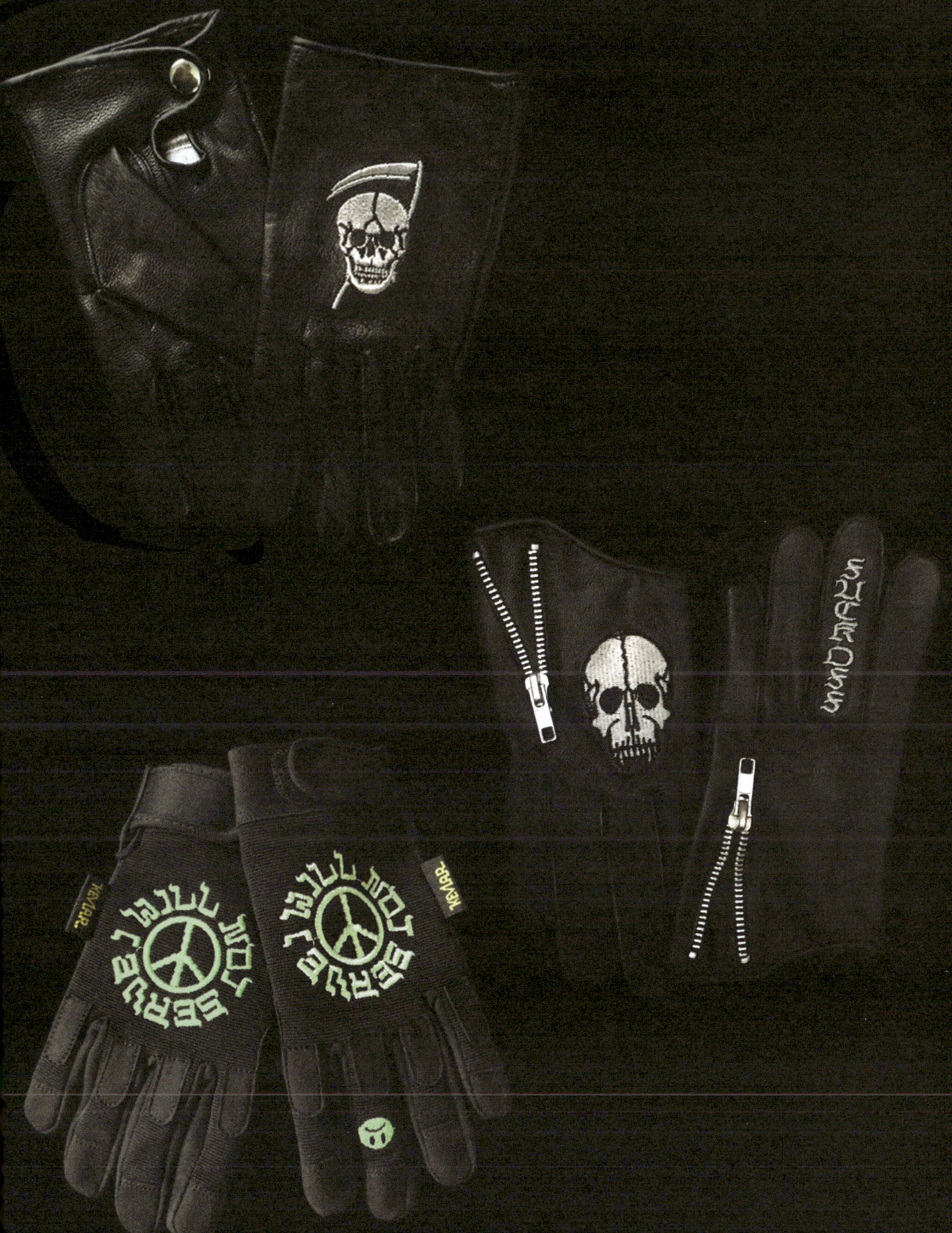

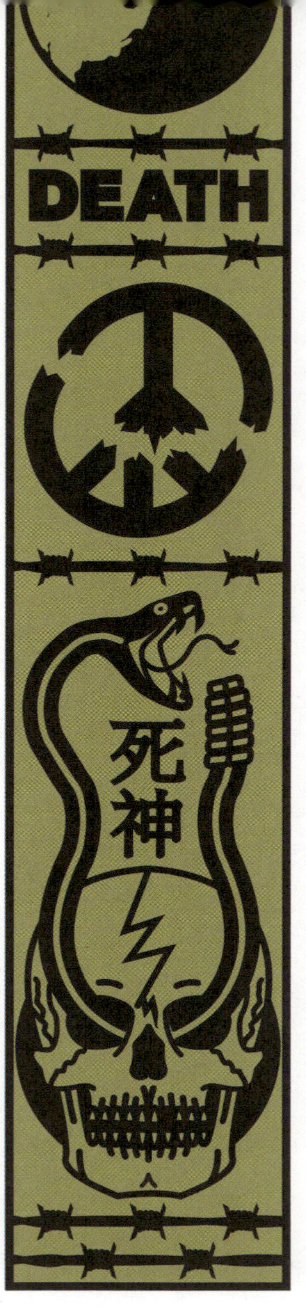
DEATH
死神

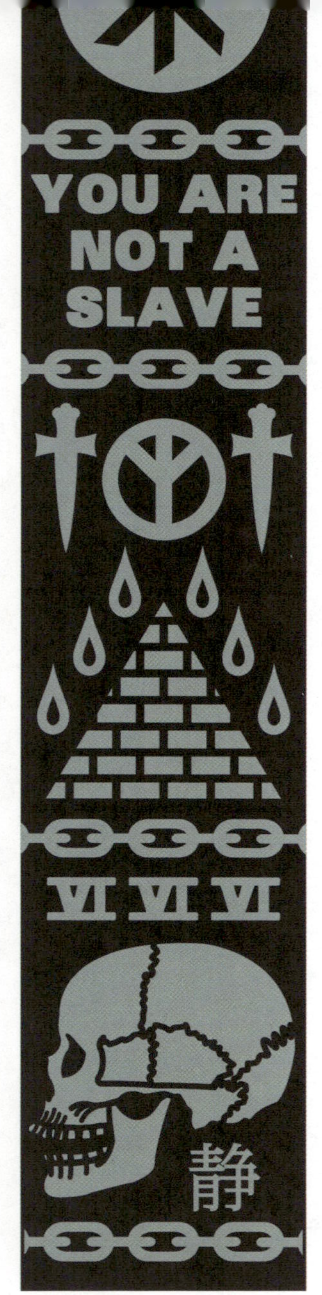
YOU ARE
NOT A
SLAVE
VI VI VI
静

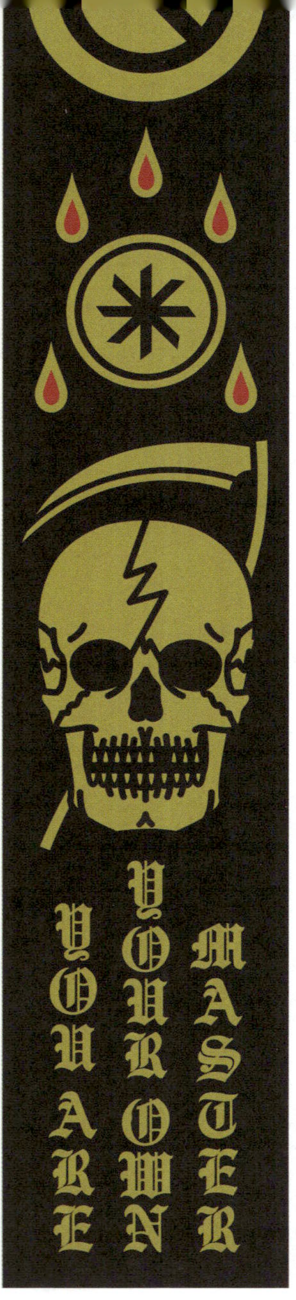
YOU ARE
YOUR OWN
MASTER

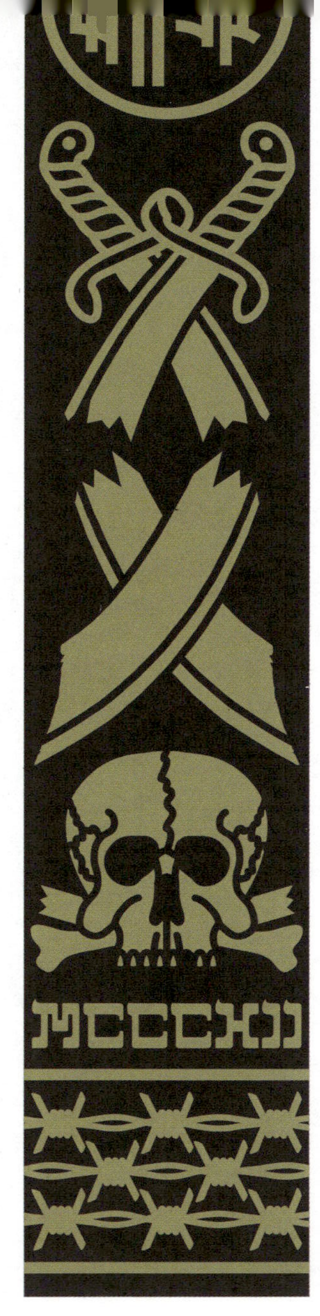
MCCCXII

MCCCXII

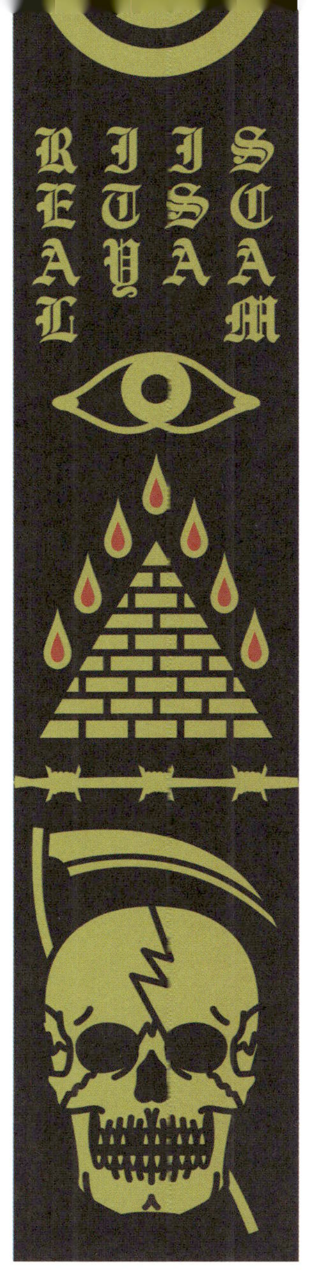
REAL
RITUAL
SCAM

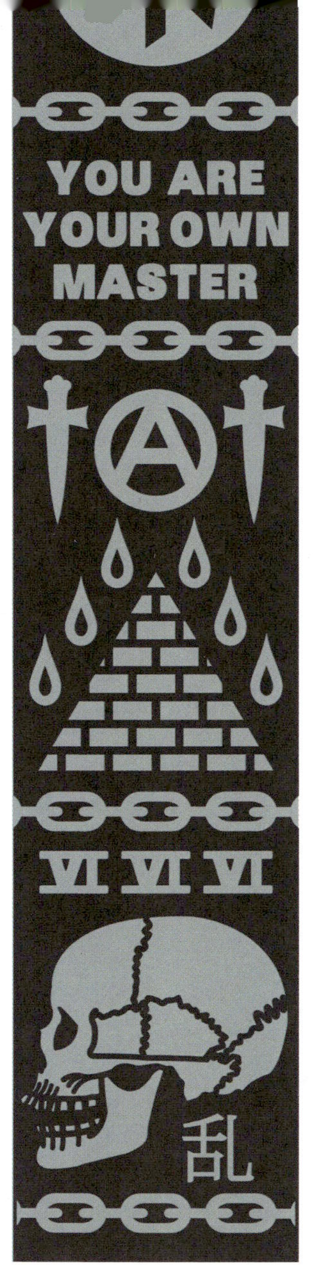
YOU ARE
YOUR OWN
MASTER
VI VI VI
乱

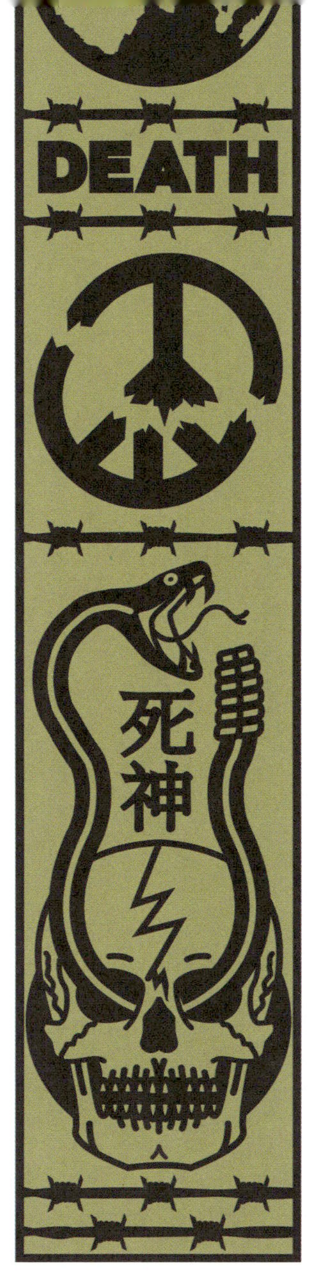
DEATH
死神

SECTION C: ARTWORK

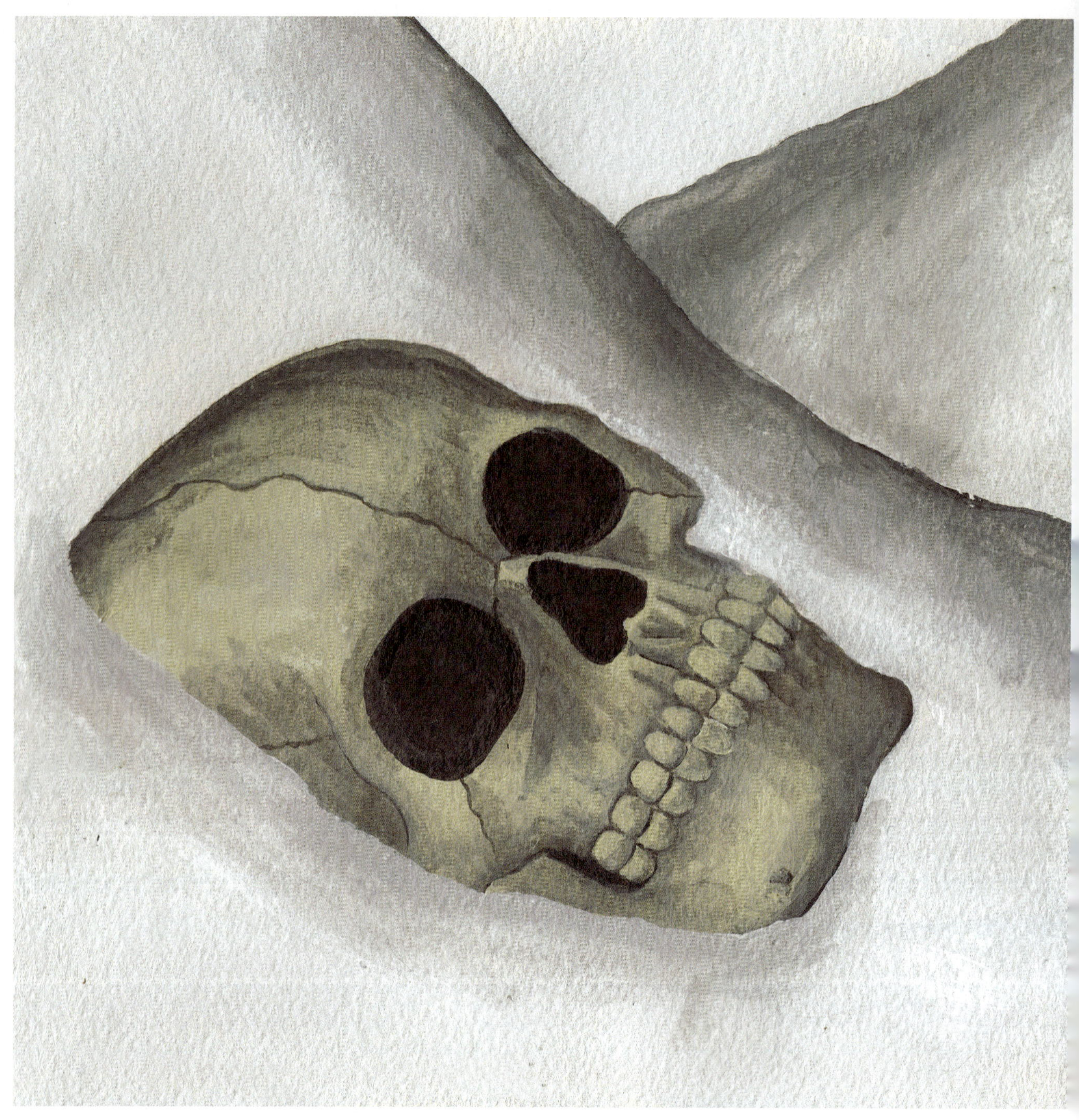

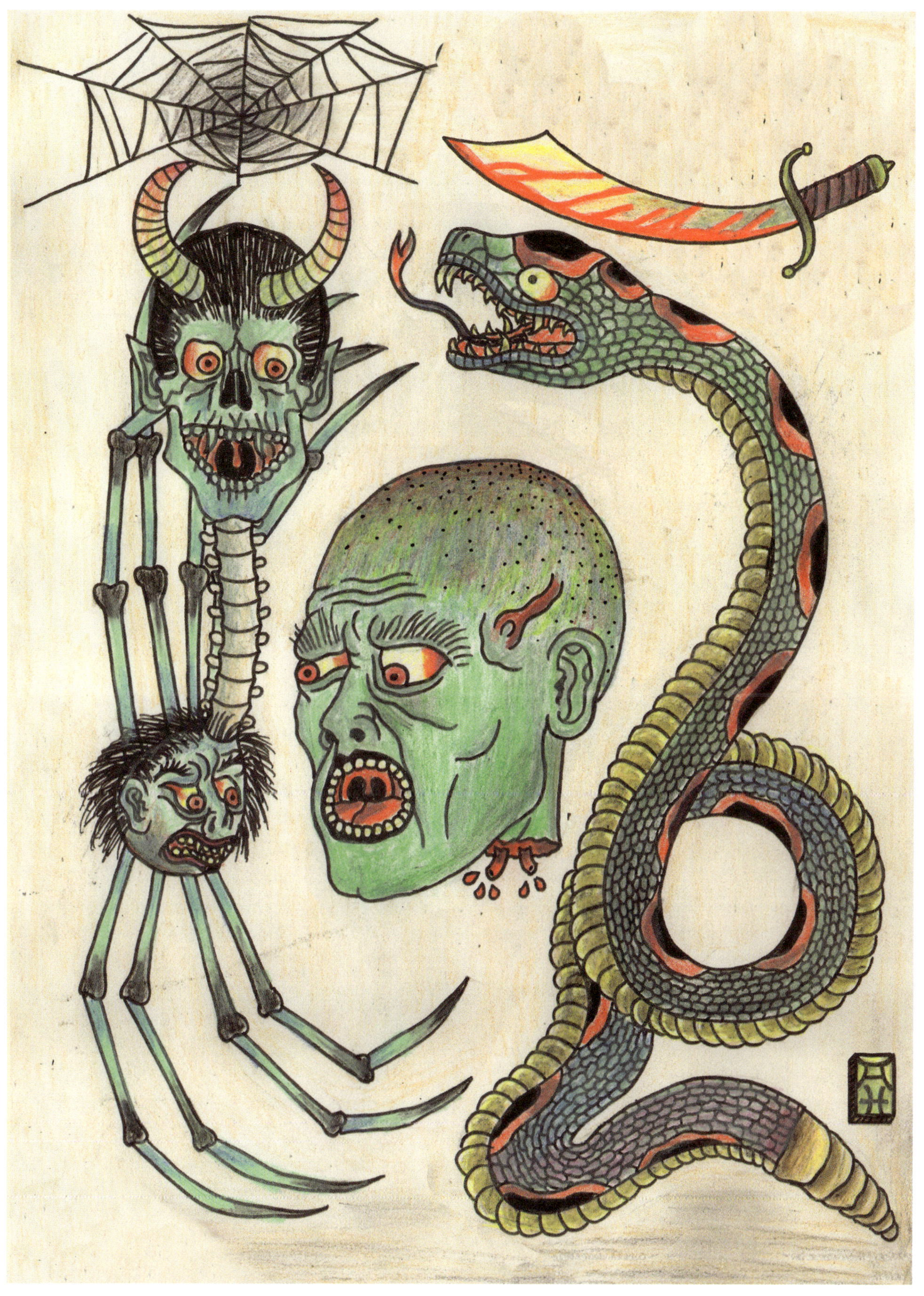

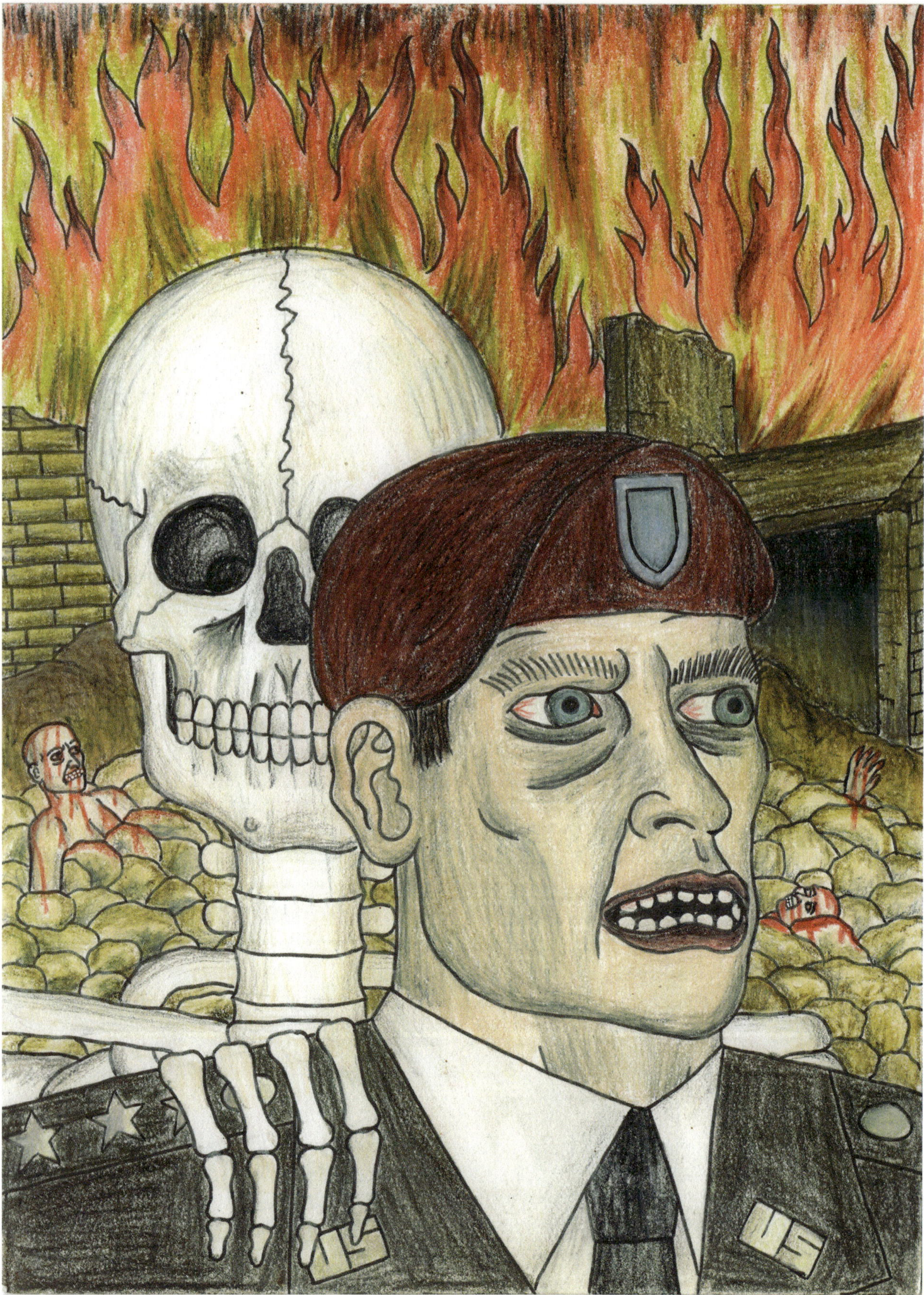

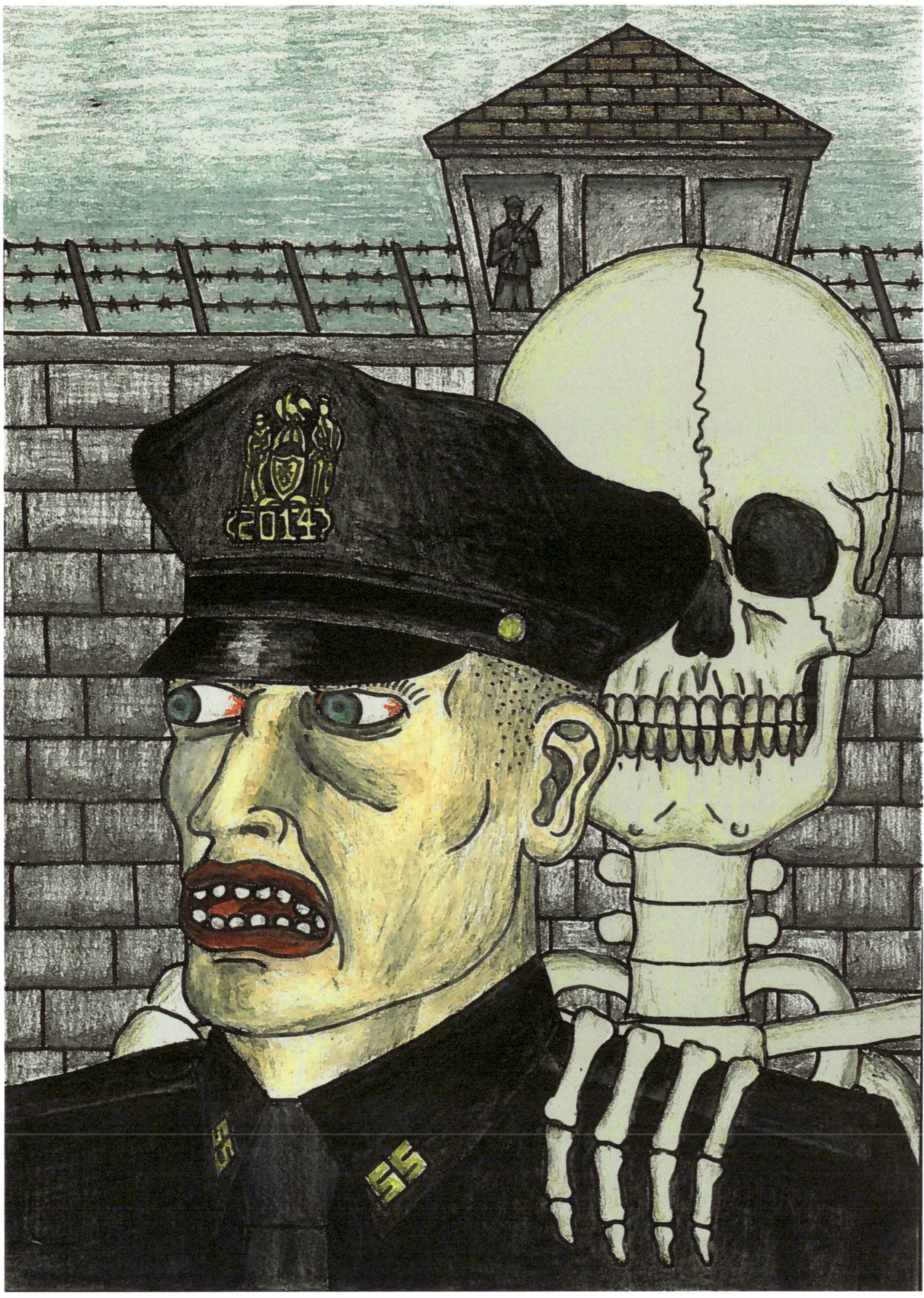

2014
SS

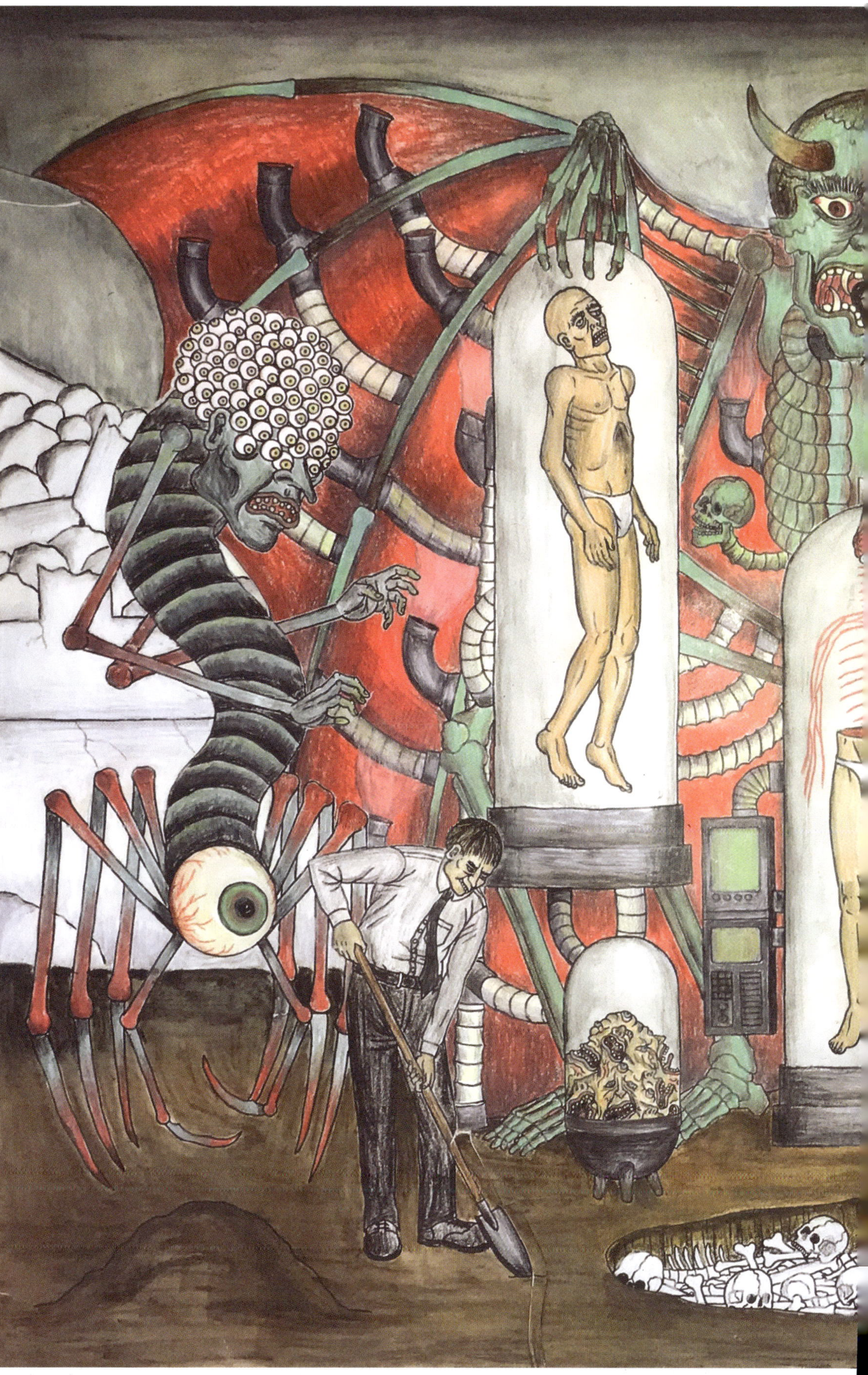

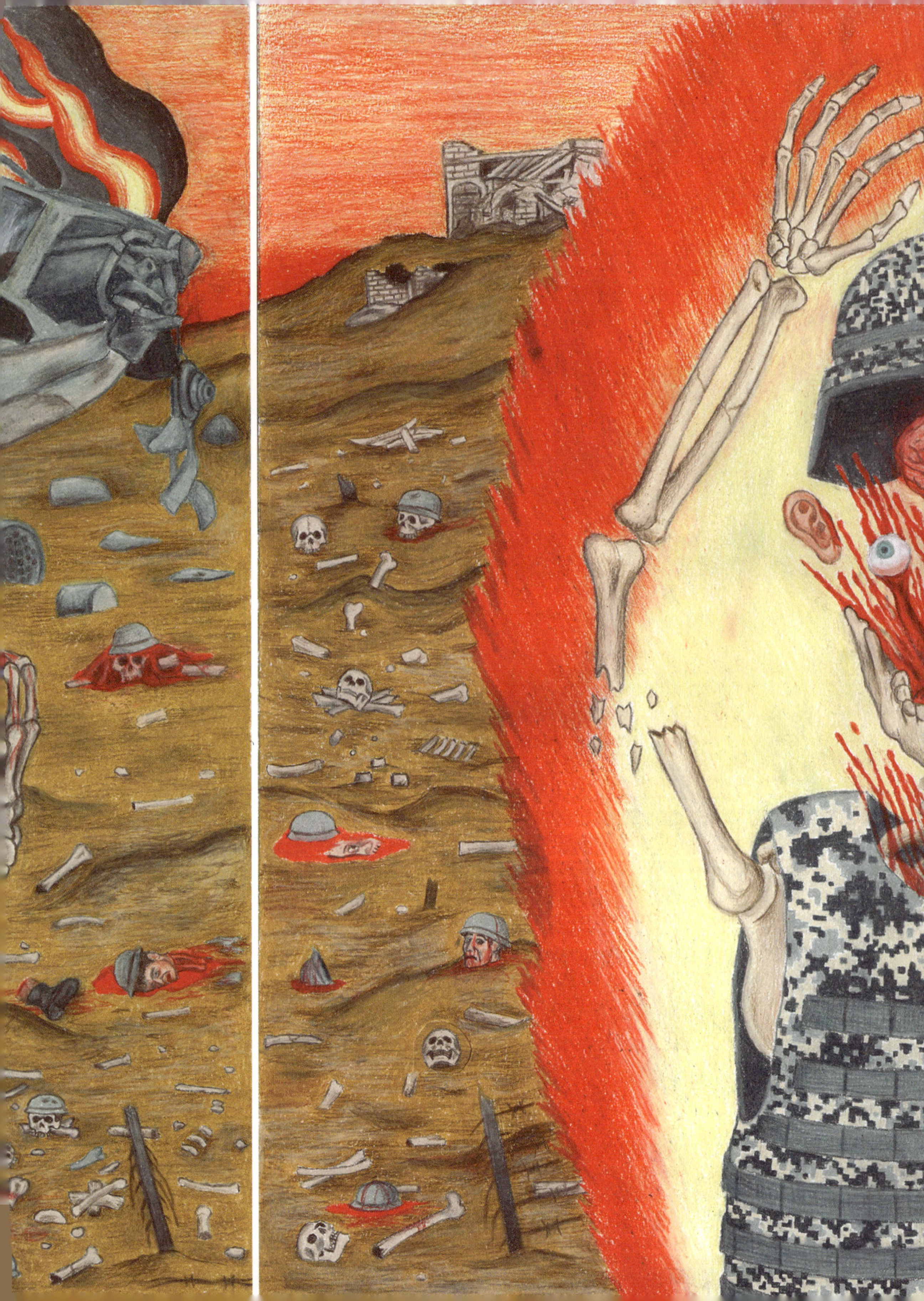

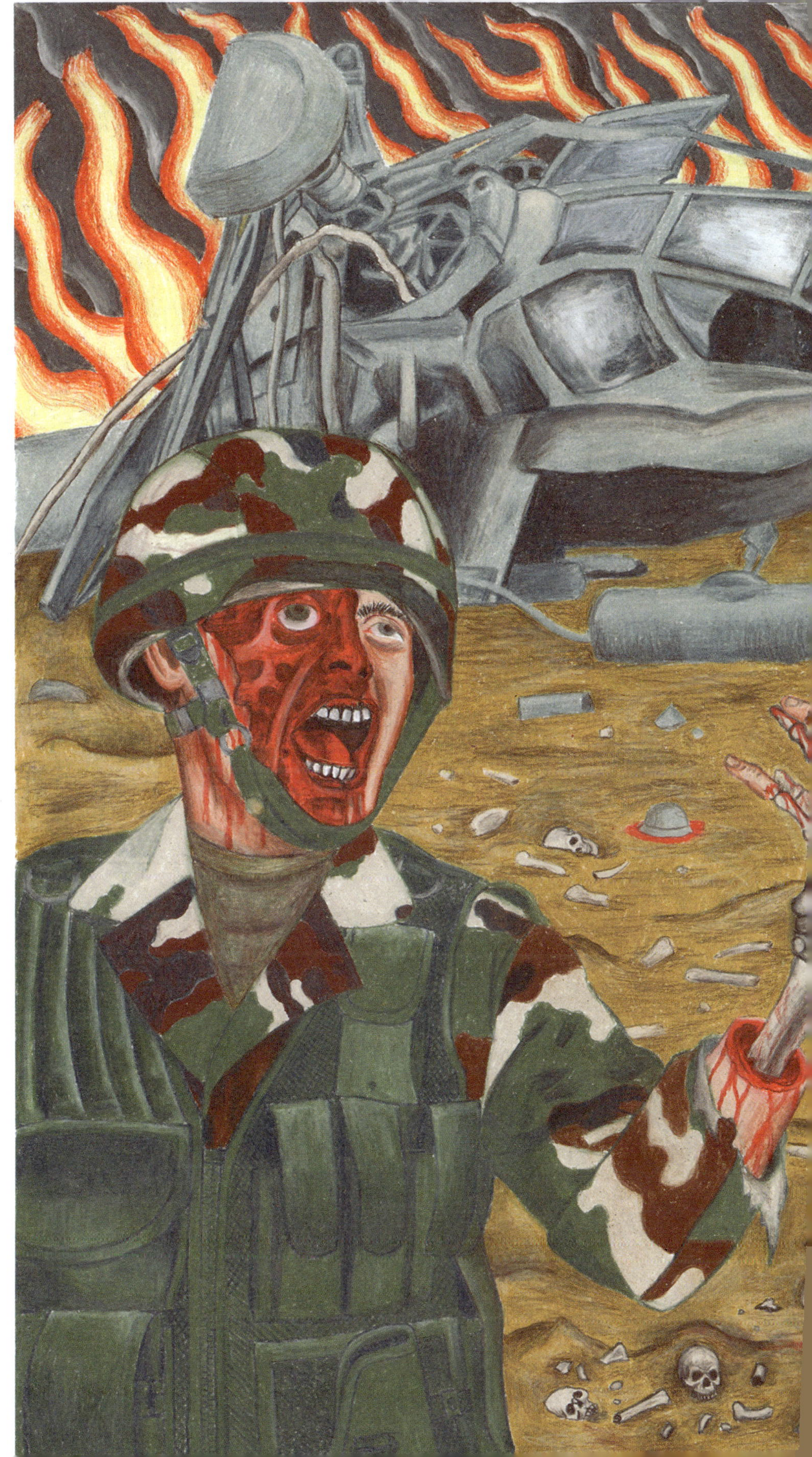

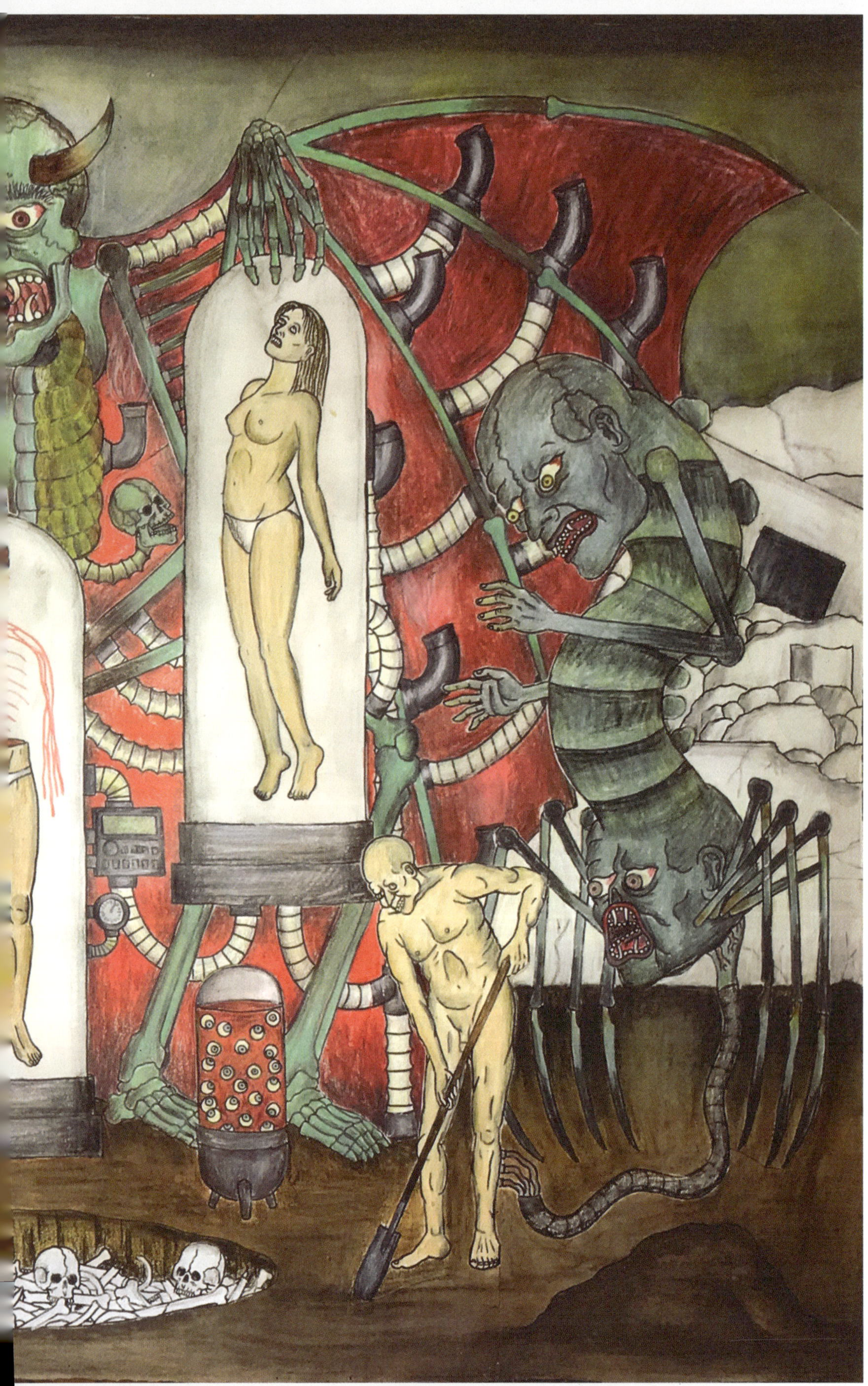

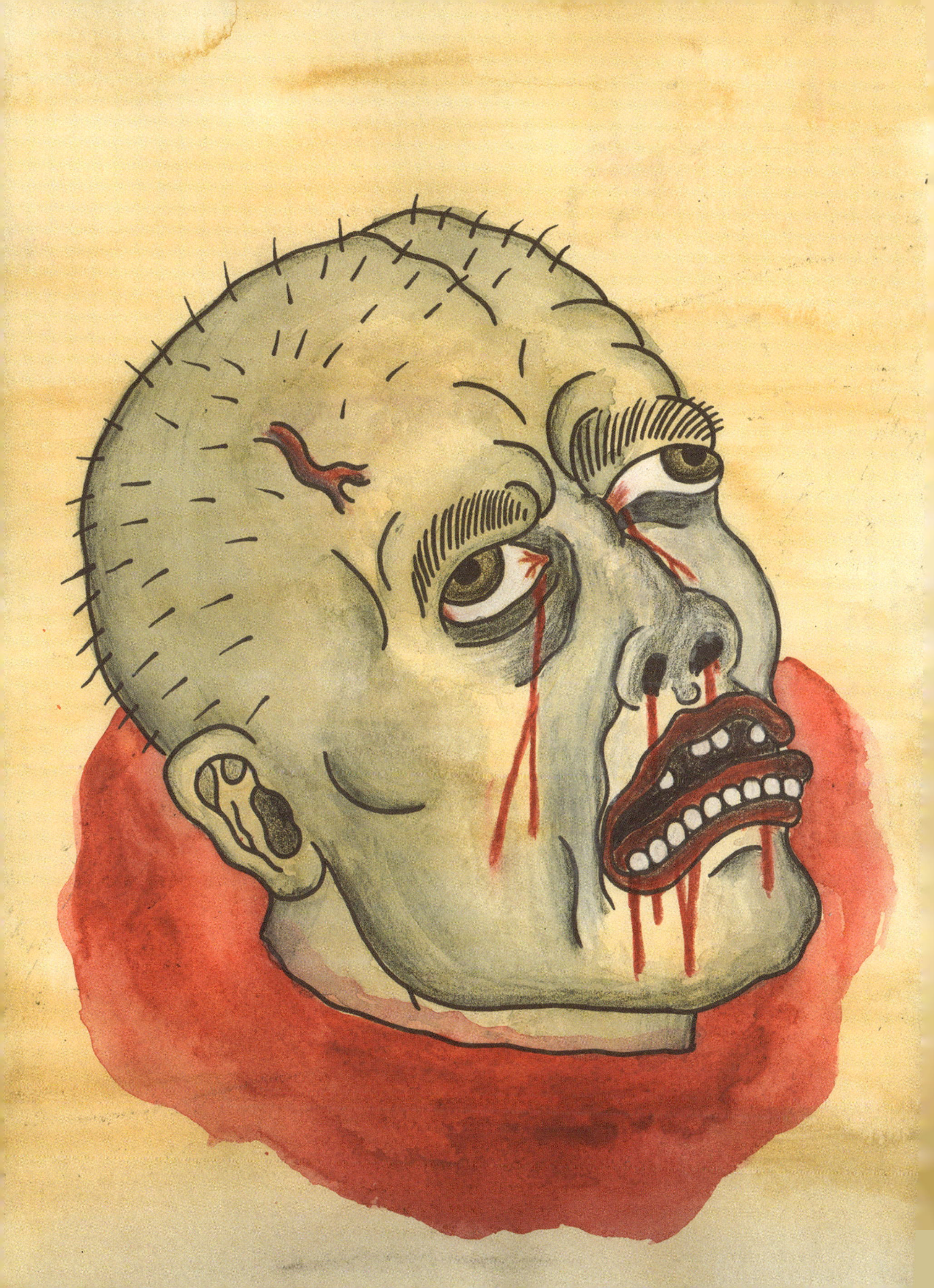

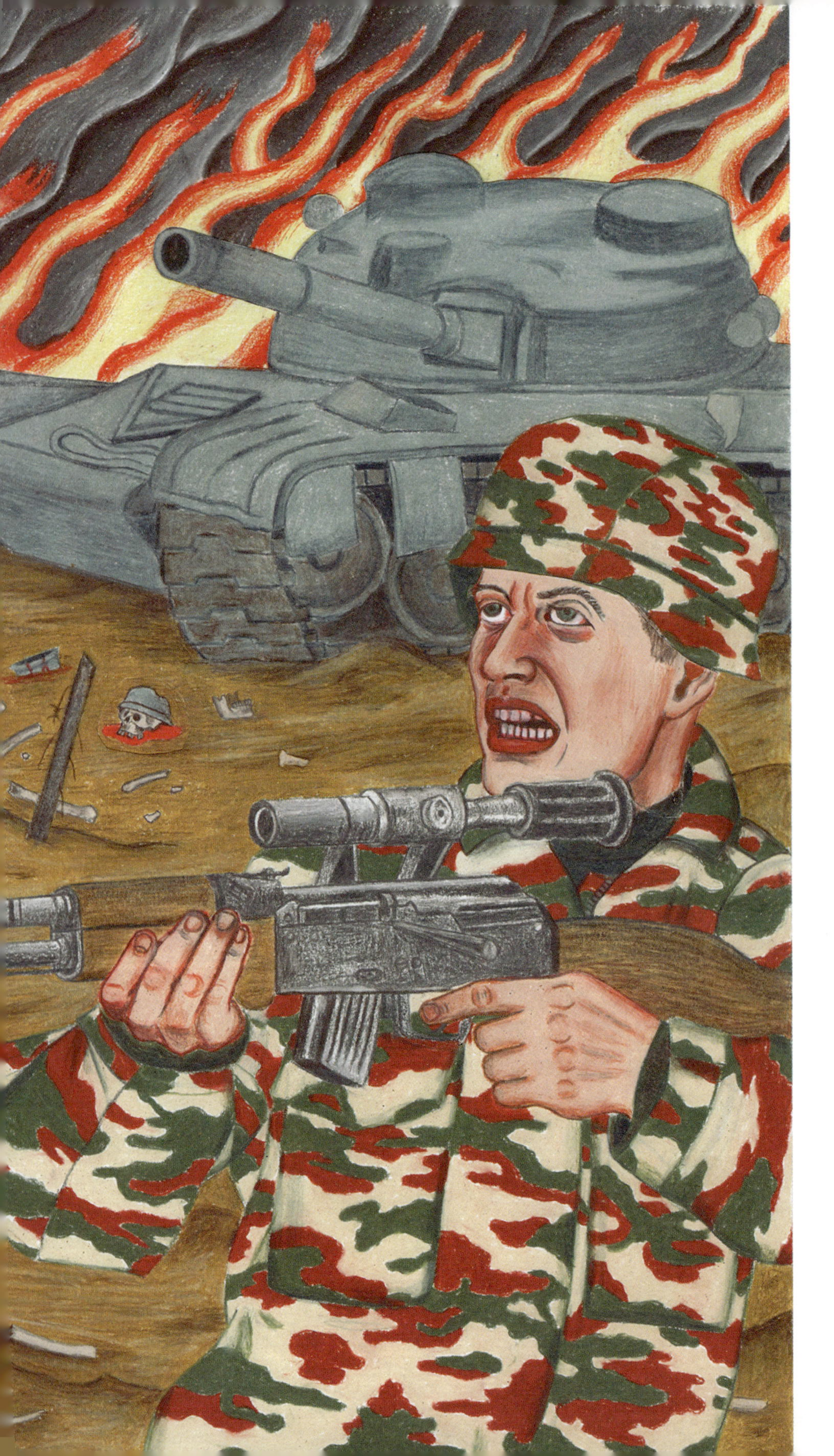

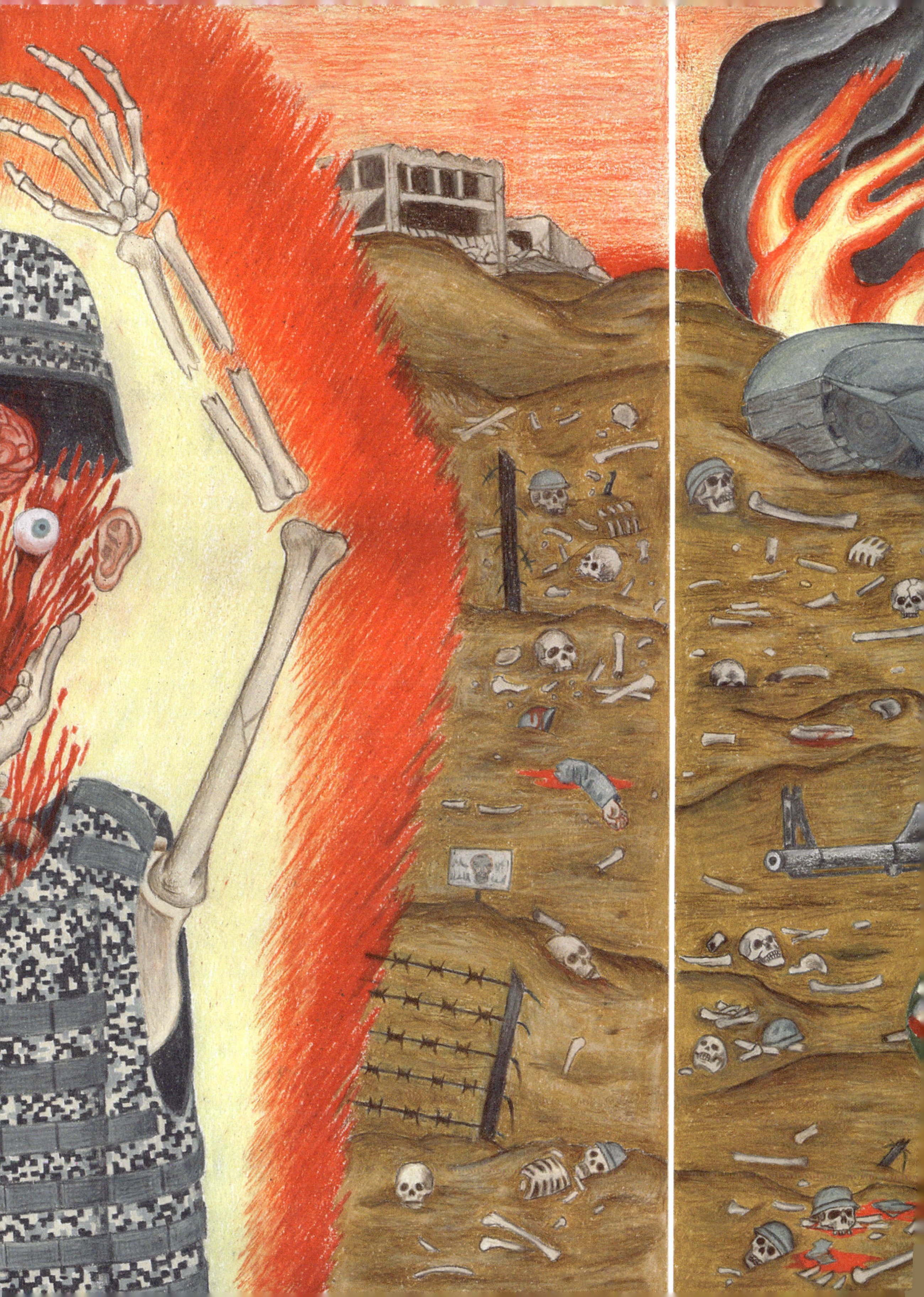

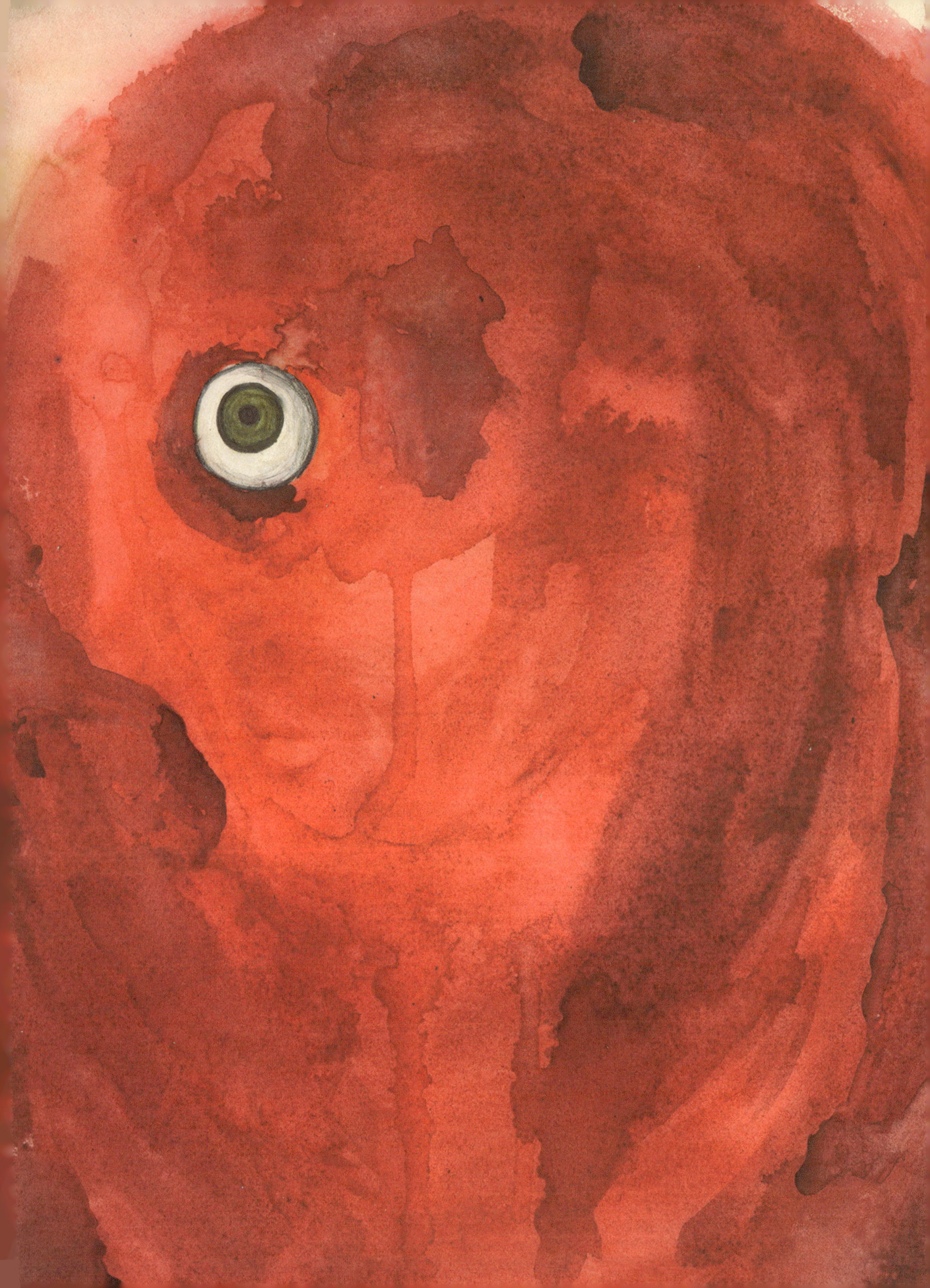

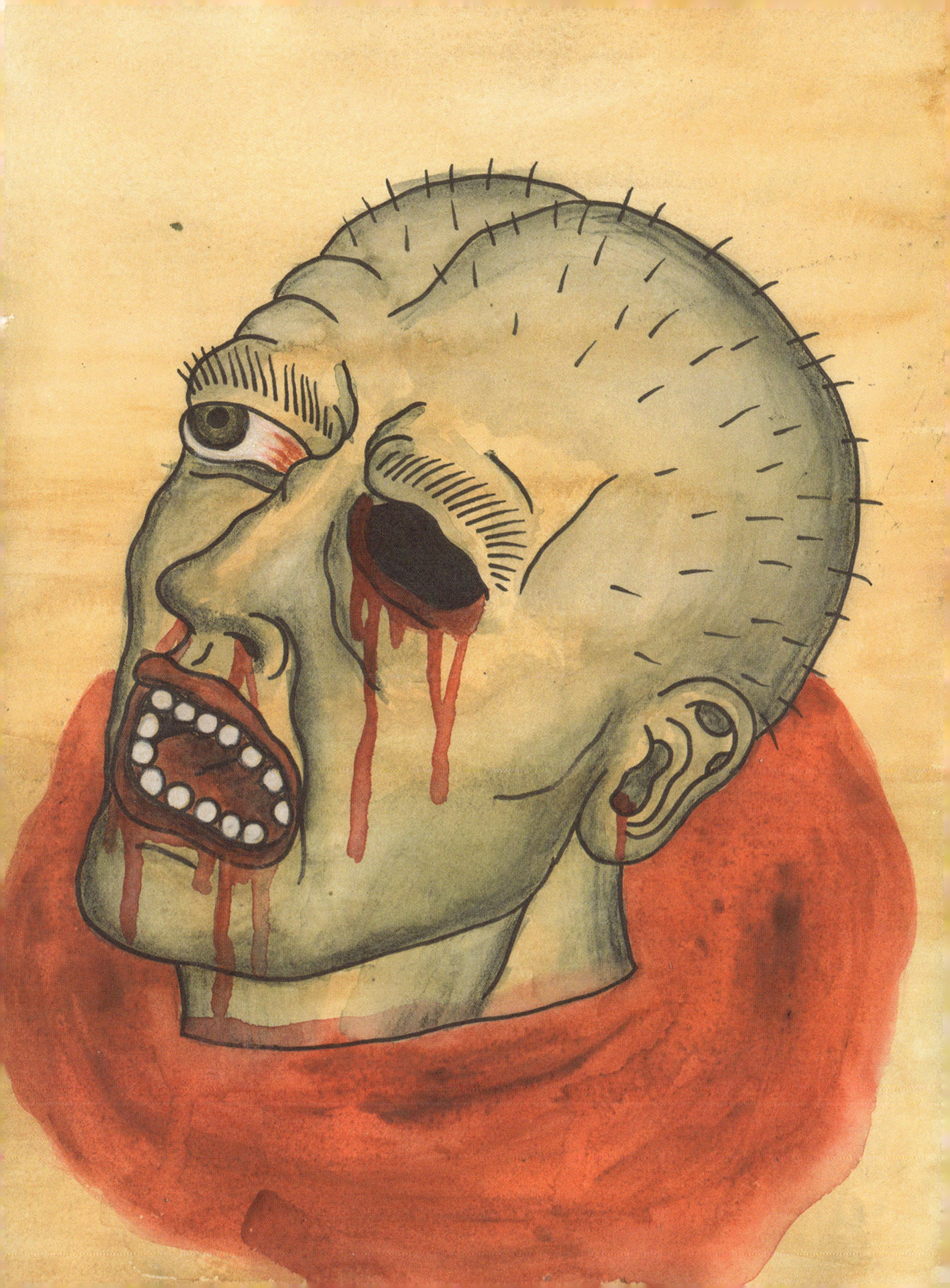

TO AVOID
ISOLATION DURING
A TERRIBLE AND
WORRYING TIME
OWNING · SHARED
THE CURRENT MOON

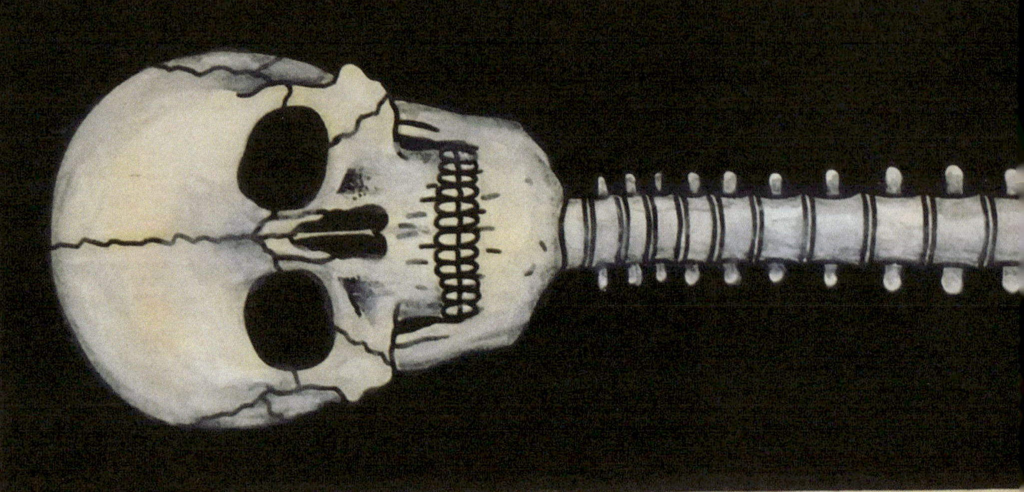

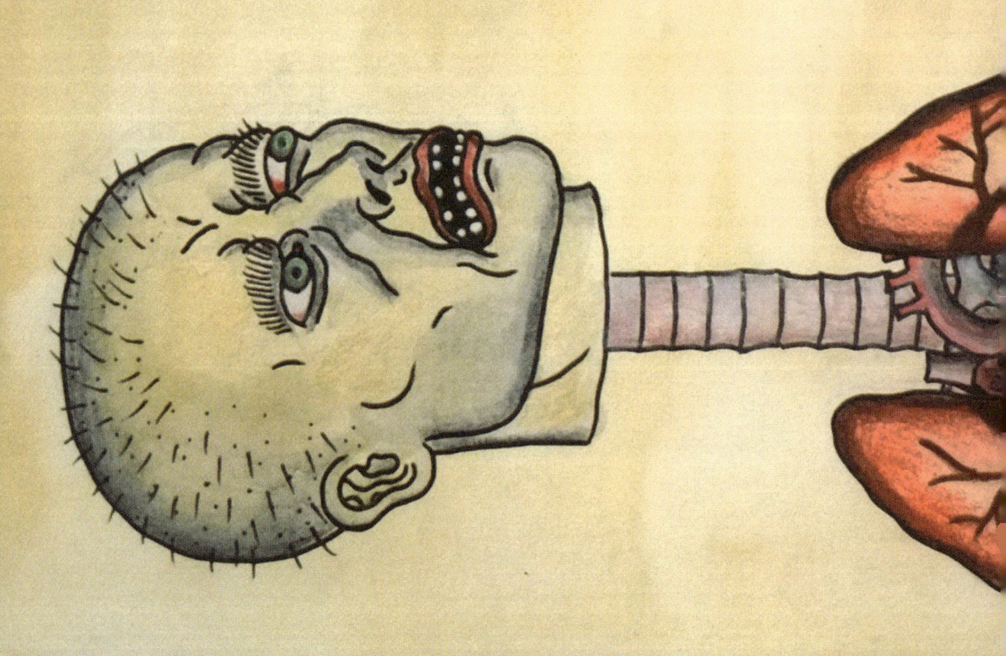

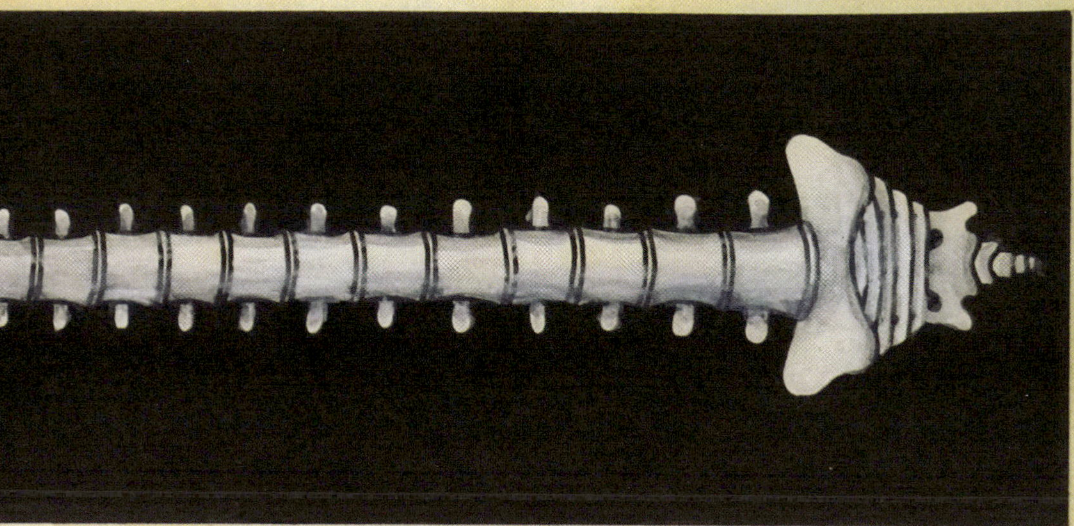
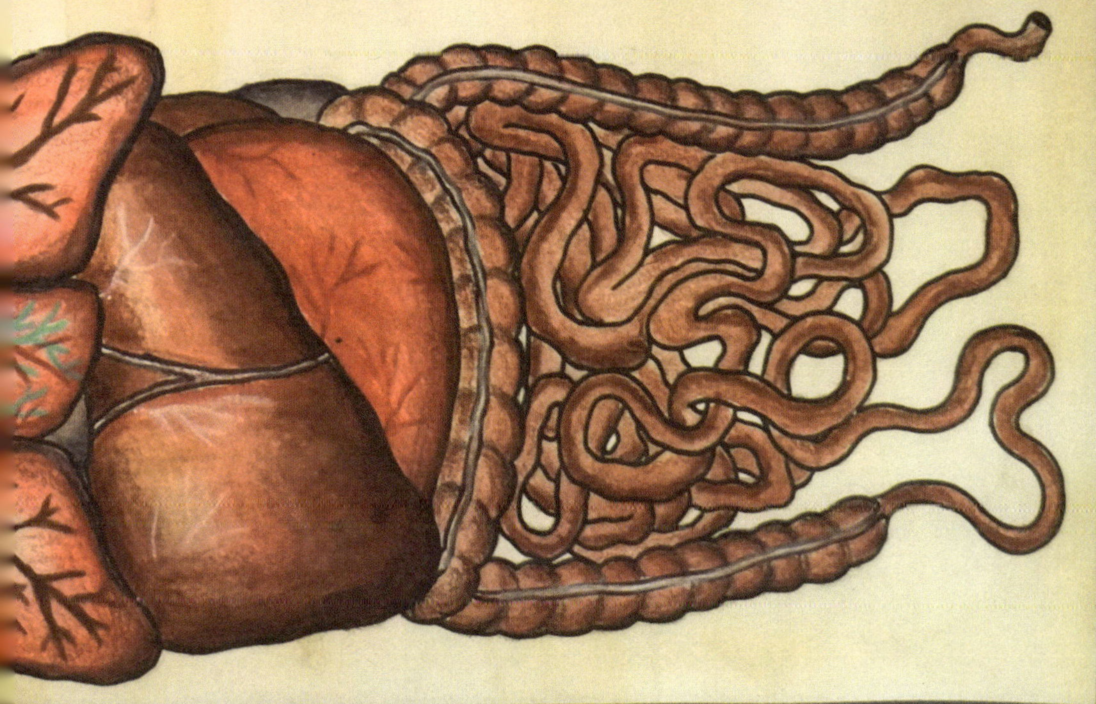

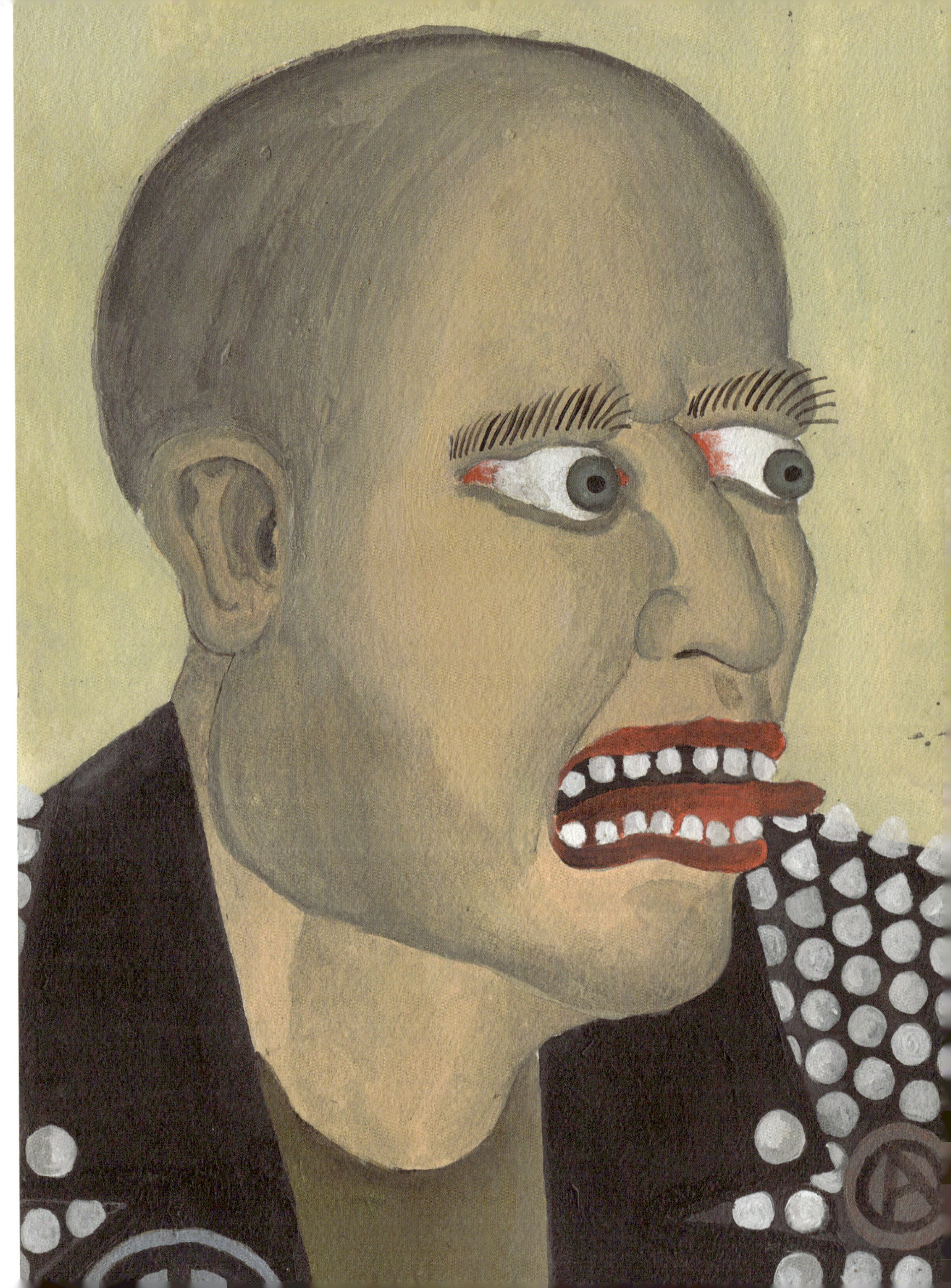

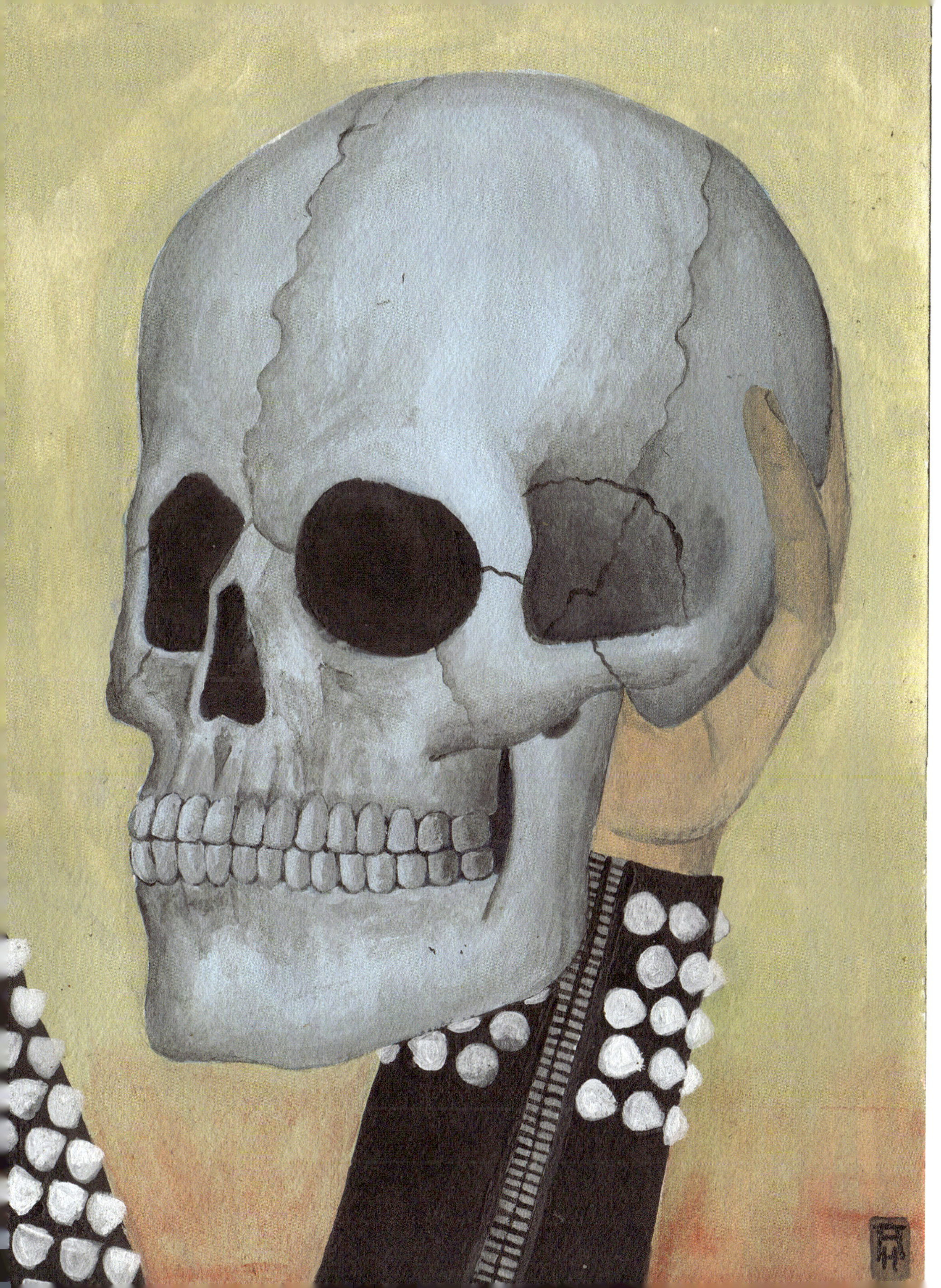

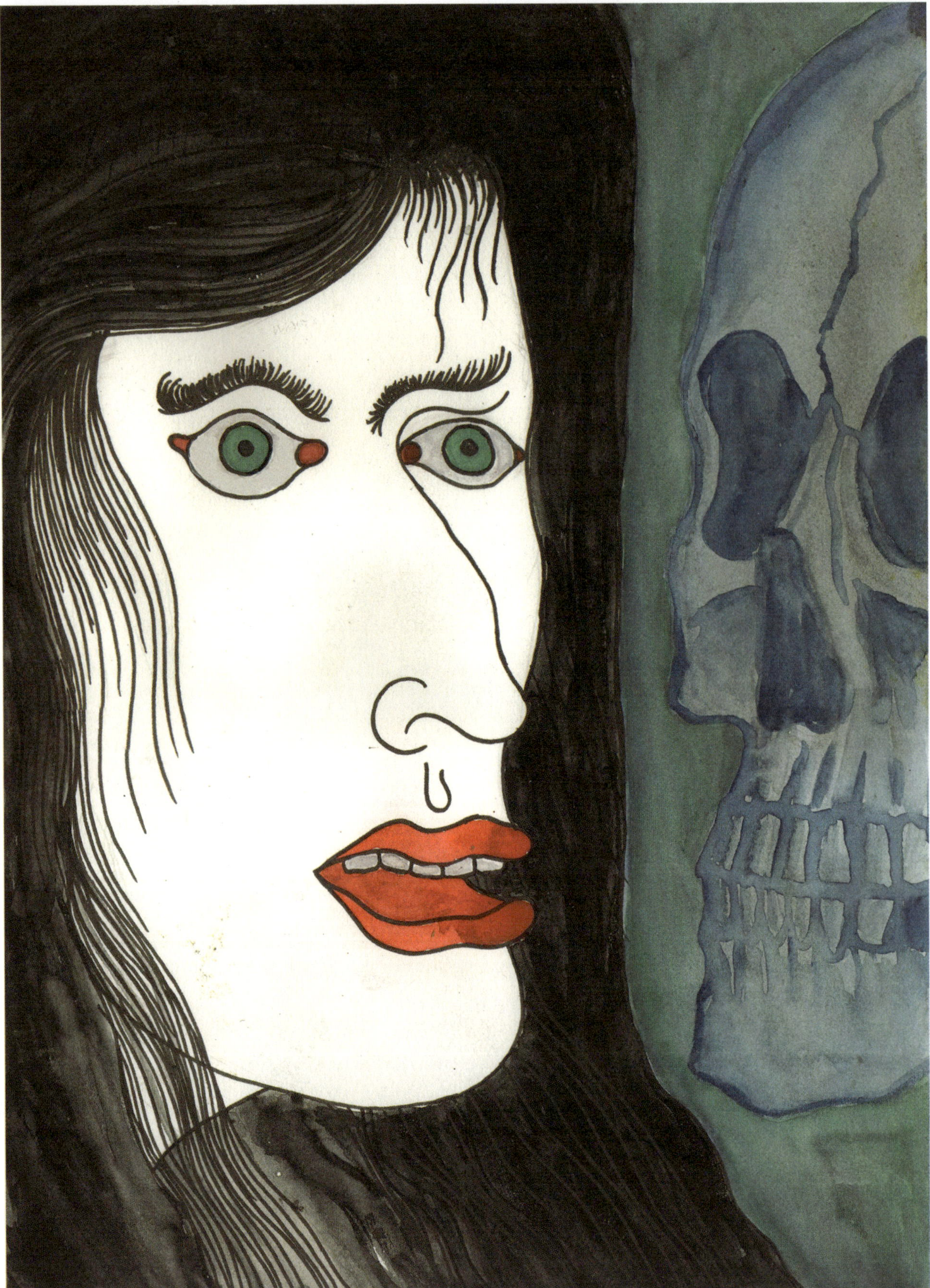

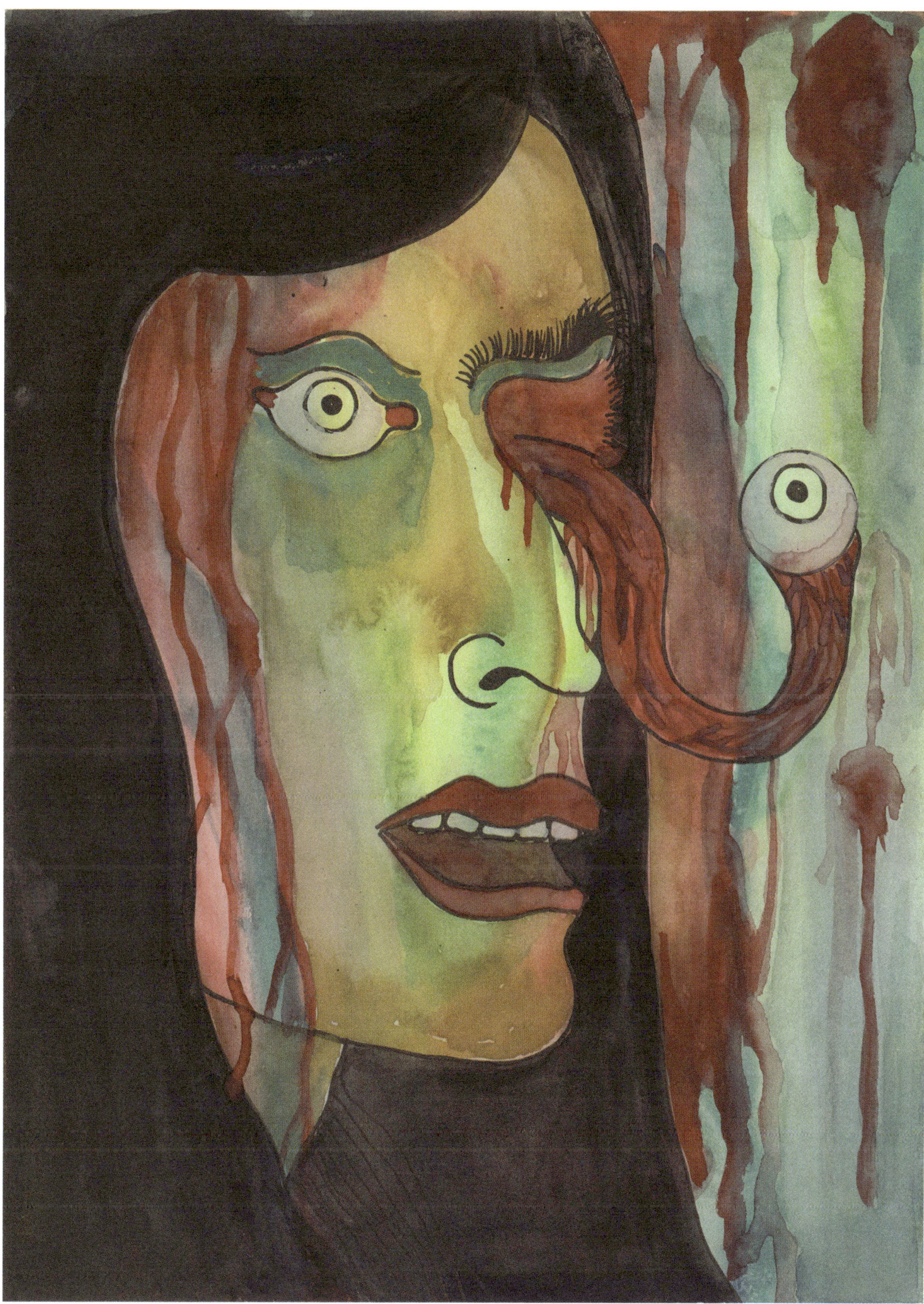

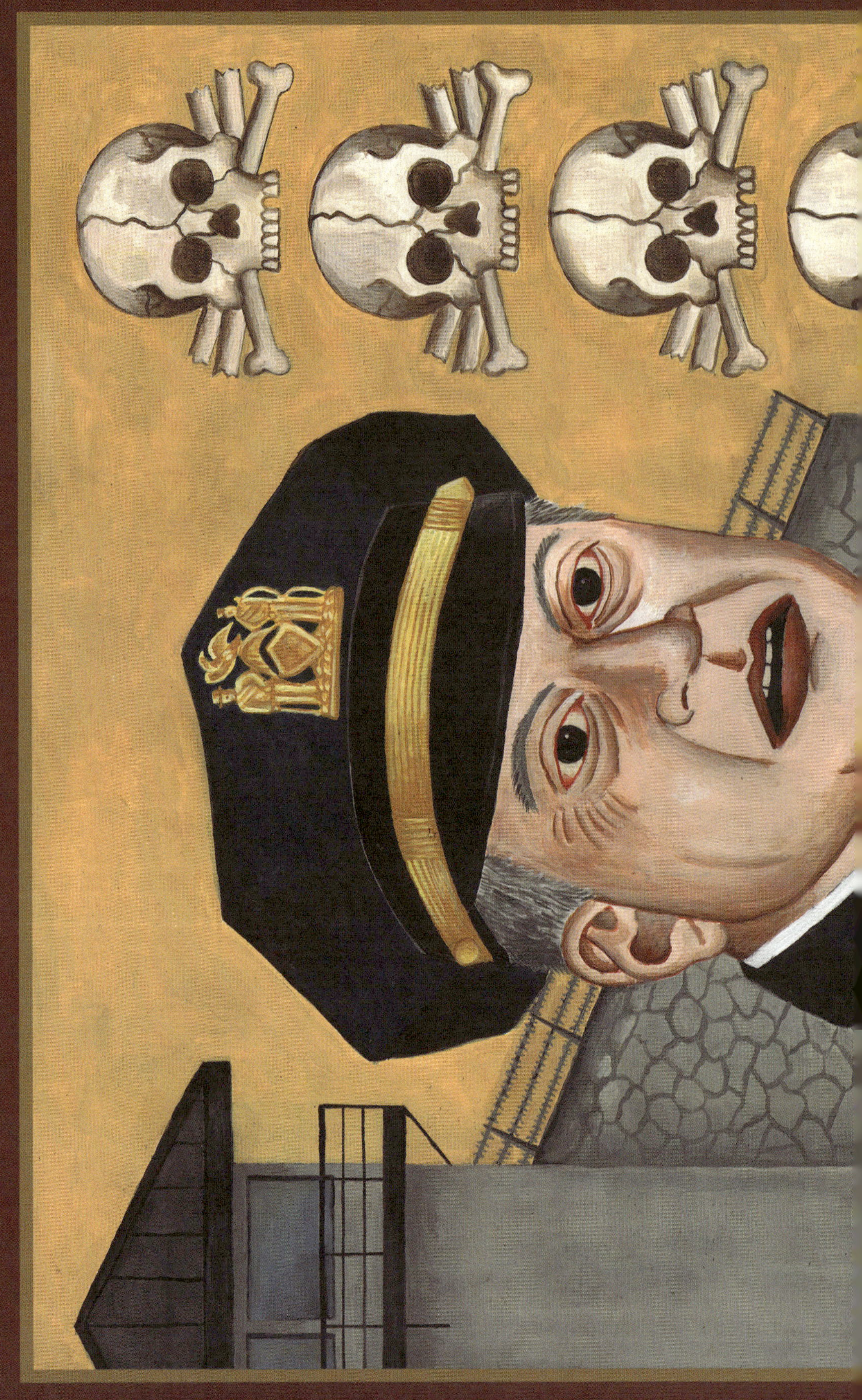

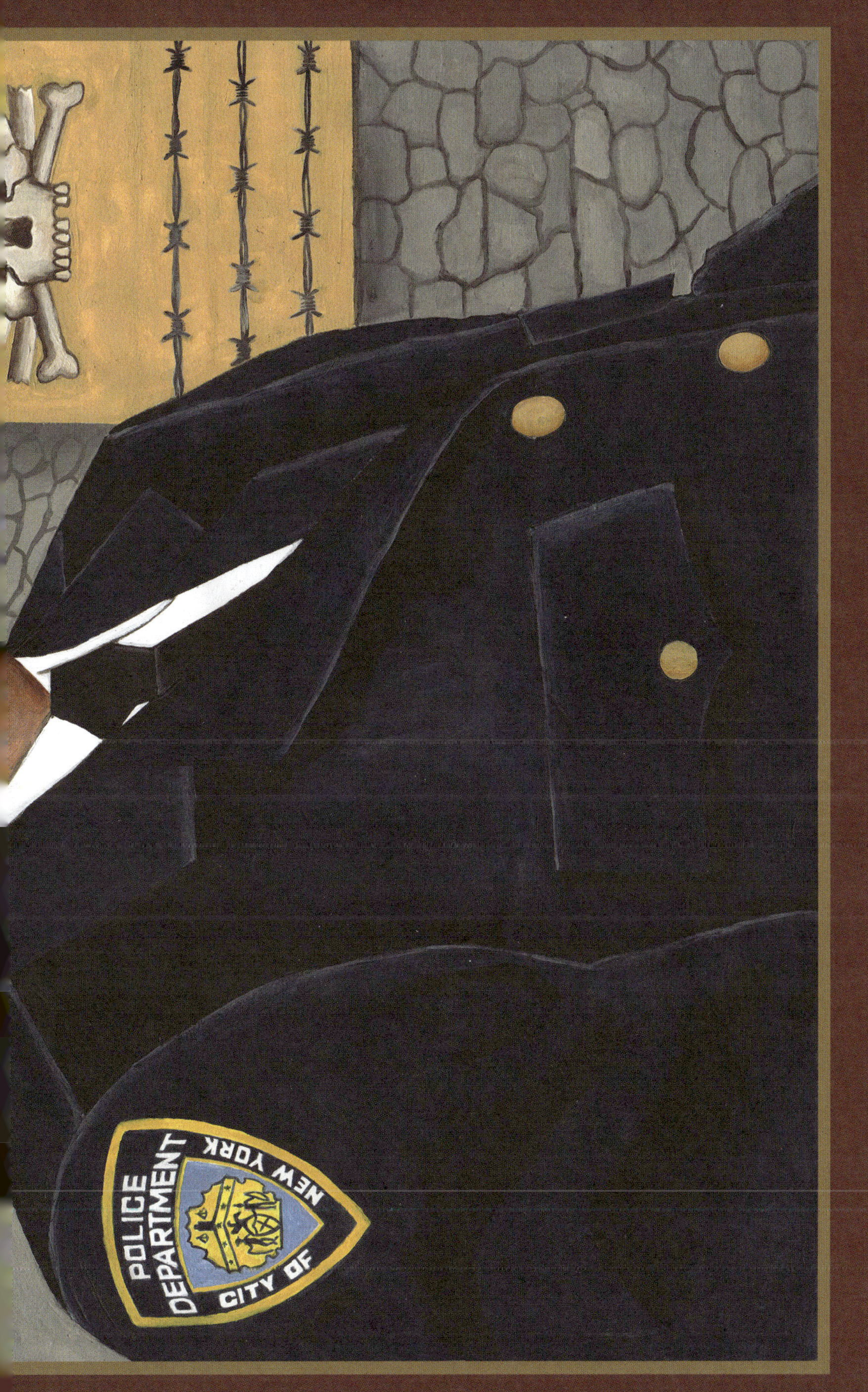
POLICE DEPARTMENT
CITY OF
NEW YORK

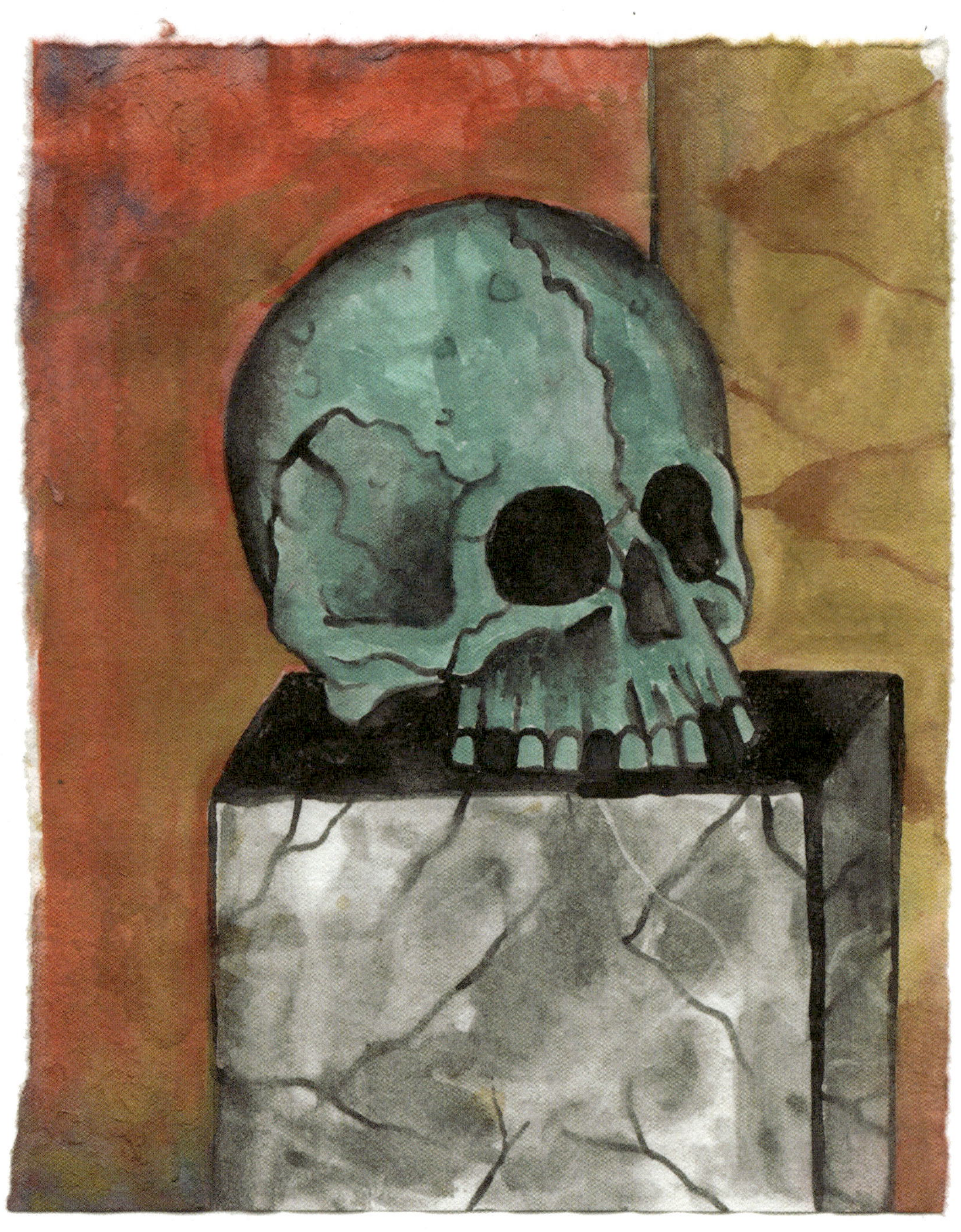

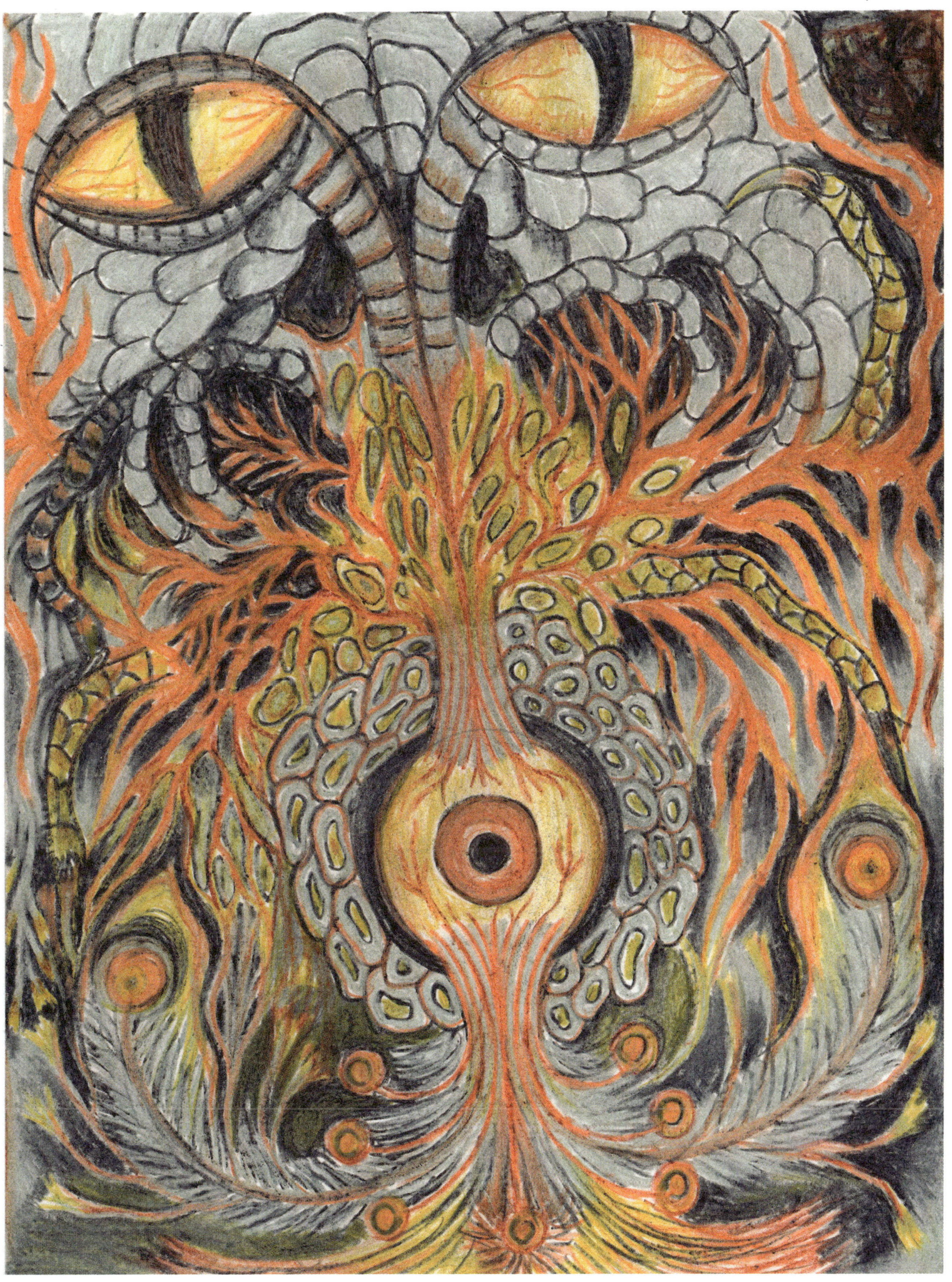

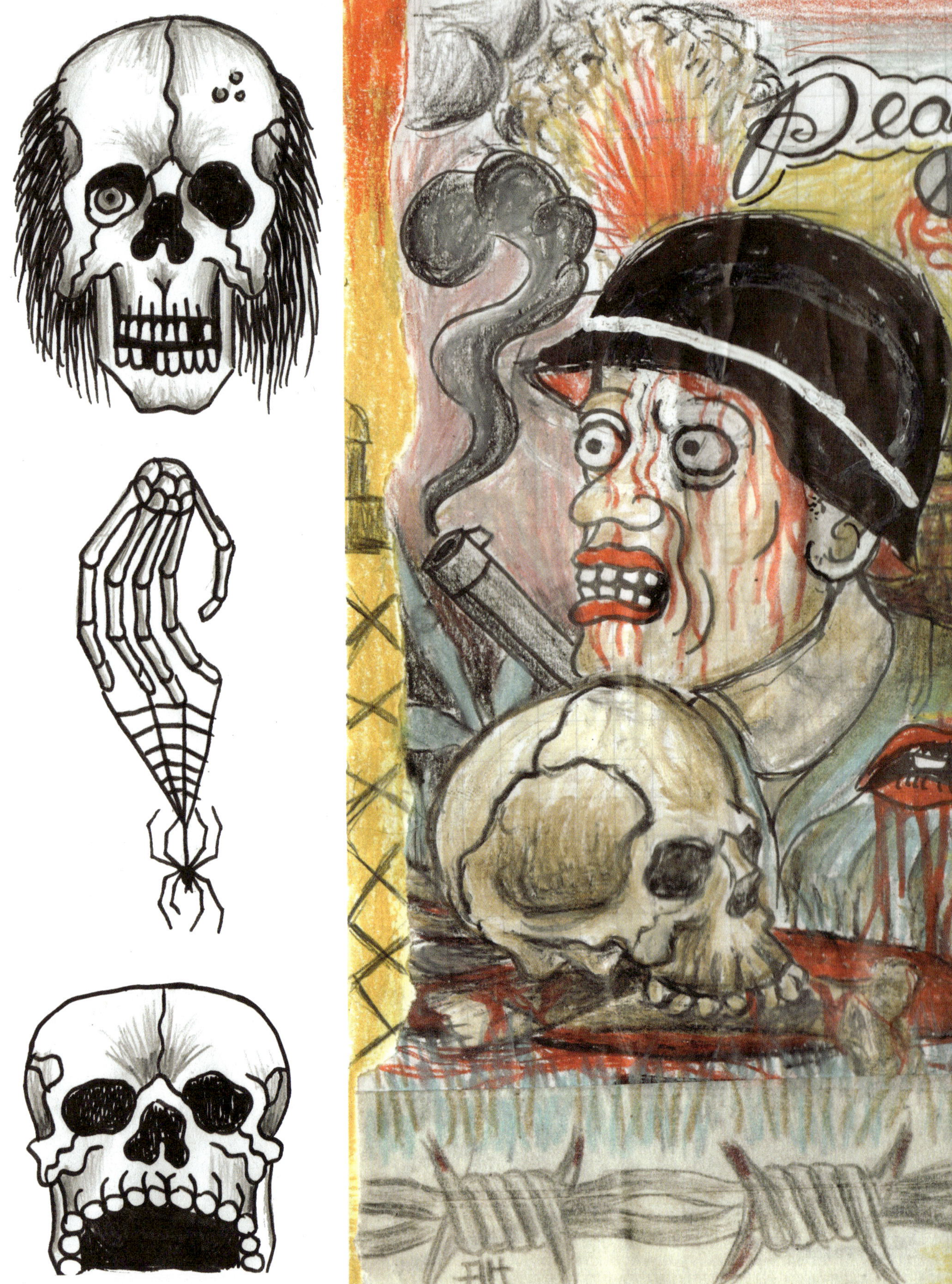
Peace

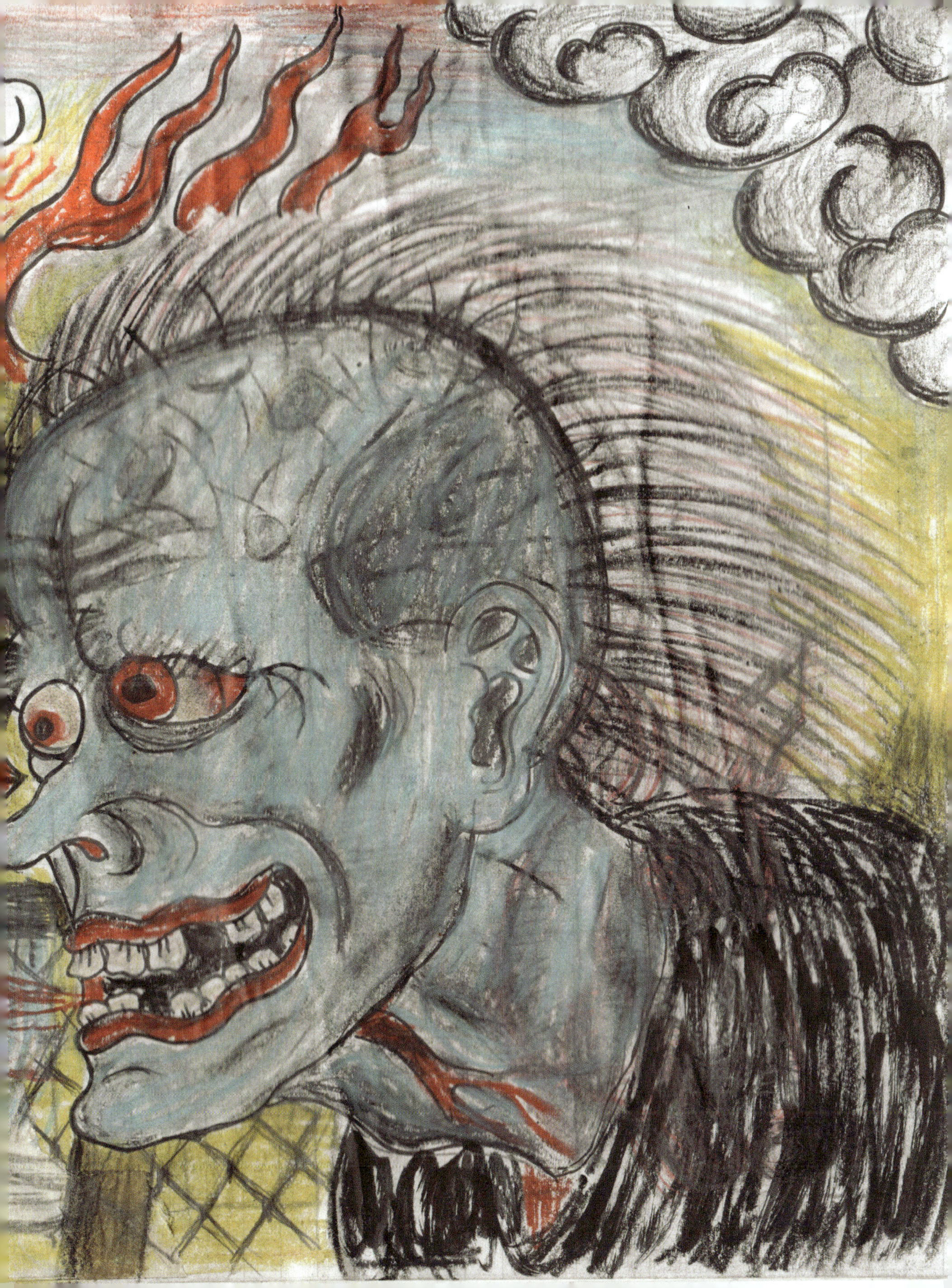

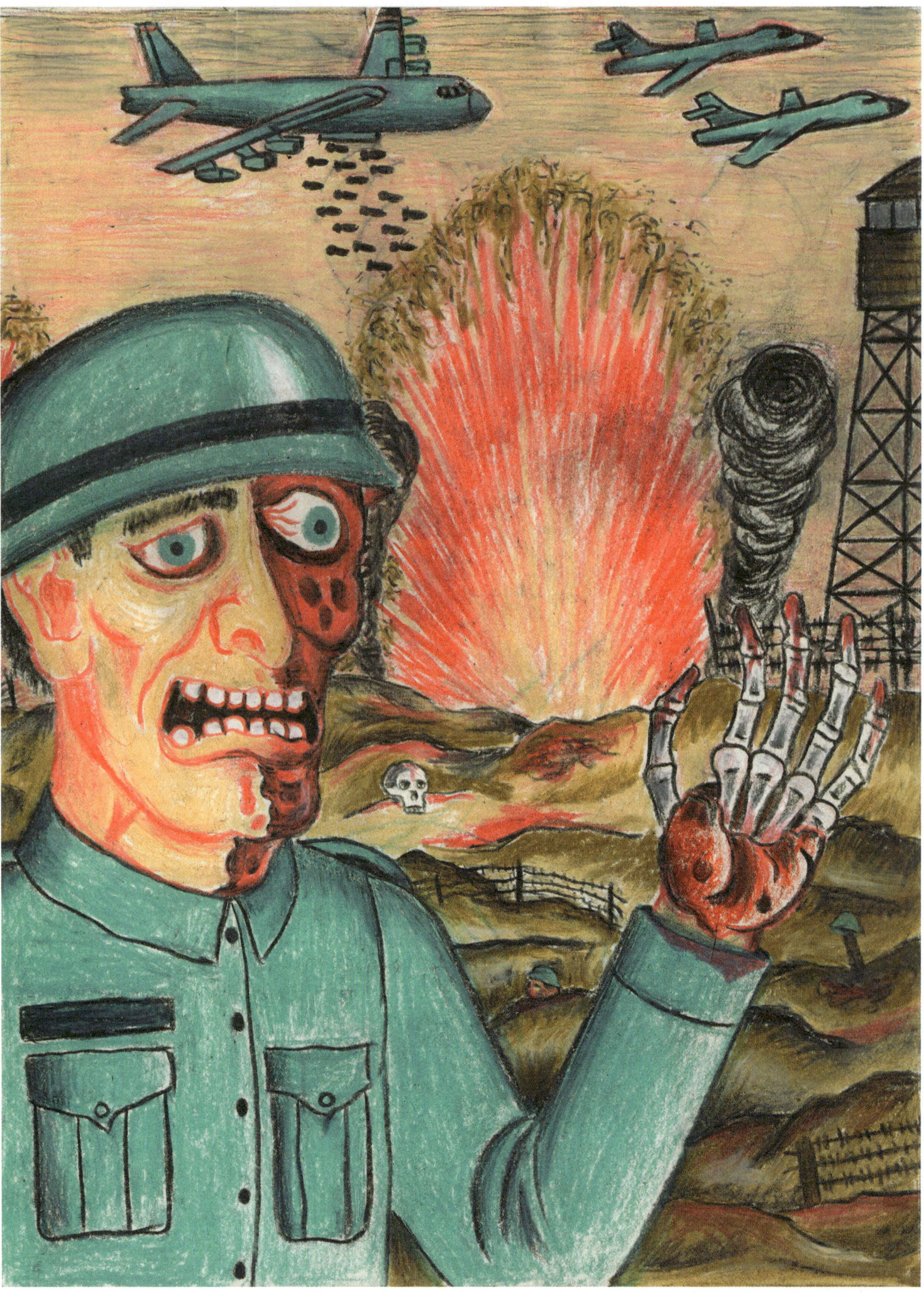

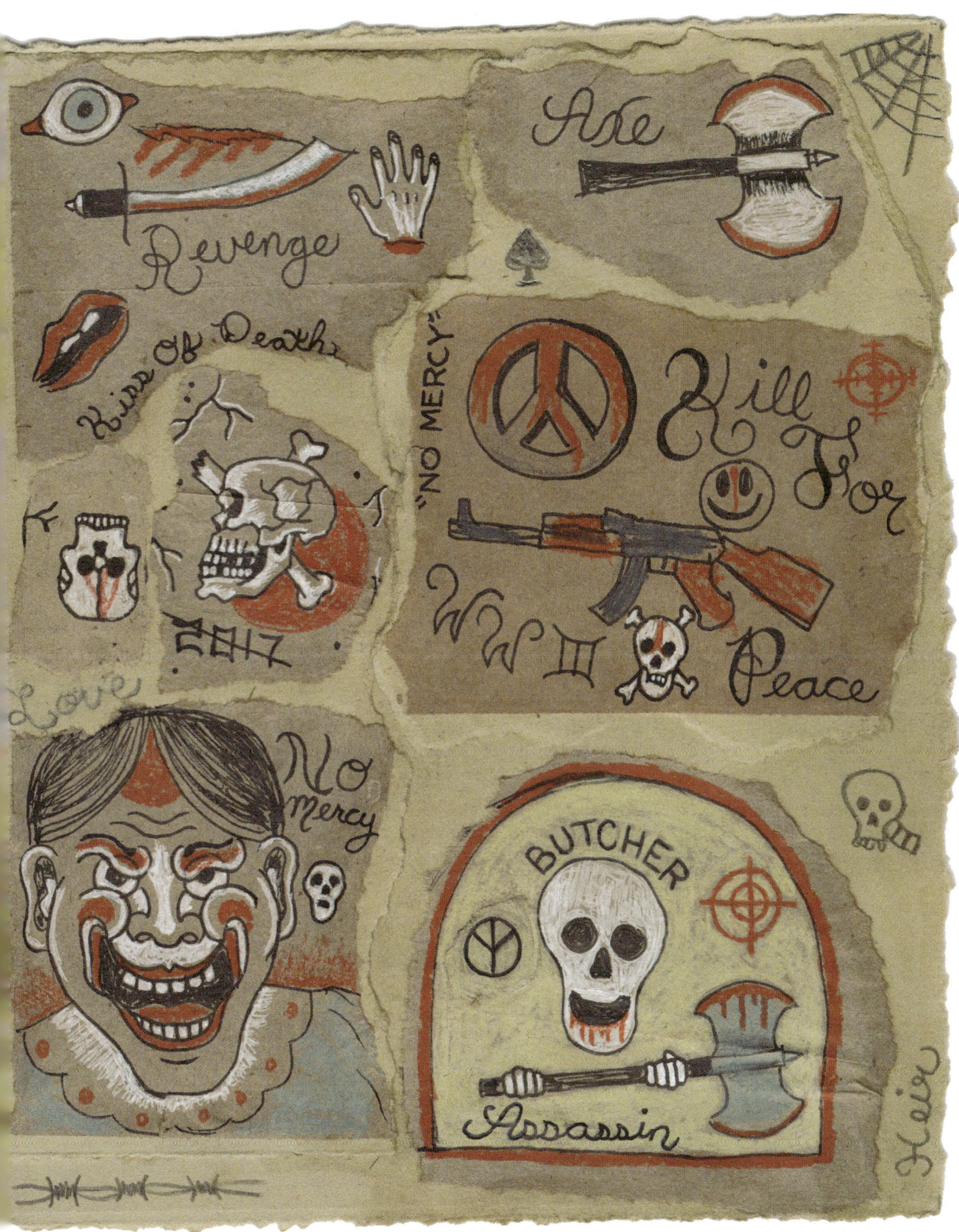
Revenge
Axe
Kiss Of Death
"NO MERCY"
Kill For
WW III
Peace
2017
Love
NO
Mercy
BUTCHER
Assassin
Hein

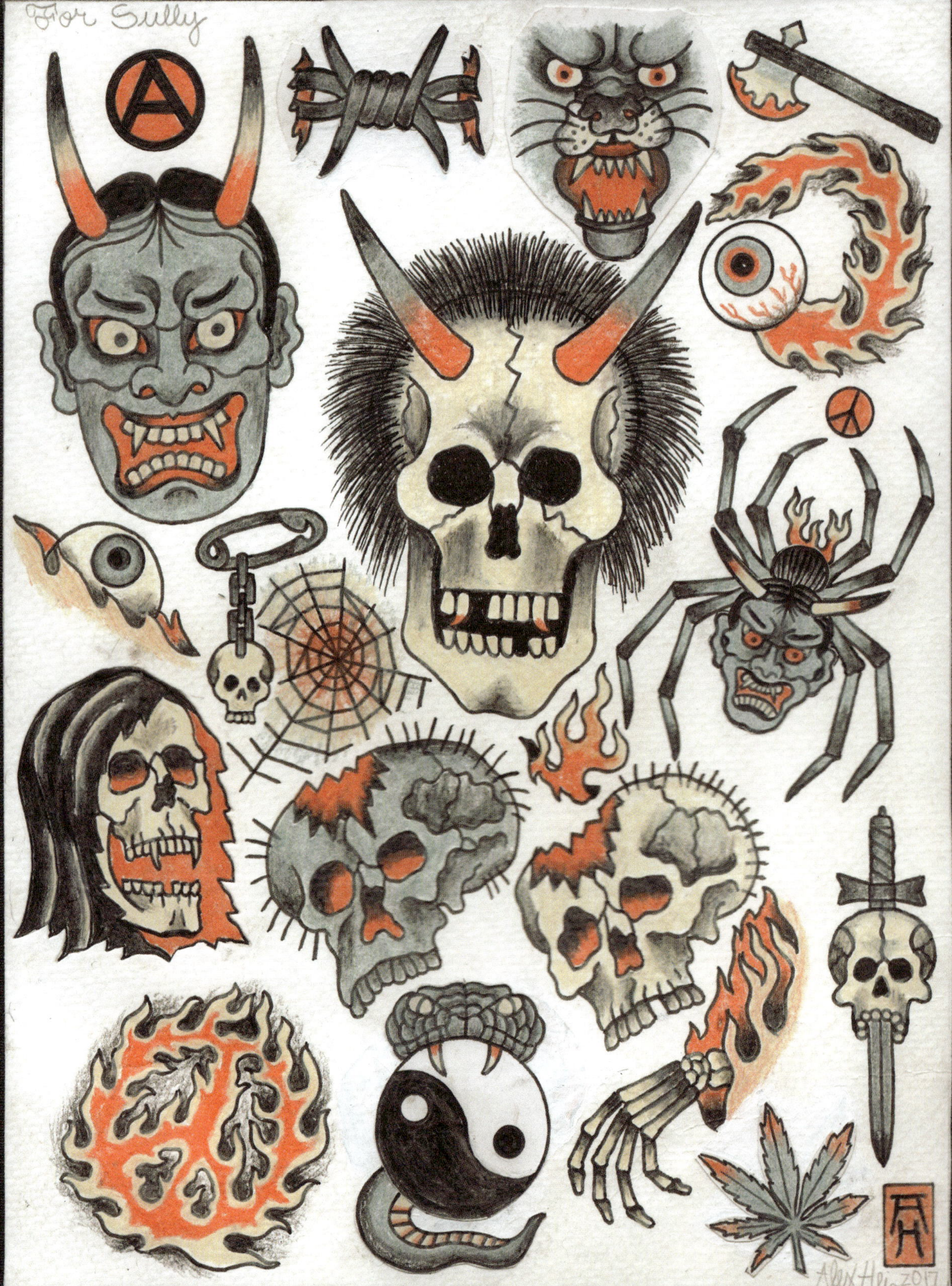
For Sully
Alex Heir 2017

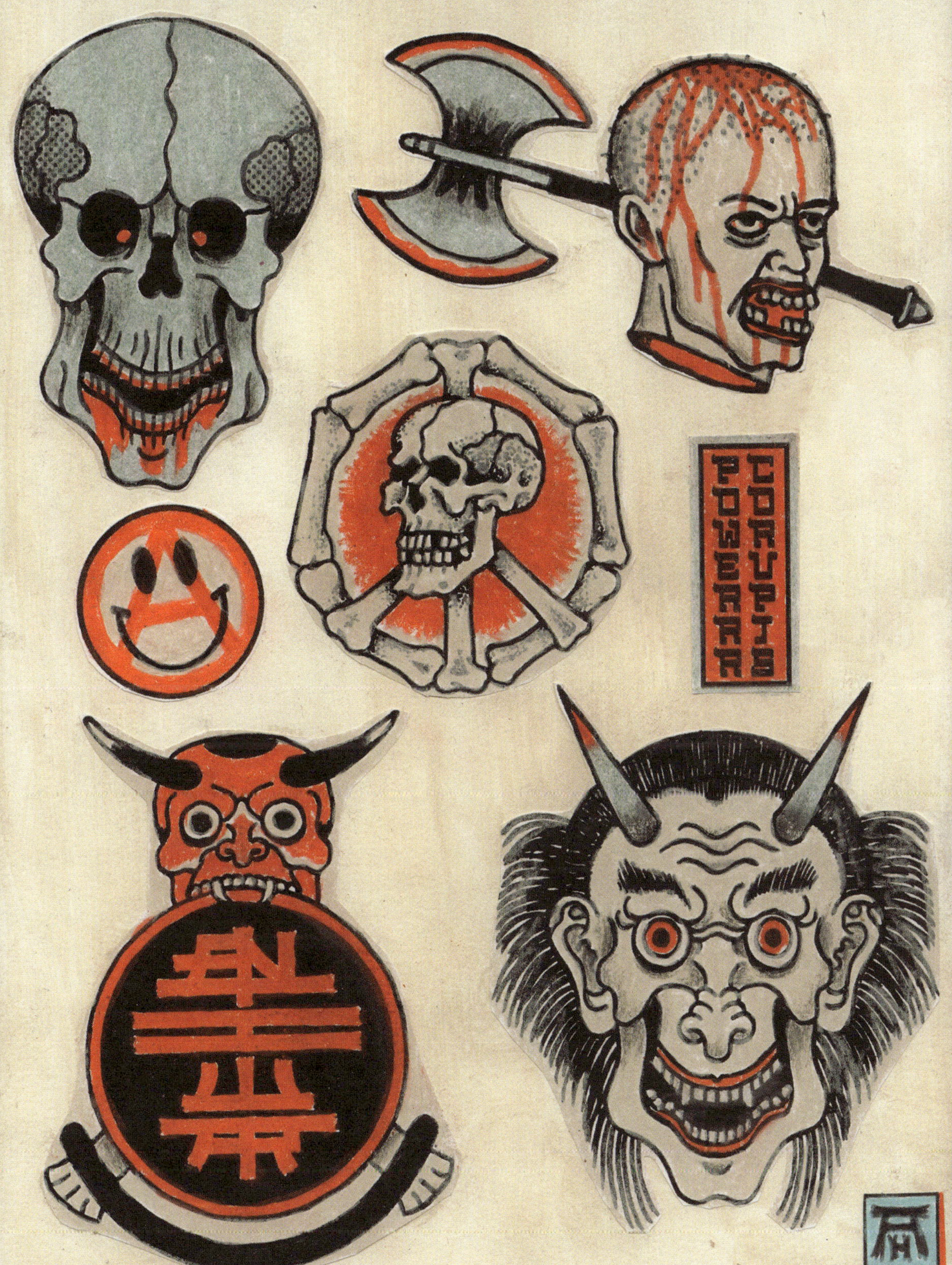

POWER
CORRUPTS

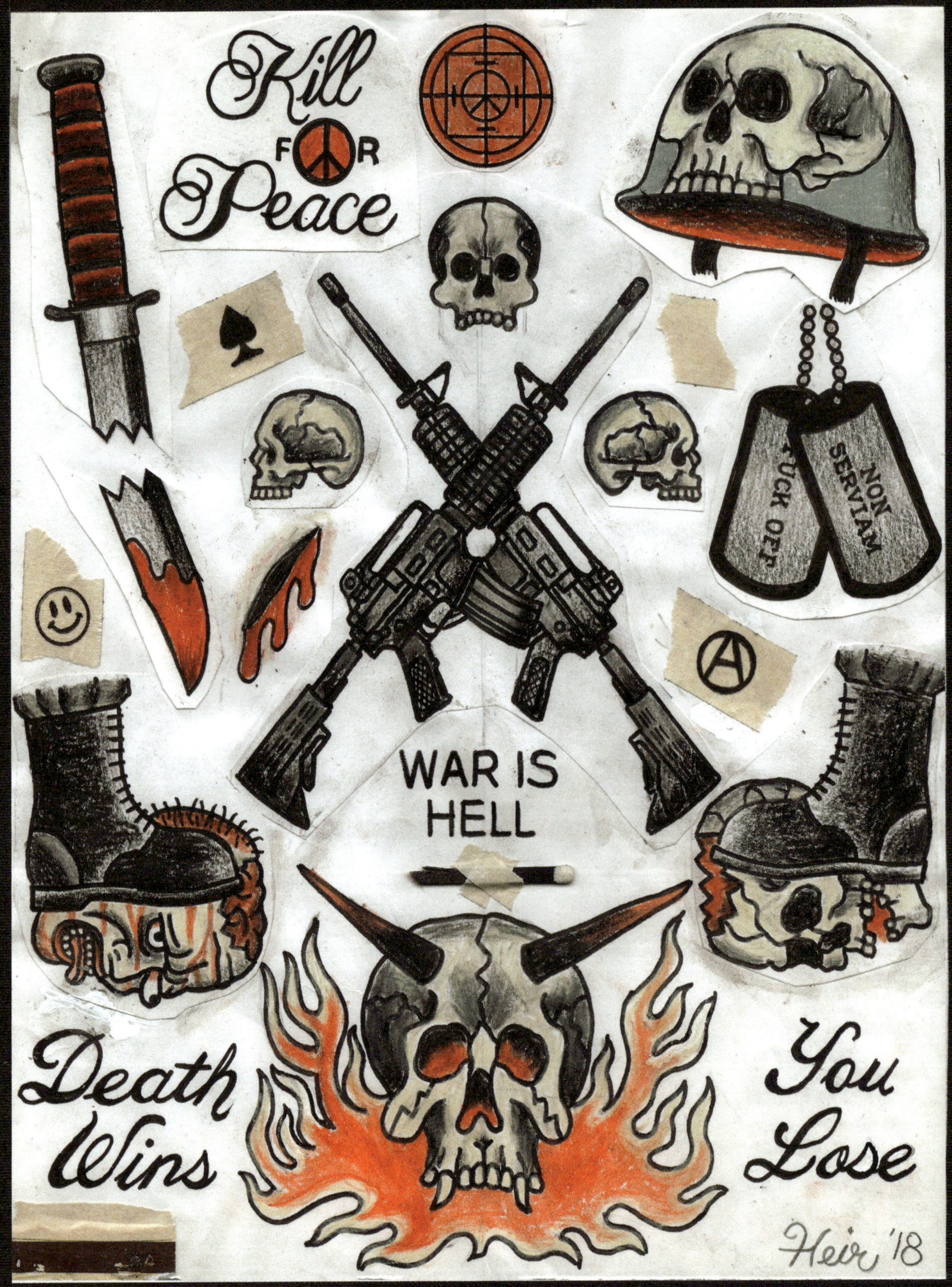

Kill FOR Peace
NON SERVIAM
FUCK OFF
WAR IS HELL
Death Wins
You Lose
Heir '18

SECTION A: COMISSSIONS

SECTION B: DEATH/TRAITORS

SECTION C: ARTWORK

156. "December," acrylic on paper, 2014
157. Flash, colored pencil on paper, 2014
158. "General," colored pencil on paper, 2014
159. "Officer," colored pencil on paper, 2014, from the collection of Chris Reyes
161-162. "Demons (Of The 21st Century)," mixed media on paper, 2014
163-166. "Warrr 2K∞," colored pencil on paper, 2018
167-169. "Severed Heads," mixed media on paper, 2014
170-171. "Anatomy," ink & colored pencil on paper, 2014, from the Collection of Dan Bailey
172-173. "Thanks, Joe," acylic on paper, 2014, from the collection of Joe Chatt
174. "Woman Having A Deadly Vision," ink & watercolor on paper, 2015
175. "Ghost," ink & watercolor on paper, 2015
176-177. "Sergeant," acrylic on paper, 2016
178. "Skull," watercolor on rice paper, 2016
179. Untitled LSD drawing, colored pencil on paper, 2017
180-181. Skull doodles, 2017, "Peace," mixed media on paper, 2017
182. "Mutilated land mine victim," colored pencil on paper, 2017
183. Flash, ink & colored pencil on paper, 2018
184. Flash, ink & colored pencil on paper, 2017, from the collection of Sully
185-186. Flash, ink & colored pencil on paper, 2018

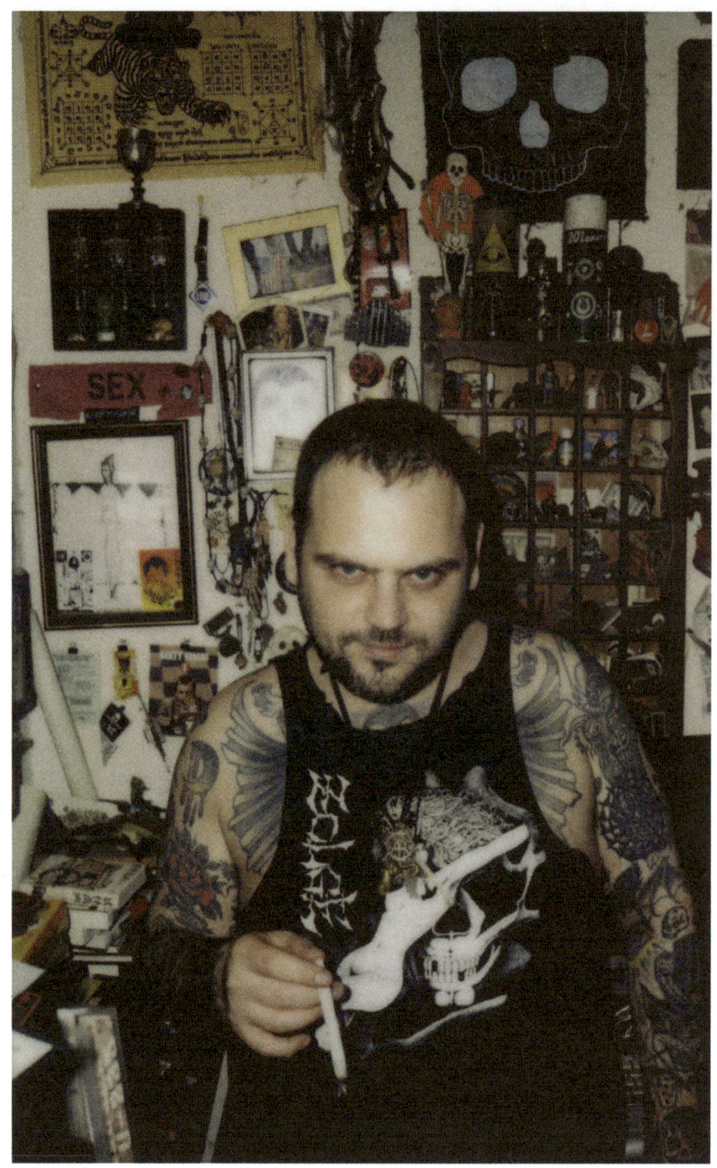

Alexander Heir has been running his Brooklyn based clothing brand Death/Traitors since 2007, in addition to creating art and illustrations for a myriad of punk, hardcore, and other underground bands & artists. He has shown work across the United States, as well as Europe and South America, in addition to fronting industrial punk band L.O.T.I.O.N. This is the second collection of his work published by Sacred Bones.